The *Flora* and *Fauna*

OF **COASTAL BRITISH COLUMBIA** AND THE **PACIFIC NORTHWEST**

The *Flora* and *Fauna*

of COASTAL BRITISH COLUMBIA
and the PACIFIC NORTHWEST

Collin Varner

VICTORIA · VANCOUVER · CALGARY

▶ To Aidan, Owen, Ava, Shaya, Nash, Reese, Kendle, Logan,
and all other young upcoming naturalists

Heritage House Publishing Company Ltd.
heritagehouse.ca

Published simultaneously in the United States of America by University of Washington Press,
under the title *The Flora and Fauna of the Pacific Northwest Coast*.

CATALOGUING INFORMATION AVAILABLE FROM LIBRARY AND ARCHIVES CANADA

978-1-77203-091-4 (pbk)
978-1-77203-092-1 (epdf)

Edited by Amy Haagsma
Proofread by Eva van Emden
Cover and interior design by Jacqui Thomas
Cover images by Collin Varner
All interior photos are by Collin Varner unless otherwise indicated; see photo credits on page 448
Map by Eric Leinberger

The interior of this book was produced on FSC®-certified, acid-free paper, processed chlorine free,
and printed with vegetable-based inks.

We acknowledge the financial support of the Government of Canada through the Canada Book Fund (CBF)
and the Canada Council for the Arts, and the Province of British Columbia through the British Columbia
Arts Council and the Book Publishing Tax Credit.

22 21 20 19 18   1 2 3 4 5

Printed in China

CONTENTS

Introduction 7

Glossary 15

FLORA

Flowering Plants 17

Berries 105

Ferns 118

Shrubs and Bushes 124

Trees 140

Fungi and Allies 157

Invasive Plants 194

Marine Plants 269

FAUNA

Birds 283

Land Mammals 350

Amphibians 362

Reptiles 366

Insects and Associates 370

Marine Life 410

Acknowledgements 448

Photo Credits 448

Bibliography 449

Index 450

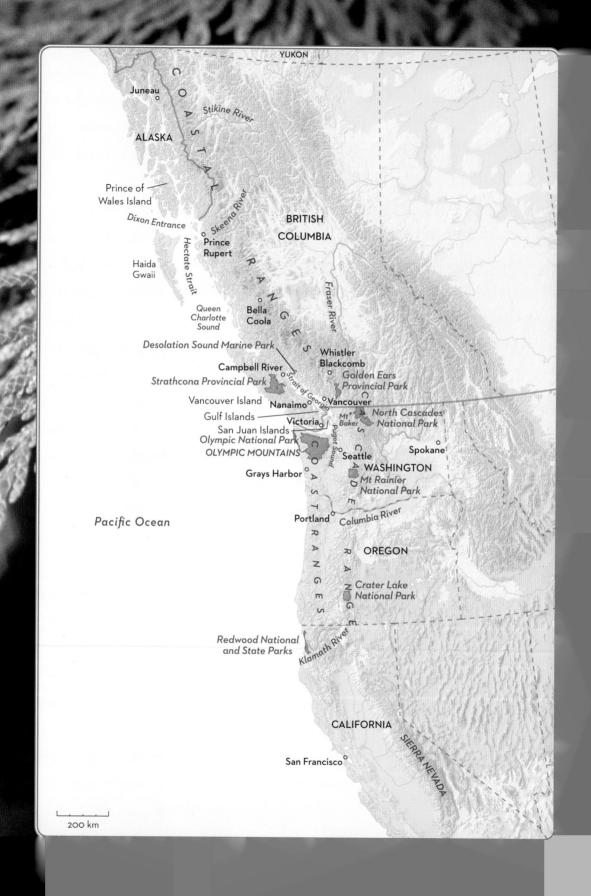

YUKON

Juneau

Stikine River

ALASKA

COASTAL

Prince of
Wales Island

Dixon Entrance

BRITISH
COLUMBIA

Skeena River

Prince
Rupert

Haida
Gwaii

Hectate Strait

Fraser River

RANGES

*Queen
Charlotte
Sound*

Bella
Coola

Desolation Sound Marine Park

Whistler
Blackcomb

Campbell River

*Golden Ears
Provincial Park*

Strathcona Provincial Park

Strait of Georgia

Vancouver Island

Nanaimo

Vancouver

Gulf Islands

Victoria

Mt
Baker

North Cascades
National Park

San Juan Islands

Olympic National Park

Puget Sound

OLYMPIC MOUNTAINS

Spokane

Seattle

Grays Harbor

WASHINGTON

*Mt Rainier
National Park*

Pacific Ocean

Portland

Columbia River

RANGES

OREGON

COAST

*Crater Lake
National Park*

RANGES

*Redwood National
and State Parks*

Klamath River

CALIFORNIA

SIERRA NEVADA

San Francisco

200 km

INTRODUCTION

THIS BOOK DESCRIBES OVER 800 PLANTS AND ANIMALS, ranging from common to not so common, that can be found in the coastal Pacific Northwest. It is not intended to present an exhaustive list of every species within the region, but rather to provide an overview of the numerous species that are common across as well as representative of the Pacific Northwest.

The vast majority of species included in this book were photographed by the author on his exploration of the coastal region over a period of several years. Written with the average observer in mind, the book has an intentional bias towards plant and animal species that are visible to the typical viewer rather than more obscure species. However, it it is also a designed to be a quick, useful resource for readers of all levels of expertise.

For the purposes of this book, the Pacific Northwest is defined as the region stretching from Juneau, Alaska, to San Francisco, California, from the mainland coast to approximately 100 kilometres (60 miles) inland, as well as the various coastal islands.

Despite the Pacific Northwest being a very large and diverse region, the species within it are relatively uniform. Yet venture another 50 kilometres (30 miles) inland, and the ecosystem is vastly different. The species covered by this book are the delights that the ambler encounters, from the intertidal to the subalpine areas. The book therefore does not include the fish not readily visible in rivers and the ocean, but it does include the salmon that spawn in coastal waters and the tiny fish found in tide pools.

DISCLAIMER Although this book mentions some of the traditional uses of edible plants for medicinal or other purposes, the author does not advocate the use of these plants for such purposes. Many plants in this region, including those with some medicinal uses, can be harmful or even poisonous. The author and publisher do not recommend experimentation with plants found in the wild and are not responsible for misidentification by readers of any species found in this book.

▶ How to use this book

This book was written to be accessible to anyone, from amateur enthusiasts to professionals. Gardeners and nature lovers will enjoy discovering the rich sampling of flora and fauna that can be found right in their own backyard. Hikers and campers will delight in identifying plants and animals encountered on the trail and in the forest. And academics and those working in the field will find a useful, general overview of the species within the Pacific Northwest as a whole.

Keep this book in your car, or put it in your backpack for a day's hike, a birdwatching excursion, or an extended camping trip, so you can look up the species you find and learn more about them. Use it to engage with your surroundings and deepen your understanding of the region and the environment. This increased knowledge will add to your enjoyment of being outdoors, bring you closer to nature, and help you get more out of your experiences. Familiarize yourself with the species that can be found within the Pacific Northwest, and then see what you can find.

▶ What you will find inside

This book is divided into two main sections, flora and fauna, and then further categorized into groupings of related species. For each species, you will find a general description, including dimensions, colouring, and other points that may be useful in finding or identifying the particular species. Also included is information on where the species can be found, in terms of both its preferred habitat and its specific location.

In rare cases, species fall under more than one category. For the purposes of this book, they are given a complete description in only one category, and a note referring the reader to this description is given in the second category. For an example, see goat's beard on pages 87 and 138.

Etymologies of common names, genus names, and species names have also been provided where they may be of interest. Many of the flora species also note any traditional uses of the plant. Descriptions for invasive plants include the species' origin, method of reproduction (how it spreads), and any particular concerns associated with the species.

For a complete alphabetized list of all the species and scientific family groupings in the book, refer to the index, beginning on page 450. Species are listed here by common name.

▶ The varied environment of the Pacific Northwest

The Pacific Northwest comprises thousands of kilometres (or miles) of coastline, including an extensive mainland coast and numerous inlets and coastal islands. For an overview of the region, see the map on page 6. Notable islands include Prince of Wales Island, off the coast of Alaska; Vancouver Island and the Haida Gwaii, both part of British Columbia; and the San Juan Islands, in Washington.

It is at the ocean's edge that thousands of rivers and streams, which can be thousands of kilometres or miles long, finally empty their fresh water into the ocean. With the fresh water comes silt. Some of the silt accumulates, forming small islands within the rivers. However, the majority gets deposited at the mouths of the rivers as nutrient-rich deltas. Some of these deltas are so large that they support thousands of hectares (or acres) of farmland, producing some of the finest crops in North America.

To most people, Mount Rainier, Mount Baker, and the peaks of the Whistler Blackcomb region conjure up images of wonderful snowfalls and winter sports. But these mountains are quickly expanding as all-season destinations with endless opportunities for outdoor recreation, such as hiking, cycling, canoeing, and observing nature. This book looks at our mountains when they are dressed in green, red, yellow, blue, and all the colours in between.

The environment of the Pacific Northwest is influenced by forces from all directions. From the east, inland rivers bring nutrients from the mainland; from the west, the coast is shaped by the ocean tides and winds, as well as human activities such as shipping and boating. Species introduced accidentally, most often from Europe and Asia, tend to thrive in the Pacific Northwest due to its temperate climate and high levels of precipitation. Interestingly, the reverse does not also hold true—species carried west across the Pacific Ocean do not tend to take hold in other areas.

▶ A diverse range of species

In the Pacific Northwest, healthy rivers and streams support millions of spawning salmon fighting the water's currents to create new life. These salmon are an important food source for bald eagles, crows, gulls, black bears, and grizzly bears. Salmon carcasses that have been dragged into the forest provide nutrients to the coniferous and deciduous trees and their undergrowth.

The combination of brackish water at the mouths of rivers and the soft, silty river bottoms create a welcoming environment for Dungeness crabs and white sturgeon. The tidal flats around these areas are covered in grasses and sedges and are home to an amazing assortment of shorebirds and migratory birds.

Mild, wet winters and dry summers offer a diverse growing range for plant life. Coastlines, meadows, and forests left moist by winter provide ideal spring growing conditions for plants to flower and set seed or fruit. The succession of coastal blooms in spring rivals the mountainous beauty of the subalpine meadows.

Flowering begins with spring gold and fawn lily, continuing with western buttercup, red paintbrush, blue-eyed Mary, Henderson's shooting star, common camas, chocolate lily, stonecrop, gumweed, and Hooker's onion, and then carrying into mid-June with the exquisite yellow-flowering brittle pricklypear cactus. These blooms decorate the shorelines, but within the forests, another show of colours flares.

Salmonberry and Indian plum are usually the first to appear, followed by thimbleberry, false Solomon's seal, fairyslipper, spotted coralroot, heart-leaved twayblade, fringecup, and foam flower. The new growth, seeds, and fruit produced by this succession of plants supply food and shelter for thousands of birds, mammals, and insects. By midsummer, the meadow plants have faded away, the grass has turned golden brown, and the soil is brick dry.

The broad elevation range, from low to alpine, makes the Pacific Northwest one of North America's most diversified growing areas. In lower areas, warmer temperatures allow for lush growth and larger trees. The first plants to flower are wild ginger, devil's club, wintergreen, orchids, honeysuckles, trailing violets, wild sarsaparilla, and tiger lily. Mid-elevation plants flower later, while the subalpine to alpine meadows and slopes hold off until July, August, or even September. The short growing season in higher elevations forces the native plants to flower in concert, with the best viewing times between mid-July and mid-August.

This range of elevation also means that plants flower at different times throughout the region. For every 305 metres (1,000 feet) of rise, for example, there is at least a week's delay in flowering time, so red elderberry flowers in mid-April at low elevations but not until mid-July at higher elevations.

▶ Exploring the region

To begin exploring the incredible Pacific Northwest, I recommend starting with the coastal islands and the adjacent mainland shoreline.

The best time to explore the shoreline is when the tide is out, or ebbing. This allows for at least four hours of exploring marine life on the exposed shelves, rocks, tide pools, and sand. The more common marine life to be seen are limpets, mussels, sea urchins, starfish, mud-flat snails, purple olives, acorn barnacles, anemones, and purple shore crabs, along with tiny sculpins and clingfish. The shorelines are also covered in beautiful kelp and other seaweeds, with interesting names such as Turkish towel, sea sacs, feather boa, seersucker, sea palm, and sea cauliflower. The exposed rocks present a smorgasbord or sushi bar for the local fauna, such as gulls, crows, sandpipers, bald eagles, turkey vultures, oystercatchers, mink, river otters, black bears and grizzly bears, wolves, black-tailed deer, and blue herons.

Walking along the shoreline, you may also see humpback whales, grey whales, orcas, and sea lions, as well as tufted puffins, pigeon guillemots, common murres, marbled murrelets, and rhinoceros auklets. Whale-, bear-, and birdwatching tours are available from Seattle, Vancouver, and Vancouver Island.

There are many treasures in the Pacific Northwest, just waiting to be discovered!

GLOSSARY

anther	The pollen-bearing (top) portion of the stamen
axil	The angle made between a stalk and the stem on which it is growing
biennial	A plant that completes its life cycle in two growing seasons
bivalve	A mollusk having two valves or two shells encasing the mollusk, such as a clam or an oyster
boss	A knob-like stud, as in the points on yellow cedar cones
bract	A modified leaf below the flower
calyx	The collective term for sepals, the outer parts of a flower
carapace	The shell that protects a crab
catkin	A spike-like or drooping flower cluster, either male or female, found in species such as cottonwood
coniferous	Having evergreen leaves, usually needle-like or scaled
corm	A swollen underground stem capable of producing roots, leaves, and flowers
deciduous	Having parts (leaves, bark) that shed annually, usually in the autumn
dioecious	Having male and female flowers on separate plants
ephemeral	Lasting for only a short time; usually refers to seasonal creeks, rivulets, and ponds
epiphyte	A plant that grows on another plant for physical support without robbing the host of nutrients
herbaceous	A non-woody plant that dies back into the ground every year
holdfast	A hard root-like structure used by seaweeds to attach themselves to rocks and the ocean floor

lenticel	A raised organ that replaces stomata on a stem
node	The place on a stem where the leaves and axillary buds are attached
obovate	Oval in shape with the narrower end pointing downward, like an upside-down egg
panicle	A branched inflorescence
perennial	General term for a plant that lives above the ground throughout the year
petiole	The stalk of a leaf
pinnate	A compound leaf with the leaflets arranged on both sides of a central axis
pinnule	The leaflet of a pinnately compounded leaf
rhizome	An underground modified stem
riparian	The area along the sides of creeks, ponds, and waterways where plants grow
saprophyte	A plant that lives on dead or decaying matter
scape	A leafless stem rising from the ground that may support one or many flowers
sepal	The outer parts of a flower; usually green
sori	Spore cases
stipe	A stem or stalk, such as on a mushroom, bull kelp, or the maidenhair fern
stolon	A stem or branch that runs along the surface of the ground and takes root at the nodes or apex, forming new plants
stomata	The pores in the epidermis of leaves; usually white
style	The stem of the pistil (female organ)

FLOWERING PLANTS

WAPATO ARROWHEAD/DUCK POTATO

Sagittaria latifolia

WATER PLANTAIN FAMILY Alismataceae

Description Wapato is a herbaceous freshwater perennial that can grow to 90 cm/36 in. tall. The arrow-shaped leaves, up to 25 cm/10 in. long, grow on long, slightly arching stalks. The waxy white flowers are produced in whorls of three on long leafless stems.

Traditional use The starchy tubers were an important food source and trading item.

Etymology The common name wapato is from the Chinook, meaning "tuberous plant." When wapato leaves and small tubers can be seen floating on the water, it usually is an indication of ducks or muskrats that have dislodged the plants for their starchy tubers (hence the name "duck potato").

Habitat Low elevations, shallow ponds, sloughs, lake edges, and slow-moving streams.

Season Depending on location, it blooms from June to early July.

KNEELING ANGELICA

Angelica genuflexa

CARROT FAMILY Apiaceae

Description Kneeling angelica is a hollow-stemmed, taprooted, herbaceous perennial to 1.5 m/4.9 ft. tall. Its tiny white-pinkish flowers are displayed in compound umbels 10–15 cm/4–6 in. across. It is the bent leaf stalks that support the pinnately compound leaves that give this plant its common and Latin names.

Traditional use The hollow stems were used as breathing straws when hiding under water.

Habitat Common along the coast in most areas, at low to mid elevations.

Season In full flower by the end of July.

▶ SEA-WATCH ANGELICA

Angelica lucida

CARROT FAMILY Apiaceae

Description Sea-watch angelica is a taprooted, herbaceous perennial to 1.4 m/4.6 ft. tall. The small white flowers are held in small heads, which form a compound umbel to 15 cm/6 in. across. The hairless leaves are more rounded than kneeling angelica and lack the bend in the leaf stalk.

Traditional use The stems were peeled and eaten.

Etymology The common name of sea-watch angelica is a bit obscure. However, if you see the autumn stalks on the bluffs above the Pacific coastline, it looks as if they are keeping watch over the sea.

Habitat Mainly seen in moist seepage areas along the coast.

Season Flowers from July to August.

▶ BEACH CARROT

Glehnia littoralis ssp. *leiocarpa*

CARROT FAMILY Apiaceae

Description Beach carrot is a prostrate, taprooted perennial that calls coastal dunes and sandy beaches home. The thick, leathery leaves usually clasp the stem beneath the sand for added protection against the harsh west coast weather. The small white flowers are clustered in unique designs.

Habitat Sandy beaches and dunes from Alaska to California.

Season Flowers from June to July.

▶ COW PARSNIP INDIAN CELERY

Heracleum lanatum

CARROT FAMILY Apiaceae

Description Cow parsnip is a tall, hollow-stemmed, herbaceous perennial 1–3 m/ 3.3–10 ft. high. Its small white flowers are grouped in flat-topped, umbrella-like terminal clusters to 25 cm/10 in. across. It produces numerous small, egg-shaped seeds, 1 cm/0.5 in. long, with a pleasant aroma. The large woolly compound leaves are divided into three leaflets, one terminal and two lateral, to 30 cm/12 in. across. Giant cow parsnip (*H. mantegazzianum*) is an introduced species that grows to 4 m/13 ft. in height and can be seen in urban areas.

Traditional use The stems were peeled and eaten raw. The discarded skin is considered poisonous.

Etymology The genus name, *Heracleum*, is fitting for this plant of Herculean proportions.

Habitat Moist forests, meadows, marshes, and roadsides from low to high elevations.

Season Flowering starts at the end of June in lower areas and at the end of July at higher elevations.

CAUTION Both species can cause severe blistering and rashes when handled.

▶ SPRING GOLD FINE-LEAVED DESERT PARSLEY

Lomatium utriculatum

CARROT FAMILY Apiaceae

Description Spring gold is an early-flowering herbaceous perennial 5–30 cm/2–12 in. tall. Its tiny conglomerated flowers are a bright canary yellow and held in umbels. The finely dissected leaves resemble a fern or carrot leaf.

Habitat Dry grassy slopes, meadows, and outcrops.

Season It has a long flowering period, from mid-March to early June.

▶ WATER PARSLEY

Oenanthe sarmentosa

CARROT FAMILY Apiaceae

Description Water parsley is a semi-aquatic herbaceous perennial to 1 m/3.3 ft. in height. Its flowers are white, faintly fragrant, and borne in flat-topped clusters. The leaves are pinnately divided two to three times, with deeply toothed leaflets. The overall appearance of the plant is weak and sprawling.

Traditional use The roots were chewed and soaked in water; the infused water was taken for headaches.

Habitat Low-elevation marshes and swamps; occasionally found in ditches.

Season Flowers from mid-June to July.

CAUTION The entire plant is considered poisonous.

▶ MOUNTAIN SWEET CICELY

Osmorhiza chilensis

CARROT FAMILY Apiaceae

Description Mountain sweet cicely is a herbaceous perennial to 1 m/3.3 ft. in height. Its thick greenish flowers are small and hard to see in the forest; the thin seeds that develop are brown black and catch easily on socks and other clothing. The leaves are divided into threes, then into threes again, for a total of nine leaflets. The licorice-scented root is reputed to have aphrodisiac powers.

Habitat Cool moist forests at low to mid elevations.

Season Flowers from the end of May to June, and sets seed very quickly.

▶ PACIFIC SANICLE
Sanicula crassicaulis
CARROT FAMILY Apiaceae

Description Pacific sanicle is a herbaceous perennial 0.2–1 m/0.7–3.3 ft. in height. Its small yellow flowers are held up in rounded terminal clusters to 1 cm/0.5 in. across. The leaves are mainly basal and palmately lobed, with light venation.

Habitat Dry forests, around rocky outcrops, and beaches.

Season Flowers from May to June.

▶ WATER PARSNIP
Sium suave
CARROT FAMILY Apiaceae

Description Water parsnip is a lanky perennial that grows to 0.5–1.5 m/1.7–5 ft. in height. The tiny white flowers (0.3 cm/0.1 in.) are borne in masses resembling the spokes of an umbrella. The 7 to 15 finely toothed leaflets are supported by sheathed stalks.

Traditional use The roots were considered important food and were eaten raw or cooked.

Habitat Sloughs, lake, and pond edges at low to mid elevations.

Season Flowers from July to August.

CAUTION Be careful when identifying this plant: many look-alikes are extremely poisonous.

▶ SPREADING DOGBANE

Apocynum androsaemifolium

DOGBANE FAMILY Apocynaceae

Description Spreading dogbane is a herbaceous perennial to 80 cm/32 in. in height. Its pink flowers are bell shaped, to 0.8 cm/0.3 in. long, and hang in beautiful clusters at the branch ends. The egg-shaped leaves are in opposite pairs, to 8 cm/5 in. long, and droop in hot temperatures. When broken, the red stems exude a milky juice.

Traditional use The stem fibres were used for cordage.

Habitat Exposed areas, dry forest edges, and road-sides at low elevations.

Season Flowers from June to July.

▶ WATER PLANTAIN

Alisma plantago-aquatica

WATER PLANTAIN FAMILY Alismataceae

Description Water plantain is a semi-aquatic perennial to 1.2 m/4 ft. tall. The lance-oblong-shaped leaves are to 30 cm/1 ft. long and are basal (at the bottom of the plant). The small whitish flowers are borne on long leafless stems that give the plant its height.

Etymology The common and Latin names both refer to the leaves' resemblance to plantain.

Habitat In urban areas, it is commonly seen in moist ditches. In lower-lying rural areas, it is common in slow-moving marshes and sloughs.

Season Flowers from July to August.

▶ SKUNK CABBAGE

Lysichiton americanus

ARUM FAMILY Araceae

Description Skunk cabbage is a herbaceous perennial to 1.5 m/5 ft. in height and as much as 2 m/6.6 ft. across. The small greenish flowers are densely packed on a fleshy spike and surrounded by a showy yellow spathe, the emergence of which is a sure sign that spring is near. The tropical-looking leaves can be over 1 m/3.3 ft. long and 50 cm/20 in. wide.

Traditional use Skunk cabbage roots were cooked and eaten in spring in times of famine. It is said that this poorly named plant has saved the lives of thousands.

Habitat Common at lower elevations in wet areas such as springs, swamps, seepage areas, and floodplains.

Season Flowers from May to July.

▶ WILD SARSAPARILLA

Aralia nudicaulis

GINSENG FAMILY Araliaceae

Description Wild sarsaparilla is a herbaceous perennial to 40 cm/16 in. in height. The easily over-looked flowers are greenish white, five petalled, and held in small rounded clusters; they are replaced by small clusters of dark-purple berries in August. Sarsaparilla produces from its rhizomes a central stem that has three compound leaves divided again into three to five leaflets.

Habitat Moist forests at low to mid elevations.

Season Flowers in June; ripe seed by August.

▶ WILD GINGER

Asarum caudatum

BIRTHWORT FAMILY Aristolochiaceae

Description Wild ginger is a trailing evergreen perennial that forms patches several metres or feet wide. Its bell-shaped solitary flower is purplish brown, to 5 cm/2 in. across, with three pointed lobes. The heart-shaped leaves, to 10 cm/4 in. across, are formed in opposite pairs in the nodes. The whole plant has a mild ginger fragrance when crushed.

Traditional use The scented plants were put in bathwater, and the roots were boiled and drunk as a tea to ease stomach problems.

Habitat Moist shaded forests with rich humus, at low to mid elevations.

Season Flowers from mid-May to August.

▶ PATHFINDER

Adenocaulon bicolor

ASTER FAMILY Asteraceae

Description Pathfinder is a herbaceous perennial to 1 m/3.3 ft. tall. Its tiny white flowers are inconspicuous compared with the large (10–15 cm/4–6 in. long) heart-shaped bicoloured leaves. The mature seeds are hooked, allowing them to attach to passing animals and people's clothing. The leaves flip over when walked through, revealing the silvery underside and thus marking the path.

Habitat Shaded forests at low to mid elevations.

Season Flowers from June to July.

► SILVER BURWEED

Ambrosia chamissonis

ASTER FAMILY Asteraceae

Description Silver burweed is a coastal herbaceous perennial to 1 m/3.3 ft. in height/length. Its flowers are separate, with males in terminal heads and females in the lower-leaf axils. The felty leaves are deeply divided, silvery green, and to 7 cm/3 in. long.

Habitat Coastal sandy beaches, between logs and rocks.

Season Flowers from June to August.

► PEARLY EVERLASTING

Anaphalis margaritacea

ASTER FAMILY Asteraceae

Description Pearly everlasting grows to 80 cm/32 in. in height and produces heads of small yellowish flowers surrounded by dry white bracts. The leaves are lance shaped, green above, and covered with a white felt underneath. If picked before they go to seed, the flowers remain fresh looking long after they are brought in.

Habitat Common on disturbed sites, roadsides, and rock outcrops.

Season Flowering starts toward the end of July.

▶ ALPINE PUSSYTOES

Antennaria alpina

ASTER FAMILY Asteraceae

Description Alpine pussytoes is a mat-forming herbaceous perennial to 12 cm/5 in. in height. Its flowers are creamy white and held in tight terminal clusters. The leaves are soft, woolly white, and mainly basal.

Etymology As the common name implies, the flower heads resemble cat paws.

Habitat Dry, exposed sites at subalpine to alpine elevations.

Season Flowers from the end of July to August.

▶ MOUNTAIN ARNICA

Arnica latifolia

ASTER FAMILY Asteraceae

Description Mountain arnica is an unbranched herbaceous perennial to 60 cm/24 in. in height. Its showy yellow flowers grow to 5 cm/2 in. across and light up the mountain slopes by midsummer; they usually grow in groups of three, each with 8 to 12 ray petals. The stem leaves are coarsely toothed and broadly lanceolate and form in two to four opposite pairs. Mountain arnica is usually seen with one terminal flower and two to three more on the lower secondary stems.

Habitat One of the most common arnicas; it prefers moist slopes and meadows at mid to subalpine elevations.

Season Flowers from July and August.

▶ NODDING BEGGARTICKS

Bidens cernua

ASTER FAMILY Asteraceae

Description Nodding beggarticks is a herbaceous annual to 1 m/3.3 ft. tall. Its flowers consist of six to eight yellow ray florets surrounding yellow-orange disc florets. As the flowers mature, they take on a relaxed or nodding appearance. The stem leaves are opposite, sawtoothed, and to 20 cm/8 in. in length.

Etymology The genus name, *Bidens*, means "two toothed," in reference to the two barbed bristles on top of the seed (fruit). The common name beggarticks comes from the shape of the seed or fruit and its ability to stick to passersby like a tick.

Origin Nodding beggarticks and common beggarticks (*B. frondosa*) are thought to have been introduced as garden ornamentals from eastern North America.

Habitat Both species can be seen growing together in wet soils and ditches and along lake and pond shores.

Season Flowers from August to September, with the seed ripening between September and October.

Reproduction By its barbed seed. This plant has ingeniously evolved a method of seed dispersal through its ability to attach itself to clothes, fur, and waterfowl.

Concerns Has become a problem due to its ability to overshadow native plants around lakes and ponds.

▶ EDIBLE THISTLE

Cirsium edule

ASTER FAMILY Asteraceae

Description Edible thistle is a showy biennial and sometimes perennial to as tall as 2 m/6.6 ft. in favourable conditions. The well-armed leaves are alternating and lance shaped, with spined lobes. The beautiful pinkish-purple flowers nod when young. Short-style thistle (*C. brevistylum*) is similar, except the styles are shorter.

Traditional use As with most thistles native to the Pacific Northwest, the taproots and lower stem provide emergency food when peeled.

Habitat Lightly covered forest edges and moist meadows.

Season Flowers from July to September, depending on elevation.

HORSEWEED CANADIAN FLEABANE

Conyza canadensis var. glabrata

ASTER FAMILY Asteraceae

Description Horseweed is an easily overlooked North American annual to 1.5 m/5 ft. tall. The lanceolate leaves, 2–10 cm/1–4 in. long, get smaller and almost stalkless as they progress up the stalks. The small ray flowers are white to off-white, numerous, and insignificant looking.

Etymology Some authorities say that horses relish the plant, while others say it bothers their nostrils. It could be both.

Habitat Fields, roadsides, and gardens at low elevations. Horseweed is considered a weed in North America, especially in agricultural areas, where it can greatly reduce crop harvests.

Season Flowers from July to September.

MOUNTAIN DAISY SUBALPINE DAISY

Erigeron peregrinus

ASTER FAMILY Asteraceae

Description Mountain daisy is a showy herbaceous perennial to 60 cm/24 in. in height. Its light- to dark-purple flowers grow to 6 cm/2 in. across and are usually borne singly. The lance-shaped basal leaves are 1–20 cm/0.5–8 in. long and form in clumps; smaller lance-shaped leaves clasp the flower stems. This beautiful plant is often seen in association with Arctic lupine (*Lupinus arcticus*), valerian (*Valeriana sitchensis*), and mountain arnica (*Arnica latifolia*).

Habitat Moist meadows and slopes at mid to subalpine elevations.

Season Flowers from mid-July to August, and into September at higher elevations.

WOOLLY SUNFLOWER WOOLLY ERIOPHYLLUM

Eriophyllum lanatum

ASTER FAMILY Asteraceae

Description Woolly sunflower is a herbaceous perennial to 60 cm/24 in. in height. Its bright-yellow flowers are borne singly, 3–4 cm/1.5 in. across, with 8 to 11 petals surrounding a centre disc. The woolly leaves to 8 cm/3 in. long are artemisia green and deeply lobed.

Etymology The genus name, *Eriophyllum*, also one of its common names, refers to the woolly leaves.

Habitat Dry exposed slopes and outcrops at low to mid elevations.

Season Flowers from mid-May to July.

GUMWEED

Grindelia integrifolia

ASTER FAMILY Asteraceae

Description Gumweed is a herbaceous perennial to 1 m/3.3 ft. in height. Its yellow ray flowers grow to 5 cm/2 in. across, with the bracts covered in a gummy latex. The basal leaves are yellowish green, 5–30 cm/2–12 in. long and lance shaped. Gumweeds are halophytes—they need salt, which they get from salt spray from the ocean.

Traditional use The latex was used to treat asthma, bronchitis, and whooping cough.

Habitat Coastal bluffs, grassy slopes, beaches, and saltwater flats. One of the most common and welcome flowers on the coast.

Season Flowers prolifically from June to September.

▶ WHITE-FLOWERED HAWKWEED

Hieracium albiflorum

ASTER FAMILY Asteraceae

Description White-flowered hawkweed is a herbaceous perennial to 0.4–1 m/1.3–3.3 ft. tall. Its creamy white flowers are 1 cm/0.5 in. across and, like the dandelion, the head is made up of only ray flowers. The leaves are mainly basal, lanceolate, and hairy.

Etymology The common name hawkweed comes from a Greek myth that the juice of the plant would clear the eyes of a hawk.

Habitat Disturbed sites and open coniferous forests at low to mid elevations.

Season Flowers from June to July at low elevations and from June to August at higher elevations.

▶ FLESHY JAUMEA MARSH JAUMEA

Jaumea carnosa

ASTER FAMILY Asteraceae

Description Fleshy jaumea is a small perennial salt-marsh plant that is 15–25 cm/6–10 in. tall and quite often prostrate. It has opposite succulent green leaves on soft pinkish-green stems. The small narrow ray flowers are yellow and usually solitary. It spreads by an extensive rhizome system. Jaumea is a halophyte. It has adapted to grow in salt-rich soils and salt-laden air.

Habitat Tidal flats and marshes.

Season Flowers from spring to summer.

▶ APARGIDIUM

Microseris borealis

ASTER FAMILY Asteraceae

Description Apargidium is a bog-loving perennial 10–50 cm/4–20 in. tall. The leaves are all basal lance oblong shaped, smooth edged to slightly toothed, and 10–25 cm/4–10 in. long. The yellow flowers are solitary and up to 4 cm/1.5 in. across and consist of ray flowers only, much like a dandelion.

Habitat Mostly coastal and montane in sphagnum bogs and wet meadows.

Season Flowers from June to September.

▶ COLTSFOOT

Petasites palmatus

ASTER FAMILY Asteraceae

Description Coltsfoot is a large-leaved herbaceous perennial to 60 cm/24 in. in height. Its purplish white flowers emerge before the leaves in late winter; they are grouped together to form terminal clusters approximately 10 cm/4 in. across on a 60 cm/24 in. stalk. The leaves have seven to nine lobes and grow to 30 cm/12 in. across. They are green above and have a white woolly belly.

Traditional use The leaves were used to cover berries in steam-cooking pits.

Etymology The genus name, *Petasites*, is from the Greek word *petasos*, meaning "hat." Japanese children once used the large leaves as hats.

Habitat Moist to wet areas at low to mid elevations.

Season Flowers from May to June.

SWEET COLTSFOOT ALPINE COLTSFOOT

Petasites frigidus

ASTER FAMILY Asteraceae

Description Sweet coltsfoot is a herbaceous perennial to 50 cm/20 in. in height. Its white to pink flowers are grouped together to form open clusters held above the leaves, which are white and woolly below and deeply lobed into three to five segments.

Traditional use The leaves were used to cover berries in steam-cooking pots.

Etymology The genus name, *Petasites*, comes from the Greek word *petasos*, meaning "hat," referring to the large basal leaves. Japanese children once used the large leaves of *P. japonica* as hats.

Habitat Bogs, lake edges, and wet meadows at subalpine to alpine elevations.

Season Flowers from late July to August.

ARROW-LEAVED GROUNDSEL

Senecio triangularis

ASTER FAMILY Asteraceae

Description Arrow-leaved groundsel is a clump-forming herbaceous perennial 30–150 cm/12–60 in. in height. Its yellow flowers grow to 1.5 cm/0.75 in. across and form in flat-topped clusters. The triangular leaves are 4–20 cm/2–8 in. long, squared at the base, and evenly toothed.

Habitat Moist sites from mid to alpine elevations.

Season Flowers from July to September, depending on elevation.

▶ CANADA GOLDENROD

Solidago canadensis

ASTER FAMILY Asteraceae

Description Canada goldenrod is a herbaceous perennial of various heights, from 0.3 m/1 ft. to 1.5 m/5 ft. Its small golden flowers are densely packed to form terminal pyramidal clusters. The many small leaves grow at the base of the flowers; they are alternate, lance linear, and sharply saw-toothed to smooth.

Habitat Roadsides, wastelands, and forest edges at low to mid elevations.

Season Flowers from July to August.

▶ VANILLA LEAF

Achlys triphylla

BARBERRY FAMILY Berberidaceae

Description Vanilla leaf is a herbaceous perennial to 30 cm/12 in. in height. Its small white flowers are formed on a spike that stands above the leaf. The small fruit (achene) is crescent shaped and greenish to reddish purple. The wavy leaves have long stems and are divided into three leaflets, one on each side and the third at the tip. When dried, the leaves have a faint vanilla-like scent.

Traditional use The leaves were used as an insect repellant.

Habitat Dry to moist forests at low to mid elevations.

Season Flowers from mid-May to June.

AMERICAN SEAROCKET

Cakile edentula

MUSTARD FAMILY Brassicaceae

Description American searocket is a coastal, sprawling annual to 50 cm/20 in. in height. Its pink to mauve flowers form toward the end of the stems and are up to 8 cm/3 in. long. The odd-looking leaves are oblong, to 7 cm/2.75 in. long, and, like the stems, fleshy. When ripe, the pod-like fruit break up easily in the waves.

Habitat Coastal sandy beaches; prefers long shallow tides.

Season Flowers from mid-June to July.

LITTLE WESTERN BITTERCRESS

Cardamine oligosperma

MUSTARD FAMILY Brassicaceae

Description Little western bittercress is a taprooted annual or biennial, depending on whether it germinates in the spring or in the fall. It is 10–40 cm/ 4–16 in. tall. Its basal leaves are deeply divided and form a rosette; the stem leaves are alternate and a simpler form of the basal leaves. The small white flowers have four petals, each to 4 cm/1.5 in. long. The erect seedpods, or siliques, are typical of the mustard family. (See similar species on p. 223.)

Etymology The species name, *oligosperma*, translates to "few seeded."

Habitat A weedy plant that can survive in a variety of damp locations, as well as on roadsides and in gravel areas, at mid elevations.

Season Flowers from May to July.

BRITTLE PRICKLY-PEAR CACTUS

Opuntia fragilis

CACTUS FAMILY Cactaceae

Description Brittle prickly-pear cactus is a mat-forming, well-armed perennial to 60 cm/24 in. across. Its yellow flowers are tissue-like and to 5 cm/2 in. across. The leaves are modified succulent stems, each carrying very pointed spines to 3 cm/1 in. long.

Traditional use The sturdy, sharp spines were used to pierce ears.

Habitat Dry exposed sites with well-drained soil.

Season Flowers from June to July.

TWINFLOWER

Linnaea borealis

HONEYSUCKLE FAMILY Caprifoliaceae

Description Twinflower is an attractive trailing evergreen to 10 cm/4 in. in height. Its nodding pink flowers are fragrant, to 0.5 cm/0.25 in. long, and borne in pairs at the end of slender, Y-shaped stems. The evergreen leaves are 1 cm/0.5 in. long, oval, shiny dark green above, and paler below, with minute teeth on the upper half.

Etymology The genus, *Linnaea*, is named for Carl Linnaeus, a Swedish botanist and the founder of the binomial system for plant and animal classification. Twinflower is said to have been his favourite flower.

Habitat Common in forests at low to mid elevations across Canada.

Season Flowers from mid-June to July.

► CLIMBING HONEYSUCKLE

Lonicera ciliosa

HONEYSUCKLE FAMILY Caprifoliaceae

Description Climbing honeysuckle is a deciduous woody vine capable of climbing trees to 8 m/26 ft. in height. Its orange flowers are trumpet shaped, to 4 cm/1.5 in. long, and form in clusters in the terminal leaves. By late summer, bunches of bright-red berries are produced in the cup-shaped leaves. The leaves are oval, 5–8 cm/2–3 in. long, and, like all honeysuckles, opposite. This species is the showiest of the native honeysuckles. Its main pollinators are hummingbirds and moths.

Habitat Scattered in low-elevation Douglas fir forests; more common near the ocean.

Season Flowering starts at the end of May.

CAUTION The berries are poisonous.

► PURPLE HONEYSUCKLE HAIRY HONEYSUCKLE

Lonicera hispidula

HONEYSUCKLE FAMILY Caprifoliaceae

Description Purple honeysuckle is a crawling vine to 4 m/13 ft. long. Its pinkish-purple flowers grow to 2 cm/1 in. long and develop bright-red berries by the end of the summer. The leaves are similar to those of the climbing honeysuckle: opposite, with the top pair fused to form a cup. The young stems and leaves are lightly haired.

Habitat Dry coniferous forests near the ocean.

Season Flowers from June to July.

CAUTION The berries are poisonous.

▶ FIELD CHICKWEED

Cerastium arvense

PINK FAMILY Caryophyllaceae

Description Field chickweed is a low-growing perennial to 30 cm/12 in. in height. Its showy white flowers are 1–1.5 cm/0.25–0.75 in. across, with five deeply notched petals. The leaves are opposite, to 3 cm/1 in. long, and vary from lanceolate to linear.

Etymology The species name, *arvense*, means "field."

Habitat Dry areas (especially in spring) on rock bluffs, in fields, and on high beaches. Field chickweed is the dominant white flower seen in meadows and grassy outcrops on the coast.

Season Flowers from May to June.

▶ SEABEACH SANDWORT

Honckenya peploides

PINK FAMILY Caryophyllaceae

Description Seabeach sandwort is a herbaceous perennial to 30 cm/12 in. in height. Its odd-looking flowers are greenish white, to 1.5 cm/0.75 in. across, and held in terminal-leaf whorls. The fleshy leaves are elliptical, pale green, opposite, and to 5 cm/2 in. long. Sandwort can be seen growing as a single plant or as a mat to 1 m/3.3 ft. across.

Etymology The genus name is after Gerhard August Honckeny (1724–1805), an 18th-century German botanist.

Habitat Upper sandy beaches, between rocks and logs.

Season Flowers from July to August.

▶ ORACHE

Atriplex patula

GOOSEFOOT FAMILY Chenopodiaceae

Description Orache is a fleshy annual 0.3–1 m/1–3.3 ft. long. Its leaves are variable; the upper leaves are lanceolate, toothed, and alternate, and the lower leaves are larger, more arrowhead shaped, opposite, and 5–8 cm/2–3 in. long. The inconspicuous green flowers form in clusters, both terminal and in the axils of the leaves. The seeds and fruit are enclosed by two triangular bracts. Orache is in the spinach family and is prepared in the same way as spinach. Moderation is recommended.

Habitat Saline soils along the coast.

Season In flower and fruit from July to October.

▶ SEA ASPARAGUS AMERICAN GLASSWORT

Salicornia virginica

GOOSEFOOT FAMILY Chenopodiaceae

Description Sea asparagus is an edible perennial to 30 cm/12 in. in height. Its tiny yellow-green flowers grow in threes in small sunken cavities along the succulent stems. The scale-like leaves are almost non-existent. As its name suggests, the young stems of this wild green vegetable can be collected and eaten raw or cooked. They have a salty flavour, but it can be masked with a few herbs.

Habitat Common along the BC and Washington coastline in areas with little wave action. It can form dense colonies of up to hundreds of square metres or feet in tidal flats and salt marshes.

Season Flowers from July to August.

► BUNCHBERRY DWARF DOGWOOD

Cornus canadensis

DOGWOOD FAMILY Cornaceae

Description Bunchberry, a perennial no higher than 20 cm/8 in. tall, is a reduced version of the Pacific dogwood tree (*C. nuttallii*). The tiny greenish flowers are surrounded by four showy white bracts, just like the flowers of the larger dogwood. The evergreen leaves, 4–7 cm/2–3 in. long, grow in whorls of five to seven and have parallel veins like the larger tree. The beautiful red berries form in bunches (hence the name) just above the leaves in August.

Traditional use Bunchberries were eaten by coastal Indigenous groups. They were usually eaten raw, with grease, in late summer to early autumn.

Habitat From low to high elevations in cool, moist coniferous forests and bogs.

Season Bunchberry and Pacific dogwood have a habit of flowering twice, once in the spring and then again in the late summer.

► SPREADING STONECROP

Sedum divergens

STONECROP FAMILY Crassulaceae

Description Spreading stonecrop is a mat-forming perennial 10–15 cm/4–6 in. in height. Its yellow flowers have five petals held in clusters by stems 10–15 cm/4–6 in. tall. The green to red leaves are plump, round, succulent, and less than 1 cm/0.5 in. across.

Etymology The genus name, *Sedum*, comes from the Latin, meaning "to sit," referring to the way the leaves are placed.

Habitat Rocky bluffs, exposed talus slopes at low to high elevations.

Season Flowers from June to August, depending on elevation.

BROAD-LEAVED STONECROP

Sedum spathulifolium

STONECROP FAMILY Crassulaceae

Description Broad-leaved stonecrop is a rhizomatous spreading succulent to 8 cm/3 in. tall. The spoon-shaped leaves are flattened more than those of most sedums. The attractive yellow flowers are formed in flat-topped clusters, which contrast well with the green to reddish leaves.

Etymology Stonecrop's old meaning was to crop or remove the leaves or plants from stone.

Habitat Mainly found on coastal bluffs to mid elevations.

Season Flowers from June to August.

BEACH MORNING GLORY SHORE BINDWEED

Convolvulus soldanella

MORNING GLORY FAMILY Convolvulaceae

Description Beach morning glory is a creeping herbaceous perennial to 50 cm/20 in. long. The beautiful funnel-like flowers are to 6 cm/2.5 in. long and alternating pinkish purple and white.

Etymology The species name, *soldanella*, is from the Italian word *soldo*, a small coin, referring to the round leaves.

Habitat Sandy coastal areas from the Haida Gwaii to California.

Season Flowers from July to September.

MANROOT BIGROOT

Marah oreganus

CUCUMBER FAMILY Cucurbitaceae

Description Manroot is a climbing herbaceous perennial to lengths of over 7 m/23 ft. It has separate female and male flowers that grow on the same plant: the white bell-shaped female flowers reach 1 cm/0.5 in. across and are formed singly, and the male flowers grow in small clusters. The fleshy fruit, to 8 cm/3 in. across, resembles miniature bristly rugby balls. In August, the bottoms of the fruit burst open to reveal the large seeds, 2 cm/1 in. long. The palmate leaves alternate from the stalk and grow 10–20 cm/4–8 in. across.

Traditional use A mixture was made from the plant to treat venereal disease.

Habitat Open fields, hillsides, and forest edges at low elevations.

Season In fruit and flower from July to September.

SLOUGH SEDGE

Carex obnupta

SEDGE FAMILY Cyperaceae

Description Slough sedge is a wetland plant to 1.5 m/5 ft. in height. Its inflorescence (flower head) is made up of dark-brown male and female drooping spikes. The leaves are typical, grass-like, and not as long as the flowering stem.

Traditional use Slough sedge was and still is an important basket-weaving material. The leaves are gathered in summer, split in half, and then hung to dry and bundled for fall and winter use.

Habitat Wet meadows, swamps, marshes, and lake edges at lower elevations.

Season Flowers from June to July.

▶ LARGE-HEADED SEDGE

Carex macrocephala

SEDGE FAMILY Cyperaceae

Description Large-headed sedge is a perennial rhizome-spreading sand-dune plant 6–30 cm/2–12 in. tall. The large seed head, to 6 cm/2 in. long, is dense and spike-like. The grooved leaves are clustered near the stem base but often surpass the flowering head in height.

Etymology The species name breaks down to *macro*, "large," and *cephala*, "head."

Habitat Large drifts can be seen on coastal sand dunes.

Season Flowers from June to July.

CAUTION This plant is not pleasant to step on in bare feet.

▶ BLACK ALPINE SEDGE

Carex nigricans

SEDGE FAMILY Cyperaceae

Description Black alpine sedge is a perennial that forms loose clumps of stems up to 30 cm/12 in. tall. The female flowers have dark bracts, and the fruit is dark coloured and long beaked. The channelled leaves form compact clumps at the base of the stems.

Habitat Usually found near wet areas, snowbanks, ponds, snowmelt streams, and brooks. Black alpine sedge is one of the more dominant sedges at high elevations.

Season Flowers from July to August, depending on elevation.

► NARROW-LEAVED COTTON GRASS

Eriophorum angustifolium

SEDGE FAMILY Cyperaceae

Description Cotton grass is a rhizomatous herbaceous perennial to 70 cm/28 in. in height. The inconspicuous flowers are held on triangular stems 30–70 cm/12–28 in. long. When mature, the flowers are covered with silky white hairs (hence the name cotton) to 3 cm/1 in. long. The flat leaves look like grass.

Etymology The species name, *angustifolium*, means "narrow leaved."

Habitat Peat bogs at low to high elevations; tolerates shallow water.

Season Seeds from June to July.

► TULE HARD-STEMMED BULRUSH

Scirpus lacustris

SEDGE FAMILY Cyperaceae

Description Tule is a semi-aquatic perennial that can grow to 3 m/10 ft. in height. The flowers, or inflorescence, are terminal and resemble the outline of an umbrella. The few leaves the plants have are mainly basal and usually reduced to sheaths.

Traditional use Tule stems were used extensively on the west coast for making mats and in basketry.

Etymology The species name, *lacustris*, means "pertaining to lakes."

Habitat Lake edges, ponds, marshes, and muddy or sandy areas near creeks. It is usually associated with fresh water; however, it will also grow in brackish water.

Season Flowers from July to September.

▶ ROUND-LEAVED SUNDEW

Drosera rotundifolia

SUNDEW FAMILY Droseraceae

Description There are about a hundred species of sundew around the world, and all of them eat insects. BC's native round-leaved sundew is a small perennial, 5–25 cm/2–10 in. high, with inconspicuous white flowers. It is the leaves that make this plant a curiosity. They are equipped with fine red hairs, each tipped with a shiny globe of reddish secretion. Small insects are attracted to the secretion and get stuck in it; the leaf then slowly folds over and smothers the unsuspecting visitors. The plant's favourite foods are mosquitoes, gnats, and midges.

Traditional use The whole plant is acrid, and the leaves were once used to remove warts, corns, and bunions.

Habitat Peat bogs throughout the west coast. It can be seen growing with the more narrow-leaved great sundew (*D. anglica*).

Season Flowers from June to August.

▶ COMMON HORSETAIL

Equisetum arvense

HORSETAIL FAMILY Equisetaceae

Description Common horsetail is a herbaceous perennial to 75 cm/30 in. in height. It has two types of stems, fertile and sterile, both hollow except at the nodes. The fertile stems are unbranched, to 30 cm/12 in. in height, and lack chlorophyll; they bear spores in the terminal head. The green sterile stems grow to 75 cm/30 in. in height and have leaves whorled at the joints. Horsetails are all that is left of the prehistoric Equisetaceae family, some members of which grew to the size of trees.

Traditional use The young fertile shoots of both common horsetail and giant horsetail (*E. telmateia*) were eaten raw or boiled.

Habitat Low wet seepage areas, meadows, damp sandy soils, and gravel roads from low to high elevations.

Season Spores are produced from May to July.

▶ SCOURING RUSH

Equisetum hyemale

HORSETAIL FAMILY Equisetaceae

Description Scouring rush is a herbaceous perennial to 1.7 m/5.6 ft. in height. Its dark-green stems are all alike, with black rings separating the hollow sections. They are branchless and rough or scratchy to the touch. Like ferns, horsetails do not produce flowers or fruit but reproduce from spores. These are borne in hard, pointed terminal cores.

Traditional use The abrasive stems were used as sandpaper, and the dark roots were used to make baskets.

Habitat Usually close to fresh water, by streams and rivers or at the base of moist slopes with loose rich soil.

Season Spores are produced from July to August.

▶ SWAMP HORSETAIL

Equisetum fluviatile

HORSETAIL FAMILY Equisetaceae

Description Swamp horsetail is a herbaceous perennial that spreads by spores and rhizomes. It grows to 0.3–1 m/1–3.3 ft. in height. Many, but not all, stems have whorls of short branches; fertile and sterile stems look alike.

Traditional use Used for sanding and filing; the early spring shoots were eaten.

Etymology The species name, *fluviatile*, means "growing in a stream."

Habitat Ponds, swamps, ditches, and other sluggish waters with mud bottoms at low to mid elevations.

Season Spores are produced from June to August.

▶ WHITE MOUNTAIN HEATHER

Cassiope mertensiana

HEATHER FAMILY Ericaceae

Description White mountain heather is a low-growing shrub to 30 cm/12 in. in height and up to several metres or feet wide. Its nodding flowers are bell shaped and pure white; they grow singly on small stalks arising from the leaf axils. The tiny evergreen leaves are scale-like and arranged in four rows.

Habitat Common at subalpine and alpine elevations; can be seen growing with pink mountain heather (*Phyllodoce empetriformis*).

Season Flowers from July to August.

▶ LITTLE PRINCE'S PINE MENZIES' PIPSISSEWA

Chimaphila menziesii

HEATHER FAMILY Ericaceae

Description Little prince's pine is the daintier of the two *Chimaphila* spp., reaching a maximum height of only 15 cm/6 in. Its creamy-white flowers are slightly fragrant, range from one to three per stem, and nod above the foliage. The leaves are alternate, to 5 cm/2 in. long, serrately edged, and a darker green than those of the larger prince's pine (*C. umbellata*).

Etymology The species is named for Dr. Archibald Menzies, a surgeon and botanist who sailed with Captain George Vancouver.

Habitat Cool coniferous forests at low to mid elevations. Both species are often found growing in the same area.

Season Flowers from June to July.

▶ PRINCE'S PINE

Chimaphila umbellata

HEATHER FAMILY Ericaceae

Description Prince's pine is a small evergreen shrub to 30 cm/12 in. in height. The white to pink flowers are waxy and formed in loose nodding clusters held above the foliage; the resulting brownish seed capsules are erect and persist through the winter. The leathery leaves form in whorls, grow to 5 cm/2 in. long, and are sharply toothed.

Traditional use The leaves were steeped and used as a cold remedy.

Habitat Cool coniferous forests at low to mid elevations.

Season Flowers from June to July.

▶ KINNIKINNICK BEARBERRY

Arctostaphylos uva-ursi

HEATHER FAMILY Ericaceae

Description Kinnikinnick is a trailing, mat-forming evergreen that rarely grows above 25 cm/10 in. in height. Its fragrant pinkish flowers bloom in spring and are replaced by bright-red berries 1 cm/0.5 in. across by late summer. The small oval leaves grow to 3 cm/1 in. long and are leathery and alternate. Grouse and bears feed on the berries.

Traditional use The leaves were dried and smoked, sometimes mixed with other plants.

Etymology Kinnikinnick is an eastern Indigenous word used to describe a tobacco mix.

Habitat Dry rock outcrops and well-drained forest areas from sea level to high elevations.

Season Flowers and berries from June to September, depending on elevation.

▶ KINNIKINNICK HYBRID

Arctostaphylos × media

HEATHER FAMILY Ericaceae

Description This hybrid is a naturally occurring cross between kinnikinnick (A. *uva-ursi*) and hairy manzanita (A. *columbiana*). The result is a faster-spreading and taller (to 90 cm/36 in. tall) shrub than A. *uva-ursi*. The branches are redder, and the undersides of the bluish-green leaves are slightly hairy, which contrasts well with the light-pink flowers.

Habitat Well-drained exposed rock outcrops at low to mid elevations.

Season Flowers from June to July.

▶ ONE-SIDED WINTERGREEN

Orthilia secunda

HEATH FAMILY Ericaceae

Description One-sided wintergreen is an evergreen perennial to 20 cm/8 in. in height. Its flowers, as the common name suggests, grow on one side of the stem; they are very small, white, and bell shaped, with a protruding, straight style. The leaves are mostly basal, toothed, oval, and green.

Etymology *Secunda* is from *secund*, meaning "one-sided."

Habitat Cool coniferous forests at low to high elevations.

Season Flowers from June and July.

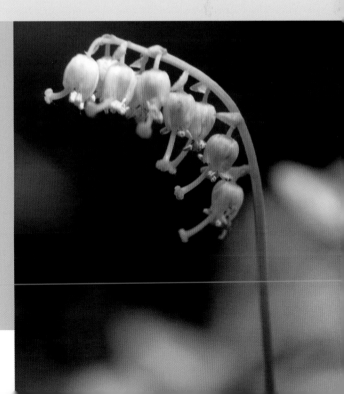

PINK MOUNTAIN HEATHER

Phyllodoce empetriformis

HEATHER FAMILY Ericaceae

Description Pink mountain heather is a mat-forming evergreen shrub 10–50 cm/4–20 in. in height. Its rose-pink flowers are bell shaped to 1 cm/0.5 in. long and held out on long slender stalks. With their stiff needle-like leaves, to 1 cm/0.5 in. long, the branches resemble miniature conifers. A hike into alpine meadows is well worth the effort to see this beautiful fragrant plant.

Habitat Rocky sites at subalpine elevations.

Season Flowers from July to August.

WHITE-VEINED WINTERGREEN

Pyrola picta

HEATHER FAMILY Ericaceae

Description White-veined wintergreen is an attractive evergreen perennial to 30 cm/12 in. in height. Its drooping flowers are yellowish green with a waxy finish; they grow to 1 cm/0.5 in. across and have a protruding, curved style. The basal leaves are 5–7 cm/ 2–3 in. long and have leathery, dark-green-and-white venation.

Etymology The species name, *picta*, means "painted," in reference to the beautiful leaves.

Habitat Cool coniferous forests at low to mid elevations.

Season Flowers from June and July.

▶ PINK WINTERGREEN

Pyrola asarifolia

HEATHER FAMILY Ericaceae

Description Pink wintergreen is an evergreen perennial to 40 cm/16 in. in height. Its pinkish flowers, to 1 cm/0.5 in. across, are carried on 30–40 cm/12–16 in. stems. The leaves are roundish to elliptical, 5–8 cm/2–3 in. long, and formed in a basal rosette. It can form extensive carpets, up to 2 m by 8 m/6.5 ft. by 25 ft.

Etymology *Pyrola* is from *pyrus* ("pear"), indicating that the leaves are sometimes pear shaped.

Habitat Moist forests with rich soil at low to mid elevations.

Season Flowers from June to July.

▶ GREEN-FLOWERED WINTERGREEN

Pyrola chlorantha

HEATHER FAMILY Ericaceae

Description Green-flowered wintergreen is an evergreen perennial to 25 cm/10 in. in height. Its greenish-yellow flowers are bowl shaped, to 1 cm/0.5 in. across, and have a protruding, curved style. The leaves are basal, roundish, and smaller than most wintergreen. This species is far daintier than pink wintergreen (*P. asarifolia*).

Etymology *Chlorantha* means "green flowered."

Habitat Cool coniferous forests at low to mid elevations.

Season Flowers from June to July.

▶ BEACH PEA

Lathyrus japonicus

PEA FAMILY Fabaceae

Description Beach pea is a climbing herbaceous perennial to 1.5 m/5 ft. long. Its flowers vary from dark purple to blue and are produced in loose clusters of two to eight. The leaves have 6 to 12 opposite-facing leaflets, with curly tendrils on the tips. At the bottom of the leaf stem are two triangular leaf-like stipules, good identifiers for this species. The small seeds grow in pods 3–7 cm/1–3 in. long.

Traditional use Beach pea seeds were eaten raw or boiled and cured in seal oil.

Habitat Sandy beaches, among the logs.

Season Flowers from May to July.

▶ ARCTIC LUPINE

Lupinus arcticus

PEA FAMILY Fabaceae

Description Arctic lupine is a herbaceous perennial to 60 cm/24 in. in height. Its pea-like flowers are light to dark blue and grow in a long terminal cluster; the resulting small seeds are contained in hairy pods to 4 cm/1.5 in. long. The basal leaves are long-stemmed and have six to eight leaflets with pointed tips. Arctic lupine is often seen in association with western anemone (*Anemone occidentalis*), partridgefoot (*Luetkea pectinata*), wood betony (*Pedicularis bracteosa*), and white-flowered rhododendron (*Rhododendron albiflorum*).

Habitat Most abundant in mid to subalpine elevations.

Season Flowers from July to August at high elevations.

▶ LARGE-LEAVED LUPINE

Lupinus polyphyllus

PEA FAMILY Fabaceae

Description Large-leaved lupine and its cultivars are the lupines you are most likely to see in parks and gardens. In its natural setting, large-leaved lupine grows to 1.5 m/5 ft. in height. The blue pea-like flowers are borne in clusters to 40 cm/16 in. long. The large leaves consist of 10 to 17 leaflets, to 12 cm/5 in. long. The seeds are in hairy pods to 5 cm/2 in. long.

Etymology The species name, *Polyphyllus*, means "with many leaves."

Habitat Moist sunny areas from sea level to mid elevations.

Season Flowers from June to July.

▶ SPRINGBANK CLOVER

Trifolium wormskioldii

PEA FAMILY Fabaceae

Description Springbank clover is a herbaceous perennial that is usually prostrate to 30 cm/12 in. in height. The flowers, to 3 cm/1 in. across, are pink to reddish purple and often white tipped. The finely toothed leaves are typically clover shaped, with three leaflets joined at one point.

Traditional use Springbank clover was an important vegetable on the west coast. The rhizomes were dug up, cleaned, and steamed and eaten or stored for winter use.

Etymology The species name commemorates Danish botanist Morten Wormskjold.

Habitat Common among the coastline in moist areas from sea level to mid elevations.

Season Flowers from June to August.

▶ GIANT VETCH

Vicia gigantea

PEA FAMILY Fabaceae

Description Giant vetch is a succulent herbaceous perennial to 2 m/6.5 ft. in length. The pea-like flowers vary in subtle colours from whitish yellow to pinkish purple and are formed in one-sided clusters of 6 to 20. The leaves are equipped with a terminal tendril to aid in climbing. The seed pods when ripe are to 5 cm/2 in. long and black.

Traditional use The seeds were eaten in small quantities.

Habitat Common among the coast in upper shore-lines.

Season Flowers from June to July, with seed pods from the end of July to September.

▶ PINK CORYDALIS

Corydalis sempervirens

BLEEDING HEART FAMILY Fumariaceae

Description Pink corydalis is an annual or biennial to 60 cm/24 in. in height. Its showy pink flowers grow up to 3 cm/1 in. long and have a splash of yellow on the tip. The bluish-green leaves are alternate and multi-divided; they make the plant stand out in a woodland setting even when not in flower.

Habitat Both dry and moist forests at low to mid elevations.

Season Flowers from mid-May to June.

PACIFIC BLEEDING HEART

Dicentra formosa

BLEEDING HEART FAMILY Fumariaceae

Description BC's native bleeding heart is very familiar, thanks to its resemblance to the many cultivated varieties. It is a herbaceous perennial to 40 cm/16 in. in height, with pinkish heart-shaped flowers that hang in clusters of 5 to 15. The delicate fern-like leaves are basal but sweep upward so much that they almost hide the flowers. Under good growing conditions, bleeding hearts can cover hundreds of square metres or feet.

Etymology The species name *formosa* means "beautiful."

Habitat Open broad-leaved forests with nutrient-rich topsoil.

Season Flowering starts in mid-April and lasts until the end of May, with the entire plant collapsing by the beginning of July.

SWAMP GENTIAN

Gentiana douglasiana

GENTIAN FAMILY Gentianaceae

Description Swamp gentian is a showy annual to 25 cm/10 in. in height. Its white, symmetrical flowers grow to 1.5 cm/0.75 in. across and are usually solitary. The stem leaves are elliptical and opposite, to 1 cm/0.5 in. long, with the basal leaves sitting in a rosette.

Etymology The genus is named after King Gentius of Illyria (second century BC), who is said to have discovered the medicinal properties of these plants.

Habitat Bogs and wet meadows at low to high elevations.

Season Flowers from mid-June to mid-July.

▶ KING GENTIAN

Gentiana sceptrum

GENTIAN FAMILY Gentianaceae

Description King gentian is a swamp-loving herbaceous perennial to 60 cm/24 in. tall. The showy blue flowers are to 5 cm/2 in. long and have dark-green dots on the inside. The leaves are oblong lanceolate, opposite, and stemless. With a little imagination this beautiful plant could look like a sceptre (hence the species name *sceptrum*).

Habitat Lake edges and wet meadows at low to mid elevations. I have found king gentian from sea level to lakeside at 1,000 m/3,300 ft.

Season Flowers at the end of summer, from August to November, depending on elevation.

▶ GOLDEN-EYED GRASS

Sisyrinchium californicum

IRIS FAMILY Iridaceae

Description Golden-eyed grass is an iris-like perennial up to 40 cm/16 in. tall. The yellow flowers are to 2 cm/1 in. across and have six petals each, with six purplish veins. The leaves are to 30 cm/12 in. long, mainly basal, dull green, and narrow.

Etymology The genus name, *Sisyrinchium*, is the name Theophrastus gave to the iris; the species name lets us know this interesting plant grows in California.

Habitat Wet soil pockets along the coast. The most northerly place it can be found is the west coast of Vancouver Island. I took the photos for this book at Clo-oose, on Vancouver Island.

Season Flowers midsummer.

▶ SATIN FLOWER

Sisyrinchium douglasii

IRIS FAMILY Iridaceae

Description Satin flower is an early-flowering perennial to 30 cm/12 in. tall. The satiny flowers have six petals and are reddish purple and to 4 cm/ 1.5 in. across. The narrow green leaves make the plant look like a clump of grass when out of flower.

Etymology The species name, *douglasii*, commemorates the famous explorer and botanist David Douglas, who discovered this plant in 1826 near the Columbia River.

Habitat Unlike golden-eyed grass, satin flower requires dry, rocky bluffs and meadows at low to mid elevations.

Season Flowers from March to May.

▶ YERBA BUENA

Satureja douglasii

MINT FAMILY Lamiaceae

Description Yerba buena is a fragrant trailing herbaceous perennial to 1 m/40 in. long. Its inconspicuous flowers are white or slightly purple and borne in the leaf axils. The egg-shaped leaves grow opposite each other to 3 cm/1 in. long and are bluntly toothed and scented when crushed.

Traditional use The leaves were steeped for a refreshing tea.

Etymology The common name yerba buena, meaning "good herb," was given to this plant by missionary Spanish priests in California.

Habitat Dry open forests.

Season Flowers from June to July.

COOLEY'S HEDGE-NETTLE

Stachys cooleyae

MINT FAMILY Lamiaceae

Description Cooley's hedge-nettle is a herbaceous perennial to 1 m/3.3 ft. in height. Its purple-red flowers are trumpet-like with a lower lip; they grow to 4 cm/1.5 in. long and are grouped in terminal clusters. The leaves are mint-like with toothed edges, opposite, finely hairy on both sides, and to 15 cm/6 in. long. The stems are square and finely hairy.

Etymology Cooley's hedge-nettle was first documented in 1891 by Grace Cooley, a professor from New Jersey who saw it near Nanaimo.

Habitat Moist open forests and streamsides at low elevations.

Season Flowers from June to mid-July.

COMMON BUTTERWORT

Pinguicula vulgaris

BLADDERWORT FAMILY Lentibulariaceae

Description Common butterwort is an insect-eating perennial to 15 cm/6 in. tall. The violet-looking flowers are held singly on leafless stems. What looks to be petals are actually lobes on a spurred tube flower. The basal greenish-yellow leaves are equipped with a slimy substance that traps insects; the leaf then lets out juices that digest the insect.

Habitat At the bottom of seepage areas and in bogs and wet meadows at low to subalpine elevations.

Season Flowers from June to August, depending on elevation.

▶ NODDING ONION

Allium cernuum

LILY FAMILY Liliaceae

Description Nodding onion is a herbaceous perennial to 45 cm/18 in. in height. Over a dozen small pink flowers are held in the distinctive nodding umbels. The grassy leaves are basal, to 30 cm/12 in. long, and similar to those of a green onion. Both bulbs and leaves smell of onion. The district of Lillooet was once covered in nodding onions; in the Salish language, *Lillooet* means "place of many onions."

Etymology The species name, *cernuum*, means "nodding."

Traditional use The cooked onions were a delicacy.

Habitat Dry grassy slopes, rocky outcrops, and forest edges at lower elevations.

Season Flowers from June to August.

▶ HOOKER'S ONION

Allium acuminatum

LILY FAMILY Liliaceae

Description Hooker's onion is a herbaceous perennial to 30 cm/12 in. in height. Its rose-coloured flowers are held in upright umbels, unlike those of nodding onion (A. *cernuum*). The leaves are grass-like and wither by blooming time. When crushed, the entire plant smells like onion.

Traditional use The small bulbs were eaten raw or steamed.

Etymology The species name, *acuminatum*, refers to the tapering flower petals.

Habitat Dry grassy slopes and crevices at low elevations.

Season Flowers from mid-May to June.

▶ HARVEST LILY

Brodiaea coronaria

LILY FAMILY Liliaceae

Description Harvest lily is a herbaceous perennial from corms to 30 cm/12 in. in height. Its purple, trumpet-shaped flowers are 4 cm/1.5 in. long and grow in clusters of three to five. The leaves are grass-like and wither by the time flowers are noticeable.

Traditional use The corms were harvested for winter consumption.

Habitat Prefers well-drained grassy slopes.

Season Flowers from the end of June to July.

▶ FOOL'S ONION

Brodiaea hyacinthina

LILY FAMILY Liliaceae

Description Fool's onion is a herbaceous perennial from corms to 30 cm/12 in. in height. The small star-shaped flowers are white with fine stripes of green and held up in terminal clusters on thin stems up to 60 cm/24 in. long. The grass-like leaves are basal and have usually disappeared by the time the flowers are noticeable.

Traditional use The corms were collected and eaten raw or boiled.

Habitat Rocky outcrops and grassy slopes.

Season Flowers at the beginning of June.

▶ COMMON CAMAS

Camassia quamash

LILY FAMILY Liliaceae

Description Common camas is a herbaceous perennial from bulb to 70 cm/20 in. in height. It has six beautiful blue-purple petals to 4 cm/1.5 in. across. The long grass-like leaves are slightly shorter than the flowering stem. Great camas (*C. leichtlinii*) is very similar but taller, to 1.2 m/4 ft. The best way to distinguish the two species is by the petals of the great camas, which twist around the fruit as they wither.

Traditional use The bulbs were an important food source. Wars were fought over ownership of certain meadows.

Habitat Moist meadows in spring, dry meadows in summer, and on grassy slopes at low elevations.

Season Flowers from mid-April to May.

▶ QUEEN'S CUP

Clintonia uniflora

LILY FAMILY Liliaceae

Description Queen's cup is a herbaceous perennial 8–15 cm/3–6 in. in height. Its white, cup-shaped flowers grow to 3 cm/1 in. across, usually with only one borne at the end of a slender stalk. The cobalt-blue fruit is round to pear shaped and singular. The two to five bright-green leaves are broadly lance shaped, basal, and fleshy.

Etymology The genus name commemorates DeWitt Clinton, governor of New York State, botanist, and developer of the Erie Canal.

Habitat Cool moist coniferous forests at low to high elevations.

Season Flowers start in mid-June at lower elevations; the berries turn blue by mid-August and last until October.

HOOKER'S FAIRYBELLS

Disporum hookeri

LILY FAMILY Liliaceae

Description Hooker's fairybells is an elegant branching herbaceous perennial to 1 m/3.3 ft. in height. Its white flowers hang in pairs, or sometimes in threes, with the stamens extending beyond the petals. This distinguishes Hooker's fairybells from Smith's fairybells (*D. Smithii*), whose stamens do not extend beyond the petals.

Traditional use Some Indigenous groups ate the berries; however, most considered them poisonous.

Etymology The common name commemorates Joseph Dalton Hooker (1817–1911), a prominent English botanist.

Habitat Cool moist forests at low elevations.

Season Flowers from the end of May to June. By August, the flowers have been replaced by yellow-red berries.

CHOCOLATE LILY

Fritillaria lanceolata

LILY FAMILY Liliaceae

Description Chocolate lily is a herbaceous perennial from bulb to 80 cm/32 in. in height. Its nodding flowers are dark brownish purple with greenish-yellow mottlings. Each bell-shaped flower has six petals to 3 cm/1 in. across. The leaves are lanceolate and formed in one or two whorls of two to five leaves. This is one of the Pacific coast's most prized spring flowers.

Traditional use The bulbs were boiled or steamed and eaten by most Pacific Northwest peoples.

Etymology The genus name, *Fritillaria*, refers to the flower's checkered pattern, reminiscent of old dice boxes.

Habitat Exposed grassy bluffs and meadows and dry to moist soil at low to mid elevations.

Season Flowers from April to May.

▶ BLACK LILY RICE ROOT

Fritillaria camschatcensis

LILY FAMILY Liliaceae

Description Black lily is a herbaceous perennial to 60 cm/24 in. in height. Its nodding flowers have six petals and are bell shaped, purple brown, and to 3 cm/1 in. across. The leaves are in whorls, lance shaped, and to 8 cm/3 in. long. Chocolate lily (*F. lanceolata*) is a less sturdy species with thinner leaves and mottled flowers.

Traditional use The bulbs were boiled or steamed and eaten by most Pacific Northwest peoples.

Etymology The common name rice root comes from the large white bulbs, which are covered with rice-like scales. The genus name, *Fritillaria*, refers to the flower's checkered pattern, reminiscent of old dice boxes.

Habitat Open forests and moist grassy fields at low to high elevations.

Season Flowering starts in mid-May.

▶ WESTERN TRILLIUM

Trillium ovatum

LILY FAMILY Liliaceae

Description The western trillium's beautiful flowers are made up of three white petals, approximately 5 cm/2 in. long, and three green sepals, elevated on a stem 30–50 cm/12–20 in. tall. The flowers change from white to pink to a mottled purple before withering away. The dark-green leaves, usually arranged in whorls of threes, are widely ovate and up to 15 cm/6 in. long. Development, logging, and over-picking have led to a dramatic decrease in wild trilliums. They are now protected by law.

Traditional use The fleshy rhizomes were used for medicinal purposes.

Habitat Moist forested areas at low elevations.

Season Flowering starts at the beginning of April.

▶ TIGER LILY

Lilium columbianum

LILY FAMILY Liliaceae

Description Tiger lily is an elegant herbaceous perennial to 1.5 m/5 ft. tall. Its drooping flowers go from deep yellow to bright orange. A vigorous plant can have 20 or more flowers. Shortly after the flower buds have opened, the petals curve backward to reveal maroon spots and anthers. The leaves are lance shaped, usually in a whorl, and 5–10 cm/2–4 in. long. It is said that anyone who smells a tiger lily will develop freckles.

Traditional use The bulbs were boiled or steamed and then eaten.

Habitat A diverse range, including open forests, meadows, rock outcrops, and the sides of logging roads, at low to subalpine elevations.

Season Flowering starts in mid-May.

▶ FALSE LILY OF THE VALLEY

Maianthemum dilatatum

LILY FAMILY Liliaceae

Description False lily of the valley is a small herbaceous perennial to 30 cm/12 in. in height. Its small white flowers appear in April to May, clustered on 5–10 cm/2–4 in. spikes. The slightly fragrant flowers are quickly replaced by berries 0.6 cm/0.25 in. across; the berries go through summer a speckled green and brown but turn ruby red by the autumn. The dark-green leaves are alternate, heart shaped, and slightly twisted, to 10 cm/4 in. long.

Traditional use The berries were eaten but were not highly regarded.

Etymology The genus name, *Maianthemum*, is from the Greek words *Maios* ("May") and *anthemion* ("blossom").

Habitat Moist coastal forests at low elevations.

Season Flowers bloom in early May, and berries start showing in mid-June.

FALSE SOLOMON'S SEAL

Smilacina racemosa

LILY FAMILY *Liliaceae*

Description False Solomon's seal is a herbaceous perennial to 1 m/40 in. in height. Its fragrant white flowers are borne terminally in 5–10 cm/2–4 in. triangle-shaped racemes. The large ovate leaves, 10–15 cm/4–6 in. long, are stalked and almost clasp the long arching stems. The red fruit grows in terminal clusters and is round, full, and abundant.

Traditional use The berries were eaten occasionally but are not recommended for consumption.

Habitat Usually seen in large showy patches in moist shady forests at low to mid elevations.

Season Flowers from May to June. The berries are ripe by mid-August.

STAR-FLOWERED SOLOMON'S SEAL

Maianthemum stellatum

LILY FAMILY *Liliaceae*

Description Star-flowered Solomon's seal is a smaller, more refined plant than false Solomon's seal (*Smilacina racemosa*). It grows to a height of 60–70 cm/24–28 in. and has attractive white star-shaped flowers that grow in open terminal clusters. The broad lance-shaped leaves grow on short stalks and are alternate and 15 cm/6 in. long; they are usually folded down the midrib and have somewhat clasping bases. The round immature fruit is green with dark stripes; it ripens slowly, turning dark bluish black. The star-shaped flowers and striped fruit distinguish this species from other *Maianthemum spp.*

Traditional use As with false Solomon's seal, the berries do not have much flavour but were eaten on occasion.

Etymology The species name, *stellatum*, references the star-shaped flowers.

Habitat Moist shaded forests, often in association with devil's club (*Oplopanax horridus*) at low to mid elevations.

Season Flowers from May to June. Berries are seen by mid-August.

▶ INDIAN HELLEBORE CORN LILY

Veratrum viride

LILY FAMILY Liliaceae

Description Indian hellebore is a tall, herbaceous perennial 1–2 m/3.3–6.6 ft. in height. Its strongly ribbed, grass-green leaves are ovate to elliptical and 10–30 cm/4–12 in. long, with a passing resemblance to corn leaves. The numerous yellowish-green flowers hang in drooping panicles from the upper portion of the plant.

Traditional use Indian hellebore was thought to have magical powers and was highly valued by virtually all coastal people. Although it is poisonous, it was used as medicine and to ward off evil spirits. It was known as *skookum* ("strong") medicine.

Habitat Moist open forests at low to high elevations and wet alpine meadows and swales.

Season Flowering starts in June at lower elevations and at the end of July at higher elevations.

CAUTION This plant is extremely poisonous.

▶ DEATH CAMAS

Zigadenus venenosus

LILY FAMILY Liliaceae

Description Death camas is a herbaceous perennial from bulb to 50 cm/20 in. in height. Its small creamy flowers are 1 cm/0.5 in. across and neatly arranged in terminal racemes on stems to 50 cm/20 in. long. The grass-like leaves are mainly basal and to 30 cm/12 in. long and have a deep groove like a keel down the centre. The entire plant is poisonous and when out of flower can be confused with the edible common camas (*Camassia quamash*).

Traditional use The bulbs were mashed and used as arrow poison.

Habitat Rocky outcrops and grassy slopes at low elevations.

Season In full flower by mid-June.

CAUTION The entire plant is poisonous.

▶ WESTERN PINK FAWN LILY

Erythronium revolutum

LILY FAMILY Liliaceae

Description Western pink fawn lily is a herbaceous perennial to 30 cm/12 in. in height. The nodding pink flowers are adorned with golden anthers. The seed takes five to seven years to form a corm and put up its first flower; picking of the flowers has greatly reduced the numbers of this plant. The leaves are basal, lance shaped, to 20 cm/8 in. long, and mottled white to dark green.

Habitat Open forests at low elevations, usually in sandy soil by rivers and streams.

Season Flowers from April to May.

▶ WESTERN WHITE FAWN LILY

Erythronium oregonum

LILY FAMILY Liliaceae

Description Western white fawn lily is a herbaceous perennial to 25 cm/10 in. in height. The nodding white flowers are adorned with golden anthers. The seed takes five to seven years to form a corm and put up its first flower; picking of the flowers has greatly reduced the numbers of this plant. The basal leaves are lance shaped, to 20 cm/8 in. long, and mottled white to brown, much like a fawn.

Traditional use The bulbs were eaten raw or steamed.

Etymology The species name, *oregonum*, means it is from Oregon.

Habitat Open forests and rocky outcrops at low elevations.

Season Flowers from April to May.

▶ YELLOW GLACIER LILY

Erythronium grandiflorum

LILY FAMILY Liliaceae

Description Yellow glacier lily is a herbaceous perennial to 30 cm/12 in. in height. You will have to go high into the mountains to see the lily's bright-yellow flowers. The 20 cm/8 in. long leaves are not mottled and are in pairs clasping the back stem. Yellow glacier lily can be seen by retreating or melting snowpacks, sometimes in the thousands.

Traditional use The bulbs, or corms, were eaten raw or steamed.

Habitat Open moist slopes at mid to subalpine elevations.

Season Flowers from June to July at high elevations.

▶ GROUND CEDAR

Diphasiastrum complanatum

CLUBMOSS FAMILY Lycopodiaceae

Description Appropriately named, ground cedar looks as if someone has poked small western red cedar branches into the ground. Its upright stems grow to 30 cm/12 in. in height and are formed on horizontal stems that creep along the ground just below the soil surface.

Habitat Dry to moist coniferous forests at low to mid elevations.

Season Can be observed year-round.

▶ RUNNING CLUBMOSS

Lycopodium clavatum

CLUBMOSS FAMILY Lycopodiaceae

Description Running clubmoss is a curious creeping evergreen that looks as if it is made of bright-green pipe cleaners. Like all clubmosses, it has no flowers and reproduces by spores. These are held in terminal cones on vertical stalks to 25 cm/ 10 in. in height. The evergreen leaves are lance shaped and arranged spirally around the stem. Running clubmoss grows horizontally across the ground, with irregular rooting. The spores are used medicinally and in industry.

Habitat Dry to moist coniferous forests at low to high elevations.

Season Can be observed year round.

▶ GROUND PINE PRINCESS PINE

Lycopodium dendroideum

CLUBMOSS FAMILY Lycopodiaceae

Description At first sight, princess pine groves look like miniature Norfolk Island pines: the stiff stems of the clubmosses attain heights of barely 30 cm/12 in. but are bushy and forked like miniature trees. They can form large patchy carpets to 15 m by 15 m/50 ft. by 50 ft. The solitary cones grow on the tips of the vertical stems.

Habitat Dry to moist coniferous forests at low to mid elevations.

Season Can be observed year round.

▶ DEER CABBAGE

Fauria crista-galli

BUCKBEAN FAMILY Menyanthaceae

Description Deer cabbage is a low-growing lush perennial to 50 cm/20 in. in height. Its white flowers are split into five wavy lobes (petals), to 2 cm/1 in. across, and sit open in clusters on stems 20–50 cm/8–20 in. long. The leaves are basal, with bumpy and rounded (crenate) lobes.

Etymology The species name, *crista-galli*, means "cockscomb," a reference to the wavy lobes.

Habitat Moist to wet forests, bogs, and seepage areas at low to high elevations.

Season Flowers from mid-June to July.

▶ BUCKBEAN BOGBEAN

Menyanthes trifoliata

BUCKBEAN FAMILY Menyanthaceae

Description Buckbean is an aquatic perennial to 30 cm/12 in. above the water. Its white flowers have five petals and straggly, protruding hairs; their foul smell attracts various insects for pollination. The succulent leaves are basally clustered and divided into three leaflets; hence the species name.

Habitat Ponds and lakes at low to mid elevations.

Season Flowers from May to June.

▶ YELLOW SAND VERBENA

Abronia latifolia

FOUR O'CLOCK FAMILY Nyctaginaceae

Description Yellow sand verbena is a prostrate perennial growing to over 1 m/3.3 ft. long. The showy yellow flowers are fragrant and formed into rounded heads to 6 cm/2 in. across. The rounded leaves, to 6 cm/2 in. across, are attached to long sticky stems that are usually covered in sand. There is also a pink sand verbena (*A. umbellata*) that grows on the upper sandy coastal beaches from Washington to California.

Habitat Upper sandy beaches and dunes.

Season Flowers from July to August.

▶ TWISTED STALK

Streptopus amplexifolius

LILY FAMILY Liliaceae

Description Twisted stalk is a branching, herbaceous perennial 1–2 m/3.3–6.6 ft. in height. Its greenish-white flowers are 1 cm/0.5 in. long and borne in leaf axils on slender twisted stalks. The fruit develops into a bright-red oval berry to 1 cm/0.5 in. long. The ovate leaves are alternate and 5–12 cm/2–5 in. long. They clasp the stem directly, with no petiole. The flowers and fruit hang from the leaf axils along the branches.

Traditional use The plants were tied to the clothing or hair for their scent.

Etymology The species name, *amplexifolius*, means "clasping leaves."

Habitat Cool moist forests at low to mid elevations.

Season Flowers at the beginning of June.

CAUTION **The berries are poisonous.**

▶ WESTERN FALSE ASPHODEL

Tofieldia glutinosa

LILY FAMILY Liliaceae

Description Western false asphodel is a herbaceous perennial to 50 cm/20 in. in height. Its creamy-white flowers are 1 cm/0.5 in. across and borne in terminal clusters on long thin stems. The plump fruit capsules are reddish purple, spongy, and very noticeable. The leaves are basal and grass-like.

Etymology The species name, *glutinosa*, means "sticky," referring to the sticky upper portions of the stem. Bees and other flying insects can access only the flowers.

Habitat Peat bogs at low to high elevations and wet alpine elevations.

Season Flowers from June to July.

▶ YELLOW POND LILY

Nuphar polysepalum

WATER LILY FAMILY Nymphaeaceae

Description Yellow pond lily is a long-stemmed aquatic perennial. Its striking yellow flowers, to 10 cm/4 in. across, are a familiar summer sight in lakes and ponds. A large round stigma dominates the centre of these large, waxy flowers. The heart-shaped floating leaves, or pads, grow to 40 cm/16 in. long. The huge rhizomes when exposed at low water levels are sought after by bears.

Traditional use The seeds, called *wokas* by Indigenous groups in California and Oregon, were gathered and used as a food source.

Etymology The genus name, *Nuphar*, means "water lily."

Habitat Ponds, lakes, and marshes at low to mid elevations.

Season Flowering begins in May and continues through the summer.

▶ ENCHANTER'S NIGHTSHADE

Circaea alpina

EVENING PRIMROSE FAMILY Onagraceae

Description Enchanter's nightshade is an easily overlooked perennial to 40 cm/16 in. in height. The flowers are very small and white to pink, with two petals. The leaves, to 6 cm/2 in. long, are heart shaped, light green, and opposite.

Etymology According to Greek mythology, Circe was a goddess—the enchantress.

Habitat Moist, shady forests at low to mid elevations.

Season Flowers from June to July.

▶ FIREWEED

Epilobium angustifolium

EVENING PRIMROSE FAMILY Onagraceae

Description Fireweed is a tall herbaceous perennial that reaches heights of 3 m/10 ft. in good soil. Its purple-red flowers grow on long showy terminal clusters. The leaves are alternate; lance shaped, like a willow's, 10–20 cm/4–8 in. long; and darker green above than below. The minute seeds are produced in pods 5–10 cm/2–4 in. long and have silky hairs for easy wind dispersal. Fireweed flowers have long been a bee-keeper's favourite.

Traditional use The stem fibres were twisted into twine and made into fishing nets, and the fluffy seeds were used in padding and weaving.

Etymology The common name fireweed comes from the fact that it is one of the first plants to grow on burned sites; it typically follows wildfires.

Habitat Common throughout BC in open areas and at burned sites.

Season Flowers from June to July at high elevations.

ALPINE FIREWEED BROAD-LEAVED FIREWEED

Epilobium latifolium

EVENING PRIMROSE FAMILY Onagraceae

Description Alpine fireweed is a showy herbaceous perennial to 40 cm/16 in. in height. The large flowers are rose to purple and contrast well with the lanceolate bluish-green leaves. The new shoots and young leaves can be used as a potherb.

Habitat Gravel bars along streams and creeks or on wet slopes at mid to high elevations.

Season Flowers in July at mid elevations and in August at higher elevations.

WESTERN STAR FLOWER

Trientalis latifolia

PRIMROSE FAMILY Primulaceae

Description Western star flower is a small herbaceous perennial 10–25 cm/4–10 in. height. Its white to pink flowers hang on very thin stalks, making them appear like stars. The oval leaves, 5–10 cm/2–4 in. long, are elevated in a whorl just under the flower stalks. There is also a northern star flower (*T. arctica*) that is more confined to bogs and swamps; it is shorter (5–20 cm/2–8 in. in height), with white flowers 1.5 cm/0.75 in. across and additional leaves on the stem below the whorl of elevated leaves.

Habitat Dry to moist coniferous forests at low elevations.

Season Flowering starts in June and continues through July.

▶ FAIRYSLIPPER

Calypso bulbosa

ORCHID FAMILY Orchidaceae

Description Fairyslipper is a delicate herbaceous perennial from corms to 20 cm/8 in. in height. Its flower is light purple; the lower lip is lighter and decorated with spots, stripes, and coloured hairs. The single leaf is broadly lanceolate and withers with the flower; a new leaf appears in late summer and remains through the winter. This is one of the most beautiful of the Pacific Northwest's native orchids.

Traditional use The Haida boiled and ate the corms in small quantities; they have a rich, buttery flavour.

Habitat Mostly associated with Douglas fir and grand fir forests.

Season Flowers from April to May.

▶ RATTLESNAKE PLANTAIN

Goodyera oblongifolia

ORCHID FAMILY Orchidaceae

Description Rattlesnake plantain is an evergreen perennial to 40 cm/16 in. in height. Its numerous small flowers are greenish white, orchid shaped, and produced on a spike 20–40 cm/8–16 in. high; they have a tendency to grow on one side of the spike. The evergreen leaves are basal, rosette-like, and 5–10 cm/2–4 in. long. They are criss-crossed by whitish veins, creating the rattlesnake pattern that gives the plant its common name.

Habitat Usually found in dry to moist coniferous forests with a moss-dominated understory.

Season Flowering starts at the end of July.

HEART-LEAVED TWAYBLADE

Listera cordata

ORCHID FAMILY Orchidaceae

Description Heart-leaved twayblade is a single-stemmed herbaceous perennial to 20 cm/8 in. in height. Its flowers have a forked bottom lip and range from pale green to purplish. Twayblades have two heart-shaped opposite leaves that grow midway up the stem. Northwestern twayblade (*L. caurina*) is very similar except it has oval leaves.

Etymology The species name, *cordata*, refers to the heart-shaped leaves.

Habitat Most often associated with moist coniferous forests at low to mid elevations.

Season Flowers from June to July, depending on elevation.

ELEGANT REIN ORCHID

Piperia elegans

ORCHID FAMILY Orchidaceae

Description Elegant rein orchid is a herbaceous perennial to 50 cm/20 in. in height. Its tiny flowers are greenish white, with a protruding spur to 1 cm/0.5 in. long. It's worth getting a close look at these beautiful, delicate flowers. Elegant rein orchid has only two leaves, which wither by the time the flowers appear.

Habitat Dry open coniferous forests at low elevations.

Season Flowers from July to August.

WHITE REIN ORCHID WHITE BOG ORCHID

Platanthera dilatata

ORCHID FAMILY Orchidaceae

Description White rein orchid is a stately herbaceous perennial to 1 m/3.3 ft. in height. Its brilliant white flowers, to 2.5 cm/1 in. across, are slightly fragrant and beautifully displayed on long spikes. The leaves are clasping and broadly lanceolate and get progressively smaller up the stem. This stunning orchid is usually seen in large colonies.

Traditional use Some groups believed this orchid was poisonous; others ate the fleshy roots. Care should be taken until the poisonous nature of the plant is clarified.

Habitat Wet slopes and meadows, seepage sites, and ditches.

Season Flowers from June to July.

ROUND-LEAVED BOG ORCHID

Platanthera orbiculata

ORCHID FAMILY Orchidaceae

Description Round-leaved bog orchid is a fleshy herbaceous perennial to 60 cm/24 in. in height. Its showy flowers are greenish white and to 3 cm/1 in. across. The stem has only two plump opposite-facing leaves, sitting on the ground. Round-leaved rein orchid is an unmistakable treasure to find.

Habitat Moist coniferous forests at low to mid elevations.

Season Flowers from mid-July to mid-August.

▶ SLENDER REIN ORCHID

Platanthera stricta

ORCHID FAMILY Orchidaceae

Description Slender rein orchid is one of the taller *Plantanthera* species, growing to 75 cm/30 in. in height. Its flowers are light green, without fragrance, and openly spaced on the stem. The bottom leaves are broadly lanceolate and get progressively narrower up the stem. Slender rein orchid is usually seen in large patches.

Habitat Wet forests and meadows and seepage areas at mid elevations.

Season Flowers from June to July.

▶ LADIES' TRESSES

Spiranthes romanzoffiana

ORCHID FAMILY Orchidaceae

Description This unusual orchid, with its wonderful name, ladies' tresses, is a herbaceous perennial to 50 cm/20 in. tall. Its lightly scented flowers are creamy white and 1 cm/0.5 in. long. They spiral around the stem in three vertical rows. The leaves are lanceolate, to 20 cm/8 in. long, and basal.

Etymology The spiralling rows of flowers were thought to resemble a woman's braided hair.

Habitat A diverse growing range: dry grassy fields and forests, bogs, streamsides, and upper beaches.

Season Flowers from July to September.

▶ OREGON OXALIS

Oxalis oregana

WOODSORREL FAMILY Oxalidaceae

Description Oregon oxalis is a delicate-looking perennial to 15 cm/6 in. tall. The white to pinkish flowers are borne singly on slender stalks that are shorter than the leaves. The shamrock-like leaves have three heart-shaped leaflets to 15 cm/6 in. tall. Both the flower and leaf stalks arise from the base.

Traditional use Small amounts of the leaves were eaten, but the leaves contain oxalic acid and should not be considered a food source.

Etymology The genus name, *Oxalis*, means "acid," "sour," or "sharp," in reference to the taste of the leaves.

Habitat Moist forested areas at low to mid elevations.

Season Flowers from April to June.

▶ CALIFORNIA POPPY

Eschscholzia californica

POPPY FAMILY Papaveraceae

Description California poppy is a herbaceous perennial to 50 cm/20 in. tall with a long taproot. The flowers are electric golden orange, to 5 cm/2 in. across, and borne singly on low stalks. The dull-green fern-like leaves contrast well with the flowers.

Etymology California poppy is California's state flower. When the first Spanish explorers came up the California coast, the poppies were so abundant they thought the hills were on fire.

Habitat Dry rocky soils. In Washington and southern BC, the California poppy is considered a garden escapee.

Season Flowers throughout the summer, depending on when the seeds germinated.

▶ MOUNTAIN SORREL

Oxyria digyna

BUCKWHEAT FAMILY Polygonaceae

Description Mountain sorrel is a rather interesting plant you will likely come across when hiking the coastal mountains. Its flowers are greenish to pinkish and formed in dense panicles to 20 cm/8 in. long. The green leaves are rounded, to 4 cm/1.5 in. across, and held out on long arching stems 10–50 cm/4–20 in. long. The leaves are sour tasting but are edible in small amounts.

Habitat Open rocky sites at mid to high elevations.

Season Flowers from July to September.

▶ WATER SMARTWEED

Polygonum amphibium

BUCKWHEAT FAMILY Polygonaceae

Description Water smartweed is a semi-aquatic perennial to 6 cm/2 in. long. The rose-pink flowers are formed in the terminal spikes 5–20 cm/2–8 in. above the water's surface. The dark-green leaves are to 15 cm/6 in. long and oblong lance shaped. They usually lie flat on the water's surface.

Etymology The genus name, *Polygonum*, is from the Greek words *poly* ("many") and *gonu* ("knees").

Habitat Lakes, ponds, and muddy shorelines when water levels drop. Low to mid elevations.

Season Flowers from July to August.

BEACH KNOTWEED

Polygonum paronychia

BUCKWHEAT FAMILY Polygonaceae

Description Beach knotweed, as the name suggests, is a prostrate coastal dune plant. The small white to pink flowers occur in the upper leaf axils; each has five corolla lobes. The leaves are mostly linear, with rolled edges and bristly midribs on the undersides.

Traditional use In Europe, a poultice of beach knotwood was used to treat inflammation.

Habitat Sand dunes and beaches along the coastline from BC to California.

Season Flowers from July to August.

WESTERN DOCK

Rumex occidentalis

BUCKWHEAT FAMILY Polygonaceae

Description Western dock is a strongly taprooted perennial to 8 cm/3 in. in height. The greenish flowers are held in dense clusters on the upper branched stems. The numerous basal leaves are heart to lance shaped with a heart-shaped to square base.

Etymology The genus name, *Rumex*, means "sour."

Habitat Damp or wet conditions, in fields and along coastlines, at low to mid elevations.

Season Flowers from June to July, with seeds persisting until September.

WESTERN SPRING BEAUTY

Claytonia lanceolata

PURSLANE FAMILY Montiaceae

Description Western spring beauty is a herbaceous perennial from a marble-sized corm to 10–20 cm/4–8 in. tall. The beautiful white to pink flowers have five petals, with darker-pink veins.

Traditional use The corms were eaten raw or cooked, often being stored for winter food.

Etymology The genus name, *Claytonia*, commemorates John Clayton (1686–1773). Clayton has been described as one of the greatest botanists in America. He corresponded with some of the greats of the day: George Washington, Thomas Jefferson, Carl Linnaeus, and John Bartram.

Habitat Mid to high elevations; usually seen chasing the snowpack as it melts.

Season As its common name suggests, flowering is usually from May to June.

SIBERIAN MINER'S LETTUCE

Claytonia sibirica

PURSLANE FAMILY Montiaceae

Description Siberian miner's lettuce is a small annual to 30 cm/12 in. in height. Its small white to pink flowers are five petalled and produced in abundance on long, thin, fleshy stems. The basal leaves are long stemmed, opposite, ovate, and, like the stems, succulent. Another species, miner's lettuce (*C. perfoliata*), differs in that its upper leaves are disc shaped and fused to other flower stems.

Traditional use The leaves were used for medicinal purposes.

Etymology Siberian miner's lettuce was first discovered in Russia, where it was a staple food for miners. Early prospectors and settlers found both species of miner's lettuce made excellent early-season salad greens.

Habitat Moist forest areas at low to mid elevations. Siberian miner's lettuce prefers cool moist forest floors.

Season Flowers from mid-April to July, depending on elevation.

▶ HENDERSON'S SHOOTING STAR

Dodecatheon hendersonii

PRIMROSE FAMILY Primulaceae

Description Henderson's shooting star is a herbaceous perennial 20–50 cm/8–20 in. in height. Its attractive flowers are flaming pink, with five petals that sweep backward. The leaves are basal and broadly ovate.

Etymology The pointing anthers and windswept petals give this plant its name.

Habitat Meadows and rocky knolls at low elevations. Not common, making it a prize to find.

Season Flowers from April to May.

▶ BANEBERRY

Actaea rubra

BUTTERCUP FAMILY Ranunculaceae

Description Baneberry is a herbaceous perennial to 1 m/3.3 ft. in height. Its tiny white flowers are formed in rounded clusters, with protruding stamens that give them a fuzzy look. The ripened fruit are formed in elongated clusters of red, or sometimes white, berries. The crinkly leaves are coarsely toothed and divided two to three times into threes.

Habitat Moist cool forests at low to mid elevations.

Season Flowers at the beginning of June, with attractive berries by mid-August.

CAUTION The entire plant is poisonous.

▶ WESTERN ANEMONE WESTERN PASQUE FLOWER

Anemone occidentalis

BUTTERCUP FAMILY Ranunculaceae

Description Western anemone is a herbaceous perennial 15–30 cm/6–12 in. tall when in flower and 30–60 cm/12–24 in. tall when in seed. Its flowers are 5 cm/2 in. across, creamy white, and often seen with blue-tinged sepals. The leaves are highly dissected and mainly basal, with a cluster of small leaves just under the flower. The seed heads are uniquely shaped like mop tops and can be seen in the hundreds by mid- to late summer.

Traditional use Some First Nations used an infusion of anemones to treat tuberculosis, but it is now considered poisonous, as is much of the buttercup family.

Habitat Alpine and subalpine meadows.

Season Starts flowering as soon as the snow disappears, from the end of June to July. Seed heads are dominant by the end of July to August.

▶ RED COLUMBINE

Aquilegia formosa

BUTTERCUP FAMILY Ranunculaceae

Description Red columbine is a herbaceous perennial to 1 m/3.3 ft. in height. The drooping red-and-yellow flowers are up to 5 cm/2 in. across and have scarlet spurs arching backward; they are almost translucent when the sun shines on them. The leaves are sea green above and paler below, to 8 cm/3 in. across, and twice divided by threes. In the head of the flower is a honey gland that can only be reached by hummingbirds and long-tongued butterflies. The hole that can sometimes be seen above this gland is caused by frustrated bumblebees chewing their way to the nectar.

Etymology The common name columbine means "dove," for the five arching spurs that are said to resemble five doves sitting around a dish.

Habitat Moist open forests, meadows, and creeksides at low to high elevations.

Season Flowers from June to mid-July.

WHITE MARSH MARIGOLD

Caltha leptosepala

BUTTERCUP FAMILY Ranunculaceae

Description White marsh marigold is a fleshy herbaceous perennial to 25 cm/10 in. in height. Its attractive white flowers are borne one to two per stem and are 2–4 cm/1–1.5 in. across, with a greenish-yellow centre. The rounded to heart-shaped leaves are mostly basal and are longer than they are wide.

Traditional use The leaves and buds were eaten both raw and cooked, but this is not recommended.

Habitat It is very happy to have its roots in frigid water at subalpine elevations.

Season In full flower by mid-July.

SUBALPINE BUTTERCUP MOUNTAIN BUTTERCUP

Ranunculus eschscholtzii

BUTTERCUP FAMILY Ranunculaceae

Description Subalpine buttercup is a perennial 10–25 cm/4–10 in. in height. Its shiny yellow flowers, to 3 cm/1 in. across, have five petals and look as if they have been varnished; this sheen helps distinguish it from the fan-leaved cinquefoil (*Potentilla flabellifolia*). The buttercup's basal leaves are twice divided by three and form a stalkless collar under the flowers.

Etymology The species is named for Russian doctor and plant collector Johann Friedrich von Eschscholtz (1793–1831).

Habitat Meadows, seepage areas, and damp slopes at subalpine and alpine elevations.

Season Flowers from July to August.

WESTERN BUTTERCUP

Ranunculus occidentalis

BUTTERCUP FAMILY Ranunculaceae

Description Western buttercup is a perennial 30–70 cm/12–28 in. in height. Its bright-yellow flowers are to 2.5 cm across and have five to eight petals (five is the norm), half as broad as they are long. The basal leaves are twice divided by three, with the stem leaves becoming smaller and more linear as they progress upward.

Habitat Forest edges, moist meadows, and coastal bluffs at low to mid elevations. Western buttercup often grows with camas and chocolate lily.

Season Flowers from April to May.

FALSE BUGBANE

Trautvetteria caroliniensis

BUTTERCUP FAMILY Ranunculaceae

Description False bugbane is a large-leaved perennial 50–80 cm/20–32 in. in height that spreads freely by rhizomes. Its white flowers have sepals but no petals—the fuzzy-looking flowers are actually stamens. These are held up in flat-topped terminal clusters to 80 cm/32 in. in height. The basal leaves are maple shaped, deeply divided into five lobes, and 15–30 cm/6–12 in. across. The stem leaves are smaller.

Etymology The genus is named for 19th-century Russian botanist Ernst Rudolf von Trautvetter (1809–1889).

Habitat Moist forests, floodplains, and streamsides at low to mid elevations.

Season Flowers from mid-June to mid-July.

▶ WESTERN MEADOWRUE

Thalictrum occidentale

BUTTERCUP FAMILY *Ranunculaceae*

Description Western meadowrue is a graceful herbaceous perennial to 1 m/3.3 ft. in height. It is dioecious; the male flowers, to 0.5 cm/0.25 in. long, have dangling purple-green stamens and anthers, and the females are greenish white, with 5 to 15 tiny pistils that mature into slender, pointed dry seeds. The blue-green leaves are divided two to three times into fan-shaped stalked leaflets.

Traditional use The seeds were crushed and rubbed into the hair and body as a perfume.

Habitat Most abundant at mid elevations in damp meadows and at forest edges.

Season Flowers from the end of May to June.

▶ GOAT'S BEARD

Aruncus dioicus

ROSE FAMILY *Rosaceae*

Description Goat's beard is a deciduous shrub to 3 m/10 ft. in height. The plants are dioecious: male and female flowers appear on separate plants. The tiny white flowers are compacted into hanging panicles up to 60 cm/24 in. long. The leaves are compounded three times (thrice pinnate), and the leaflets are bright green with a toothed edge, tapering to a point. With a little imagination, the hanging flowers look like a goat's beard.

Traditional use The roots were steeped, and the warm tea was given to an expecting woman just before giving birth. It was thought the tea would help her heal.

Habitat Moist open woodlands, creeksides, and wet rocky slopes at lower elevations.

Season Flowers from June to early July.

► LARGE-LEAVED AVENS

Geum macrophyllum

ROSE FAMILY Rosaceae

Description Large-leaved avens is a herbaceous perennial to 90 cm/3 ft. in height. Its bright-yellow flowers resemble buttercups. They are approximately 0.6 cm/0.25 in. across and are produced singly or in small clusters. The unique round fruit has bristly bent protruding styles that catch on fur and clothing, an excellent way of dispersing the seed. The irregularly shaped larger leaves are 15–20 cm/6–8 in. across, while the stem leaves are smaller and three-lobed.

Traditional use The roots were boiled and used medicinally.

Habitat Prefers moist soil in open forests and beside pathways, trails, and roads at low elevations.

Season Flowering starts at the end of April and continues irregularly through August.

► PARTRIDGEFOOT

Luetkea pectinata

ROSE FAMILY Rosaceae

Description Partridgefoot is a mat-forming miniature sub-shrub to 12 cm/5 in. tall. Its cream-coloured flowers form in compact terminal clusters to 2 cm/1 in. long. The evergreen leaves are finely dissected and resemble the feathered leggings on grouse and ptarmigan.

Etymology The genus, *Luetkea*, honours Count Fyodor Petrovich Litke (1797–1882), born Friedrich Benjamin Lütke, a supporter of the Russian Academy of Sciences in St. Petersburg and commander of a Russian ship that charted the coast of Alaska in 1827.

Habitat Meadows and slopes at subalpine to alpine elevations.

Season Flowers from mid-July to August, trickling into September.

▶ SILVERWEED

Potentilla anserina ssp. *pacifica*

ROSE FAMILY Rosaceae

Description Silverweed grows to only 30 cm/12 in. in height but can take over several hectares or acres in favourable conditions. The yellow flowers are produced singly on a leafless stalk. The compound leaves reach 25 cm/10 in. in length and have 9 to 19 toothed leaflets; they are bicoloured: grass green above and felty silver below (hence the common name). Silverweed spreads quickly thanks to its fast-growing stolons, which root at the nodes.

Traditional use The cooked roots were an important food source.

Etymology The genus name, *Potentilla*, means "powerful," a reference to its medicinal properties.

Habitat Saline marshes, meadows, and wet runoff areas near the ocean.

Season Flowering starts in mid-May and continues through June and July.

▶ FAN-LEAVED CINQUEFOIL

Potentilla flabellifolia

ROSE FAMILY Rosaceae

Description Fan-leaved cinquefoil is a herbaceous perennial to 30 cm/12 in. in height. Its yellow flowers, to 2 cm/1 in. across, have five petals that surround a central button. The leaves have three leaflets that are deeply notched and spread out like a fan.

Traditional use Infusions of *Potentilla* were used in Europe for sore throats and cramps in the stomach, heart, and abdomen.

Etymology The species name *flabellifolia* means "fan shaped."

Habitat Moist slopes and meadows at high elevations.

Season Flowers from July to August.

▶ MARSH CINQUEFOIL

Potentilla palustris

ROSE FAMILY Rosaceae

Description Marsh cinquefoil is a perennial aquatic that can grow to 80 cm/32 in. out of the water. The beautiful wine-coloured flowers are to 2 cm/ 1 in. across and held in loose terminal clusters. They emit a fetid odour, which attracts pollinating insects. The strawberry-like leaves are alternating and divided into five to seven leaflets.

Traditional use The stems were used medicinally.

Habitat Lake edges, ponds, and bogs, from low to mid elevations.

Season Flowers from July to September.

▶ VILLOUS CINQUEFOIL

Potentilla villosa

ROSE FAMILY Rosaceae

Description Villous cinquefoil is a rhizomatous herbaceous perennial to 30 cm/12 in. in height. The bright-yellow flowers have five petals, each marked with an orange basal dot. The basal leaves are compound, with three leaflets with silky-haired undersides.

Etymology The species name, *villosa*, means "hairy."

Habitat Rocky shorelines at low elevations to rocky slopes in the alpine.

Season Flowers from June to September, depending on elevation.

▶ CLEAVER BEDSTRAW

Galium aparine

MADDER FAMILY Rubiaceae

Description Cleaver is a sprawling, clinging, or climbing annual to 60 cm/24 in. long. Its small white flowers are stalked from the leaf axils. The resulting fruit are annoying little burrs covered with hooked bristles. The bristly leaves are very narrow and to 5 cm/2 in. long and grow in whorls of six to eight. The back-angled bristles on the square stems and leaves help the plants climb over and through other plants.

Traditional use The abrasive parts of the plant were rubbed between the hands to remove pitch.

Habitat Most commonly seen on or near beaches climbing over rocks and logs, in disturbed sites, and in broad-leaved forests.

Season Flowers in the spring, with the burrs maturing in July.

▶ COAST BOYKINIA

Boykinia elata

SAXIFRAGE FAMILY Saxifragaceae

Description Coast boykinia is a herbaceous perennial to 60 cm/24 in. in height. Its small white flowers are produced on long slender stalks 25–60 cm/10–24 in. tall. The grass-green leaves are to 8 cm/3 in. across and somewhat heart shaped, with five to seven lobes, and are supported on long slender hairy stems. When in flower, boykinia is very attractive.

Etymology The species name, *elata*, means "tall."

Habitat Moist forests, wet cliff faces, and streamsides at low to mid elevations.

Season Flowers from June to July.

▶ SMALL-FLOWERED ALUMROOT

Heuchera micrantha

SAXIFRAGE FAMILY Saxifragaceae

Description Small-flowered alumroot is a perennial to 60 cm/24 in. in height. Its small white flowers are abundant and held on scapes (stems) up to 60 cm/ 24 in. tall. The heart-shaped leaves have long hairy stems and are basal. The leaves are slightly longer than they are broad and distinguish this plant from smooth alumroot (*H. glabra*), which has leaves that are broader than they are long.

Etymology The common name alumroot is given because the roots are very astringent.

Habitat Wet cliff faces and stream banks at low to high elevations.

Season Flowers by the beginning of June.

▶ LEATHERLEAF SAXIFRAGE

Leptarrhena pyrolifolia

SAXIFRAGE FAMILY Saxifragaceae

Description Leatherleaf saxifrage is a moisture-loving perennial 15–30 cm/6–12 in. in height. Its tiny white flowers are held in round terminal clusters. The leathery leaves, to 7 cm/3 in. long, are dark green on top and a lighter green underneath. As cold weather comes to the meadows, the stems and seed heads turn brilliant red.

Habitat Wet meadows at subalpine elevations.

Season Flowers from July to August, with a red colouring from mid-September to October.

▶ FRINGED GRASS OF PARNASSUS

Parnassia fimbriata

SAXIFRAGE FAMILY Saxifragaceae

Description Fringed grass of parnassus is not a grass but a herbaceous perennial to 40 cm/16 in. in height. The curious-looking white flowers are produced one per stem and have five veined, fringed petals. The glossy green leaves are kidney shaped and to 5 cm/2 in. across. Despite its common name, fringed grass of Parnassus does not grow on Greece's Mount Parnassus.

Habitat Enjoys having its feet in wet meadows or on stream edges at mid to alpine meadows.

Season Flowers from July to September, depending on elevation.

▶ ALASKA SAXIFRAGE

Saxifraga ferruginea

SAXIFRAGE FAMILY Saxifragaceae

Description Alaska saxifrage is a perennial 20–40 cm/8–16 in. in height. Its small white flowers to 1 cm/0.5 in. across have five petals; the upper three petals are slightly broader and have two yellow dots. The leaves are basal, wedge shaped, and toothed above the middle.

Etymology The genus name, *Saxifraga*, means "rock breaking." It was thought that these plants could break rocks.

Habitat Rock crevices, stream banks, and seepage areas at low to high elevations.

Season Flowers from May to July, depending on elevation.

▶ MERTEN'S SAXIFRAGE WOOD SAXIFRAGE

Saxifraga mertensiana

SAXIFRAGE FAMILY Saxifragaceae

Description Merten's saxifrage is a low-growing perennial with flowering stems to 40 cm/16 in. in height. The white flowers grow in open clusters, have five petals, and are replaced by pinkish bulblets that make new plants. The rounded succulent leaves are to 10 cm/4 in. across, with a heart-shaped base, and are irregularly toothed.

Etymology The species name commemorates Karl Heinrich Mertens (1796–1830), a German botanist and naturalist.

Habitat Moist gravel stream banks, even on large moist mossy rocks. Low to high elevations.

Season Flowers in spring and summer, depending on elevation.

▶ TOLMIE'S SAXIFRAGE

Saxifraga tolmiei

SAXIFRAGE FAMILY Saxifragaceae

Description Tolmie's saxifrage is a mat-forming perennial to 40 cm/16 in. across. Its white flowers, to 1 cm/0.5 in. across, have five petals with stamens between each; the stems, 5–10 cm/2–4 in. tall, produce one to four flowers each. The small shiny leaves are succulent and slightly curled to prevent desiccation from strong sunlight.

Habitat By the snowmelt line on rocky slopes at subalpine to alpine elevations.

Season Flowers from late July to August.

▶ FRINGECUP

Tellima grandiflora

SAXIFRAGE FAMILY Saxifragaceae

Description Fringecup is a perennial to 80 cm/32 in. in height. Its fringed flowers are greenish, fragrant, 1 cm/0.5 in. long, and produced on 60–80 cm/24–32 in. scapes (stems). The basal leaves are round to heart shaped, deeply notched, and 5–8 cm/2–3 in. across; the scape leaves are smaller. When out of flower, fringecup can be confused with the piggyback plant.

Traditional use The plants were crushed and boiled, and the resultant infusion was used to treat illness.

Habitat Moist, cool forests along the coast.

Season Flowers from the end of April to the end of June.

▶ FOAM FLOWER

Tiarella trifoliata

SAXIFRAGE FAMILY Saxifragaceae

Description Foam flower is a herbaceous perennial to 50 cm/20 in. in height. Each wiry stem supports several tiny white flowers. The trifoliate leaves, to 7 cm/3 in. across, are all basal except for one, located approximately halfway up the stem; this is good for identification. There is another species of foam flower (*T. trifoliata* var. *unifoliata*) that is very similar except for its solid leaf.

Etymology The massed flowers are thought to resemble foam.

Habitat Shaded moist woods at low to mid elevations. Common in cool forests.

Season Flowers from mid-May to July.

PIGGYBACK PLANT

Tolmiea menziesii

SAXIFRAGE FAMILY Saxifragaceae

Description The piggyback plant gets its unusual name from the way it reproduces. By late summer, young plants can be seen growing at the base of the leaves. As autumn approaches, the leaves fall to the ground, allowing the young plants to take root. Mature plants can grow to a height of 70 cm/28 in. The flowers are small, reddish purple, and inconspicuous. The dark-green leaves are rough, with five to seven lobes, and up to 10 cm/4 in. across.

Habitat Moist forests at low to mid elevations. A common plant in forests, but it blends well with other plants and is often overlooked.

Season Flowering starts in mid-May.

RED PAINTBRUSH

Castilleja sp.

FIGWORT FAMILY Scrophulariaceae

Description The many species of paintbrush are difficult to distinguish. They range in height from 20 cm/8 in. to 80 cm/32 in., and there is frequent hybridization within their diverse growing range, making identification even harder. Red paintbrush is a perennial with small lance-shaped leaves. Its actual flowers are small and inconspicuous. It is the showy red bracts that attract all the attention.

Habitat Low-elevation grassy meadows and rocky outcrops to moist subalpine and alpine meadows.

Season Flowers from June to August, depending on elevation.

▶ SMALL-FLOWERED BLUE-EYED MARY

Collinsia parviflora

FIGWORT FAMILY Scrophulariaceae

Description Small-flowered blue-eyed Mary is a herbaceous perennial 5–30 cm/2–12 in. tall. Its flowers are 0.5–1 cm/0.25–0.5 in. long, white on the upper lips, and blue on the bottom. The leaves are 1–4 cm/0.5–1.5 in. long and vary in shape from oblong to lanceolate; the upper leaves form in whorls. Large-flowered blue-eyed Mary (*C. grandiflora*) is similar but has larger flowers (1–1.5 cm/0.5–0.75 in.). Both species can be seen growing together.

Habitat Open grass-covered rock outcrops at low to mid elevations.

Season Flowers as early as March, with full colour by April and May.

▶ YELLOW MONKEY-FLOWER

Mimulus guttatus

FIGWORT FAMILY Scrophulariaceae

Description Yellow monkey-flower can be annual or perennial; it normally self-seeds, disappears, and then germinates as an annual in the spring. It can grow to 80 cm/32 in. in height. Its beautiful yellow flowers are two lipped and to 5 cm/2 in. long, with many small dots and one larger dot on the lower lip. The lower leaves are oval and grow in pairs, while the upper leaves hug the stem. Chickweed monkey-flower (*M. alsinoides*) is smaller, to 20 cm/8 in. high, and often grows with the larger variety; its flowers are much smaller and have only a single dot on the lower lip.

Habitat Wet cliffs and ledges at low elevations.

Season Flowers from May to August.

LEWIS'S MONKEY-FLOWER PINK MONKEY-FLOWER

Mimulus lewisii

FIGWORT FAMILY Scrophulariaceae

Description Lewis's monkey-flower is a clump-forming herbaceous perennial to 90 cm/36 in. in height. Its flowers are snapdragon shaped, 2–5 cm/1–2 in. long, and pinkish red, with a yellow throat. The leaves are 7–10 cm/3–4 in. long and opposite and clasp the stems. When in flower, the clusters are a fabulous sight in the upper mountains.

Etymology The species is named for Captain Meriwether Lewis of the Lewis and Clark Expedition.

Habitat Cold stream edges and wet meadows from mid to subalpine elevations.

Season Flowers from July to August.

MOUNTAIN MONKEY-FLOWER

Mimulus tilingii

FIGWORT FAMILY Scrophulariaceae

Description Alpine monkey-flower is a herbaceous perennial 5–20 cm/2–8 in. in height. Its bright-yellow flowers are almost duplicates of those of yellow monkey-flower (*M. guttatus*) except that they grow on very short leafy stems. It is most often seen forming a beautiful low mat in alpine regions.

Habitat Damp meadows and edges of cold streams at subalpine elevations.

Season In full flower from mid-August to mid-September.

BRACTED LOUSEWORT WOOD BETONY / FERNLEAF

Pedicularis bracteosa

FIGWORT FAMILY Scrophulariaceae

Description Bracted lousewort is a herbaceous perennial to 1 m/3.3 ft. in height. Its odd-looking flowers are pale yellow to pinkish-purple and shown off on 7–20 cm/3–8 in. spikes. The green leaves are gracefully dissected to the point of resembling ferns; hence its common name fernleaf. This species is the tallest of the louseworts.

Traditional use The leaf shapes were incorporated into the design of baskets.

Etymology The unfortunate common name of lousewort was given because it was thought that cattle grazing on it would be more readily infested with lice.

Habitat Common in moist open forests at mid to high elevations.

Season Flowers from the end of July to August.

PARROT'S BEAK

Pedicularis racemosa

FIGWORT FAMILY Scrophulariaceae

Description Parrot's beak is a herbaceous perennial with several greenish to red stems up to 80 cm/32 in. tall. The white, light purple, or yellowish flowers are borne in small racemes at the top of the stems. Each flower (to 4 cm/1.5 in. long) is divided into a curved or coiled beak-like upper lip. The leaves are alternating to 10 cm/4 in. long, linear, and finely toothed.

Habitat Conifer forests and meadows at mid to high elevations.

Season Flowers from July to August.

DAVIDSON'S PENSTEMON

Penstemon davidsonii

FIGWORT FAMILY Scrophulariaceae

Description Davidson's penstemon is an evergreen mat-forming shrub. Its showy flowers are unusually large (3 cm/1 in. long), blue purple, and produced in mass on stems 5–10 cm/2–4 in. tall. The leaves are 1 cm/0.5 in. long, opposite, and evergreen.

Etymology The species is named for Dr. George Davidson, an avid collector of western plants.

Habitat Rocky slopes and cliffs at mid to high elevations.

Season Flowers from June to August, depending on elevation.

SLENDER BLUE PENSTEMON

Penstemon procerus

FIGWORT FAMILY Scrophulariaceae

Description Slender blue penstemon is an upright herbaceous perennial 10–60 cm/4–24 in. in height. Its blue-purple flowers have the typical penstemon shape, funnel-like with a five-lobed calyx; they are neatly arranged in whorls on the top portion of the stems. The basal leaves appear in tufts, while the stem leaves are opposite and lance shaped.

Habitat Drier meadows and slopes at mid to alpine elevations.

Season In full flower from the end of July to August.

▶ AMERICAN BROOKLIME

Veronica americana

FIGWORT FAMILY Scrophulariaceae

Description American brooklime is a herbaceous perennial with flowering stems to 1 m/40 in. tall. The light blue–mauve flowers are produced in loose clusters and have two obvious stamens. The leaves are opposite, usually with three to five pairs per flowering stem, and oval to lance shaped.

Traditional use The leaves are edible and can be used as a potherb or raw in salads. Brooklimes were once considered an important medicine in Europe and among North American Indigenous groups.

Habitat Ditches, ponds, and marsh edges at low to mid elevations.

Season Flowers from July to September.

▶ CATTAIL

Typha latifolia

CATTAIL FAMILY Typhaceae

Description Cattails are semi-aquatic perennials that can grow to 2.5 m/8 ft. in height. The distinctive "tail," a brown spike, is 15–20 cm/6–8 in. long, 3 cm/1 in. wide, and made up of male and female flowers. The lighter-coloured male flowers grow at the top and usually fall off, leaving a bare spike above the familiar brown female flowers. The sword-shaped leaves are alternate and spongy at the base.

Traditional use The long leaves were used to weave mats, and the fluffy seeds were used to stuff pillows and mattresses.

Habitat Common at low to mid elevations, at lakesides and riversides and in ponds, marshes, and ditches.

Season Seed heads can be seen from July to December.

▶ STINGING NETTLE

Urtica dioica

NETTLE FAMILY Urticaceae

Description Stinging nettle is a herbaceous perennial to over 2 m/6.6 ft. high. Its tiny flowers are greenish and produced in hanging clusters to 5 cm/2 in. long. The leaves are heart shaped at the base, tapered to the top, coarsely toothed, and to 10 cm/4 in. long. The stalks, stems, and leaves all have stinging hairs that contain formic acid; many people have the misfortune of encountering this plant the hard way.

Traditional use The young leaves were boiled as a spinach substitute.

Etymology The genus name, *Urtica*, is from the Latin word *uro* ("to burn").

Habitat Thrives in moist, nutrient-rich, somewhat shady disturbed sites, where it can form great masses. Stinging nettles are usually an indicator of nitrogen-rich soil.

Season Flowering starts at the beginning of May.

▶ SEA BLUSH

Plectritis congesta

VALERIAN FAMILY Valerianaceae

Description Sea blush is a seaside annual to 50 cm/ 20 in. in height. Its small pink flowers are crowded into rounded terminal clusters. The leaves, 1–4 cm/ 0.5–1.5 in. long, are oval and face opposite to each other.

Etymology The genus name, *Plectritis*, is Greek for "plaited," and the species name means "congested"; both refer to the flowers.

Habitat Meadows and rock outcrops from slightly inland to the ocean.

Season Flowers from April to June. Can be seen with fawn lily, camas, blue-eyed Mary, and chocolate lily.

▶ SITKA VALERIAN

Valeriana sitchensis

VALERIAN FAMILY Valerianaceae

Description Sitka valerian is a herbaceous perennial to over 1 m/3.3 ft. in height. Its pinkish tubular flowers are slightly fragrant, grow in flat-topped clusters, and are supported on long succulent stems. The leaves are thick, to 25 cm/10 in. long, and divided into five to seven coarsely toothed segments. The roots are the source of the drug valerian, which is used as both a stimulant and an antispasmodic.

Habitat Moist mid-level stream banks, subalpine to alpine meadows, and slopes.

Season Flowers in June at mid elevations and from July to September at higher elevations.

▶ STREAM VIOLET

Viola glabella

VIOLET FAMILY Violaceae

Description Stream violet is a herbaceous woodland perennial to 25 cm/10 in. in height. Its showy yellow flowers, to 2 cm/1 in. across, each have five petals; the top two petals are often pure yellow, while the bottom three have purple lines. The heart-shaped leaves are toothed and grow to 5 cm/2 in. across. The flowers and leaves can be used in salads or steeped for tea.

Habitat Needs a moist environment, such as open forests and meadows, at low to high elevations. Common at all elevations.

Season Flowers in mid-May at lower elevations and in mid-July at higher elevations.

▶ EVERGREEN VIOLET

Viola sempervirens

VIOLET FAMILY Violaceae

Description Evergreen violet is a small creeping perennial to 8 cm/3 in. in height, the smallest of the yellow flowering violets in the Pacific Northwest. Its yellow flowers are solitary and 1–5 cm/0.5–2 in. across, with delicate brown veins on the bottom petals. The evergreen leaves grow to 3 cm/1 in. across and are broadly heart shaped and leathery. It spreads by sending out slender trailing stems. It is said that violets worn around the head will dispel the fumes of wine and prevent headache and dizziness.

Habitat Dry to moist forests at low to mid elevations. Common in forested areas, often hiding under bushes or fallen leaves.

Season Flowering starts in mid-March.

BERRIES

▶ OREGON GRAPE

Mahonia nervosa

BARBERRY FAMILY Berberidaceae

Description Oregon grape is a small spreading understory shrub that is very noticeable when the upright bright-yellow flowers are in bloom. By midsummer, the clusters of small green fruit, 1 cm/0.5 in. across, turn an attractive grape blue. The leaves are evergreen, holly-like, waxy, and compound, usually with 9 to 17 leaflets. The bark is rough, light grey outside, and brilliant yellow inside. Another species, tall Oregon grape (*M. aquifolium*), grows in a more open and dry location, is taller (2 m/6.6 ft.), and has fewer leaflets (five to nine).

Traditional use When steeped, the shredded stems of both species yield a yellow dye that was used in basket making. The tart berries were usually mixed with sweeter berries for eating.

Etymology The species name, *aquifolium*, means "holly-like."

Habitat Dry coniferous forests in southern coastal BC and Washington.

Season Flowers at the end of May. The berries begin to turn blue by August and persist through autumn.

▶ SOOPOLALLIE SOAPBERRY / CANADIAN BUFFALO BERRY

Shepherdia canadensis

OLEASTER FAMILY Elaeagnaceae

Description Soopolallie is a deciduous bush 1–3 m/3.3–10 ft. in height. The tiny star-like bronze male and female flowers are borne on separate bushes. The bitter berries are bright red and grow in small clusters along the stems. The leaves and stems are covered with orange dots, giving them a rusty appearance.

Traditional use The froth of the berries was used to make ice cream.

Etymology Soopolallie is Chinook for "soapberry," referring to the way the berries froth up when beaten with water.

Habitat Forest edges and upper beaches at low to mid elevations.

Season Flowers from the end of March to April. The berries ripen by mid-July.

► CROWBERRY

Empetrum nigrum

CROWBERRY FAMILY Empetraceae

Description Crowberry is a low heather-like shrub to 30 cm/12 in. in height. The small purplish flowers are borne two to three in the leaf axils. The plants are mostly dioecious, with male and female flowers on separate plants. The crow-black berries are to 1 cm/0.5 in. across and edible. However, some will find the taste does not agree with them.

Traditional use The berries were an important food source for the Inuit but were not so highly regarded along the coast.

Habitat Bogs and bluffs along the coast.

Season Flowers from April to June, with the berries ripening from August to October, depending on elevation. I can remember going out in the beginning of October to pick them for Thanksgiving stuffing.

► SALAL

Gaultheria shallon

HEATHER FAMILY Ericaceae

Description Salal is a prostrate to mid-sized bush that grows to 0.5–4 m/20 in.–13 ft. in height. In spring, the small pinkish flowers (1 cm/0.5 in. long) hang like strings of tiny Chinese lanterns. The edible dark-purple berries grow to 1 cm/0.5 in. across and ripen by mid-August or September. Both the flowers and the berries display themselves for several weeks. The dark-green leaves are 7–10 cm/3–4 in. long, tough, and oval shaped. Salal is often overlooked by berry pickers, but the ripe berries taste excellent fresh and make fine preserves and wine.

Traditional use Salal was an important food source for most indigenous peoples. The berries were eaten fresh, often mixed with other berries, or crushed and placed on skunk cabbage leaves to dry. The dried berry cakes were then rolled up and preserved for winter use.

Habitat Dry to moist forested areas along the entire coast.

Season Flowering starts at the beginning of May, and the fruit starts to ripen at the beginning of August.

▶ WESTERN TEA-BERRY

Gaultheria ovatifolia

HEATHER FAMILY Ericaceae

Description Western tea-berry is a small to prostrate evergreen bush. The bell-shaped flowers are to 0.5 cm/0.25 in. long, white to pinkish, and, like the berries, quite often found hiding beneath the leaves. The red berries are edible, 0.6 cm/0.25 in. across, and grooved into segments. The heart-shaped leaves are alternate, 1.5–4 cm/0.75–1.5 in. long, finely toothed, shiny above, and dull below. Alpine wintergreen (*G. humifusa*) is an even smaller bush; it is generally seen at higher elevations.

Traditional use The ripe berries were eaten as they were being picked, but they were too sparse to be collected.

Habitat Moist coniferous forests and bogs at mid to subalpine elevations.

Season Flowers from July to August, depending on elevation.

▶ OVAL-LEAVED BLUEBERRY

Vaccinium ovalifolium

HEATHER FAMILY Ericaceae

Description The oval-leaved blueberry is one of BC's most recognized and most harvested blueberries. It is a mid-sized bush to 2 m/6.6 ft. in height. The bell-shaped pinkish flowers appear before the leaves and are followed by the classic blue berries. Rubbing the berries reveals a covering of dull bloom and a darker berry. The soft green leaves are smooth edged, alternate, and egg shaped (no point) and grow to 4 cm/1.5 in. in length.

Traditional use Oval-leaved blueberries were a valuable and delicious food source. They were eaten fresh, often mixed with other berries, or dried for future use. As with all blueberries, they were also mashed to create a purple dye used to colour basket materials.

Habitat Moist coniferous forests from sea level to high elevations. Black huckleberry (*V. membranaceum*) and Cascade huckleberry (*V. deliciosum*) also grow in this type of habitat.

Season The fruit ripens as early as July at lower elevations and into September at higher elevations.

▶ EVERGREEN HUCKLEBERRY

Vaccinium ovatum

HEATHER FAMILY Ericaceae

Description Evergreen huckleberry is an attractive mid-sized shrub to 3 m/10 ft. in height. In spring, it is covered in clusters of bell-shaped pinkish flowers. By late summer, the branches are weighed down by the many small blue-black berries (0.7 cm/0.25 in. across). This is a favourite late-season bush among avid berry pickers.

Traditional use The late-producing berries were in high demand for their flavour.

Habitat Coniferous forests at low elevations along the coast.

Season Flowering starts in early May, and the berries ripen from early September to December.

▶ RED HUCKLEBERRY

Vaccinium parvifolium

HEATHER FAMILY Ericaceae

Description One of the most graceful of all BC's berry bushes, the red huckleberry grows on old stumps, where it can attain heights of 3–4 m/10–13 ft. The combination of almost translucent red berries (1 cm/0.5 in. across), a lacy zigzag branch structure, and oval pale-green leaves (2.5 cm/1 in. long) is unmistakable. The small greenish to pink flowers are inconspicuous.

Traditional use The berries were eaten fresh, often mixed with other berries, or dried for winter use. Their resemblance to salmon eggs made them ideal for fish bait.

Habitat Coastal forested areas at lower elevations.

Season Flowering starts in mid-April, and the berries ripen by the beginning of July.

▶ BOG BLUEBERRY

Vaccinium uliginosum

HEATHER FAMILY Ericaceae

Description Bog blueberry is a small deciduous bush to 60 cm/24 in. in height. At high elevations, it may reach only 10 cm/4 in. in height. The tiny pink flowers give way to dark-blue berries that have a waxy coating. The berries are delicious. The leaves are green above and pale on the underside, to 3 cm/1 in. long, with no teeth.

Traditional use The berries were eaten fresh or dried into cakes for winter use.

Habitat Low elevated bogs along the coast to sub-alpine scrub.

Season The berries are ripe by July in lower areas.

▶ STINK CURRANT BLUE CURRANT

Ribes bracteosum

CURRANT AND GOOSEBERRY FAMILY Grossulariaceae

Description Stink currant is an unarmed deciduous bush 2–4 m/6.6–13 ft. in height. The small greenish flowers give way to 15–25 cm/6–10 in. long clusters of blue-black berries that are covered in a whitish bloom, giving them a blue-grey appearance. The maple-like leaves are to 20 cm/8 in. across, with five to seven pointed lobes. When crushed, the leaves emit a musky odour. The name stink currant is not deserved for this attractive plant. Maybe a more fitting name would be musk currant.

Traditional use The berries were eaten raw or dried into cakes for winter use.

Habitat Rich wet soils along creeks and seepage areas at low to subalpine elevations.

Season The berries are ripe by July in lower areas.

▶ BLACK GOOSEBERRY

Ribes lacustre

CURRANT AND GOOSEBERRY FAMILY Grossulariaceae

Description Black gooseberry is an armed shrub to 2 m/6.6 ft. in height. Its delicate reddish flowers are disc shaped and to 0.7 cm/0.25 in. across and hang in drooping clusters of 7 to 15. The small, dark-purple berries are bristly and hang in clusters of three to four. The leaves are maple shaped, with five lobes 5 cm/2 in. across. The branches are covered with small golden spines, with larger spines at the nodes. Use caution when picking the berries: the spines can cause an allergic reaction in some people.

Traditional use The berries were eaten.

Habitat Moist open forests and lake edges at low to high elevations.

Season The berries ripen from July to August.

▶ GUMMY GOOSEBERRY   STICKY GOOSEBERRY

Ribes lobbii

CURRANT AND GOOSEBERRY FAMILY Grossulariaceae

Description Gummy gooseberry is a spiny-stemmed shrub to 1.2 m/4 ft. in height. Its attractive flowers make it stand out in spring. The flowers have showy large recurved red sepals with white petals and stamens hanging down. The large berries are hairy; they start off green and ripen to purple. The leaves are small, with three to five lobes; the leaves and stems are sticky.

Traditional use The berries were eaten, but only in small quantities. I find them unpalatable.

Etymology The species name, *lobbii*, is named after William Lobb (1809–1864), who collected plants in North and South America for Veitch Nurseries.

Habitat Open forests along the coast at low to mid elevations.

Season The berries ripen by July.

▶ RED-FLOWERING CURRANT

Ribes sanguineum

CURRANT AND GOOSEBERRY FAMILY Grossulariaceae

Description Red-flowering currant is an upright deciduous bush 1.5–3 m/5–10 ft. in height. Its flowers range in colour from pale pink to bright crimson and hang in 8–12 cm/3–5 in. panicles. The bluish-black berries, 1 cm/0.5 in. across, are inviting to eat but are usually dry and bland. The leaves are 5–10 cm/ 2–4 in. across and maple shaped, with three to five lobes. Currants and gooseberries are both in the genus *Ribes*; a distinguishing feature is that currants have no prickles, while gooseberries do.

Habitat Dry open forests at low to mid elevations.

Season Flowers from mid-May to June.

▶ BLACKBERRIES

Rubus spp.

ROSE FAMILY Rosaceae

Of the three Pacific Northwest blackberry species, only one is native to the region. The two introduced species require more sunshine to thrive. The three are easy to identify.

>> Trailing blackberry

Rubus ursinus

Description The first to bloom and set fruit, it is often seen rambling over plants in and out of forested areas. The berries are delicious, and the leaves can be steeped as a tea. The trailing blackberry, which is native to the Pacific Northwest, can tolerate more shade than the Himalayan blackberry. The trailing blackberry is usually seen at the forest edge. Blooming starts at the end of April, and the fruit sets by mid-July.

>> Himalayan blackberry

R. discolor

Description This blackberry was introduced from India and has now taken over much of the Pacific Northwest. It is heavily armed, grows rampant to 10 m/33 ft., and is a prolific producer of berries. Blooming starts in mid-June, and the fruit sets by mid-August.

>> Cutleaf blackberry

R. laciniatus

Description Introduced from Europe, this berry is very similar to the Himalayan blackberry but less common. It can be found in open wasteland, at forest edges, and in ditches. Blooming starts in mid-June, and the fruit sets by mid-August.

▶ THIMBLEBERRY

Rubus parviflorus

ROSE FAMILY Rosaceae

Description Thimbleberry is an unarmed shrub to 3 m/10 ft. in height. Its large white flowers open up to 5 cm/2 in. across and are replaced by juicy bright-red berries. The dome-shaped berries are 2 cm/1 in. across and bear little resemblance to a thimble. The maple-shaped leaves grow up to 25 cm/10 in. across, and, when needed, make a good substitute for bathroom tissue.

Traditional use The large leaves were used to line cooking pits and cover baskets. The berries were eaten fresh or dried, often mixed with other berries.

Habitat Common in coastal forests at low to mid elevations.

Season Flowering starts in mid-May, and the fruit matures at the end of July to early August.

▶ BLACK RASPBERRY BLACKCAP

Rubus leucodermis

ROSE FAMILY Rosaceae

Description Black raspberry is an armed deciduous shrub to 2 m/6.6 ft. in height. Its white flowers are small, to 3 cm/1 in. across, and borne in terminal clusters of three to seven. The resulting fruit (1 cm/0.5 in. across) starts off red but turns dark purple to black by July or August. The leaves have three to five leaflets supported on long, arching, well-armed stems. Black raspberries can be distinguished from other raspberries by the bloom, a whitish waxy coating, on the stems.

Traditional use The berries were eaten raw or dried into cakes for winter consumption.

Habitat Open forests and forest edges at low to mid elevations.

Season Flowers in June. The berries ripen from July to August, depending on elevation.

▶ CREEPING RASPBERRY FIVE-LEAVED BRAMBLE

Rubus pedatus

ROSE FAMILY Rosaceae

Description Creeping raspberry is an unarmed trailing perennial 0.2–1 m/0.7–3.3 ft. long. Its white flowers, to 2 cm/1 in. across, are produced singly. The small edible berries are glossy red and form in clusters of one to five. The compound leaves have five coarsely toothed leaflets to 2.5 cm/1 in. across.

Traditional use The berries were eaten as they were picked but were not widely used because they are small and difficult to gather.

Habitat Found mostly at mid elevations in moist coniferous forests but can also be seen at low to sub-alpine elevations.

Season Flowers in June. The berries ripen from August to September.

▶ SALMONBERRY

Rubus spectabilis

ROSE FAMILY Rosaceae

Description Salmonberry is one of BC's tallest native berry bushes. Though it averages 2–3 m/6.6–10 ft. in height, the bush can grow up to 4 m/13 ft. high. The bell-shaped pink flowers are 4 cm/1.5 in. across; they bloom at the end of February and are a welcome sight. Flowering continues until June, when both the flowers and the ripe fruit can be seen on the same bush. The soft berries range in colour from yellow to orange to red, with the occasional dark purple, and are shaped like blackberries. The leaves are compound, with three leaflets, much like the leaves of a raspberry. Weak prickles may be seen on the lower portion of the branches; the tops are unarmed.

Traditional use The high water content of the berries prevented them from being stored for any length of time. They were generally eaten shortly after harvesting.

Etymology The berry's common name comes from its resemblance to the shape and colour of salmon eggs.

Habitat Common on the coast in shaded damp forests.

Season The berries are harvested from mid-June to mid-July.

▶ COASTAL STRAWBERRY

Fragaria chiloensis

ROSE FAMILY Rosaceae

Description Coastal strawberry is a deciduous maritime perennial that grows to 30 cm/12 in. in height. Its white flowers are five petalled and to 3 cm/1 in. across, with approximately 20 orange stamens. The red fruit is small (1.5 cm/0.75 in. across) and tasty. The leathery leaves are basal and divided into three leaflets that are obovate, coarsely toothed, and woolly beneath. Strawberry leaves can be steeped to make a refreshing tea.

Etymology The species name refers to this plant's extensive range, from Alaska to Chile.

Habitat Usually seen on exposed rocky outcrops or in sand near the ocean.

Season Flowers from June to July.

▶ WOODLAND STRAWBERRY

Fragaria vesca

ROSE FAMILY Rosaceae

Description The woodland strawberry is an unarmed herbaceous perennial to 20 cm/8 in. in height. Its white flowers are 1–3 cm/0.4–1.2 in. across and have five petals and a yellow centre. The delicious fruit, 1–3 cm/0.4–1.2 in. across, is a smaller version of the cultivated strawberry. The leaves are 3–5 cm/1.2–2 in. across and compound, with three coarsely toothed leaflets. The blue-leaf, or wild, strawberry (*F. virginiana*) is similar but has bluish-green leaves, and the terminal teeth on its leaflets are shorter than the teeth on either side; the terminal teeth of the woodland strawberry are longer than the others.

Traditional use The juicy fruit was eaten fresh, and the leaves were steeped for tea.

Habitat Found mainly in lower-elevation open forests, but can also be found at mid to high elevations.

Season Flowers from May to June.

▶ SASKATOON BERRY SERVICE BERRY

Amelanchier alnifolia

ROSE FAMILY Rosaceae

Description Depending on growing conditions, the Saskatoon berry can vary from a 1 m/3.3 ft. shrub to a small tree 7 m/23 ft. in height. The white showy flowers are 1–3 cm/0.5–1 in. across and often hang in pendulous clusters. The young reddish berries form early and darken to a purple black by midsummer. The berries are up to 1 cm/0.5 in. across. The light bluish-green leaves are deciduous, oval shaped, and toothed above the middle.

Traditional use The berries were eaten fresh, often mixed with other berries, or dried for future use. On the Great Plains, the berries were mashed with buffalo meat to make pemmican. The hard, straight wood was a favourite for making arrows.

Habitat Shorelines, rocky outcrops, and open forests at low to mid elevations.

Season Flowering starts in mid-April, and the berries are fully ripe by the first week of August.

▶ HIGHBUSH CRANBERRY

Viburnum edule

HONEYSUCKLE FAMILY Caprifoliaceae

Description Highbush cranberry is usually seen as a straggling bush 3 m/10 ft. in height. Its small white flowers, to 1 cm/0.5 in. across, are borne in rounded clusters nestled between the paired leaves. The resulting red berries, to 1.5 cm/0.5 in. across, grow in clusters of two to five. The leaves are opposite and mostly three lobed.

Traditional use The tart berries were generally preserved for several months before eating.

Habitat Open forests and forest edges at low to mid elevations.

Season Flowers from the end of May to June. The berries ripen in September and last through October.

FERNS

MAIDENHAIR FERN

Adiantum pedatum

POLYPODY FAMILY Polypodiaceae

Description Maidenhair fern is a delicate-looking fern with an almost tropical appearance. The fan-shaped fronds carry the dainty green leaflets (pinnules), which contrast well with the dark stems (stipes) that grow up to 60 cm/24 in. in length. The reproducing sori under the pinnules are visible in late summer and fall.

Traditional use The shiny black stipes were used in basket making.

Etymology The genus name, *Adiantum*, meaning "unwetted," refers to the way the fronds repel water.

Habitat Moist cliff faces at low to mid elevations.

GREEN SPLEENWORT

Asplenium viride

POLYPODY FAMILY Polypodiaceae

Description Green spleenwort is a small rock fern to 15 cm/6 in. in height. The leaves and stipe are green, and the leaflets are round to oval. This feature distinguishes it from the similar-looking maidenhair spleenwort (*A. trichomanes*), whose stipe is purplish brown. The two species hybridize to produce *Asplenium × adulterinum*.

Habitat Usually seen growing in crevices of calcareous rocks at mid to high elevations.

▶ LADY FERN

Athyrium filix-femina

POLYPODY FAMILY Polypodiaceae

Description Lady fern is a tall fragile fern to 2 m/ 6.6 ft. in height. The apple-green fronds average 30 cm/12 in. across and are widest below the centre, tapering at the top and bottom. The diamond shape distinguishes the lady fern from the similar-looking spiny wood fern (*Dryopteris expansa*), whose fronds have an abrupt triangular form. The fronds die off in winter and emerge again in April. The horseshoe-shaped sori appear on the back of the fronds in spring.

Traditional use The young fronds (fiddleheads) were sometimes eaten in April.

Habitat Common in damp forests at low to mid elevations; often associated with deer ferns and spiny wood ferns.

▶ DEER FERN

Blechnum spicant

POLYPODY FAMILY Polypodiaceae

Description Deer fern can be distinguished from licorice fern (*Polypodium glycyrrhiza*) and sword fern (*Polystichum munitum*) by its two distinct types of fronds, sterile and fertile. The sterile fronds grow up to 75 cm/30 in. long, are tapered at both ends, and usually lie flat. The fertile, or spore-producing, fronds are erect from the centre of the plant and can grow up to 75 cm/30 in. in height. Deer fern is a good winter browse for deer.

Habitat Moist forested areas with plenty of rainfall. Not as common as sword fern but can be seen in most moist forested areas.

▶ SPINY WOOD FERN

Dryopteris expansa

POLYPODY FAMILY Polypodiaceae

Description Spiny wood fern is an elegant plant to 1.5 m/5 ft. tall. The pale-green fronds are triangular, average up to 25 cm/10 in. across, and die off in winter. In spring, the rounded sori are produced on the underside of the fronds. Spiny wood fern is similar in appearance and requirements (shade, water, and soil conditions) to lady fern (*Athyrium filix-femina*).

Traditional use Some groups dug up the rhizomes in the fall and ate them steamed.

Habitat Common in moist forests at low to mid elevations.

▶ PARSLEY FERN MOUNTAIN FERN

Cryptogramma crispa

POLYPODY FAMILY Polypodiaceae

Description Parsley fern is a small evergreen to 30 cm/ 12 in. in height. It has two sets of fronds, sterile and fertile (spore producing). The sterile fronds are evergreen, deeply dissected, and parsley green and grow to 20 cm/8 in. in height. The fertile fronds have less-congested foliage; their leaf margins are rolled and cover the sori, and they grow to 30 cm/ 12 in. in height. The fertile fronds emerge in spring.

Etymology The species name, *crispa*, refers to the crisped look of the fronds.

Habitat Dry sites, typically on rocky outcrops or slopes at low to high elevations.

▶ OAK FERN

Gymnocarpium dryopteris

POLYPODY FAMILY Polypodiaceae

Description Oak fern is a deciduous plant to 40 cm/ 16 in. in height that is usually seen in patches. The fragile-looking leaves are triangular and appear to be in three segments. The stipe, or stem, is golden brown.

Habitat Moist open forests at low to high elevations; especially common at mid elevations. Looking like a soft green carpet, it can cover hundreds of square metres or feet on the slopes of open forests.

▶ LICORICE FERN

Polypodium glycyrrhiza

POLYPODY FAMILY Polypodiaceae

Description Licorice fern is a small evergreen fern commonly seen on mossy slopes and on the trunks of bigleaf maple trees. The dark-green fronds grow to 50 cm/ 20 in. long and 5–7 cm/2–3 in. wide and have a golden stem (stipe). The round spores are produced in a single row under the leaves. The rhizomes have a licorice taste; hence the fern's common name. Leather polypody (*P. scouleri*) is a coastal species that can be seen on the trunks of conifers not far from the ocean. Its appearance is more rounded than that of licorice fern, and its rhizomes are not licorice flavoured.

Traditional use The roots were eaten fresh or cooked and used as a cold and throat medicine.

Habitat Low-elevation forests, where it grows on trunks and branches of large trees, and sometimes on shady outcrops. Commonly seen growing on the trunks of bigleaf maple trees.

▶ BRACKEN FERN

Pteridium aquilinum

POLYPODY FAMILY Polypodiaceae

Description Bracken fern is BC's tallest native fern, often reaching to 3 m/10 ft. or more in height. It is also the most widespread fern in the world. The tall, arching fronds are dark green, with a golden-green stem (stipe). They are triangular and grow singly from rhizomes in spring.

Traditional use The rhizomes were peeled and eaten fresh or cooked, and the fiddleheads were boiled and eaten. However, it is not advisable to eat this fern, as it has now been proven to be a health hazard.

Habitat A diverse growing range, from dry to moist and open to forested regions.

▶ WESTERN SWORD FERN

Polystichum munitum

POLYPODY FAMILY Polypodiaceae

Description Western sword fern is the Pacific Northwest's most common fern. It is evergreen and can grow to 1.5 m/5 ft. in height. The fronds are dark green, with side leaves (pinnae) that are sharply pointed and toothed. A double row of sori forms on the underside of the fronds in midsummer, turning orange by autumn. The fronds are in high demand in eastern Canada and the United States for floral decorations.

Traditional use The ferns were used to line steaming pits and baskets and were placed on floors as sleeping mats.

Etymology The species name, *munitum*, means "armed," referring to the side leaves that resemble swords.

Habitat Dry to moist forest near the coast at lower elevations, where it can form pure groves.

SHRUBS AND BUSHES

▶ DEVIL'S CLUB

Oplopanax horridus

GINSENG FAMILY Araliaceae

Description Devil's club is a deciduous shrub 1–3 m/3.3–10 ft. in height. Its small white flowers are densely packed into pyramidal clusters approximately 15 cm/6 in. long. The flowers bloom in May and are replaced by showy scarlet berries in August; these are not considered edible. The large leaves are maple-like, alternate, and to 30 cm/12 in. across, with spines in the larger veins on both sides. The stems are sprawling, awkward looking, and very well armed, with spines to 1 cm/0.5 in. long.

Traditional use Next to hellebore, devil's club was coastal indigenous peoples' most valued medicinal plant. Infusions and poultices were used to relieve arthritis, fevers, colds, and infections.

Etymology The species name, *horridus*, comes to mind when you accidentally encounter this shrub.

Habitat Moist forested areas with rich soil at low to mid elevations.

Season Red berries appear by August and last through September.

▶ CALIFORNIA HAZELNUT BEAKED HAZELNUT

Corylus cornuta var. californica

BIRCH FAMILY Betulaceae

Description California hazelnut is a broad spreading shrub 2–5 m/3.3–16 ft. tall. The male flowers are formed in hanging catkins in early spring. Their pollen is mainly wind distributed to the small female flowers that have beautiful protruding red stigmas. A very close look is needed to see them. The toothed leaves are alternate, to 8 cm/3 in. long, with a heart-shaped base. They give the forest a wonderful autumn-yellow colour.

Traditional use The nuts were an important and delicious food. They were often traded to areas where the hazelnuts did not grow.

Habitat Open moist forests along the coast.

Season The hazelnuts are noticeable by the end of June and ripen by August or September.

▶ BLACK TWINBERRY

Lonicera involucrata

HONEYSUCKLE FAMILY Caprifoliaceae

Description Black twinberry is a deciduous shrub 1–3 m/3.3–10 ft. in height. Its yellow flowers are tubular and borne in pairs, to 2 cm/1 in. long. The inedible berries are shiny black, cupped in a moon bract, and to 1 cm/0.5 in. across. The leaves are broadly lance shaped, tapering to a point, opposite, and 5–15 cm/2–6 in. long.

Traditional use The berries were mashed and the purple juice used to dye roots for basketry. The Haida rubbed the berries into their scalps to prevent their hair from turning grey. It was said that eating the berries drove a person mad.

Habitat Moist to wet open forests at low to high elevations.

Season Flowers by the end of May; the berries ripen by the end of June.

▶ RED TWINBERRY

Lonicera utahensis

HONEYSUCKLE FAMILY Caprifoliaceae

Description Red twinberry is a deciduous shrub to 1.5 m/5 ft. in height. Its twin flowers are a creamy yellow, to 1.5 cm/0.75 in. long. The twin berries are an attractive fleshy red, to 1 cm/0.5 in. across. The leaves grow to 5 cm/2 in. long and are more rounded than those of the black twinberry.

Habitat Open forests and forest edges; common at mid elevations.

Season Flowers from mid-May to June.

▶ BLUE-BERRIED ELDER BLUE ELDERBERRY

Sambucus caerulea

HONEYSUCKLE FAMILY Caprifoliaceae

Description Blue-berried elder ranges from a bush to a small tree to 6 m/20 ft. in height. Its flowers are similar to those of the red-berried elder but are in flat-topped clusters, not pyramidal. The mature berries are dark blue with a white coating of the bloom, giving them a soft-blue appearance. The leaves are compound, with five to nine oval, lance-shaped leaflets.

Traditional use Though the raw berries are edible, they were usually eaten cooked.

Habitat Dry open sites at low elevations. The blue-berried elder is found in inland areas and the Gulf Islands and San Juan Islands.

Season The berries start to turn blue by mid-August and, if not eaten by birds or people, last into October.

▶ RED-BERRIED ELDER RED ELDERBERRY

Sambucus racemosa

HONEYSUCKLE FAMILY Caprifoliaceae

Description Red-berried elder is a bushy shrub to 6 m/20 ft. in height. Its small flowers are creamy white and grow in pyramidal clusters 10–20 cm/4–8 in. long. The berries that replace them take up to three months to turn bright red; they are poisonous to people when eaten raw but are a favourite food for birds. The leaves are compound and 5–15 cm/2–6 in. long, with five to nine opposite leaves.

Traditional use The pithy branches were hollowed out and used as blowguns. The berries were either steamed or boiled.

Habitat Moist coastal forest edges and roadsides.

Season Flowers in May and sets mature berries in July.

▶ SNOWBERRY

Symphoricarpos albus

HONEYSUCKLE FAMILY Caprifoliaceae

Description Snowberry is an erect deciduous shrub to 2 m/6.6 ft. in height. Its small white to pink flowers turn into an abundance of very noticeable white berries 1–2 cm/0.5–1 in. across. Older plants produce a smaller oval leaf to 2 cm/1 in. long, while younger, more vigorous plants have wavy leaves to 5 cm/2 in. long. The leaves have a sweet fragrance when wet. Snowberries are best appreciated in winter, when the bright-white berries stand out against the surrounding grey.

Traditional use Thin branches were bound together to make brooms.

Etymology The genus name, *Symphoricarpos*, refers to the clustering of the berries.

Habitat Open forested areas at low to mid elevations.

Season The berries form in September.

CAUTION **The berries are poisonous.**

▶ RED-OSIER DOGWOOD

Cornus stolonifera

DOGWOOD FAMILY Cornaceae

Description Red-osier dogwood is a mid-sized deciduous shrub to 5 m/16 ft. in height. Its small white flowers (0.7 cm/0.25 in. across) are grouped together to form dense round clusters approximately 10 cm/4 in. across. The leaves are typical of dogwood: opposite and to 10 cm/4 in. long, with parallel veins. Younger branches are pliable and have an attractive red colour.

Traditional use The small branches were used for weaving, as barbecue racks and fuel for smoking salmon, and in latticework for fishing weirs.

Habitat Moist to wet areas, usually forested, at low to mid elevations.

Season Flowering starts in late May, and the berries ripen by the end of July to August.

▶ COMMON JUNIPER

Juniperus communis

CYPRESS FAMILY Cupressaceae

Description Common juniper is a prostrate conifer that rarely exceeds 1 m/3.3 ft. in height and 4 m/13 ft. in diameter. Its bluish-green needles are very sharp and prick when handled. The light-green "berries," which are actually cones, turn a dark bluish black in the second year. These mature "berries" are used to flavour gin. Common juniper is the only circumpolar conifer in the northern hemisphere.

Traditional use The wood was used only medicinally, as it rarely attains a size large enough for woodworking or carving.

Habitat Found on dry rocky outcrops from low to alpine elevations and occasionally in bogs.

Season Berries can be seen from July to December.

▶ HAIRY MANZANITA

Arctostaphylos columbiana

HEATHER FAMILY Ericaceae

Description Hairy manzanita is an evergreen shrub to 4 m/13 ft. in height. Its small pinkish-white flowers are to 0.7 cm/0.25 in. long, urn shaped, and formed in terminal clusters. By midsummer, they develop into mealy brown-red berries. The dull-green leaves are oval shaped, hairy, and to 5 cm/2 in. long.

Traditional use The berries were eaten raw or cooked. Caution should be taken—the berries are thought to cause serious constipation.

Etymology The common name manzanita is Spanish for "small apples," in reference to the fruit.

Habitat Rocky southwestern-facing areas at low elevations that are exposed to the sun.

Season Flowers in late spring, with berries by midsummer, between July and August.

▶ COPPERBUSH

Elliottia pyroliflorus

HEATHER FAMILY Ericaceae

Description Copperbush is another plant from the heather family. It is a deciduous bush to 2 m/6.6 ft. tall, with exfoliating copper-coloured bark. The pink to copperish flowers and long protruding, curved style make this bush unique. Even the seeds retain the curved style. The leaves are grass green, alternating, lance shaped, and to 5 cm/2 in. long.

Etymology The genus, *Elliottia*, is named after Stephen Elliott (1771–1830), a botanist at Charleston, South Carolina.

Habitat Moist forested areas at mid to subalpine elevations.

Season Flowers in June at mid elevations and in mid-July at subalpine elevations.

▶ WESTERN BOG LAUREL

Kalmia microphylla

HEATHER FAMILY Ericaceae

Description BC's native laurel is a small lanky evergreen no more than 60 cm/24 in. high. Its beautiful pink flowers, 2.5 cm/1 in. across, have a built-in pollen dispenser. A close look reveals that some of the stamens are bent over; these spring up when the flower is disturbed, dusting the intruder with pollen. The leaves are opposite, lance shaped, 2–4 cm/1–1.5 in. long, shiny dark green above, and felty white below, with its edges strongly rolled over. The plant is poisonous and should not be confused with Labrador tea (*Rhododendron groenlandicum*), which it resembles from above.

Traditional use The leaves were boiled and used in small doses for medicinal purposes.

Habitat Peat bogs and lakeshores at low to high elevations.

Season Flowers in early May.

CAUTION The plant is poisonous.

LABRADOR TEA

Rhododendron groenlandicum

HEATHER FAMILY Ericaceae

Description Most of the year, Labrador tea is a small gangly shrub to 1.5 m/5 ft. in height. In spring, the masses of small white flowers turn the shrub into the Cinderella of the bog. The evergreen leaves are lance shaped, alternate, and 4–6 cm/2 in. long, with the edges rolled over. The leaves can be distinguished from those of the poisonous bog laurel (*Kalmia microphylla*) by their flat-green colour on top and rust-coloured hairs beneath. To be safe, pick the leaves only when the shrub is in flower.

Traditional use The leaves have long been used by indigenous groups across North America as infusions. Early explorers and settlers quickly picked up on this caffeine substitute. Caution must be taken—not all people can drink it.

Habitat Peat bogs, lakesides, and permanent wet meadows at low to alpine elevations.

Season Flowering starts in mid-May, with the best viewing at the end of May, or early June at lower elevations.

FALSE AZALEA FOOL'S HUCKLEBERRY

Menziesia ferruginea

HEATHER FAMILY Ericaceae

Description False azalea is an upright deciduous shrub to 3 m/10 ft. in height. Its flowers, which resemble a huckleberry's, are a dull-copper colour, bell shaped, and to 1.3 cm/0.5 in. long, with long stems. The small fruit (0.5 cm/0.25 in. long) is a dry, four-valved capsule that is not edible. The leaves are elliptical, bluish green on top, whitish green below, and 3–6 cm/1.2–2.4 in. long. They appear to grow in whorls.

Etymology The genus name, *Menziesia*, is after Archibald Menzies, a naval surgeon and botanist who sailed with Captain George Vancouver and collected plants on the west coast.

Habitat Moist forested sites, especially in wetter areas at low to high elevations.

Season Flowers from May to July, depending on elevation.

▶ WHITE-FLOWERED RHODODENDRON

Rhododendron albiflorum

HEATHER FAMILY Ericaceae

Description White-flowered rhododendron is a deciduous bush to 2 m/6.6 ft. in height. Its showy white-cream flowers are to 2 cm/1 in. long and grow in clusters of two to four along the stems. The leaves are alternate and 3–7 cm/1–2 in. long, and the upper surface is shiny but also slightly hairy.

Traditional use The leaves were used for tea by some indigenous groups; others boiled the buds to use as a sore-throat remedy or chewed them to treat stomach ulcers.

Habitat Moist open slopes or on the edges of coniferous forests at subalpine elevations.

Season Flowers from mid-July to the beginning of August.

▶ PACIFIC RHODODENDRON COAST RHODODENDRON

Rhododendron macrophyllum

HEATHER FAMILY Ericaceae

Description Pacific rhododendron is an evergreen shrub that can reach heights of up to 8 m/26 ft. tall. Its beautiful pink flowers are five lobed and to 4 cm/1.5 in. long. The leathery leaves are evergreen (lasting two to three years) and are 10–20 cm/ 4–8 in. long. Pacific rhododendron is the state flower of Washington. Archibald Menzies discovered this plant at Port Discovery, Washington, in 1792 while voyaging with Captain George Vancouver.

Habitat Moist forests from southern Vancouver Island to northern California.

Season Flowers in June.

▶ MOCK ORANGE

Philadelphus lewisii

HYDRANGEA FAMILY Hydrangeaceae

Description In flower, mock orange is a showy deciduous bush to 4 m/13 ft. in height. Its fragrant four-petalled flowers are white with a yellow centre and grow to 3 cm/1 in. across. The leaves are similar to those of cultivated varieties: opposite and to 5 cm/2 in. long, with three prominent veins. As the common name suggests, the flowers resemble orange blossoms.

Traditional use The hard straight wood was used for arrows, pipe stems, fish spears, and combs.

Habitat Moist forested sites at low to mid elevations.

Season Flowers from May to July; the air is filled with perfume until June

▶ CALIFORNIA WAX MYRTLE

Myrica californica

SWEET GALE FAMILY Myricaceae

Description California wax myrtle is an evergreen shrub to small tree 6–10 m/20–33 ft. tall. The flowers are produced on a spike 0.5–3 cm/0.25–1 in. long and range from reddish to greenish in colour. The fruit that follows are purple berries to 0.7 cm/0.25 in. across that are covered with a waxy coating (hence the common name of wax myrtle). The leaves are to 8 cm/3 in. long, and wedge shaped, with small dark spots on them.

Habitat Coastal forests at low elevations, from southern Vancouver Island (especially Chesterman Beach in Tofino, BC, where there are hundreds) to Long Beach, California.

Season Flowers in the spring.

▶ SWEET GALE

Myrica gale

SWEET GALE FAMILY Myricaceae

Description Sweet gale is an aromatic shrub to 1–3 m/3.3–10 ft. in height. Its flowers are displayed in yellowish male and female catkins, which appear in spring before the leaves. The fruit are tiny cone-like brown husks that persist through the winter. The thin leaves are flat green above and whitish below, coarsely toothed above the middle, and to 5 cm/2 in. long.

Etymology The genus name, *Myrica*, means "perfume," a reference to the sweet-scented leaves.

Habitat Prefers to have its feet wet in shallow fresh water, including ponds, lakes, and swamps, at low to mid elevations. When out of flower, it blends with hardhack (*Spiraea douglasii*).

Season Flowers in April, and the tiny fruit can be seen throughout the year.

▶ REDSTEM CEANOTHUS

Ceanothus sanguineus

BUCKTHORN FAMILY Rhamnaceae

Description Redstem ceanothus is a deciduous bush to 3 m/10 ft. in height. Its fragrant tiny flowers grow in terminal clusters 10–15 cm/4–6 in. long. The oval leaves are finely toothed, to 10 cm/4 in. long, with three major veins.

Traditional use The wood was sometimes used in smoking deer meat.

Etymology The species name, *sanguineus*, means "bloody red," referring to the colour of the new twigs.

Habitat Open forests and forest edges on dry sites, at low to mid elevations. Snowbush (*C. velutinus*) also grows in these habitats and blooms at about the same time.

Season Blooms from the end of May to June.

▶ OCEANSPRAY ARROW-WOOD

Holodiscus discolor

ROSE FAMILY Rosaceae

Description Oceanspray is an upright deciduous shrub to 5 m/16 ft. in height. Its small creamy-white flowers are densely packed to form inverted-pyramidal clusters to 20 cm/8 in. long. The fruiting clusters turn an unattractive brown and persist through winter. The leaves are wedge shaped, flat green above, pale green and hairy below, and to 5 cm/2 in. long.

Traditional use The straight new growth was a favourite for making arrows; hence its common name of arrow-wood. The wood is extremely hard and was used to make harpoon shafts, teepee pins, digging tools, and drum hoops.

Etymology The species name, *discolor*, refers to the two-coloured leaf.

Habitat Dry open forests at low to mid elevations; often found on rocky outcrops.

Season In full flower by the end of June.

▶ NINEBARK

Physocarpus capitatus

ROSE FAMILY Rosaceae

Description Ninebark is an upright deciduous shrub to 4 m/13 ft. in height. Its tiny white flowers are grouped into rounded clusters to 7 cm/3 in. across. The fruit are reddish-brown inflated seed capsules. The maple-shaped leaves are three to five lobed, shiny green above, paler below, and to 7 cm/3 in. long. Despite its name, it is debatable whether the shaggy bark has nine layers.

Traditional use Ninebark was used medicinally.

Etymology The species name, *capitatus*, refers to the rounded heads of the flowers.

Habitat Usually seen in moist sites, in open forests, and at streamsides and lakesides, but also in dry rocky areas at lower elevations.

Season Flowers from mid- to late July.

▶ BALDHIP ROSE WOODLAND ROSE

Rosa gymnocarpa

ROSE FAMILY Rosaceae

Description The baldhip rose is the Pacific Northwest's smallest native rose. It is often prostrate to 1.5 m/5 ft. in height. The tiny pink flowers are five petalled, delicately fragrant, 1–2 cm/0.5–1 in. across, and usually solitary. The compound leaves are smaller than those of the Nootka rose and have five to nine toothed leaflets. The spindly stems are mostly armed, with weak prickles. A good identifier is this rose's unusual habit of losing its sepals, leaving the hip bald. Rosehips have a higher concentration of vitamin C than oranges and make an excellent jelly or marmalade.

Etymology The species name, *gymnocarpa*, means "naked fruit."

Habitat Dry open forests at lower elevations, from southern BC to the redwood forests of California.

Season Flowers in June.

▶ NOOTKA ROSE

Rosa nutkana

ROSE FAMILY Rosaceae

Description The largest of the Pacific Northwest's native roses, the Nootka rose grows to 3 m/10 ft. in height. The showy pink flowers are five petalled, fragrant, 5 cm/2 in. across, and usually solitary. The compound leaves have five to seven toothed leaflets and are armed with a pair of prickles underneath. The reddish hips are round, plump, and 1–2 cm/0.5–1 in. across and contrast well with the dark-green foliage.

Traditional use Rosehips were strung together to make perfume. They were eaten only in times of famine, as the hips can cause irritation when passed if their fine fibres are not completely removed before eating.

Habitat Open low-elevation forests throughout BC.

Season Flowering begins in mid-May, and the hips start to develop colour by the beginning of August.

▶ SWAMP ROSE CLUSTERED WILD ROSE

Rosa pisocarpa

ROSE FAMILY Rosaceae

Description Swamp rose is a weakly armed bush to 1.5 m/5 ft. tall. Its pale-pink flowers are formed in small clusters (not singly); hence the common name of clustered wild rose. The hips are small and pea sized. The leaves consist of five to seven pointed leaflets with two thorns at the base.

Etymology The species name, *pisocarpa*, means "with pea-like fruit."

Habitat Low-lying swampy areas along the coast.

Season Flowers from May to June.

▶ SUBALPINE SPIREA

Spiraea densiflora

ROSE FAMILY Rosaceae

Description Subalpine spirea is a deciduous mountain shrub to 70 cm/28 in. tall. The small pink flowers are crowded together to form flat-topped terminal clusters to 5 cm/2 in. across. The alternate leaves are toothed above the middle and up to 5 cm/2 in. long.

Traditional use Some species' branches were used to make garlands.

Etymology The genus name, *Spiraea*, is from *spirea*, meaning "spiral" or "twisted."

Habitat Creeksides, lakesides, and wet meadows at mid to subalpine elevations.

Season Flowers from late July to August.

▶ HARDHACK STEEPLEBUSH

Spiraea douglasii

ROSE FAMILY Rosaceae

Description Hardhack is an upright deciduous bush to 2 m/6.6 ft. in height. Its tiny pink flowers group together to form fuzzy pyramidal clusters up to 15 cm/ 6 in. tall. The resulting brown fruiting clusters persist on the bush through winter. The alternate leaves are elliptical to oval, toothed above the middle, 5–10 cm/2–4 in. long, dark green above, and a felty paler green below.

Traditional use The tough wiry branches were used to make halibut hooks, scrapers, and hooks for drying and smoking salmon.

Habitat Prefers moist conditions; can be seen growing in ditches and bogs and at lakesides from low levels to subalpine meadows.

Season Flowering begins in mid-June and fades by August.

▶ GOAT'S BEARD

Aruncus dioicus

ROSE FAMILY Rosaceae

This species description is located on page 87 among other members of the Rose family in the Flowering Plants section.

▶ FALSEBOX MOUNTAIN LOVER

Paxistima myrsinites

STAFF TREE FAMILY Celastraceae

Description Falsebox is a small evergreen shrub to 75 cm/30 in. in height. Its tiny maroon flowers go unnoticed by all but a curious few. The evergreen leaves are elliptical, leathery, tooth edged, and to 3 cm/1 in. long. Falsebox is an attractive bush more noticed for its foliage than its flowers.

Etymology The species name, *myrsinites*, is Greek for "myrrh," in reference to the fragrant flowers.

Habitat Forested mountain slopes at low to mid elevations.

Season Flowers from May to June or later.

▶ INDIAN PLUM

Oemleria cerasiformis

ROSE FAMILY Rosaceae

Description Indian plum is an upright deciduous shrub or small tree to 5 m/16 ft. in height. Its white flowers, which usually emerge before the leaves, are 1 cm/0.5 in. across and hang in clusters 6–10 cm/2–4 in. long. The small plum-like fruit grow to 1 cm/0.5 in. across; they start off yellowish and red and finish a bluish black. They are edible, but a large seed and bitter taste make them better for the birds. The leaves are broadly lance shaped, light green, and 7–12 cm/3–5 in. long and appear in upright clusters.

Traditional use Small amounts were eaten fresh or dried for winter use.

Etymology The species name, *cerasiformis*, means "cherry shaped," a reference to the fruit.

Habitat Restricted to low elevations on the southern coast and Gulf Islands; prefers moist open broad-leaved forests.

Season Flowers from March to April, with ripe fruit by the end of June.

TREES

▶ VINE MAPLE

Acer circinatum

MAPLE FAMILY Aceraceae

Description Vine maple is a shrub or small tree 3–9 m/10–30 ft. in height. It is often multi-stemmed, with older trees occasionally becoming prostrate. The leaves resemble those of Japanese maples: they are opposite and 7–13 cm/3–5 in. across, with seven to nine serrated lobes. The winged seeds are 4 cm/1.5 in. long, starting out green and becoming reddish brown by autumn. The bark is smooth and pale green on younger trees and dull brown on older ones. The autumn leaves create an incredible colour show.

Traditional use The wood was used to make bows, arrows, spoons, handles, and snowshoe frames.

Habitat Moist shaded woods at lower elevations. A common understory tree.

Season Very noticeable from October to November.

▶ DOUGLAS MAPLE

Acer glabrum

MAPLE FAMILY Aceraceae

Description Douglas maple is a small deciduous tree to 10 m/33 ft. in height. Its long palmate leaves are opposite and 5–10 cm/2–4 in. across and have three to five sharp lobes. The leaves of the closely related vine maple (A. *circinatum*) have seven to nine lobes. The pairs of winged seeds, or samaras, grow to 5 cm/2 in. across and are joined at right angles.

Traditional use The hard, durable wood was used in many ways, including for snowshoe frames, drum hoops, tongs, throwing sticks, bowls, and masks.

Habitat Dry open forested sites at low to mid elevations.

Season The leaves turn a brilliant orange in the autumn.

▶ BIGLEAF MAPLE

Acer macrophyllum

MAPLE FAMILY Aceraceae

Description The bigleaf maple is the largest native maple on the west coast, often exceeding heights of 30 m/100 ft. Its huge leaves, which are dark green, five lobed, and 20–30 cm/8–12 in. across, are excellent identifiers. In early spring, it produces beautiful clusters of scented yellow-green flowers, 7–10 cm/3–4 in. long. The mature winged seeds (samaras), 5 cm/2 in. long, act as whirligigs when they fall; they are bountiful and an important food source for birds, squirrels, mice, and chipmunks. The fissured brown bark is host to an incredible number of epiphytes, most commonly mosses and licorice ferns.

Traditional use The plentiful wood was important in indigenous culture as a fuel and for carvings, paddles, combs, fish lures, dishes, and handles. The large leaves were used to line berry baskets and steam pits.

Habitat Dominant in lower forested areas. Its shallow root system prefers moist soils, mild winters, and cool summers.

Season Flowers from April to May, with the winged seeds seen in July.

▶ RED ALDER

Alnus rubra

BIRCH FAMILY Betulaceae

Description The largest native alder in North America, the red alder grows quickly and can reach 25 m/81 ft. in height. Its leaves are oval shaped, grass green, and 7–15 cm/3–6 in. long, with a coarsely serrated edge. Hanging male catkins, 7–15 cm/3–6 in. long, decorate the bare trees in early spring. The fruit (cones) are 1.5–2.5 cm/0.75–1 in. long; they start off green, then turn brown, and persist through winter. The bark is thin and grey on younger trees and scaly when older. Red alder leaves give a poor colour display in autumn, when they are mainly green or brown.

Traditional use The soft straight-grained wood is easily worked and was used for making masks, bowls, rattles, paddles, and spoons. The red bark was used to dye fishnets, buckskins, and basket material.

Habitat Moist wooded areas, disturbed sites, and stream banks at low to mid elevations.

▶ SITKA ALDER

Alnus sinuata

BIRCH FAMILY Betulaceae

Description The Sitka alder is a deciduous shrub or small tree 3–7 m/10–23 ft. high. Its coarse leaves are double serrated, grass green, and 7–10 cm/3–4 in. long. In early spring, it becomes covered in pollen-producing catkins 10–15 cm/4–6 in. long and female cones 2 cm/1 in. long.

Traditional use The soft straight-grained wood is easily worked and was used for making masks, bowls, rattles, paddles, and spoons. The red bark was used to dye fishnets, buckskins, and basket material.

Habitat As with most alders, it prefers moist conditions, from the coast of the Arctic Circle to the high mountains of California. Often grows on avalanche sites.

Season In leaf from April to November.

▶ PAPER BIRCH CANOE BIRCH

Betula papyrifera

BIRCH FAMILY Betulaceae

Description Paper birch is a medium-sized tree reaching heights of 20 m/66 ft. Its serrated leaves are 8–12 cm/3–5 in. long, rounded at the bottom, and sharply pointed at the apex. Male and female catkins can be seen in early spring, just before the leaves appear. The white peeling bark is a good identifier on younger trees. There is also a red-bark variety that can be confused with the native bitter cherry (*Prunus emarginata*).

Traditional use The bark was used to make canoes, cradles, food containers, writing paper, and coverings for teepees. The straight-grained wood was used for arrows, spears, snowshoes, sleds, and masks.

Etymology The species name, *papyrifera*, means "to bear paper."

Habitat Rare in low-elevation coastal forests but common in interior forests; prefers moist soil and will tolerate wet sites.

▶ PACIFIC DOGWOOD

Cornus nuttallii

DOGWOOD FAMILY Cornaceae

Description Pacific dogwood ranges from being a multi-trunked shrub to a medium-sized tree as tall as 20 m/66 ft. Its leaves are elliptical, deep green above, lighter green below, and to 10 cm/4 in. long. The flowers are not quite as they seem: the four to seven showy white petals are actually bracts that surround small greenish-white flowers. Clusters of small red berries, 1 cm/0.5 in. across, appear by late summer. The bark is dark brown and smooth on young trees and scaly and ridged on older ones. The flower is the floral emblem of BC, and the tree is protected by law.

Traditional use The hard wood was used to make bows, arrows, harpoon shafts, and, more recently, knitting needles.

Etymology The painter and ornithologist John James Audubon named this tree after his friend Thomas Nuttall, the first person to classify it as a new species.

Habitat Coastal forests at low elevations.

Season Flowering starts in mid-April; there is often a second, smaller show in September.

▶ ARBUTUS PACIFIC MADRONE

Arbutus menziesii

HEATHER FAMILY Ericaceae

Description The arbutus is often seen as a contorted shrub or small tree, but in ideal conditions it can attain heights of 30 m/100 ft. Its leaves are leathery, glossy dark green above, silvery white below, and to 15 cm/6 in. long. They are similar to the leaves of the rhododendron, which is in the same family. The panicles of white flowers produced in the spring are followed by clusters of orange-red berries 1 cm/0.5 in. across. The reddish-brown bark peels away every year to reveal a greenish underbark; the beautiful colours of the thin peeling outer bark are the key identifiers. The arbutus is Canada's only native broadleaf evergreen tree.

Traditional use The leaves and bark were steeped as tea and used to cure colds and stomach aches. The wood was also used to make tools or carvings, but rarely, as it cracks very easily.

Habitat Dry coastal forests. Southwestern BC is the northern extent of its range.

Season Flowers in the spring.

GARRY OAK

Quercus garryana

BEECH FAMILY Fagaceae

Description Even when stunted or windblown, Garry oak is the coast's stateliest deciduous tree. It ranges from 3 m/10 ft. to 25 m/82 ft. in height, and the male and female flowers are borne separately, but on the same tree. Like those of most white oaks, the leaves of the Garry oak are deeply round lobed and to 12 cm/5 in. long. (Red or black oaks have pointed lobes.) The acorns are 2 cm/1 in. long, with a bumpy cap. The light-grey bark is tough, with thick edges.

Traditional use The acorns were eaten raw, boiled, or roasted. The hard wood was used to make small tools.

Etymology The plant explorer David Douglas, who discovered the tree, dedicated it to his friend Nicholas Garry, deputy governor of the Hudson's Bay Company.

Habitat Dry slopes and meadows on southeastern Vancouver Island, the Gulf Islands, and the San Juan Islands and elsewhere in Washington and Oregon.

Season The acorns ripen in the autumn.

CASCARA

Rhamnus purshiana

BUCKTHORN FAMILY Rhamnaceae

Description Cascara can be a multi-trunked shrub to a small tree to 9 m/30 ft. in height. Its leaves are oblong with prominent veins, glossy, grass green, and 7–13 cm/ 3–5 in. long. The flowers are small, greenish yellow, and rather insignificant. The berries are 0.5 cm/0.25 in. across and look like small cherries; they are red at first, turning bluish black in late summer. The smooth bark is silvery grey and resembles an elephant's hide on older trees. The bark was collected commercially for years and used as the key ingredient in laxatives.

Traditional use The bark was boiled, and the infusion was used as a laxative.

Habitat Prefers moist, nutrient-rich sites in the shade of larger trees at low elevations.

Season The small flowers are produced in the spring, while the bluish-black berries are seen at the end of summer.

▶ BLACK HAWTHORN

Crataegus douglasii

ROSE FAMILY Rosaceae

Description Black hawthorn is an armed scraggly shrub or bushy tree to 9 m/30 ft. in height. The leaves are roughly oval, coarsely toothed above the middle, and to 6 cm/2 in. long. The clusters of white flowers are showy but bland in smell. The edible fruit is purple black and to 1 cm/0.5 in. long and hangs in bunches. Older bark is grey, patchy, and very rough.

Traditional use The 3 cm/1 in. thorns were used as tines on herring rakes.

Habitat Prefers moist soil beside streams, in open forests, or near the ocean.

Season Flowers in May. The berries ripen by mid-June.

▶ BITTER CHERRY

Prunus emarginata

ROSE FAMILY Rosaceae

Description Bitter cherry is a small to medium-sized tree, 5–15 m/16–50 ft. in height. Its bark is very distinctive: reddish brown with orange slits (lenticels). It is thin and smooth and peels horizontally. The white flowers (1 cm/0.5 in. across) put on a wonderful show in April. The immature green fruit, 1 cm/0.5 in. across, appear in early June and are bright red by midsummer. The leaves are quite different from those of the familiar Japanese cherries; they are alternate, 3–8 cm/1–3 in. long, very finely toothed, and usually rounded at the tip. The cherries are extremely bitter and considered inedible to humans but are an important food source for birds. The fruit pits do not break down when digested, so birds carry them kilometres or miles from the parent tree.

Traditional use The shiny red bark was used to make baskets, mats, and bags. The hard wood makes excellent fuel.

Habitat Scattered in disturbed forests at low to mid elevations.

Season Flowers from the end of April to May.

▶ SITKA MOUNTAIN ASH

Sorbus sitchensis

ROSE FAMILY Rosaceae

Description Sitka mountain ash is a small multi-stemmed bush or thicket 1.5–4.5 m/5–15 ft. in height. Its compound bluish-green leaves have 7 to 13 leaflets, 11 being the norm. The tiny white flowers are in terminal clusters, 5–10 cm/2–4 in. across. From August to September, the bushes and trees display a wonderful show of bright red-orange berries. The bark is thin and shiny grey. The native mountain ash should not be confused with the larger European mountain ash (*S. aucuparia*), an introduced species that has naturalized well, as its berries are a favourite with birds. The European ash, or rowan, is rich in history. In the United Kingdom, it was planted near homes to protect owners from witches and in cemeteries to keep the dead in their graves. Christ is believed to have been crucified on a cross made from mountain ash, cedar, holly pine, or cypress.

Habitat Sitka mountain ash stays primarily where its name suggests: in the mountains. European ash can be found at lower elevations, especially near townships.

Season Flowers in the spring, followed by masses of orange berries by the end of summer.

▶ COTTONWOOD

Populus balsamifera ssp. *trichocarpa*

WILLOW FAMILY Salicaceae

Description Cottonwood is the tallest deciduous tree in the Pacific Northwest. It is also one of the fastest growing, attaining heights of 45 m/150 ft. and trunk diameters of 2–3 m/6.6–10 ft. Its leaves are heart shaped, alternating, shiny dark green above, pale green below, and 7–15 cm/3–6 in. long. The tiny seeds on female trees hang on 7–13 cm/3–5 in. catkins and are covered in white fluffy hairs known as "cotton." The deeply furrowed bark and large sticky buds are identifiers in winter. In early summer, bits of cotton can be seen filling the skies, transporting the seeds many kilometres or miles away from the parent trees. The wood is used commercially to make tissue paper.

Traditional use The sticky gum from the buds was boiled and used to stick feathers on arrow shafts and to waterproof baskets and birchbark canoes.

Habitat Low moist to wet areas across BC, Washington, and Oregon. Requires sunshine and will not tolerate heavy shade.

Season The buds appear in winter, and the seeds are dispersed in early summer, covered in the fluffy cotton-like hairs.

▶ PACIFIC CRAB APPLE

Malus fusca

ROSE FAMILY Rosaceae

Description Pacific crab apple is a deciduous shrub or small tree 2–10 m/6.6–33 ft. in height. Its leaves are 5–10 cm/2–4 in. long and similar to those of orchard apple trees, except that they often have bottom lobes. The flowers are typical apple blossoms: white to pink, fragrant, and in clusters of 5 to 12. The fruit that follows is 1–2 cm/0.5–1 in. across and green at first, turning yellowy reddish. On older trees, the bark is scaly and deeply fissured. The Pacific crab apple is the coast's only native apple.

Traditional use The small apples were an important food source, and the hard wood was used to make digging sticks, bows, handles, and halibut hooks.

Habitat High beaches, moist open forests, swamps, and stream banks at lower elevations.

Season Flowers from the end of April to May.

▶ TREMBLING ASPEN

Populus tremuloides

WILLOW FAMILY Salicaceae

Description Trembling aspen is a slender deciduous tree to 25 m/82 ft. in height. Its small heart-shaped leaves are finely toothed and grow to 8 cm/3 in. long; the leaf stalks are long and flattened, which is why the leaves tremble in the slightest breeze. Trembling aspens are dioecious (male and female flowers appear on separate trees).

Traditional use The wood was used for small dug-out canoes, tent poles, and drying racks.

Habitat Damp soils in open sites and forests at low to mid elevations.

► WILLOWS

Salix spp.

WILLOW FAMILY Salicaceae

Native willows are easy to identify as a genus but hard to distinguish as a species. This is due to the variable leaf shapes within the same species, male and female flowers appearing on separate plants, flowering before leaves appear, and hybridization between species. The two most common willows are Scouler's willow and Pacific willow.

>> Scouler's willow

Salix scouleriana

Description Scouler's willow is a shrub or tree 5–12 m/16–40 ft. in height. Its leaves are 5–8 cm/2–3 in. long, felty, narrow at the base, and rounded at the tip. The flowers appear before the leaves; the males are to 4 cm/1.5 in. long, and the females are to 6 cm/2.5 in. long. Can be found scattered in disturbed spots in young forests at low to mid elevations.

Season In leaf from April to November.

>> Pacific willow

S. lucida ssp. *lasiandra*

Description Pacific willow is a shrub or tree 6–12 m/20–40 ft. in height. Its leaves are 10–15 cm/4–6 in. long and lance shaped, with finely toothed edges. The flower appears with the leaves; the males are to 7 cm/3 in. long, and the females are to 12 cm/5 in. long. Can be found scattered in disturbed spots in young forests at low to mid elevations.

Season In leaf from April to November.

▶ YELLOW CYPRESS YELLOW CEDAR

Cupressus nootkatensis

CYPRESS FAMILY Cupressaceae

Description Yellow cypress is a slow-growing large conifer of conical habit that often exceeds 45 m/150 ft. in height. Its thin greyish-brown bark can be shed in vertical strips. The reddish-brown cones are round and to 1–2 cm/0.5–1 in. across, with four to six scales tipped with pointed bumps (bosses). (Red cedar, in comparison, has egg-shaped cones.) The bluish-green leaves are prickly to touch and more pendulous than the red cedar's.

Traditional use The wood was used for carving fine objects, such as bentwood boxes, chests, and intricate canoe paddles. The bark is soft; women used it to make clothing, blankets, baskets, rope, and hats.

Etymology Yellow cypress was first documented in Nootka Sound on the west coast of Vancouver Island in 1791 by Archibald Menzies; hence the species name.

Habitat Moist forests on the southern coast at mid to high elevations.

▶ ROCKY MOUNTAIN JUNIPER

Juniperus scopulorum

CYPRESS FAMILY Cupressaceae

Description Rocky mountain juniper is usually seen as a shrub, but on occasion it can form a beautiful weathered tree to 9 m/30 ft. in height. The bluish-green leaves are in two forms: the juvenile growth is prickly, while the mature growth is softer and resembles the leaves of western red cedar (*Thuja plicata*). The reddish-brown bark is thin and stringy, also like that of the red cedar. The trees are dioecious; male and female flowers are on separate trees. The soft blue female cones are knobby and to 0.7 cm/0.5 in. across and grow in abundance.

Traditional use Juniper wood was considered one of the best for making bows. The branches were burned as an incense and fumigant.

Habitat Dry exposed sites.

▶ WESTERN RED CEDAR

Thuja plicata

CYPRESS FAMILY Cupressaceae

Description Western red cedar is a fast-growing large conifer with heights exceeding 60 m/200 ft. Its bark sheds vertically and ranges from cinnamon red on young trees to grey on mature trees. The bases of older trees are usually heavily flared, with deep furrows. The egg-shaped cones are 1 cm/0.5 in. long and green when young, turning brown and upright when mature. (Yellow cypress, in comparison, has round cones). The bright-green leaves are scale-like, with the appearance of overlapping shingles. Western red cedar is BC's provincial tree. On old stumps, springboard marks can be seen 2–3 m/6.6–10 ft. above the ground. Early fallers used to stand on springboards when sawing or chopping the trees down; the springboards allowed them to get away from the tree's flared base. The shingle industry is now the biggest user of red cedar.

Traditional use First Nations know this tree as "the tree of life." It supplied them from birth to death, from cradle to coffin. The wood was used to make dugout canoes, fishing floats, paddles, bowls, masks, totem poles, ornamental boxes, and spear and arrow shafts. The bark was shredded for clothing, diapers, mats, blankets, baskets, and medicine.

Habitat Thrives on moist ground at low elevations. Will tolerate drier or higher sites but will not attain gigantic proportions.

▶ PACIFIC SILVER FIR

Abies amabilis

PINE FAMILY Pinaceae

Description Pacific silver fir is a straight-trunked, symmetrical conifer to 60 m/200 ft. in height. The bark on young trees is smooth grey, with prominent resin blisters. As the tree ages, the bark becomes scaly, rougher, and often lighter in colour. The cones are dark purple, barrel shaped, and to 12 cm/ 5 in. long. They sit erect on the upper portion of the tree. The needles are a lustrous dark green on the upper surface and silvery white below, with a notched tip.

Traditional use The soft wood was used for fuel, but little else. The sap was enjoyed as a chewing gum.

Etymology The species name, *amabilis*, means "lovely fir."

Habitat Moist forests at mid to high elevations.

▶ GRAND FIR

Abies grandis

PINE FAMILY Pinaceae

Description Grand fir is a remarkably fast-growing conifer that reaches heights of over 90 m/300 ft. Its bark is thin and blistery on young trees, roughened into oblong plates divided by shallow fissures on older trees. The cones are erect, cylindrical, to 10 cm/4 in. long, and green to brown. The needles are dark green and flat, 2–4 cm/1–1.5 in. long, and grooved on top, with two white bands of stomata below.

Traditional use The wood was used as fuel and to make canoes, fishhooks, and hand tools. The boughs were brought inside as an air purifier.

Etymology This is the tallest of the true firs and was aptly named "grand" by botanist and explorer David Douglas.

Habitat A low-elevation species on the coast; most commonly found in moist areas, where it grows with Douglas fir and western red cedar.

▶ SUBALPINE FIR

Abies lasiocarpa

PINE FAMILY Pinaceae

Description Subalpine fir is a thin spire-like tree to 40 m/130 ft. in height; firs that grow closer to the timberline are much smaller dwarfed shrubs. The leaves are bluish green, 2–3 cm/1 in. long, and pungent when crushed. The bark on the young tree is smooth and grey, but it roughens as the tree ages. The deep purple cones are 5–10 cm/2–4 in. long and stand erect on the upper portion of the tree; as with all true firs, the cones disintegrate as winter approaches, leaving a central core on the tree.

Traditional use The bark, pitch, wood, and boughs were widely used. The bark and pitch were used medicinally, the wood was used as a fuel, and the boughs were used as bedding.

Habitat This fir is the dominant conifer on subalpine slopes.

▶ SITKA SPRUCE

Picea sitchensis

PINE FAMILY Pinaceae

Description Sitka spruce is often seen on rocky outcrops as a twisted dwarf tree, though in favourable conditions it can exceed 90 m/300 ft. in height. Its reddish-brown bark is thin and patchy, a good identifier when the branches are too high to observe. The cones are golden brown and to 8 cm/3 in. long. The needles are dark green, to 3 cm/1 in. long, and sharp to touch. Sitka spruce has the highest strength-to-weight ratio of any BC, Washington, or Oregon tree. It was used to build the frame of Howard Hughes's infamous plane, the *Spruce Goose*.

Traditional use The new shoots and inner bark were a good source of vitamin C. The best baskets and hats were woven from spruce roots, and the pitch (sap) was often chewed as a gum.

Habitat A temperate rainforest tree that does not grow farther than 200 km/125 mi. from the ocean.

▶ WHITEBARK PINE

Pinus albicaulis

PINE FAMILY Pinaceae

Description Whitebark pine can reach heights of 20 m/66 ft., but it is often seen as a stunted bush under 3 m/10 ft. Its needles are slightly curved, to 8 cm/3 in. long, purplish when young, and green when mature.

Habitat Exposed dry sites at subalpine elevations. A related species, western white pine (*P. monticola*) can be seen at slightly lower elevations.

▶ SHORE PINE

Pinus contorta

PINE FAMILY Pinaceae

Description Depending on where they are growing, shore pines vary dramatically in size and shape. By the shoreline, they are usually stunted and twisted from harsh winds and nutrient-deficient soil. A little farther inland, they can be straight trunked and to 20 m/66 ft. in height. The small cones, 3–5 cm/1–2 in. long, are often slightly lopsided and remain on the tree for many years. The dark-green needles are 4–7 cm/2–3 in. long and grow in bundles of two. The nuts are edible but small and hard to reach. Another variety, lodgepole pine (*P. contorta* var. *latifolia*), grows straighter and taller, to 40 m/132 ft.

Traditional use The straight wood was used for teepee poles, torches, and arrow and harpoon shafts.

Habitat The coastal variety grows in the driest and wettest sites, from low to high elevations.

▶ WESTERN WHITE PINE

Pinus monticola

PINE FAMILY Pinaceae

Description Western white pine is a medium-sized symmetrical conifer to 40 m/132 ft. in height. Its bark is silvery green grey when young and dark brown and scaly when old. The cones are 15–25 cm/6–10 in. long and slightly curved. The bluish-green needles are 5–10 cm/2–4 in. long and grow in bundles of five.

Traditional use The bark was peeled into strips and sewn together with roots to make canoes. The pitch was used for waterproofing.

Etymology The species name, *monticola*, means "growing on mountains."

Habitat Moist to wet soils on the southern coast at low to high elevations.

▶ DOUGLAS FIR

Pseudotsuga menziesii

PINE FAMILY Pinaceae

Description Douglas fir is a fast-growing tall coni-fer 90 m/300 ft. in height. Its bark is thick, corky, and deeply furrowed. The ovate cones are 7–10 cm/3–4 in. long and have three forked bracts protrud-ing from the scales; the cones hang down from the branches, unlike the cones of true firs, which stand up. The needles are 2–3 cm/1 in. long and pointed at the apex, with a slight groove on the top and two white bands of stomata on the underside. It is the state conifer of Oregon.

Traditional use The wood was used for teepee poles, smoking racks, spear shafts, fishhooks, and firewood.

Etymology The common name commemorates the botanist and explorer David Douglas.

Habitat Tolerates dry to moist conditions from low to high elevations. Reaches its tallest size near the coast.

▶ WESTERN HEMLOCK

Tsuga heterophylla

PINE FAMILY Pinaceae

Description Western hemlock is a fast-growing pyrami-dal conifer to 60 m/200 ft. in height. Its reddish-brown bark becomes thick and deeply furrowed on mature trees. The plentiful cones are small (2–2.5 cm/0.75–1 in. long), conical, reddish when young, and brown when mature. The flat green leaves are 0.7–2 cm/0.25–0.75 in. long. The ends of the branches (main leaders) and new shoots are nodding, giving the tree a soft, pendulous appearance that is good for identification. Western hemlock is the state tree of Washington.

Traditional use The wood has long been used for spear shafts, spoons, dishes, roasting spits, and ridgepoles. The bark was boiled to make a red dye for wool and basket material.

Habitat Flourishes on the Pacific coast, from Alaska to Oregon, from low elevations to 1,000 m/3,300 ft., where it is replaced by mountain hemlock (*T. mertensiana*).

► MOUNTAIN HEMLOCK

Tsuga mertensiana

PINE FAMILY Pinaceae

Description Mountain hemlock is a smaller, stiffer tree than western hemlock (*T. heterophylla*). It is often stunted by its harsh environment, but with good conditions it can slowly grow to 40 m/132 ft. in height. The reddish-brown bark is rough and deeply ridged, even on young trees. The cones are up to 8 cm/3 in. long, compared with 2.5 cm/1 in. for the western hemlock's. The bluish-green leaves are equal in length, to 2 cm/0.75 in. long.

Etymology The species name commemorates the German botanist Franz Karl Mertens.

Habitat Typically found at higher elevations, often associating with Pacific silver fir (*Abies amabilis*) and subalpine fir (*A. lasiocarpa*). Well adapted to the short growing season and heavy snowpacks. Does not naturally grow at lower elevations.

► WESTERN YEW

Taxus brevifolia

YEW FAMILY Taxaceae

Description Western yew is a small conifer 3–25 m/10–83 ft. in height. It is usually seen as a straggly shrub or small tree in the understory of larger trees. Its thin brownish bark is scale-like, exposing reddish-purple patches that distinguish it from the European species. Female trees produce a beautiful but poisonous red berry that ripens in August or September. The flat needles are 3 cm/1 in. long and dark green above, with white bands below. The cancer-fighting drug paclitaxel is extracted from yew bark.

Traditional use Western yew was considered the best wood for making bows.

Habitat Found intermittently on a variety of forested sites at low to mid elevations.

CAUTION The berries are poisonous.

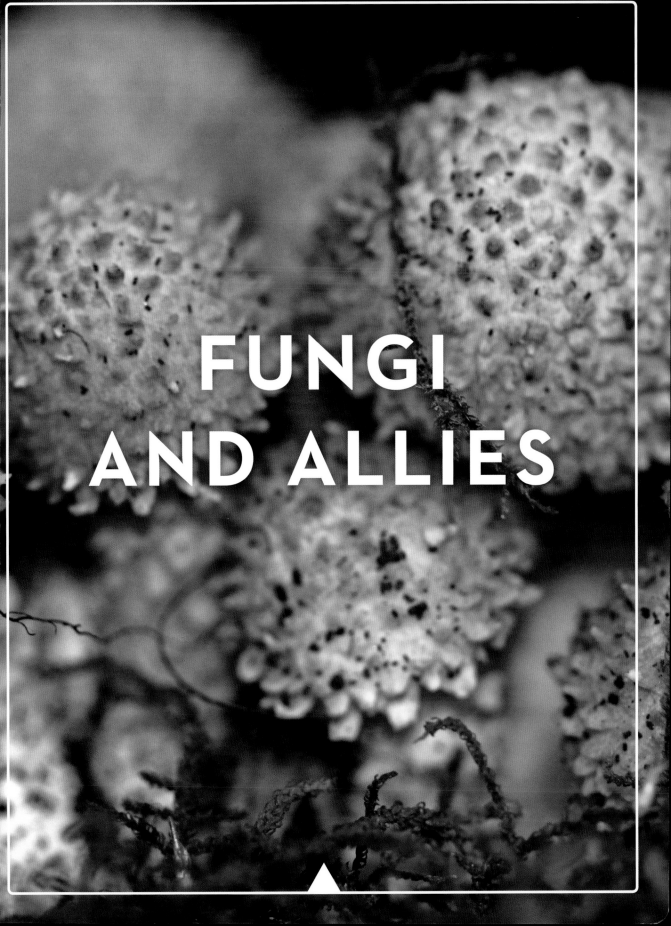

FUNGI
AND ALLIES

▶ CANDY STICK

Allotropa virgata

INDIAN PIPE FAMILY Monotropaceae

Description Appropriately named, candy stick is a red-and-white-striped saprophyte 15–60 cm/6–24 in. in height. Its flowers have white to pink sepals and a central red ovary with 10 very noticeable red stamens. The leaves are reduced to small lance-shaped scales.

Etymology The species name, *virgata*, is Latin for "striped."

Habitat Moist coniferous forests at low to mid elevations. Not common; a treasure to find.

Season Flowers from June to July

▶ PINESAP

Monotropa hypopitys

INDIAN PIPE FAMILY Monotropaceae

Description Pinesap is a curious-looking fleshy saprophyte to 30 cm/12 in. in height. Its flowers and stem are yellowish pink. Approximately 5 to 10 flowers grow on only one side of the curved stem; they start off pointing downward but turn to face upward as they mature, and the colour darkens.

Etymology The genus name, *monotropa*, means "one-sided."

Habitat Moist coniferous forests at low to mid elevations.

Season Can be seen by midsummer.

▶ PINEDROPS

Pterospora andromedea

HEATHER FAMILY Ericaceae

Description Pinedrops is the tallest (to 1 m/3.3 ft.) of the Pacific Northwest's saprophytes. Its bell-shaped flowers are a mix of colours—yellow, red, white, and finally brown, when the plants are spent. The hanging flowers were thought to look like pine-drops from the conifers that they grow under. The scale-like leaves are lance shaped and clasp the sticky reddish stems.

Habitat Deep rich humus soils in coniferous forests at low to mid elevations. I found a wonderful group of pinedrops growing at 2,200 m/7,260 ft. in a pon-derosa forest in the Sierra Nevada mountains.

Season Flowers from mid- to late summer, depend-ing on elevation.

▶ SPOTTED CORALROOT

Corallorhiza maculata ssp. maculata

ORCHID FAMILY Orchidaceae

Description Spotted coralroot is a perennial sapro-phyte to 50 cm/20 in. tall. The flower tips are white with red spots.

Etymology The genus name, *Corallorhiza*, means "coral-like roots," and the species name, *maculata*, means "spotted."

Habitat Shaded coniferous forests at low to mid elevations.

Season Can be seen in mid- to late summer.

▶ NAKED BROOMRAPE   ONE-FLOWERED CANCER ROOT

Orobanche uniflora

BROOMRAPE FAMILY Orobanchaceae

Description Naked broomrape is a parasitic annual to 15 cm/6 in. in height. Its single flower is purple with a whitish throat and to 2 cm/1 in. long; there are usually one to three flower stalks on each plant. Naked broomrape receives its nourishment from the roots of other plants.

Habitat Rocky outcrops, open slopes, and wherever broad-leaved stonecrops grow.

Season Flowers from mid-April to July.

▶ DWARF MISTLETOE

Arceuthobium tsugense

SANDALWOOD FAMILY Santalaceae

Description Dwarf mistletoe is a parasitic flowering plant that receives its nutrition and water from its conifer host. Once a conifer is infected with mistletoe, it takes two to three years for the mistletoe's vegetative growth (buds, flowers, and seeds) to appear. The mature sticky seeds are explosively expelled from the parent plant onto other branches and trees. Severe infestations can cause witch's broom, contorted branches, growth loss, and even death of the host tree.

Habitat Usually seen on western hemlock branches.

Season Can be seen throughout the year.

▶ VANCOUVER GROUNDCONE

Boschniakia hookeri

BROOMRAPE FAMILY Orobanchaceae

Description As opposed to dwarf mistletoe, which is parasitic on the above-ground branches of conifers, Vancouver groundcone is a parasite on the roots of salal. It is a herbaceous perennial to 13 cm/5 in. tall and has a mix of colours, including yellow, orange, and purple. The small tube-shaped flowers are yellow to purple and protrude above the scale-like leaves. The overall size and shape of this plant does look like a malformed cone that has dropped to the ground.

Traditional use The potato-like stem base was eaten raw in small quantities.

Habitat Low elevations. You will most likely see salal growing above or nearby.

Season Flowers in the spring.

▶ INDIAN PIPE

Monotropa uniflora

INDIAN PIPE FAMILY Monotropaceae

Description Indian pipe is a fleshy ghost-like herbaceous perennial to 25 cm/10 in. in height. It has a single white flower to 3 cm/1 in. long; this starts off nodding but stands erect when mature. The white leaves are scale-like and clasp the stem. The entire plant turns black at the end of the growing season. The plant is usually seen growing in clumps of up to 25 stems.

Etymology The species name, *uniflora*, means "single flower."

Habitat Coniferous forests with nutrient-rich soil and deep shade at low elevations.

Season Flowers in early July.

▶ FLY AGARIC

Amanita muscaria

AMANITA FAMILY Amanitaceae

Description Fly agaric is a very common toadstool with a convex cap. It flattens out as it emerges, from 10 cm/4 in. to 20 cm/8 in. across. The scarlet-coloured cap is smooth, with the exception of the whitish veil remnants, and the gills and stalk are white to cream coloured. Fly agaric is probably the most recognized mushroom in the world. It is illustrated in many fairy-tale books, often seen with an elf sitting on it.

Habitat A woodland mushroom that can also be seen in city yards, in parks, and along treed boulevards, often in association with broadleaf trees and conifers. The yellow-capped fly agaric (A. *muscaria* var. *formosa*), can often be seen growing with the red-capped variety (see photo).

Season Fruitbodies can be seen from late June to November.

Edibility Very poisonous. Over the last millennium, some people have used it as a hallucinogenic. Please do not try this.

▶ DEATH CAP

Amanita phalloides

AMANITA FAMILY Amanitaceae

Description Death cap is a deadly poisonous introduced mushroom. The mature cap is flattened, olive green to yellow green, and to 15 cm/6 in. across. The cap sometimes has the warty remains of the veil. The gills are white, and the stalk is white to light whitish green and to 18 cm/7 in. tall. When in its button stage, it can be confused with puffballs. If collecting puffballs, cut them in half—the insides should be all white, with no gills.

Habitat Open mixed forests. More associated with broadleaf trees than conifers.

Season Fruitbodies can be seen from July to November.

Edibility Deadly poisonous. Death cap has caused more deaths than any other mushroom.

▶ GEMMED AMANITA

Amanita gemmata

AMANITA FAMILY Amanitaceae

Description Gemmed amanita is a beautiful but poisonous Pacific Northwestern mushroom. The cap is to 12 cm/5 in. across and light to dark yellow, and it usually retains the white, warty parts of the veil. The gills and the stalk are white, and the stalk is to 12 cm/5 in. in height.

Habitat Mixed forests and treed areas, such as urban parks, boulevards, and yards.

Season I have seen the best concentrations of gemmed amanita in late spring, but fruitbodies can also be seen into the autumn.

Edibility As handsome as this mushroom is, it is very poisonous.

▶ PANTHER CAP

Amanita pantherina

AMANITA FAMILY Amanitaceae

Description Panther cap is a very apt name for this spotted mushroom. The cap is to 20 cm/8 in. across and can vary from light to dark brown, with white veil remnants dotting the surface. The gills are white; the stalk is white to off-white and to 20 cm/8 in. in height.

Habitat Mixed forests; often found under Douglas firs.

Season I have seen the best concentrations in May; however, the fruitbodies can also be seen through the summer and autumn, depending on location.

Edibility Poisonous.

▶ SHAGGY MANE SHAGGY INK CAP

Coprinus comatus

SHAGGY CAP FAMILY Coprinaceae

Description Shaggy mane is another aptly named edible mushroom. The cylindrical shaggy cap is white with a brown top and to 8 cm/3 in. across. It is supported on a smooth white stalk to 20 cm/8 in. in height. As the mushroom ages, the white cap and gills start turning inky black from the bottom up; hence the common name of the shaggy ink cap.

Habitat Open mixed forests, lawns, and on hard-packed soils on roadsides and trailsides. The best concentrations are seen when the rain arrives in late summer and autumn.

Season Shaggy mane can be seen from April to June and from September to November.

Edibility Considered one of the best eating mushrooms when young and white. When the caps start showing their inky transition, they are too late to be edible.

▶ ALCOHOL INKY TIPPLER'S BANE

Coprinus atramentarius

INK CAP FAMILY Coprinaceae

Description Alcohol inky is a very common but short-lived mushroom. The elongated bell-shaped cap is to 10 cm/4 in. across and pale grey with brownish tints. The stalk and gills are white to pinkish; the stalk is to 15 cm/6 in. in height. The entire fruitbody turns black as it ages.

Traditional use An ink was made from the spent caps.

Etymology The species name, *atramentarius*, means "inky."

Habitat Forested areas, lawns, roadsides, and old stumps.

Season Fruitbodies can be seen from May to November.

Edibility This mushroom should not be eaten by people who consume alcohol. Even a tiny portion of alcohol before, during, or after eating the mushroom will set off poisonous reactions. The common name of Tippler's bane suggests this.

WOOLLY INK CAP

Coprinus lagopus

INK CAP FAMILY Coprinaceae

Description Woolly ink cap is a very short-lived mushroom, often lasting only hours. I have found patches and gone home to get my camera, only to come back and find they had expired. The caps are to 7 cm/2.5 in. across and start off a beautiful bell-shaped woolly grey; however, they soon turn into a dark inverted cap with exposed dark ribs. The stalks are white and to 20 cm/8 in. in height. It is an unusual sight to see the dark inverted caps supported on the white stalks.

Habitat In bark mulch, leaf compost, and organic matter under conifers.

Season Fruitbodies can be seen from late June to October.

Edibility Probably too small and fast expiring to be of any interest.

CROWDED WHITE CLITOCYBE

Clitocybe connata

DIVERSE FUNGI FAMILY Tricholomataceae

Description Crowded white clitocybe is an unusually shaped mushroom that is often seen in multiple clusters. The caps are greyish to white and 5–15 cm/2–6 in. across. The gills are mainly white but have shades of light pink and yellow. The stalks are to 12 cm/5 in. in height, whitish, and often fused together at the base.

Habitat I have found these mushrooms mainly trailside in gravelly areas, growing under the salmonberries.

Season Fruitbodies are seen from October to November.

Edibility Considered poisonous.

▶ FIR CONE CAP DOUGLAS FIR COLLYBIA

Strobilurus trullisatus

DIVERSE FUNGI FAMILY Tricholomataceae

Description Fir cone cap, as its common name suggests, grows mainly on old Douglas fir cones. You may have to dig down a bit to find the cone. Its cap is very small, to only 1.5 cm/0.6 in. across. It is white to pink, with white gills, and convex to flat, depending on conditions and age. The fragile stalk is to 5 cm/2 in. in height and darkens in colour toward the base.

Habitat Coniferous forests, mainly on Douglas fir cones.

Season Fruitbodies are seen from the end of August to November, always on cones.

Edibility Considered poisonous.

▶ ANGEL WINGS

Pleurocybella porrigens

OYSTER MUSHROOM FAMILY Pleurotaceae

Description Angel wings are aptly named, for when the light shines through the slightly translucent caps, they do look like they belong on an angel. The caps are pure white to antique ivory, to 10 cm/4 in. long, and fan shaped to spoon shaped. The gills may look white, pink, or yellowish, depending on the light.

Habitat Conifers' logs and stumps. I have seen them mainly on hemlocks.

Season From September to October.

Edibility After reading that several older Japanese people died after eating these mushrooms, I would not recommend their consumption.

▶ LICHEN AGARIC

Lichenomphalia umbellifera

DIVERSE FUNGI FAMILY Tricholomataceae

Description Lichen agaric caps look like tiny funneled parasols, with the gills acting as the spokes. The yellowish to orangish caps are only 3.5 cm/ 1.4 in. across and are supported by darker, shaded gills that radiate from the top of the 3.5 cm/1.4 in. tall stalk.

Habitat Mainly found on old fallen logs.

Season Fruitbodies are seen from as early as March to November.

Edibility Not recommended.

▶ SMOKY GILLED WOODLOVER

Hypholoma capnoides

STROPHARIA FAMILY Strophariaceae

Description Smoky gilled woodlover, as its name indicates, grows on decaying wood. The caps vary in colour from yellow orange to brownish and grow to 6 cm/2.5 in. across. The gills are smoky grey when young and darker purple brown when mature. The stalk is to 10 cm/4 in. height and yellowish toward the cap, darkening to brownish toward the base.

Habitat Mixed forests on conifer stumps and logs. In ideal conditions, there can be hundreds in the same location.

Season Fruitbodies are seen from mid-August to the beginning of December.

Edibility Edible and sought after. Care should be taken not to confuse it with the poisonous species sulphur tuft (*H. fasciculare*).

▶ QUESTIONABLE STROPHARIA

Stropharia ambigua

STROPHARIA FAMILY Strophariaceae

Description Questionable stropharia is one of the more beautiful mushrooms on the west coast. The cap is to 15 cm/6 in. across, yellowish to orangish, and adorned on the edges with cotton-like veil remnants. The gills are smoky grey but mature to a darker purplish black. The caps' colour and size contrast well with the pure-white stalk, which is to 18 cm/7 in. in height.

Habitat Can be found in bark mulch in new landscaping and in leaf and conifer litter in mixed forests.

Season Fruitbodies are seen from September to November.

Edibility Some Pacific Northwest fungi authorities say it tastes like old leaves. I would not recommend eating it.

▶ PRINCE

Agaricus augustus

MEADOW MUSHROOM FAMILY Agaricaceae

Description The prince mushroom is so called because of its size, and because when cooked, it makes a meal fit for a prince. The enormous cap, to 30 cm/12 in. across, is initially rounded, becomes convex, and then flattens out completely. The surface is cream coloured with large reddish-brown scales that increase in size toward the centre. The gills start off pinkish grey and then turn dark brown at maturity. The stalk is to 20 cm/8 in. in height and has a large pendulous ring; the stalk is smooth above the ring, with scales below.

Habitat Open coniferous forests and parks, especially under true cedars.

Season Fruitbodies are seen from July to November.

Edibility Choice and well sought after. The flesh has an almond aroma.

▶ FRIED CHICKEN MUSHROOM

Lyophyllum decastes

DIVERSE FUNGI FAMILY Tricholomataceae

Description Fried chicken mushrooms grow in dense clusters on the ground. The caps are 5–12 cm/ 2–5 in. across and range from yellowish brown to greyish brown to dark brown, depending on age. The gills start out white and then turn yellowish when mature. The stalks are 5–10 cm/2–4 in. in height, whitish, and darker toward the base.

Habitat On the ground in open areas, at forest edges, and on trails that are covered in bark mulch.

Season Fruitbodies are seen from mid-June to the end of October.

Edibility A lot of people search out this mushroom and have no problems; however, there are reports of others having gastric upsets. Caution should be taken.

▶ BLACK-EYED PARASOL

Lepiota atrodisca

PARASOL MUSHROOM FAMILY Lepiotaceae

Description Black-eyed parasol grows singly and in small groups. The small white cap is up to 5 cm/2 in. across and has a black-grey centre with black-grey scales that radiate out toward the edges. The white gills are held up on a smooth white stalk to 7 cm/3 in. in height.

Habitat On the ground in mixed forests.

Season This beautiful little mushroom has a short fruiting season, from October to November.

Edibility Unknown. Some small *Lepiota* spp. are deadly poisonous.

▶ BRISTLY MUSHROOM

Pholiota squarrosoides

STROPHARIA FAMILY Strophariaceae

Description On first looking at the bristly mushroom, it looks as if it is armed and dangerous. Both the caps and stalks have bristly scales. The caps are to 10 cm/4 in. across and yellowish brown. The gills range from whitish when young to rusty brown when mature. The bristly stalks are to 12 cm/5 in. in height.

Habitat Typically found growing in clusters on hardwood logs and stumps.

Season Fruitbodies are seen from August to October.

Edibility It was once thought to be edible; however, it is now known to be poisonous.

▶ VELVET ROLLRIM

Tapinella atrotomentosa

FAMILY Tapinellaceae

Description Velvet rollrim forms fruitbodies that are convex, becoming flat to funnel shaped, with an inrolled margin. The cap is to 25 cm/10 in. across and is covered with velvety dark-brown or black fur. The contrasting gills are cream yellow and forked. The thick stalk is to 8 cm/3 in. in height, off-centre, and velvety dark brown.

Habitat On the stumps of conifers.

Season Fruitbodies are seen from August to October.

Edibility Poisonous.

▶ SULPHUR TUFT

Hypholoma fasciculare

STROPHARIA FAMILY Strophariaceae

Description Sulphur tuft is probably the most common woodland mushroom and, when in full form, one of the most handsome. The caps are to 8 cm/ 3 in. across, sulphur yellow, and orangish toward the centre. The gills are yellow to start, becoming greenish grey to purplish black over time. The yellow stalks are to 10 cm/4 in. in height.

Etymology The species name, *fasciculare*, means "clustered" or "grouped," referring to the way these mushrooms grow.

Habitat Mixed forests on stumps and logs.

Season Fruitbodies are seen from August to November, though sometimes an early showing can be seen in May or June.

Edibility Poisonous.

▶ FALSE CHANTERELLE

Hygrophoropsis aurantiaca

FAMILY Paxillaceae

Description False chanterelle, when in full form, is a colourful and beautiful mushroom. Its cap is to 12 cm/5 in. across and convex to flat, becoming funnel shaped. The surface is downy and yellow orange to orange brown. The deep-orange gills extend down to the stalk and are sometimes forked. The stalk is to 10 cm/4 in. in height, smooth, hollow, and orange to orange brown.

Etymology The species name, *aurantiaca*, means "orange coloured."

Habitat Mixed forests on decayed coniferous wood. If found growing on the ground, the wood will have been buried.

Season Fruitbodies are seen from August to November.

Edibility Mildly poisonous; gastric problems have been reported.

▶ WOOLLY PINE SPIKE

Chroogomphus tomentosus

FAMILY Gomphidae

Description Woolly pine spike is peg shaped and orange when young, which makes identification a little easier. The cap is woolly orange and to 10 cm/ 4 in. across. The gills are yellowish orange and often invert themselves with age to resemble the spokes of an umbrella. The stalk is to 18 cm/7 in. in height and yellowish orange.

Habitat Mixed forests; mainly associated with hemlocks and Douglas firs—not with pines, as the common name would suggest.

Season Fruitbodies are seen from July to October, depending on rainfall.

Edibility It is said to be edible, with a mild taste.

▶ RED HOT MILK CAP

Lactarius rufus

MILKCAP FAMILY Russulaceae

Description Red hot milk cap, as its name implies, has a peppery taste. However, it is considered poisonous. The cap is to 12 cm/5 in. across and is bright red to brick red. The gills start off whitish and mature to match the cap in colour. The stalk is red and to 10 cm/4 in. in height.

Etymology The genus name, *Lactarius*, means "milk producing," referring to the white latex seen when the mushroom is scarred or broken.

Habitat Around wet areas and at bog edges under conifers.

Season Fruitbodies are seen from August to November.

Edibility Considered poisonous.

▶ TUBARIA

Tubaria furfuracea

FAMILY Tubariaceae

Description Tubaria is a small mushroom that is characterized by its fleshy cinnamon-coloured cap. The cap is to 5 cm/2 in. across; it is cinnamon brown when young and then fades to dingy white when mature. The gills are cream coloured and become cinnamon brown with age. The brownish stalk is hollow and to 5 cm/2 in. in height.

Etymology The species name, *furfuracea*, means "mealy" or "scurfy."

Habitat Solitary to gregarious on wood debris, in wood chips, and in mossy lawns.

Season Fruitbodies are seen later than with most mushrooms, from October to January.

Edibility Unknown.

▶ CUCUMBER CAP

Macrocystidia cucumis

FAMILY Marasmiaceae

Description Someone had an interesting sense of smell when they named this mushroom cucumber cap. I find it smells more like fish. The cap is to 5 cm/2 in. across and conical when young, flattening out as it matures. It is dark brown with a contrasting cream edge. The gills are pinkish yellow, becoming pink when mature. The stalk is to 5 cm/2 in. in height and velvety brown to black.

Habitat Found on decomposing wood chips and in garden beds.

Season Fruitbodies are seen from September to November.

Edibility Not edible.

▶ MARASMIELLUS

Marasmiellus candidus

FAMILY Marasmiaceae

Description Marasmiellus is easy to recognize by its small size and electric-white colour. The caps are to 4 cm/1.5 in. across, pure white when young, and light pink when older. The gills are widespread and the same colour as the cap. The stalk is to 2.5 cm/1 in. in height and white at the cap, darkening to grey black at the base.

Etymology The species name, *candidus*, means "shining" or "pure white."

Habitat I have found this beautiful little mushroom mainly on dead salmonberry canes. It also occurs on hardwood and conifer branches.

Season Fruitbodies can be seen from late September to November.

Edibility Considered not edible.

▶ ZELLER'S BOLETE

Boletus zelleri

BOLETE FAMILY Boletaceae

Description Zeller's bolete is one of the more common boletes in the Pacific Northwest. The cap is to 13 cm/5 in. across and dark reddish brown to almost black, with a wrinkled, velvety surface. The edge of the cap is often cream coloured. The tubes on the underside are yellowish. The stalk is to 11 cm/4.5 in. in height and red or yellowish with red lines.

Etymology The species name commemorates Professor Sanford Myron Zeller, who first discovered it in Seattle, Washington.

Habitat Coniferous forests and forest edges.

Season Fruitbodies are seen from summer to autumn.

Edibility Edible, with a mild taste.

▶ ADMIRABLE BOLETE

Boletus mirabilis

BOLETE FAMILY Boletaceae

Description Admirable bolete is probably the best looking of the bolete species. The cap is to 15 cm/ 6 in. across and wine red to dark red brown, with a velvet-like surface. The underside tubes are initially pale yellow and mature to a darker greenish yellow. The stalk is to 17 cm/7 in. in height, reddish brown, and generally wider at the base.

Etymology The species name, *mirabilis*, means "wonderful" or "remarkable," which it is.

Habitat Coniferous forests; usually associated with decaying hemlock.

Season Fruitbodies are seen from late summer to autumn.

Edibility Edible and sought after.

▶ GOLDEN CHANTERELLE

Cantharellus formosus

CHANTERELLE FAMILY Cantharellaceae

Description Golden chanterelle is probably the most sought-after edible fungus in the Pacific Northwest. The golden caps are initially convex and then become depressed or funnel shaped, to 13 cm/ 5 in. across. The undersides have gill-like ridges that run down to the stem. The stem is to 10 cm/4 in. in height. Both the stem and the undersides are the same colour as the cap. Golden chanterelle is the state mushroom of Oregon.

Etymology The species name, *formosus*, means "beautiful."

Habitat Coniferous forests.

Season Fruitbodies are seen from July to November.

Edibility Edible and sought after. In the Pacific Northwest, golden chanterelles are at their peak in October, when we harvest them to make our delicious Thanksgiving stuffing.

▶ RED-BELTED POLYPORE

Fomitopsis pinicola

POLYPORE FAMILY Polyporaceae

Description Red-belted polypore is known as brown crumbly rot to the BC Forest Service. Its perennial fruitbody is rounded, woody, and to over 60 cm/ 24 in. across. The colours of this fungi can be variable; it is usually seen with a dark attachment to the tree with an orangey-red margin. The undersurface is white to off-white and extends to the outer edge. Red-belted polypore is considered the most common conk in the Pacific Northwest.

Habitat Almost always on the trunks of conifers.

Season The fruitbodies can be seen year-round.

Edibility Not edible, as it is too tough, but it has been harvested for use in herbal medicines.

▶ TURKEY TAIL

Trametes versicolor

POLYPORE FAMILY Polyporaceae

Description The species name, *versicolor*, means "many colours," which turkey tail has. The annual caps are 10 cm/4 in. across, and the concentric zones may be black, grey, cream, rust brown, dark brown, or yellow. The undersides are white. Turkey tail is usually found in groups of multiple, overlapping rosettes.

Habitat Mixed forests; almost exclusively on hardwood logs and stumps.

Season Fruitbodies can be seen year-round; however, the young, colourful ones are more plentiful in summer and autumn.

Edibility Considered not palatable.

► ARTIST'S CONK

Ganoderma applanatum

POLYPORE FAMILY Polyporaceae

Description Artist's conk is known as white mottled rot to the BC Forest Service. The brown perennial fruitbodies are to 60 cm/24 in. across, flat, and often covered with powdery brown spores. The undersides are white; however, they immediately turn brown if scratched. It is from this browning that artists can get creative.

Traditional use Indigenous groups in Alaska burned artist's conk as a mosquito repellent.

Etymology The species name, *applanatum*, means "flattened out."

Habitat Mixed forests. Common on hardwood trunks, stumps, and logs.

Season Fruitbodies can be seen year-round.

Edibility Not considered palatable.

► WESTERN VARNISH SHELF

Ganoderma oregonense

POLYPORE FAMILY Polyporaceae

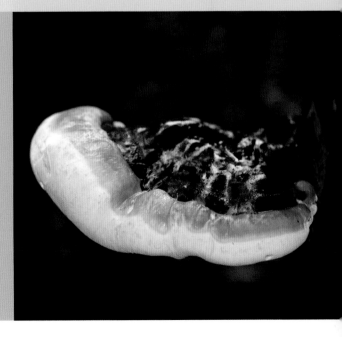

Description Western varnish shelf is a beautiful annual fungus that looks as if it has been painted with high-gloss varnish. The fruitbodies are to 30 cm/ 12 in. across and shiny, with a mix of mahogany colours in concentric zones. The undersides are white and often roll over the edge to the surface, giving a wonderful contrast of colours. As the fruitbodies age, their shine disappears, and the upper surface cracks.

Habitat Mixed forests on dead conifers, trunks, and stumps.

Season The fruitbodies can be seen year-round.

Edibility Not considered palatable.

▶ WHITE TRUNK ROT

Phellinus hartigii

POLYPORE FAMILY Polyporaceae

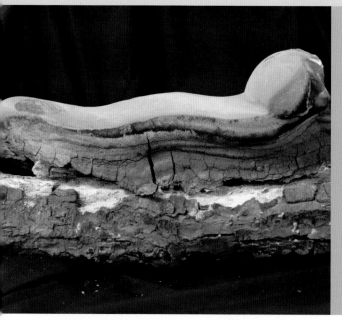

Description Trees infected with white trunk rot are very prone to wind damage. In a forest situation, this is not much of a problem. However, in a residential area or park, infected trees should be monitored. The infection spreads 1–2 m/3.3–6.6 ft. up and down from each fruiting body. The fruitbodies are perennial and extremely variable in shape, depending on whether they are growing on the trunk of a branch or the underside. When formed on the trunk, they are hoof shaped, to 15 cm/6 in. across, dark brown on top, and cream coloured to brown on the underside. When formed on the underside, they are flattened (to 60 cm/24 in. long) against the branch, with the spore-bearing layer facing outward (resupinate).

Habitat Mixed forests on conifers, mainly hemlocks, in the Pacific Northwest.

Season Fruitbodies can be seen year-round.

Edibility Not considered palatable.

▶ STRINGY BUTT ROT

Perenniporia subacida

POLYPORE FAMILY Polyporaceae

Description When you first come across stringy butt rot, it appears as if someone has thrown a bucket of thick white to cream-coloured paint on a tree. The perennial fruitbodies are leathery to crust-like; they start off as a light-brown stain and later develop white pits. The white pits amalgamate to form masses of white spongy fibres to several metres or feet long. Living trees with the fruitbodies on it (often western red cedar) should be inspected by a professional.

Habitat In mixed forests, on both hardwoods and conifers.

Season Fruitbodies can be seen year-round.

Edibility Not edible.

▶ DYER'S POLYPORE

Phaeolus schweinitzii

POLYPORE FAMILY Polyporaceae

Description Dyer's polypore, as its name suggests, has long been used for dyeing. It produces colours ranging from bright yellow to cinnamon brown. The annual fruitbodies are to 25 cm/10 in. across, yellowish when young, and reddish brown and velvety when mature. The stalk is to 7 cm/3 in. in height. To the BC Forest Service, this fungus is known as Schweinitz butt rot, named after Lewis David von Schweinitz (1780–1834), renowned as the father of American mycology.

Habitat In mixed forests, on living and dead wood, and on the forest floor near the base of infected trees. Mainly associated with conifers in the Pacific Northwest.

Season Fruitbodies are seen from July to November, and brown spent ones can be found year-round.

Edibility Not considered palatable, and may be poisonous.

▶ SULPHUR SHELF

Laetiporus conifericola

POLYPORE FAMILY Polyporaceae

Description Sulphur shelf is one of the largest and most beautiful fungi in the Pacific Northwest. There are two species in the Pacific Northwest: *L. conifericola*, which grows on conifers, and *L. gilbertsonii*, which grows on hardwoods. The tops of the fan-shaped shelves are orange, and the undersides are sulphur yellow to orange. The shelves can independently grow to 60 cm/24 in. across and can collectively be several metres or feet across. The shelves are rubbery when young but fade to white yellow and get crumbly when old. Sulphur shelves are annuals.

Habitat Both species grow in mixed forests; the fruitbodies are usually seen in dead wood. I came across a beautiful patch of *L. conifericola* on an amabilis fir log at 1,200 m/3,900 ft. elevation.

Season I have found the fresh fruitbodies only from September to November.

Edibility When young, the outer edges are considered edible. Try only a very small piece if you are a first-time user.

▶ TIGER'S EYE

Coltricia perennis

POLYPORE FAMILY Polyporaceae

Description Tiger's eye has a beautiful resemblance to an oversized, highly decorated golf tee. The beautiful caps are to 10 cm/4 in. across and have concentric zones of colours, including orange, gold, dark brown, and cinnamon brown, usually with a lighter outer edge. The undersides are a uniform light brown to dark brown. The stalk is to 5 cm/2 in. in height, thin, brown, and velvety.

Etymology The species name, *perennis*, refers to the fungi being perennial.

Habitat Coniferous forests. I have found Tiger's eye at elevations to 1,200 m/3,900 ft.

Season Fruitbodies are seen from the end of August to November, depending on elevation.

Edibility Not edible.

▶ TINDER POLYPORE   HOOF FUNGUS

Fomes fomentarius

POLYPORE FAMILY Polyporaceae

Description Tinder polypores are known to the BC Forest Service as white spongy trunk rot. The perennial fruitbodies are to 15 cm/6 in. across and 15 cm/6 in. thick; colours range from white, grey, or cream to brown. The upper surface has perennial zone lines, which can be counted much like the rings on a tree. As the fruitbodies age, they become more hoof-like. This fungus was long used as a tinder for starting fires. The infamous iceman Ötzi, who was found in 1991 in the Ötzal Alps and thought to have been frozen for over 5,000 years, is said to have been carrying a piece of tinder polypore with him.

Habitat On hardwoods in the Pacific Northwest; seen mainly on birch trees, but also seen on alder and cottonwoods.

Season Fruitbodies are seen year-round.

Edibility Not considered edible.

► LION'S MANE MUSHROOM

Hericium erinaceus

TOOTH FUNGI FAMILY Hydnaceae

Description It's not hard to see why the common name lion's mane was given to this fungus, especially when it is yellowish gold. The fruitbodies are to 40 cm/16 in. across and to 20 cm/8 in. long. The spines are to 8 cm/3 in. long; they start off white, turn to a yellowish gold, and then finish a mud brown.

Etymology The species name, *erinaceus*, means "resembling a hedgehog." Bearded hedgehog mushroom is another common name for this fungus.

Habitat In hardwood forests, mainly on maples and oaks. I have found lion's mane on older living beech trees in parks.

Season Fruitbodies are seen from late August to the beginning of November.

Edibility Edible only when bright white.

► WHITE FAIRY FINGERS

Clavaria vermicularis

CORAL AND CLUB FUNGI FAMILY Clavariaceae

Description White fairy fingers are also known as white worm coral and white spindles. The white fruitbodies are slender, fragile, unbranched, and to 15 cm/6 in. in height. Purple fairy clubs are very similar except for their colour, and they are shorter.

Etymology The species name, *vermicularis*, means "worm-like."

Habitat On the ground in open conifer forests. I have found purple fairy clubs growing up to 1,500 m/4,950 ft. in elevation in pure fir stands.

Season Fruitbodies are seen from July to September, depending on elevation.

Edibility Both species are considered edible when young.

► CRESTED CORAL FUNGUS

Clavulina coralloides

CORAL AND CLUB FUNGI FAMILY Clavariaceae

Description Crested coral fungus is very widespread across North America and Europe. The fruitbodies are white when young, purplish brown when mature, many forked or crested, and to 10 cm/ 4 in. across and in height.

Habitat On the ground or on extremely rotted conifer wood.

Season Fruitbodies are seen from July to late October.

Edibility Considered edible only in its pure-white stage.

► CAULIFLOWER MUSHROOM

Sparassis crispa

CORAL AND CLUB FUNGI FAMILY Clavariaceae

Description Cauliflower mushroom is a wood-rotting fungus that is mainly associated with Douglas fir and pine in the Pacific Northwest. The fruitbodies can become very large, to 50 cm/20 in. across by 50 cm/20 in. tall, and weigh up to 20 kg/45 lb. The fruitbodies are densely branched with wavy flesh-like leaves; they are white to cream coloured, becoming light brown with age.

Etymology The species name, *crispa*, means "finely waved" or "closely curled."

Habitat In coniferous forests on or near stumps or at the base of living trees.

Season Fruitbodies are seen from August to the end of October.

Edibility It is sought after when fresh.

▶ SWAMP BEACON

Mitrula elegans

CORAL AND CLUB FUNGI FAMILY Clavariaceae

Description Swamp beacon or matchstick fungi are very apt names for when the fungi are en masse or in troops. They do light up a murky marsh. The fruitbody is composed of a teardrop-shaped golden-yellow fertile head on a white, almost translucent, stalk to 3.5 cm/1.5 in. tall. Swamp beacons grow on decaying forest vegetation when the soil is completely saturated.

Habitat Mixed forests that have large shallow depressions, which allow winter and early-spring rains to sit for long periods.

Season Fruitbodies are seen in the spring.

Edibility Not known.

▶ ORANGE CORAL MUSHROOM

Ramaria flavigelatinosa

CORAL AND CLUB FUNGI FAMILY Clavariaceae

Description Orange coral mushroom is many branched, orangish to light yellow, and to 15 cm/ 6 in. in height. The genus *Ramaria* has hundreds of species worldwide, and the Pacific Northwest has a great collection of these. The orange coral mushroom is one of the more common ones I have found.

Etymology The genus name, *Ramaria*, is from the Latin word *ramus*, meaning "branched."

Habitat Found on the ground, mainly under hemlocks.

Season Fruitbodies are seen from September to November.

▶ PINK CORAL MUSHROOM

Ramaria formosa

CORAL AND CLUB FUNGI FAMILY Clavariaceae

Description This is one of the prettiest coral mushrooms. It is mainly branched, salmon pink with yellow tips, and to 20 cm/8 in. in height. The genus *Ramaria* has hundreds of species worldwide, and the Pacific Northwest has a great collection of these. The pink coral mushroom is one of the more common ones I have found.

Etymology The species name, *formosa*, means "beautiful."

Habitat Found in mixed forests, mainly under hemlocks.

Season Fruitbodies can be seen from August to November.

Edibility Poisonous.

▶ YELLOW CORAL MUSHROOM

Ramaria rasilispora

CORAL AND CLUB FUNGI FAMILY Clavariaceae

Description This coral mushroom is often found buried in the forest duff. It is many branched, pale yellow, and to 15 cm/6 in. in height. The genus *Ramaria* has hundreds of species worldwide, and the Pacific Northwest has a great collection of these. The yellow coral mushroom is one of the more common ones I have found.

Habitat Found in coniferous forests in the ground.

Season Fruitbodies are seen from late August to November.

Edibility Some coral mushrooms are edible, while others are poisonous. I would not recommend eating any of them.

▶ ORANGE JELLY

Dacrymyces palmatus

JELLY FUNGI FAMILY Dacrymycetaceae

Description Orange jelly has a lobed brain-like gelatinous fruitbody. It is to 10 cm/4 in. across by 2.5 cm/1 in. in height and is shiny yellow to orange. This brightly coloured fungus needs moisture to stay turgid; without moisture, it will become flaccid until the rainy weather returns.

Habitat Mixed forests on conifer wood.

Season Fruitbodies are seen in spring and autumn.

Edibility Not considered edible.

▶ SMALL STAGSHORN JELLY FUNGUS

Calocera cornea

JELLY FUNGI FAMILY Dacrymycetaceae

Description Small stagshorn fruitbodies resemble yellow modelling clay after it has been forced through a strainer. The fruitbodies are light yellow to rich yellow orange, depending on how much moisture they have in them. The fruitbodies are usually unbranched, gelatinous, and to only 2 cm/0.75 in. in height. Stagshorn jelly fungus (*C. viscosa*) is the larger species. The fruitbodies are bright yellow, forked at the tips, and to 10 cm/4 in. in height.

Etymology The species name, *cornea*, means "horny."

Habitat Mixed forests, in the cracks of barkless hardwoods.

Season Fruitbodies are seen from September to November.

Edibility Not edible.

► GOLDEN JELLY CONE

Guepiniopsis alpina

JELLY FUNGI FAMILY Dacrymycetaceae

Description As its name suggests, the fruitbodies of golden jelly cone are cone shaped, yellow to orange, and 1 cm/0.5 in. across by 2.5 cm/1 in. in height. As with most yellow jelly fungi, the more moisture they retain, the lower their colour intensity.

Habitat Mixed forests on coniferous wood.

Season Fruitbodies are seen in spring and again in autumn.

Edibility Not considered edible.

► TOOTHED JELLY FUNGUS   CAT'S TONGUE

Pseudohydnum gelatinosum

JELLY FUNGI FAMILY Tremellaceae

Description Toothed jelly fungus is fairly easy to identify, as there is no competition for its odd appearance, which resembles a cat's tongue. The gelatinous fruitbody is translucent white to tan brown; the cap is to 7.5 cm/3 in. across with minute teeth or spines on the underside.

Etymology The genus name, *Pseudohydnum*, means "false hydnum"—having teeth on the underside.

Habitat Mixed forests on coniferous wood.

Season Fruitbodies are seen from September to November.

Edibility Edible; however, it is said to be bland.

▶ CARBON ANTLERS

Xylaria hypoxylon

CARBON ANTLER FAMILY Xylariaceae

Description Carbon antlers are very curious looking and common throughout the year. The strap-like fruitbodies are to 7.5 cm/3 in. in height, antler branched, and black with powdery white tips. The white tips consist of masses of asexual spores (conidia).

Habitat Mixed forests on decayed hardwood, mainly alder, in the Pacific Northwest.

Season Fruitbodies are seen year-round.

Edibility Not edible.

▶ BRITTLE CINDER   FALSE CHARCOAL

Kretzschmaria deusta

CARBON ANTLER FAMILY Xylariaceae

Description Brittle cinder causes soft rot, which breaks down the lignin and cellulose of living hardwood trees. The perennial fruitbodies start off in spring as flat grey scabs, sometimes with white edges. By the end of summer, the fruitbodies look like lumps of black tar or charcoal that crumbles in your fingers.

Etymology The species name, *deusta*, means "burned."

Habitat I have found brittle cinder only on the base of our native bigleaf maples in mixed forests in the Pacific Northwest. It has also been reported on oak, beech, and lime.

Season The mature fruitbodies can be seen year-round.

Edibility Not edible.

▶ PEAR-SHAPED PUFFBALL

Lycoperdon pyriforme

PUFFBALL FAMILY Lycoperdaceae

Description Pear-shaped puffballs produce white- to cream-coloured fruitbodies that mature to light brown. They are to 4 cm/1.5 in. across and 6 cm/2.5 in. in height; they have a slightly granular surface when young and are smooth when mature. A hole develops on the top for the spores to puff out.

Etymology The species name, *pyriforme*, means "pear shaped."

Habitat Mixed forests, on decayed stumps and buried wood.

Season Fruitbodies are seen from July to early November.

Edibility Edible when young and pure white inside.

▶ GEM-STUDDED PUFFBALL COMMON PUFFBALL

Lycoperdon perlatum

PUFFBALL FAMILY Lycoperdaceae

Description Gem-studded puffball is probably the Pacific Northwest's most common puffball. The rounded fruitbodies are to 8 cm/3 in. across and 10 cm/4 in. in height, white to start, and light brown at maturity. Their surface is covered with different-sized conical spines that eventually fall off, leaving a net-like pattern. As with most puffballs, a hole develops on the top for the spores to puff out.

Etymology The genus name, *Lycoperdon*, means "wolf fart"; I don't know who thought this one up.

Habitat Common on the ground in open forests and on roadsides.

Season Fruitbodies are seen from August to November.

Edibility Edible when young and pure white inside.

▶ ROUNDED EARTHSTAR

Geastrum saccatum

EARTHSTAR FAMILY Geastraceae

Description Rounded earthstar is not that common in the Pacific Northwest and is a delight to find. The fruitbodies are to 10 cm/4 in. across when open. The outer layer splits into five to eight rays, giving it a star-like shape. The inner spore-bearing fruitbody is rounded and a darker tan colour than the outer layer.

Etymology The species name, *saccatum*, means "resembling a bag."

Habitat In mixed forests on forest litter.

Season Fruitbodies are seen from August to November.

Edibility Not edible.

▶ CHERRY TREE GUMMOSIS

FAMILY Unclassified

Description Our native cherry trees in the Pacific Northwest (*Prunus emarginata*) are susceptible to gummosis. It is not actually a pathogen, however; it is a response to biotic diseases or abiotic injury. A fallen tree could have broken a cherry tree branch or stripped the bark off the trunk. Gum exuding from the tree could be insect related or a response from infectious diseases or cankers.

Habitat Mixed forests.

Season Sap can be seen year-round on damaged or infected trees.

Edibility Not edible.

► JELLIED BIRD'S NEST FUNGI

Nidula candida

BIRD'S NEST FUNGI FAMILY Nidulariaceae

Description You will need a keen eye to find jellied bird's nest fungi. The nests are only 0.8 cm/0.3 in. across by 2 cm/0.75 in. in height. The disc-shaped eggs (peridioles) are light brown and are embedded in a sticky gel. Raindrops dissolve the gel, allowing the peridioles to splash out of the nest. The peridioles' cases eventually break down in moist weather, releasing the spores.

Etymology The species name, *candida*, means "shining" or "pure white."

Habitat Mixed forests, on decayed wood. I have found jellied bird's nest fungi mainly on the dead canes of salmonberries.

Season Nests with eggs in them are seen from March to April; empty nests can be seen year-round.

Edibility Not edible.

► FLUTED BLACK ELFIN SADDLE

Helvella lacunosa

FALSE MOREL AND ELFIN SADDLE FAMILY Helvellaceae

Description Somebody with a good imagination thought the cap of fluted black elfin saddle was an appropriate perch for an elf. The contorted, sometimes saddle-shaped cap is to 8 cm/3 in. across and grey to almost black. The stalk is to 10 cm/4 in. in height, deeply incised, and whitish to dark brown.

Etymology The species name, *lacunosa*, means "with deep holes or pits."

Habitat Mixed forests and lawns.

Season The fruitbodies can be seen in spring and autumn.

Edibility Some authorities say it is edible if cooked, but I would take caution and not eat it. Just enjoy finding it.

▶ WOOLLY CHANTERELLE

Gomphus floccosus

CHANTERELLE FAMILY Cantharellaceae

Description The fruitbodies of woolly chanterelle start off cylindrical and mature to a funnel shape. They are to 15 cm/6 in. across by 20 cm/8 in. in height. The undersides are cream to yellow, tapered, and densely ridged and wrinkled.

Etymology The species name, *fluccosus*, means "woolly."

Habitat I have found woolly chanterelles in mixed forests at sea level and in coniferous forests at 1,200 m/3,900 ft. in elevation.

Season Fruitbodies are mainly seen in the summer months in cool areas.

Edibility Edible to some, while a gastrointestinal problem to others. I would take caution and not eat it.

▶ BLISTERED CUP FUNGUS

Peziza vesiculosa

CUP FUNGI FAMILY Pezizaceae

Description Blistered cup fungus produces cup-shaped fruitbodies to 8 cm/3 in. across by 5 cm/2 in. in height. The cup is tan coloured; the inside is smooth, while the outside is rougher in texture. When mature, the fruitbodies often split and form blisters.

Etymology The species name, *vesiculosa*, means "furnished with small bladders or blisters."

Habitat Mainly seen on mature and new garden plantings with rich soil. I have seen thousands emerge in new garden plantings.

Season Fruitbodies can be seen year-round; however, a wet, mild October seems to produce more.

Edibility Poisonous unless well cooked. Probably another fungus to avoid eating

▶ ORANGE WAX CRUST

Phlebia merismoides
FAMILY Meruliaceae

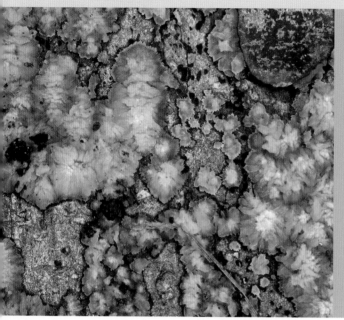

Description When young, orange wax crust has a beautiful coral colour; as it ages, it becomes pinkish to brown. The fruitbodies are formed flat against the host and can spread up to 30 cm/12 in. across. They are wrinkled to bumpy and waxy to gelatinous, depending on their moisture content.

Habitat Mixed forests, mainly on dead hardwoods, Red alder seems to be the favourite in the Pacific Northwest.

Season Fruitbodies are seen from September to November.

Edibility Not considered edible.

▶ HAIRY BLACK CAP

Pseudoplectania melaena
FAMILY Sarcosomataceae

Description When first seen, hairy black caps seem out of place, as if a piece of round bark fell to the ground. The fruitbodies start out dark brown and mature to black. They are to 5 cm/2 in. across and rounded to irregular in shape. The stalks are very small, to 1 cm/0.5 in. in height.

Etymology The genus name means "false plectania," referring to a closely related fungus.

Habitat In mixed forests on forest litter.

Season In the Pacific Northwest, I have found the fruitbodies only in early spring. They are sometimes abundant and sometimes scattered or solitary.

Edibility Not considered edible.

▶ ORANGE PEEL FUNGUS

Aleuria aurantia

CUP FUNGI FAMILY Pyronemataceae

Description When seen in grassy parks, orange peel fungus does look like orange peels discarded by picnickers. The rubbery fruitbodies are to 10 cm/ 4 in. across by 5 cm/2 in. in height. The inner cap is smooth and bright orange, while the outside is covered in fine white powder, making it appear lighter in colour.

Habitat Open areas, lawns, parks, and the sides of gravelly paths.

Season Fruitbodies are seen in late spring and autumn.

Edibility Edible; however, it is said to be tasteless.

▶ DOG VOMIT SLIME MOLD SCRAMBLED EGG SLIME MOLD

Fuligo septica

FAMILY Physaraceae

Description This yellow slime mold has a fruiting body to 20 cm/8 in. long and almost as wide and to 3 cm/1.2 in. thick. It first appears bright yellow with occasional white edging and darkens with age.

Habitat Mainly seen on rotting wood and wood chips.

Season From May to October.

Edibility Not edible.

INVASIVE PLANTS

▶ PIGWEED RED ROOT

Amaranthus retroflexus

AMARANTH FAMILY Amaranthaceae

Description Pigweed is a an annual to 1.8 m/6 ft. in height, more commonly seen at 0.9–1.2 m/ 3–4 ft. It has coarse foliage, and its small green flowers are borne in densely crowded spikes 5–15 cm/2–6 in. long. The abundant seeds are small, oval, and glossy black. The mature leaves are long stemmed, wavy edged, and to 15 cm/6 in. long. Other common species of *Amaranthus* are tumbling amaranth (*A. albus*) and prostrate pigweed (*A. graecizans*).

Traditional use The spring and early-summer leaves are excellent as potherbs or raw in salads. An extract from the plant was thought to be an antidote to snakebites.

Etymology The common name pigweed is from the pleasure hogs get from eating it. The genus name, *Amaranthus*, is from the Greek word *amarantos*, "unfading," in reference to the flowers retaining their colour for a long time.

Origin Native to tropical America; introduced or spread to the west coast by 1940.

Season Flowers from July to the first frost.

Reproduction By seed. Although pigweed is an annual, a single plant can produce over 100,000 seeds.

Concerns Pigweed's ability to produce so many seeds has made it one of agriculture's most common weeds. If not plowed under early in the season, it can infest farms and reduce field crops.

▶ GOUTWEED BISHOP'S WEED

Aegopodium podagraria

CARROT FAMILY Apiaceae

Description Goutweed is a herbaceous perennial to 50 cm/20 in. in height. Its white flowers are borne in umbrella-shaped clusters typical of the carrot family. The leaves are long stalked and usually have three leaflets on top.

Traditional use As its common name suggests, it was used to relieve the pains of gout. The botanist Carl Linnaeus also recommended that the young leaves be boiled and eaten as a green vegetable. Without more information, I would not recommend this.

Etymology The genus name, *Aegopodium*, means "goat's foot." You will need a good imagination to see the similarities between the leaves' outline and a goat's foot. The plant's appearance around ancient European monasteries gave it the common name bishop's weed.

Origin Introduced from Europe as a garden ornamental.

Season Flowers from July to August.

Reproduction By invasive rhizomes (underground stems) and seeds.

Concerns Once established in a garden, this weed is incredibly hard to eradicate. One small rhizome left behind can quickly start a new colony.

▶ WILD CHERVIL

Anthriscus sylvestris

CARROT FAMILY Apiaceae

Description Wild chervil is a taprooted perennial to 1.2 m/4 ft. in height. Its small white flowers are borne in loose umbrella-like clusters in the top portion of the plant. The leaves are triangular and finely dissected within. Care must be taken not to confuse wild chervil with the similar-looking but extremely poisonous poison hemlock (*Conium maculatum*).

Traditional use The taproots are considered edible when boiled like parsnips.

Etymology The species name, *sylvestris*, means "growing in woods or forests," which it does very well.

Origin Wild chervil was first introduced to the east coast of North America. It is a fairly recent alien to the west coast and is spreading rapidly.

Season The plant is in flower from April to June, with seeds maturing from July onward. The stems die back in late summer, but a second growth of non-flowering stems and leaves appears in autumn, and remains green throughout the winter.

Reproduction By seed.

Concerns Under ideal conditions—moist, rich soils and partial shade—wild chervil can cover several hectares or acres within a few growing seasons.

▶ WILD CARROT QUEEN ANNE'S LACE

Daucus carota

CARROT FAMILY Apiaceae

Description Wild carrot is a biennial to 1 m/3.3 ft. in height. Its small white flowers are grouped to form showy terminal clusters to 10 cm/4 in. across. The leaves are to 15 cm/6 in. long and dissected to the point that they resemble delicate ferns. If the stems are scratched, a carrot scent is released.

Traditional use Wild carrot is thought to be the parent of our present-day cultivated carrot. The seeds of wild carrot can be used to spice up soups and stews. Medicinally, a poultice from the roots was used to ease the pain of cancerous ulcers.

Etymology Both the genus and species name are Latin for "carrot." Although wild carrot was first introduced to England when Queen Elizabeth I was in reign (1533–1603), it said that Queen Anne, who reigned from 1702 to 1714, was very fond of wearing lace, and it was named in her honour.

Origin Native to Europe; first recorded in the United States in 1739.

Season Flowers from July to September.

Reproduction By seed.

Concerns Difficult to eradicate from fields, especially cultivated carrot patches.

▶ FENNEL WILD FENNEL

Foeniculum vulgare

CARROT FAMILY Apiaceae

Description Fennel is a herbaceous perennial to 1.8 m/6 ft. in height. Its beautiful golden flowers are borne in large, flat, terminal umbels to 10 cm/4 in. across. The seeds are ribbed, elliptical, and to 0.5 cm/0.2 in. long, which is half the length of the cultivated species, *F. officinalis*. The bright-green leaves are dissected so finely they give the plant a feathery appearance.

Traditional use The seeds, leaves, and roots have an anise flavour and are edible. The seeds were generally used to flavour soups, stews, and tea. The leaves and stems have long been cooked or boiled with fish. The tea made from the seeds is used as a carminative.

Etymology The genus name, *Foeniculum*, is Latin for "fennel," and the species name, *vulgare*, means "common."

Origin Native to Europe but considered more precisely indigenous to the shores of the Mediterranean Sea. The Ancient Italians are thought to be responsible for its spread. Wherever they colonized, fennel was to be found. Its use can be traced back to Roman times.

Season Flowers from July to September.

Reproduction By seed.

Concerns The seeds germinate readily in cultivated soils.

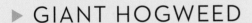

▶ GIANT HOGWEED

Heracleum mantegazzianum

CARROT FAMILY Apiaceae

Description Giant hogweed is a robust herbaceous perennial to 4.5 m/15 ft. in height. Its small white flower clusters fit together much like an umbrella, forming a giant inflorescence to 0.6–0.9 m/2–3 ft. across. The leaves are coarsely toothed and similar to a maple leaf, except that they attain sizes of 0.6–1.5 m/2–5 ft. across. Our native cow parsnip (*H. lanatum*) is similar but smaller, 1–3 m/3.3–10 ft. in height.

Traditional use Iranians used the seed as a spice (golpar), and the English fed the leaves to hogs. This plant should be considered poisonous to humans.

Etymology Hogweed's ability to grow so strongly has given it its genus name, *Heracleum*, in honour of Hercules. The species name is in honour of Paolo Mantegazza (1831–1910), an Italian anthropologist and traveller.

Origin Giant hogweed was brought over from the Caucasus Mountains of Asia as a garden curiosity. The earliest records of its being on the west coast are from 1950.

Season Flowers from June to July.

Reproduction By division and seed. A single plant can produce up to 10,000 seeds per year.

Concerns Severe skin irritation and blisters can occur if exposed to the sun after coming in contact with the sap (phototoxicity).

▶ COMMON PERIWINKLE BLUE BUTTONS / CREEPING MYRTLE

Vinca minor

DOGBANE FAMILY Apocynaceae

Description Periwinkle is a trailing, ground-covering evergreen perennial capable of covering hundreds of square metres or feet. Its attractive bluish-mauve flowers are to 2.5 cm/1 in. across, have five petals, and are borne singly on slender stems. The leaves are to 8 cm/3 in. long, shiny green, opposite, and elongated egg shaped. Greater periwinkle (*V. major*) is similar but has larger leaves, flowers, and stems.

Traditional use A tincture made from the fresh leaves was used to treat internal hemorrhages. Modern herbal stores sell extracts of periwinkle under the category of "smart drugs." It is claimed that it increases oxygen to the brain, which enhances the memory.

Etymology The genus name, *Vinca*, is from *vincio*, "to bind" or "to wind around." In the 1400s, it was thought that periwinkle had the power to ward off evil spirits.

Origin A garden escapee from Eurasia.

Season Flowers heavily from March to May.

Reproduction By seed and rooting along the stems.

Concerns Has become a problem around urban forests, where it suffocates the lower native flora. Greater periwinkle is also a garden escapee but is less invasive.

▶ HOLLY HOLY TREE / CHRIST'S THORN

Ilex aquifolium

HOLLY FAMILY Aquifoliaceae

Description The holly trees growing wild in Pacific Northwest forests rarely exceed 6 m/20 ft. in height. The heavy shade stunts their growth and seldom allows them to set fruit. In the open, they can attain heights of 13–16 m/40–50 ft. Hollies are mainly dioecious; male and female flowers are on separate trees. The fruit produced from the female flowers are approximately 0.75 cm/0.25 in. across.

Traditional use Holly leaves were steeped as an infusion and used against catarrh, pleurisy, and smallpox. While the berries are not edible by humans, birds will feast on the mature berries, and sheep, cows, and deer will browse the foliage.

Etymology The species name, *aquifolium*, is the old classic name for holly, often used as Christmas decoration. Legend has it that holly first emerged under the feet of Jesus Christ—the berries were his drops of blood; hence the common name holy tree. Holly farms were a common sight on the west coast from the 1920s to the 1960s.

Origin Introduced from Europe for hedging and its attractive berries.

Season The red berries can be seen from October to March.

Reproduction By seed in the wild, and through layering, cuttings, and grafting in cultivation.

Concerns Can over-shade the surrounding native flora.

▶ ENGLISH IVY

Hedera helix

GINSENG FAMILY Araliaceae

Description English ivy is a familiar evergreen sprawler and climber. Its greenish-yellow flowers are borne in terminal, globular umbels. The pea-sized berries produced from these are purplish black and smooth and contain two to five seeds. English ivy only produces flowers when the branches grow above their host or support (typically a tree or a fence), so ivy growing on the ground will not flower. It does not need to. It reproduces by rooting in the soil. The flowering branch leaves differ from the five-lobed lower leaves by becoming rounded with wavy edges.

Traditional use All parts are considered poisonous to humans, though birds eat the ripe berries A decoction of the flowers and wine was thought to relieve dysentery.

Etymology The species name, *helix*, is ancient Greek for "spiral shaped" and was given to plants that twine.

Origin Native to Europe, Asia Minor, and Iran.

Season Flowers in late summer, with the berries persisting throughout winter.

Reproduction By seed, mainly by birds, and vegetatively.

Concerns The combination of English ivy's quick reproduction and its ability to sprawl and climb have made it one of the worst invaders of our west coast forests.

▶ CHICORY

Cichorium intybus

ASTER FAMILY Asteraceae

Description Chicory is an attractive perennial to 1.9 m/6.2 ft. tall. The beautiful blue flowers are to 5 cm/2 in. across, with each ray having five teeth at the tips. The coarse-looking leaves get progressively smaller from the base of the stem to the tips of the branches.

Traditional use The young leaves were used in salads, and the roots were baked, ground, and used as a coffee substitute.

Origin Chicory is native to the Mediterranean.

Season Flowers from mid- to late summer.

Reproduction By seed.

Concerns Not an aggressive weed.

▶ OX-EYE DAISY

Leucanthemum vulgare

ASTER FAMILY Asteraceae

Syn. *Chrysanthemum leucanthemum*

Description Ox-eye daisy is an aromatic, herbaceous perennial to 75 cm/30 in. tall. Its flowers have the daisy's typical white ray petals and yellow centre disks, to 5 cm/ 2 in. across. The basal leaves are obovate with rounded teeth; the stem leaves are similar, though alternate.

Traditional use Has been used as an antispasmodic and diuretic and to control whooping cough.

Etymology Its synonymous name, *Chrysanthemum leucanthemum*, is from the Greek words *chrysos* ("gold") and *anthos* ("flower").

Origin This is a European introduction that has been naturalized in most of the Pacific Northwest.

Season Flowers abundantly from mid-June to August.

Reproduction By seed.

Concerns Can be a menace in cow pastures. Mainly seen as an attractive roadside weed.

▶ YARROW

Achillea millefolium

ASTER FAMILY Asteraceae

Description Yarrow is a herbaceous perennial to 1 m/3.3 ft. in height. Its many small white flowers form flat-topped clusters 5–10 cm/2–4 in. across. The aromatic leaves are so finely dissected that they appear fern-like.

Traditional use Herbal shops sell tablets, capsules, liquid formulas, and tinctures claiming relief from nose bleeds, fevers, colds, sore throats, high blood pressure, premenstrual syndrome, rheumatism, and a lot more, as well as aromatherapy. Yarrow's primary use since ancient times is for blood clotting.

Etymology Its species name, *millefolium*, means "a thousand leaves." The genus name, *Achillea*, is from the Greek general Achilles, who is said to have used yarrow to stop the bleeding of his soldiers' wounds.

Origin There is still discussion as to whether early European settlers brought yarrow over to the new world or it was already here.

Season Flowers from July to August at higher elevations.

Reproduction By seed and rhizome.

Concerns Yarrow's strong odour can taint dairy cows' and goats' milk if regularly browsed.

▶ MAYWEED STINKING CHAMOMILE

Anthemis cotula

ASTER FAMILY Asteraceae

Description Mayweed is a taprooted herbaceous perennial to 80 cm/31 in. in height. Its daisy-like flowers have approximately 12 white ray florets surrounding yellow disc florets. The leaves are alternate and finely dissected, giving the plant a feathery appearance. If the plant is rubbed, brushed against, or crushed, a foul odour is emitted.

Traditional use Mayweed's fetid odour has made it very unpopular for any culinary use. Even fleas, mosquitoes, and bees stay away. Extracts from the plant have been used as an antispasmodic and to treat hysteria. The plant was also used to treat menstrual problems in young women.

Etymology The genus name, *Anthemis*, was used by the Greek botanist Pedanius Dioscorides (AD 40–90) to describe the abundance of flowers. The species name, *cotula*, is Greek for "small cup." The base of the leaves form cups, which often hold water. The common name mayweed is from Ancient English, meaning "maiden."

Origin Native to Europe.

Season Flowers from July to September.

Reproduction By seed.

Concerns The plant's foul odour can be transferred to milk if consumed by dairy animals.

▶ COMMON BURDOCK

Arctium minus

ASTER FAMILY Asteraceae

Description Common burdock, a biennial, starts its first year of life as a basal rosette. In its second year, it sends up a robust branched stem to over 1.8 m/6 ft. in height with similar width. Its violet-coloured flowers are surrounded by hooked bracts that later form the burr, up to 2.5 cm/1 in. across. The heart-shaped basal leaves can be as long as 45 cm/18 in.; the stem leaves are smaller. Great burdock (A. *lappa*) is almost identical to common burdock, except with larger flowers set in flat-topped clusters instead of along the stem.

Traditional use The first-year taproots have long been cultivated as a food source. The young stalks can be peeled (thoroughly) and eaten raw. Burdock has been used in blood medicines and as a cure for eczema.

Etymology The common name burdock is from the burr-like seed heads and from the leaves' resemblance to curled dock (*Rumex crispus*).

Origin Native to Eurasia, it was first documented in New England in 1638.

Season Flowers from July to autumn.

Reproduction By seed.

Concerns If grazed upon, burdock can give a bitter taste to milk, and it is a serious problem if entangled in the wool of sheep.

► WORMWOOD ABSINTHIUM / VERMOUTH

Artemisia absinthium

ASTER FAMILY Asteraceae

Description Wormwood is an aromatic herbaceous perennial to 1.5 m/5 ft. in height. Its small nodding flowers are roundish, green yellow, and borne in panicles in the upper leaf axils. The lower leaves are long stacked, dissected two to three times, and up to 10 cm/4 in. long. As the leaves progress up the stems, they become shorter and less divided, until they are reduced to approximately 2.5 cm/1 in. long and stalkless.

Traditional use Wormwood has been used medicinally for hundreds of years, including to relieve depression, jaundice, gout, and digestive problems. It has also been used as a worm expeller and moth repellant.

Etymology The oil extracted from wormwood is absinthol, which is the main ingredient in absinthe. Wormwood is reputed to have grown along the path of the serpent in the Garden of Eden.

Origin Introduced to the east coast of North America from Eurasia in the early 19th century as a garden plant.

Season Flowers from July to September.

Reproduction By seed and rhizome. The plants can easily be propagated by root division in autumn or by cuttings in late summer.

Concerns If grazed on, it can taint dairy animals' milk.

► MUGWORT

Artemisia vulgaris

ASTER FAMILY Asteraceae

Description Mugwort is a very aromatic herbaceous perennial to 1.5 cm/5 ft. in height. Its tiny flowers are bell shaped, woolly, reddish brown, and massed in upright panicles. The leaves are variable in shape, most being dissected to the main rib, green above, woolly and white beneath, and to 10 cm/4 in. long.

Traditional use The raw leaves were used as one of the main ingredients for stuffing geese and as a flavouring for beer. The dried leaves were crushed and used as a condiment. Mugwort has also been highly valued in European apothecaries since medieval times.

Etymology The genus name, *Artemisia*, commemorates the Greek goddess of chastity, Artemis (the Romans' Diana).

Origin Like wormwood, mugwort was first introduced to the east coast of North America from Eurasia in the early 19th century. European settlers brought it over to grow and use for its medicinal and culinary properties.

Season Flowers from July to October.

Reproduction By seed (mainly by wind) and rhizome. The plants can easily be propagated by root division in autumn or by cuttings in late summer.

Concerns If grazed on, it can taint dairy animals' milk.

▶ ENGLISH DAISY COMMON DAISY

Bellis perennis

ASTER FAMILY Asteraceae

Description English daisy is a low-growing herbaceous perennial with flower stalks reaching up to 15 cm/6 in. in height. Its very familiar white and yellow flowers are approximately 2.5 cm/1 in. across when they are open; they shut at night and in damp weather. The long-stalked leaves are formed in a basal rosette and range in shape from oval to spoon shaped.

Traditional use The flowers were used to make a summer wine, and the leaves were used as salad greens and potherbs. Medicinally, the plant was very popular in the 14th century for its use as a mild laxative and antispasmodic and for stomach and intestinal problems.

Etymology The Latin name, *Bellis perennis*, translates to "pretty perennial," an apt name for this beautiful little plant. The common name daisy is a corruption of the Old English name "day's eye," so called because it is open during the day and shut at night.

Origin Introduced from Europe.

Season English daisy has a prolific flower display in late spring and a modest showing through autumn.

Reproduction By seed.

Concerns Can be a problem in well-kept lawns such as golf courses and lawn bowling greens.

▶ NODDING BEGGARTICKS

Bidens cernua

ASTER FAMILY Asteraceae

This species is described on page 28, among other members of the Aster family in the Flowering Plants section.

▶ MOUNTAIN BLUET

Centaurea montana

ASTER FAMILY Asteraceae

Description Mountain bluet is a taprooted herbaceous perennial to 90 cm/3 ft. in height. Its purple-blue flowers can be up to 10 cm/4 in. across. The leaves are broadly lance shaped, woolly below, and up to 15 cm/6 in. long, becoming progressively reduced upward.

Traditional use The flower petals have long been used for eyewash. The very popular French eyewash Eau de casse-lunettes used to be made from them. An application of bruised leaves to open cuts and wounds was thought to have healing powers.

Etymology The species name, *montana*, means "of the mountains," which is also reflected in its common name.

Origin Endemic to Europe.

Season Flowers from May to July, often with a secondary bloom from August to September.

Reproduction By seed and vigorous rhizomes.

Concerns Easily spreads into natural ecosystems.

▶ CORNFLOWER BACHELOR'S BUTTON

Centaurea cyanus

ASTER FAMILY Asteraceae

Description Cornflower is a taprooted annual 60–90 cm/2–3 ft. in height. Its 4 cm/ 1.5 in. flowers range in colour from striking blue to purple to pink to white. The basal leaves are lance shaped, white, woolly below, and sparsely toothed, with lobes at the base. The upper leaves are smaller, narrower, and without teeth.

Traditional use The flower petals have long been used for eyewash. The very popular French eyewash Eau de casse-lunettes used to be made from them. An application of bruised leaves to open cuts and wounds was thought to have healing powers.

Etymology The genus name, *Centaurea*, is named after Chiron, a centaur from Greek mythology: half man, half horse. The species name, *cyanus*, is Greek for "blue flower."

Origin Cornflower is a garden escapee originally brought over from Europe.

Season Flowers from June to September.

Reproduction By seed.

Concerns The cornflower, like all of the *Centaurea* species, is difficult to eradicate, but it is not as much of a concern as some of the perennial knapweeds, such as *C. maculosa*, *C. debauxii*, and *C. diffusa*.

CANADA THISTLE

Cirsium arvense

ASTER FAMILY Asteraceae

Description Canada thistle is an armed rhizomatous perennial 0.5–1.25 m/1.6–4.1 ft. in height. Its pale-purple flowers are up to 2 cm/0.75 in. tall, borne in clusters of one to five per branch, and dioecious (male and female flowers are on separate plants). No other thistle has this characteristic. The leaves are alternate, white, hairy below, and wavy, with marginal spines. Bull thistle has larger flower heads and spiny wings on the stems.

Traditional use The young stems and leaves were carefully peeled and eaten raw or boiled; the roots were peeled and roasted.

Etymology The genus name, *Cirsium*, means "swelling veins"; the juice from thistles was used to reduce the swelling on veins. The species name, *arvense*, means "growing in cultivated fields," its preferred habitat.

Origin Although called Canada thistle, it is a native of Eurasia, probably imported in a sack of tainted crop seed. Now considered one of the most invasive weeds in Canada and the United States.

Season Flowers from July to August. The female plants bear thousands of fluffy white seeds.

Reproduction Primarily vegetatively (by rhizome), and secondarily by seed.

Concerns It is capable of infesting many hectares or acres at a time, thereby reducing or eliminating crop fields.

BULL THISTLE

Cirsium vulgare

ASTER FAMILY Asteraceae

Description Bull thistle is a well-armed biennial 0.9–1.8 m/3–6 ft. in height. In its first year, it forms a ground-hugging rosette with a large taproot. In its second year, it bolts, producing an upright fibrous branching stem supporting 20 or more flowers. The purplish flower heads are up to 5 cm/2 in. across, armed, usually solitary, and at the end of the branches. The leaves are pinnately divided, prickly, hairy on top, clasping to the winged stems, and 7–30 cm/3–12 in. long. The mature seeds are 0.15 cm/0.06 in. long and are supplied with a parachute-like plume for easy wind dispersal. Thistle seeds are a favourite food of finches.

Etymology The genus name, *Cirsium*, is the Ancient Greek name for thistle.

Origin Bull thistle is a native of Eurasia. It likely came over to North America in a sack of contaminated crop seed.

Season Flowers from July to September, depending on elevation.

Reproduction By seed.

Concerns Biennials are easier to eradicate than annuals in yearly cultivated soils. However, in uncultivated soils, such as in hay fields, the presence of bull thistles can reduce the market value of the crop.

SMOOTH HAWKSBEARD

Crepis capillaris

ASTER FAMILY Asteraceae

Description Smooth hawksbeard is a taprooted annual or biennial 20–90 cm/8–36 in. in height. Its flowers resemble a dandelion's but are smaller, to 2.5 cm/1 in. across. They consist of ray florets only and are borne in multi-headed clusters. The leaves are deeply incised, 5–30 cm/2–12 in. long, and usually hairless (smooth, as the common name suggests). If the seed of hawksbeard germinates late in the season, it will sit as a leafy rosette through the winter and bloom the following May or June. This is known as a winter biennial.

Etymology The genus name, *Crepis*, is Greek for "boot" or "sandal." The pinnately cut leaves somewhat resemble a sandal.

Origin Introduced from Europe as a garden ornamental.

Season Flowers from May to November.

Reproduction By seed.

Concerns A pest in unkempt lawns, fields, and boulevards.

MOUSE-EARED CHICKWEED

Cerastium fontanum

PINK FAMILY Caryophyllaceae

Syn. *Cerastium vulgatum*

Description Mouse-eared chickweed is a sprawling herbaceous biennial or short-lived perennial to 50 cm/18–19 in. in length. Its tiny white flowers have five deeply notched petals and are borne in terminal clusters. The leaves are to 2.5 cm/1 in. long, opposite, mouse-ear shaped, and like the stems, coarsely hairy.

Traditional use The young leaves and stems can be added to a salad or used as a potherb.

Etymology The genus name, *Cerastium*, is from the Greek word *kerastes*, "horned," referring to the tiny horned seed capsules. The species name, *fontanum*, means "growing by springs" or "growing by water."

Origin Introduced from Eurasia.

Season Flowers from April to November.

Reproduction By seed and rooting at the stem nodes.

Concerns Most commonly a problem in lawns and on playing fields. It is also the alternate host of the tobacco mosaic virus.

▶ QUICKWEED SHAGGY GALINSOGA / FRINGED QUICKWEED / SHAGGY SOLDIER

Galinsoga quadriradiata

ASTER FAMILY Asteraceae

Description Quickweed is a fibrous-rooted herbaceous perennial 20–60 cm/8–24 in. in height. Its flowers have yellow disc florets surrounded by white ray florets, which are borne in terminal leafy-bracted clusters. The leaves are 2.5–8 cm/1–3 in. long, opposite, hairy, and coarsely toothed. Small-flowered quickweed (*G. parviflora*) is very similar, except it is not as hairy and its ray florets are slightly smaller.

Traditional use The fuzzy leaves were eaten raw in salads or cooked as potherbs.

Etymology The genus name, *Galinsoga*, commemorates the 18th-century Spanish physician and botanist Don Mariano Martinez de Galinsoga. The common name quickweed indicates how fast this plant can spread.

Origin Introduced from Central and Southern America.

Season Flowers from May to December.

Reproduction By seed.

Concerns Can become a serious invader in vegetable crops. Quickweed is mainly an autumn weed, often seen growing with common chickweed (*Stellaria media*).

▶ MARSH CUDWEED CHAFEWEED / LOW CUDWEED

Gnaphalium uliginosum

ASTER FAMILY Asteraceae

Description Marsh cudweed is an easily overlooked annual or biennial to 20 cm/8 in. in height. Its bland flowers are greenish brown, 0.7 cm/0.25 in. across, and formed in crowded terminal clusters. The leaves are alternate, narrow (linear), unstalked, woolly downy, and 2.5–5.5 cm/1–2 in. long. Cotton-batting cudweed (*G. chilense*) is a taller relative with more attractive flowers.

Traditional use In Europe, it was used as a gargle for inflammation of the throat (quinsy). The leaves were used to prevent chafing on steer and horses carrying large loads; hence the common name chafeweed.

Etymology The genus name, *Gnaphalium*, is from the Greek word *gnaphalion*, meaning "a plant with soft down." The species name, *uliginosum*, means "from a marshy place" or "from swamps."

Origin Marsh cudweed was introduced from Europe.

Season Flowers from August to September.

Reproduction By seed.

Concerns It has become very invasive in areas that have moist low-lying fields.

▶ ORANGE HAWKWEED
DEVIL'S PAINTBRUSH / GRIM-THE-COLLIER

Hieracium aurantiacum

ASTER FAMILY Asteraceae

Description Orange hawkweed is a herbaceous perennial 30–60 cm/12–24 in. in height. Its flowers are an electric orange red, are borne in terminal clusters of 5 to 25, and grow to 2.5 cm/1 in. across. The leaves are mainly basal, lanceolate, and, like the stem, hairy.

Traditional use Unlike other members of the chicory group, such as salsify, hawk-bits, dandelion, and goat's beard, orange hawkweed seems to have been grown as a garden ornamental.

Etymology The species name, *aurantiacum*, means "orange red." The common name Grim-the-Collier is from the black hairs that cover the flower stalk and the involucrate, a whorl of bracts below the flower.

Origin Orange hawkweed was introduced from Europe, most likely as a garden ornamental that jumped the fence.

Season Flowers from July to August.

Reproduction By extremely invasive rhizomes, stolons, and seeds.

Concerns Can very quickly dominate fields, gardens, and roadsides.

▶ COMMON HAWKWEED

Hieracium vulgatum

ASTER FAMILY Asteraceae

Syn. *H. lachenalii*

Description Common hawkweed is an upright herbaceous perennial to 80 cm/31 in. in height. Its flower heads are 2–3 cm/1–1.5 in. across, have yellow ray florets only and no disc, and are borne in terminal clusters of 5 to 20. The basal leaves are arranged as a rosette, ovate stalked, and toothed, and the stem leaves are unstalked. The Pacific Northwest has several native hawkweeds that can be confused with the introduced species. Two natives are Canada hawkweed (*H. canadense*) and narrow-leaved hawkweed (*H. umbellatum*). A specialized key is necessary for proper identification. All species of hawkweed have a milky juice in their stems and leaves, and their flowers comprise only ray florets.

Traditional use For centuries, hawkweeds have been used medicinally for diseases of the lungs, asthma, and consumption. The juice from the plant mixed with wine was thought to help digestion and dispel wind.

Etymology The species name, *vulgatum*, means "common."

Origin Common hawkweed is a native of Europe.

Season Flowers from July to September.

Reproduction By seed.

Concerns Has spread very rapidly in fields, gardens, and lawns.

▶ SPOTTED HAWKWEED MOTTLED HAWKWEED

Hieracium maculatum

ASTER FAMILY Asteraceae

Description Spotted hawkweed is an attractive herbaceous perennial 25–80 cm/ 10–32 in. in height. The yellow flowers are typical of the genus: to 2.5 cm/1 in. across, have ray florets only and no disc, and are borne in terminal clusters of 5 to 20. The leaves are 2.5–15 cm/1–6 in. long, slightly hairy, and grey green with a mottling of purple bronze.

Traditional use For centuries, hawkweeds have been used medicinally for diseases of the lungs, asthma, and consumption. The juice from the plant mixed with wine was thought to help digestion and dispel wind.

Etymology The genus name, *Hieracium*, is from the Greek *hieras* ("hawk"). It was thought that hawks that drank the juice from these plants would have improved eyesight. The English names hawkweed and hawksbit are also based on this belief.

Origin Spotted hawkweed is a garden escapee from Europe.

Season Flowers from July to August.

Reproduction By seed.

Concerns Can be a problem in gardens and on roadsides.

▶ HAIRY CAT'S EAR FALSE DANDELION

Hypochaeris radicata

ASTER FAMILY Asteraceae

Description Hairy cat's ear is a taprooted herbaceous perennial 15–60 cm/6–24 in. tall. Its yellow flowers are up to 4 cm/1.5 in. across, have ray florets only (no disc), and are borne in terminal clusters on leafless stalks (as opposed to the dandelion's flowers, which are borne singly). The leaves are 5–20 cm/2–8 in. long, obovate, round toothed, round lobed, densely hairy, and formed in a basal rosette.

Traditional use The young leaves can be eaten raw or cooked. I find the young leaves slightly bitter, even after cooking.

Etymology With considerable imagination, one can see a resemblance between the hairy leaves and a cat's ear.

Origin Native to Europe.

Season Flowers from May to October, with the main floral display in August.

Reproduction By seed.

Concerns It has become a problem in cultivated fields and lawns, where it competes for nutrients and overshadows grass.

WALL LETTUCE

Lactuca muralis

ASTER FAMILY Asteraceae

Description Wall lettuce is a taprooted annual or biennial 0.3–1.2 m/1–4 ft. in height. Its yellow flowers are 2 cm/1 in. across, have five petals, and are borne in terminal clusters. The basal leaves are 5–20 cm/2–8 in. long, are deeply cut and lobed, clasp the stem, and are glaucous underneath. The few upper leaves are reduced in size.

Traditional use The young leaves have long been used fresh in salads and as potherbs. Boiling the leaves removes some of the bitterness.

Etymology The genus name, *Lactuca*, is descriptive of the milky juice (lac) that comes from the broken stems and leaves. The species name, *muralis*, refers to where the plant commonly grows on or by the garden wall.

Origin Wall lettuce is native to Europe.

Season Flowers from July to September.

Reproduction By seed.

Concerns Competes with crops for moisture and nutrients.

PRICKLY LETTUCE WILD LETTUCE / OPIUM LETTUCE

Lactuca serriola

ASTER FAMILY Asteraceae

Syn. *Lactuca scariola*

Description Prickly lettuce is a taprooted annual or biennial 0.9–1.8 m/3–5 ft. in height. Its yellow ray florets have no disc, are to 2.5 cm/1 in. across, and are borne in terminal clusters. The alternating leaves are 5–30 cm/2–12 in. long, clasping, bluish green, and usually deeply incised. Prickly lettuce is thought to be the ancestor to our modern-day garden varieties.

Traditional use The young leaves can be eaten raw or as a potherb, and the young shoots can be cooked like asparagus. Caution should be taken, as large quantities can cause digestive problems. The milky juice in the plant contains lactucarium, a drug used for its antispasmodic, digestive, narcotic, and sedative properties. The milky juice, when dried, is like a weak opiate without being addictive or a problem to the digestive system.

Etymology The common name prickly lettuce is from the weak prickles on the under midrib and leaf margins.

Origin Introduced from Europe.

Season Flowers from July to September.

Reproduction By seed.

Concerns A problem in cultivated fields, where it competes with crops for light, nutrients, and moisture.

▶ NIPPLEWORT

Lapsana communis

ASTER FAMILY Asteraceae

Description Nipplewort is a taprooted annual 0.4–1.5 m/1.3–5 ft. in height. Its yellow flowers are 2 cm/1 in. across and composed of ray florets only, with no disc. The flowers last only a day or two, quickly followed by miniature dandelion-like seed heads. The lower leaves are egg shaped and coarsely toothed, with basal lobes. The upper leaves are reduced and narrow.

Traditional use Throughout history, nipplewort has been cultivated in Europe as a vegetable. The young leaves can be used quite enjoyably as salad greens and pot-herbs. A decoction from nipplewort was also used as treatment for sore or cracked nipples, as indicated by its common name.

Etymology The genus name, *Lapsana*, is from the Greek word *lapazo*, meaning "purge," indicating that the plant was used medicinally.

Origin Introduced from Eurasia.

Season Flowers from June to September.

Reproduction By seed.

Concerns Can be a problem in cultivated gardens.

▶ PINEAPPLE WEED DISC MAYWEED

Matricaria discoidea

ASTER FAMILY Asteraceae

Description Pineapple weed is a pleasantly scented annual to 30 cm/12 in. in height. Its green-yellow flowers are rayless (all disc) and borne in dense terminal clusters. The alternating leaves are divided one to three times, giving the plant a fern-like appearance.

Traditional use Young plants make a good substitute for chamomile in herbal tea. It was also used in midwifery and to treat uterine infections. The pineapple scent from the crushed plants makes it useful for potpourri.

Etymology The genus name, *Matricaria*, is medieval for "mother" or "womb." The species name, *discoidea*, means "disc only"; the flowers have no rays.

Origin Pineapple weed is native to North America. It was probably introduced to the west coast.

Habitat It has the ability to grow in compacted soils, usually on gravel roads and pathways and in waste areas.

Season Flowers from June to August.

Reproduction By seed.

▶ SCENTLESS MAYWEED FALSE CHAMOMILE

Matricaria perforata

ASTER FAMILY Asteraceae

Syn. *M. inodora, M. maritima, Tripleurospermum inodorum*

Description Scentless mayweed is a fibrous-rooted annual or biennial to 60 cm/24 in. in height. Its daisy-like flowers are to 5 cm/2 in. across, with a yellow disc surrounded by 12 to 20 white ray florets. The flowers are borne singly at the end of the branching stems. The alternating leaves are divided so heavily (one to three times) that it gives them a feather-like appearance.

Traditional use Because the plant is almost scentless, it was not popular in poultices or herbal teas. In Finland, an infusion of scentless mayweed was used to treat consumption.

Etymology The species name, *perforata*, refers to the perforated or pierced appearance of its foliage.

Origin Introduced from Europe as an ornamental, it can easily be distinguished from other mayweeds and chamomiles by its lack of scent.

Season Flowers from May to October.

Reproduction By seed.

Concerns Seeds germinating in the summer and autumn will overwinter as rosettes and, if not plowed under, will compete with field crops the following spring.

▶ OX-TONGUE HAWKWEED BITTERWEED

Picris hieracioides

ASTER FAMILY Asteraceae

Description Ox-tongue hawkweed is a herbaceous biennial or perennial to 90 cm/36 in. in height. Its dandelion-like flowers are to 3.5 cm/1.5 in. across, bright yellow, and in terminal clusters. The leaves are to 20 cm/8 in. long, alternating, and lance shaped, and the stems are bristly hairy.

Traditional use The young leaves are bitter; however, they can be used as a potherb. Concoctions made from the leaves have been used to relieve fevers.

Etymology The genus name, *Picris*, is from the Greek word *picros*, meaning "bitter," referring to the bitter-tasting leaves. The species name, *hieracioides*, means "resembles hawkweed."

Origin Introduced from Eurasia as a garden ornamental.

Season Flowers from July to October.

Reproduction By seed.

Concerns Ox-tongue hawkweed is quickly becoming an obnoxious pest invading fields, pastures, and rangeland.

TANSY RAGWORT

ST. JAMES WORT / STAGGERWORT / STAMMERWORT

Senecio jacobaea

ASTER FAMILY Asteraceae

Description Tansy ragwort is a branched biennial or short-lived perennial to 90 cm/3 ft. in height. Its showy yellow flowers are to 2.5 cm/1 in. across and borne in flat-topped clusters. Each flower has 10 to 15 ray florets and as many disc florets. The carrot-like leaves are 5–20 cm/2–8 in. long, two to three times pinnately cut, and reduced in size upward.

Traditional use It has long been used medicinally. The juice has been used as a wash for burns and to relieve inflammation of the eyes and sores. A poultice of the green leaves was used in relieving rheumatism, gout, and joint pain. It was also used as remedy for speech impediments. A yellow dye can be obtained by boiling the flowers.

Etymology The common name stammerwort refers to its use in treating speech impediments.

Origin Introduced from Eurasia.

Season Flowers from July to September.

Reproduction By seed.

Concerns Toxic to livestock. If it is eaten, it can cause the animals to stagger (hence the common name staggerwort).

STICKY RAGWORT

STICKY GROUNDSEL / VISCID GROUNDSEL / STINKING GROUNDSEL

Senecio viscosus

ASTER FAMILY Asteraceae

Description Sticky ragwort is a taprooted annual or biennial 10–60 cm/4–24 in. in height. Its small yellow flowers are borne at the end of the stems and have both ray and disc florets. The leaves are 2.5–10 cm/1–4 in. long, deeply lobed, sticky, and granular. The entire plant is slightly hairy and, as the common name suggests, sticky.

Traditional use The leaves are carminative (used for expelling gas) and have mild emetic properties (used to induce vomiting).

Etymology The species name, *viscosus*, refers to the plant's stickiness. On hot days, or when the plant is crushed, it emits a strong odour; hence the common name stinking groundsel.

Origin Introduced from Europe.

Season Flowers from July to September.

Reproduction By seed.

Concerns Can be a pest in gardens and on roadsides.

COMMON GROUNDSEL OLD-MAN-IN-THE-SPRING / GRIMSEL/SIMSON

Senecio vulgaris

ASTER FAMILY Asteraceae

Description Common groundsel is a taprooted annual or biennial 10–60 cm/4–24 in. in height. Its yellow flowers are to 0.7 cm/0.25 in. across, composed of disc florets only, and borne at the end of the stems. The leaves are 2–10 cm/1–4 in. long, deeply lobed, and granular; they are similar in appearance to the leaves of sticky groundsel, except they are not sticky.

Traditional use The many applications of common groundsel in medicine date back hundreds of years. Its main uses were diaphoretic (to increase perspiration), purgative (laxative), diuretic (to increase urine flow), and emetic (to induce vomiting).

Etymology The genus name, *Senecio*, is from the Latin word *senex*, "old man." This is referring to the hairy seed heads that are formed from spring to summer. When the wind blows the seeds off the plants, they are left bald; hence the common name old-man-in-the-spring.

Origin Common groundsel was introduced to the east coast of North America from Eurasia in the 1600s. The early settlers brought it over as a treatment for the beginnings of cholera.

Season Flowers mainly from April to October, but can also be seen sputtering throughout the year.

Reproduction By seed.

Concerns A problem in cultivated fields, where it competes with crops. It also has the potential to poison grazing livestock.

PERENNIAL SOW THISTLE CORN SOW THISTLE / CREEPING SOW THISTLE

Sonchus arvensis

ASTER FAMILY Asteraceae

Description Three species and one variety of sow thistle are commonly seen in the Pacific Northwest: perennial sow thistle (*S. arvensis*), annual sow thistle (*S. asper*), common sow thistle (*S. oleraceus*), and hairless or smooth perennial sow thistle (*S. arvensis* var. *glabrescens*). They can be distinguished from true thistles by their milky juice (latex) and dandelion-like yellow flowers.

Perennial sow thistle is a herbaceous perennial to 1.8 m/6 ft. in height. Its flowers are to 5 cm/2 in. across, composed of ray florets only, and borne in round or flat-topped clusters. Floral bracts supporting the flower head that are not covered with woolly hairs are most likely of the smooth variety, *S. arvensis* var. *glabrescens*. The leaves are 5–40 cm/2–16 in. long, clasping with prickly margins, and deeply lobed.

Traditional use Young leaves taste like dandelion and can be cooked like spinach.

Origin Introduced from Europe to North America. The Romans may have brought sow thistle to England.

Season Flowers from August to October.

Reproduction By seed and rhizome.

Concerns Competes aggressively with cultivated crops.

▶ ANNUAL SOW THISTLE

PRICKLY SOW THISTLE /
SPINY MILK THISTLE

Sonchus asper

ASTER FAMILY Asteraceae

Description Annual sow thistle is a taprooted annual to 1.2 m/4 ft. in height. Its yellow flowers are to 2.5 cm/1 in. across. It has ray florets only. The floral bracts have no hair and are borne in flat-topped clusters. The leaves are the identifying factor when distinguishing annual sow thistle from common sow thistle. Both species have spiny-toothed margins on the leaves, but the base of annual sow thistle's leaves have large rounded flanges as they clasp the stem. With common sow thistle, the base of the leaves is pointed as the leaves pass through the stem.

Traditional use Like other sow thistles, the young leaves are excellent in soups, casseroles, and salads. The milky juice of all sow thistles is said to be a healthy wash for the skin.

Etymology As the common name sow thistle suggests, it is a favourite food for pigs. The genus name, *Sonchus*, is derived from the Greek word *sonchos*, meaning "hollow," referring to the hollow stems.

Origin Introduced from Europe.

Season Flowers throughout the summer, from June to September.

Reproduction By seed.

Concerns A problem in cultivated fields and a host of several viruses.

▶ COMMON SOW THISTLE

HARE'S THISTLE /
HARE'S LETTUCE

Sonchus oleraceus

ASTER FAMILY Asteraceae

Description Common sow thistle is a taprooted annual to 1.2 m/4 ft. in height, more commonly seen at 0.6 m/2 ft. Its yellow flowers are to 2.5 cm/1 in. across, have ray florets only, and are borne in flat or round-topped clusters. The flowers are very similar to those of annual sow thistle. The leaves are 5–30 cm/2–12 in. long, with margins and sharply cut lobes. The base passes through the stem.

Traditional use Young leaves taste like dandelion and can be cooked like spinach. Leaves and stalks were thought to be good for nursing mothers, probably because of the association of the milky juice produced from the broken leaves and stalks. The milky juice of all sow thistles is said to be a healthy wash for the skin.

Etymology The species name, *oleraceus*, is given to cultivated plants, vegetables, and potherbs. As one of the common names suggests, it is a favourite with rabbits.

Origin Introduced from Europe.

Season Flowers from June to September.

Reproduction By seed.

Concerns A problem in cultivated fields and a host of several viruses.

COMMON TANSY

TANSY / BUTTONS /
BITTER BUTTONS / PARSLEY FERN

Tanacetum vulgare

ASTER FAMILY Asteraceae

Description Common tansy is an aromatic herbaceous perennial to 1.5 m/5 ft. in height. Its button-like yellow flowers have disc florets only, which are grouped together to form attractive flat-topped clusters. The feather-like leaves are 5–25 cm/ 2–10 in. long, alternate, and finely divided.

Traditional use An old custom of European bishops was to make tansy cakes for Easter consumption. Small doses of tansy are said to be anti-flatulent and rid the stomach of worms, while large doses are a violent irritant of the abdominal organs. Infusions of the dried flowers and seeds were used to relieve gout.

Etymology The common name tansy is thought to mean "immortal." This could be for two reasons: first, that the flowers last so long, and second, that tansy was used to preserve and protect dead bodies from corruption.

Reproduction By seed and rhizome.

Concerns Some people get skin irritations from just touching the plants.

COMMON DANDELION

LION'S TOOTH /
WET-A-BED / SWINE'S SNOUT

Taraxacum officinale

ASTER FAMILY Asteraceae

Description The common dandelion is probably the most recognized weed. It is a taprooted perennial to 50 cm/20 in. in height. Yellow ray flowers are to 5 cm/2 in. across and are borne singly on a hollow stem. The wavy green leaves grow in a basal rosette and can reach lengths of 30 cm/12 in. The flowers close as the sun disappears and reopen at the approach of sunrise.

Traditional use All parts are edible, for tea, wine, beer, and cooking. It is officially recognized in pharmacology as a remedy for kidney, liver, skin, and digestive problems.

Etymology The digested green leaves are said to make the kidneys relax in children; hence the common name wet-a-bed. The common name dandelion is the adulterated English version of the French *dent de lion*, meaning "tooth of the lion." This supposedly refers to the sharply toothed leaves.

Origin Introduced from Eurasia.

Season Flowers throughout spring and summer, with a heavy floral display from April to May.

Reproduction By seed.

Concerns Can be a problem in lawns.

▶ YELLOW SALSIFY GOAT'S BEARD / JACK-GO-TO-BED-AT-NOON

Tragopogon dubius

ASTER FAMILY Asteraceae

Description Yellow salsify is a taprooted biennial or, occasionally, short-lived perennial 30–90 cm/1–3 ft. in height. Its yellow flowers are to 7 cm/3 in. across, with pointed floral bracts extending past the ray florets. The flower heads are borne singly at the end of hollow stems. The grass-like leaves are 10–30 cm/4–12 in. long, bluish green, and clasping. The seed heads are much like a dandelion's except larger, up to 10 cm/4 in. across.

Traditional use The roots can be roasted or boiled in the same fashion as parsnips. The young stems collected before the flowers emerge can be cut into pieces and boiled like asparagus. The milky juice from the plant was taken internally for stomach aches and heartburn.

Etymology The flowers open at dawn and close by mid-afternoon; hence their common name Jack-go-to-bed-at-noon.

Origin Introduced from Europe.

Season Flowers from July to September.

Reproduction By seed.

Concerns Can be a problem in cultivated fields.

▶ SALSIFY PURPLE GOAT'S BEARD / OYSTER PLANT

Tragopogon porrifolius

ASTER FAMILY Asteraceae

Description Salsify is a taprooted biennial 0.6–1.2 m/2–4 ft. in height. Its attractive purple flowers are 5–7 cm/2–3 in. across with bright-green floral bracts extending beyond the ray florets. Each flower is borne singly at the end of a hollow stem. The long grass-like leaves are to 30 cm/12 in. long and clasp the stems at the base.

Traditional use Salsify roots have been baked, sautéed, and used in soups and stews. The roots are said to taste like oysters (hence the common name oyster plant). Decoctions of the plant were used to treat liver and stomach disorders.

Etymology The genus name, *Tragopogon*, is from the Greek, meaning "goat's beard." It was thought that the fluffy seed heads resembled a goat's beard as they fell apart. The species name, *porrifolius*, is Latin for "leaves resembling leeks."

Origin Introduced from Europe.

Season Flowers from July to August.

Reproduction By seed.

Concerns Known to compete with field crops.

▶ COCKLEBUR
Xanthium strumarium

COMMON COCKLEBUR /
BROAD-LEAVED COCKLEBUR / CLOTBUR

ASTER FAMILY Asteraceae
Syn. *X. canadense*

Description Cocklebur is a taprooted annual 0.6–1.8 m/2–6 ft. in height. Its male and female flowers are borne in the upper leaf axils. Male flower heads have one to three rows of pollen-producing discs, while female flower heads have two disks surrounded by bracts. The female flower head eventually becomes the spiny burr. In autumn, the burr contains two mature seeds, one that germinates the following spring, the other in two years or more. The stem leaves are to 12 cm/5 in. long, alternating, and heart shaped to triangular, with serrated edges.

Traditional use Cocklebur has been used to treat leucoderma, epilepsy, fevers, and venomous insect bites. A yellow hair dye was also made from the plant.

Etymology The genus name, *Xanthium*, is derived from the Greek word *xanthos*, meaning "yellow." The species name, *strumarium*, means "cushion-like" or "swollen," which refers to it being used to treat swollen necks.

Origin Thought to be native to eastern North America.

Season Flowers from late July to September.

Reproduction By seed. The seeds float in waterways or stick to passing humans or animals.

Concerns Cocklebur seedlings are poisonous to livestock.

▶ POLICEMAN'S HELMET
Impatiens glandulifera

SPOTTED TOUCH-ME-NOT /
QUICK-IN-THE-HAND /
SPECKLED JEWELS

BALSAM FAMILY Balsaminaceae

Description Policeman's helmet is a succulent annual to 1.8 m/6 ft. in height. Its flowers are to 4 cm/1.5 in. long and are borne on slender floating stems originating from the leaf axils. They are spotted and range in colour from white to red to pink to purple. The pouched bases of the flowers have a recurved spur. The leaves are 5–15 cm/2–6 in. long, finely toothed, and either opposite each other or whorled. In the base of the flower is a honey gland (hence the species name, *glandulifera*) that can only be reached by hummingbirds and long-tongued butterflies. The holes that can sometimes be seen above this gland are caused by frustrated bumblebees and wasps chewing their way to the nectar.

Traditional use A very effective ointment was made by boiling the leaves and stems in lard, letting it cool and harden, and then applying it to piles and hemorrhoids. The crushed leaves and stems could also be used fresh to relieve the itching and rash caused by poison ivy.

Origin Introduced from Asia.

Season Flowers from July to September.

Reproduction By seed.

Concerns Becoming a problem around damp forest edges, where it deprives our native plants of light.

▶ SMALL TOUCH-ME-NOT

Impatiens parviflora

BALSAM FAMILY Balsaminaceae

Description Small touch-me-not is a succulent annual 20–30 cm/8–32 in. in height. Its pale-yellow flowers are borne one to several on long stems originating from the leaf axils. The leaves are 5–13 cm/2–5 in. long, alternating, and finely sawtoothed.

Traditional use A very effective ointment was made by boiling the leaves and stems in lard, letting it cool and harden, and then applying it to piles and hemorrhoids. The crushed leaves and stems could also be used fresh to relieve the itching and rash caused by poison ivy.

Etymology The genus name, *Impatiens*, is given because of the quick-releasing seeds. The ripe seed pods are elastic and tightly coiled. When touched by falling rain, passing animals, or the curious hand, the seeds are energetically or impatiently discharged.

Origin Introduced from Asia.

Season Flowers from July to August.

Reproduction By seed.

Concerns Competes with native plants for light and moisture.

▶ COMMON FORGET-ME-NOT CHANGING FORGET-ME-NOT

Myosotis discolor

BORAGE FAMILY Boraginaceae

Description Common forget-me-not is a fibrous-rooted annual 10–30 cm/4–12 in. in height. Its tiny flowers start off yellowish and then turn light blue purple and finally dark blue purple. The leaves are 2.5–5 cm/1–2 in. long, alternating, and linear to lanceolate, with short hairs on both sides.

Traditional use The juice was used to treat pulmonary infections and snake bites.

Etymology The genus name, *Myosotis*, is Latin for "mouse ears," referring to the small fuzzy leaves. The pressed juice from the plants was used to harden and temper steel. There are many stories about how these plants received the common name forget-me-not. Most related to young men picking the flowers for their lovers, while some stories go back as far as the Garden of Eden.

Origin Introduced from Europe.

Season Flowers from April to May.

Reproduction By seed.

Concerns A roadside pest in short grassy areas.

▶ COMFREY KNITBONE / BONESET

Symphytum officinale

BORAGE FAMILY Boraginaceae

Description Comfrey is a taprooted perennial 0.9–1.5 m/3–5 ft. in height. Its bell-shaped flowers are creamy yellow to blue or purple and droop in one-sided clusters, much like a scorpion's tail. The leaves are alternating, hairy, and rough in texture and can be over 30 cm/1 ft. long at the base.

Traditional use The plant's roughness and hairiness make it a little tough to eat raw. However, when the young leaves are cooked like spinach they are very palatable, either by themselves or mixed with other greens. Comfrey was long used to set broken bones. A boiled mash was made from the roots and applied to a broken finger, arm, or leg. Within a short period of time, the mash would set as strong as any plaster.

Etymology The Greek genus name, *Symphytum*, and common names comfrey, knitbone, and boneset refer to this plant's abilities in mending broken bones.

Origin Introduced from Europe.

Season Flowers throughout the summer.

Reproduction By seed.

Concerns Once it is in a garden, it is hard to get rid of.

▶ GARLIC MUSTARD HEDGE GARLIC / JACK-IN-THE-HEDGE

Alliaria petiolata

MUSTARD FAMILY Brassicaceae

Description Garlic mustard is a taprooted biennial 0.3–1.2 m/1–4 ft. in height. Its white flowers have four petals and are borne in terminal clusters. The seed pods (siliques) that are produced from these are to 5 cm/2 in. long and upright and contain tiny blackish seeds. The basal leaves are on long stalks (petioles) and are kidney shaped, while the stem leaves are heart shaped and shorter stalked.

Traditional use The leaves, flowers, seeds, and roots are edible, either raw or cooked. The garlic odour and taste from the plant were used to spice up soups, stews, roasts, and fish. The juice from the plants was used externally to treat wounds and ulcers. The leaves were chewed for sore gums and gum ulcers.

Etymology The genus name, *Alliaria*, means "garlic smelling," which it is.

Origin Introduced from Eurasia by the early settlers; one of the first records of it was in 1868 on Long Island, New York.

Season Flowers from April to June.

Reproduction By seed.

Concerns Garlic mustard is extremely invasive—it crowds out native understory plants.

▶ MOUSE-EAR CRESS THALE CRESS / COMMON WALL CRESS

Arabidopsis thaliana
MUSTARD FAMILY Brassicaceae
Syn. *Arabis thaliana, Sisymbrium thaliana*

Description Mouse-ear cress is a taprooted annual to 40 cm/16 in. in height. Its tiny white flowers are borne on slender upright stalks to 40 cm/16 in. in height. The slightly hairy leaves mainly sit in a basal rosette, with a few smaller stem leaves.

Traditional use Mouse-ear cress is one of the most commonly used plants in the laboratory. It's easy to grow, has a short life cycle, is a heavy producer of seeds, and has a comparatively small genome. Its study in the field of genetics has been extremely helpful.

Etymology The genus name, *Arabidopsis*, means "resembles an arabis," while the species and common names commemorate the German botanist Johann Thal (1542–1583).

Origin Mouse-ear cress was introduced from Eurasia.

Season Flowers from March to June.

Reproduction By seed.

Concerns Has not become a major pest. It needs open areas to thrive.

▶ EARLY WINTER CRESS SCURVY GRASS / BARBARA'S HERB / BELLE ISLE CRESS

Barbarea verna
MUSTARD FAMILY Brassicaceae
Syn. *B. praecox*

Description Early winter cress is a taprooted biennial 30–90 cm/1–3 ft. in height. Its bright-yellow flowers are borne on a terminal flower stalk and flower stalks originating in the leaf axils. The pinnately lobed basal leaves are long stalked, while the upper leaves are reduced in size and clasping.

Similar species American winter cress (*B. orthoceras*) is very similar in appearance, but its seed pods (siliques) are shorter: 2.5–5 cm/1–2 in. long, compared with 5–8 cm/ 2–3 in. long on early winter cress.

Traditional use It has been cultivated for centuries as a vegetable. It is usually cooked like spinach. There are sources still selling the seeds.

Etymology The common name cress is very Old English for "to eat" or "to nibble on." The genus name, *Barbarea*, commemorates the fourth-century saint Barbara, probably because early winter cress was eaten at her winter festivals.

Origin Introduced from Eurasia.

Season Flowers from April to June.

Reproduction By seed.

Concerns Competes with cultivated crops for light and nutrients.

▶ WILD TURNIP WINTER RAPE

Brassica napus

MUSTARD FAMILY Brassicaceae

Description Wild turnip is a taprooted annual to 1.8 m/6 ft. in height. The flowers are typical of the mustard family: dull yellow to golden, with four petals and four sepals. The seed pods (siliques) are 5–10 cm/2–4 in. long. The leaves are alternating, heavily divided, and mostly clasping.

Similar species Wild turnip is closely related to field mustard (*B. campestris*), white mustard (*B. hirta*), Indian mustard (*B. juncea*), wild mustard or charlock (*B. kaber*), and black mustard (*B. nigra*).

Traditional use The young leaves, like those of its related species, can be eaten raw in salads or used as potherbs in soups and stews. Dried seeds ground and mixed with vinegar make a mustard paste.

Etymology The genus name, *Brassica*, was Pliny the Elder's name for cabbage-like plants, and the species name, *napus*, was Pliny's name for a turnip.

Origin All six species were introduced from Eurasia.

Season Flowers from April to July.

Reproduction By seed.

Concerns A major competitor with field crops.

▶ SHEPHERD'S PURSE SHEPHERD'S POUCH / PEPPER-AND-SALT / PICKPOCKET

Capsella bursa-pastoris

MUSTARD FAMILY Brassicaceae

Description Shepherd's purse is a taprooted annual 10–50 cm/4–20 in. in height. Its tiny flowers are borne in tight clusters that thin out along the stem as the seeds are produced. The basal leaves are to 12 cm/5 in. long and pinnately lobed; they sit in a rosette. The stem leaves are smaller, sawtoothed, and clasping, with two round lobes at their base. The seed pods (siliques) are to 0.7 cm/0.25 in. long, heart shaped or triangular, and filled with tiny seeds.

Traditional use The plant has a bitter, peppery taste. The young leaves and seeds were used as potherbs. Medicinally, shepherd's purse was one of the most used plants in the mustard family. One of its main uses was to stop hemorrhaging of all kinds.

Etymology The genus name, *Capsella*, means "small box." The species name is derived from the words *bursa*, "purse" and *pastoris*, "shepherd," in reference to the old leather purses shepherds wore on their belts.

Reproduction By seed.

Concerns Competes vigorously with cultivated crops. It is known to carry fungi that attack other members of the mustard family.

▶ HAIRY BITTERCRESS

Cardamine hirsuta

MUSTARD FAMILY Brassicaceae

Description Hairy bittercress is a thinly taprooted annual 5–30 cm/2–12 in. in height. The tiny white flowers are borne in compact racemes that thin out along the stem as the seeds are produced. The upright seed pods (siliques) are to 2.5 cm/1 in. long. The basal rosette of leaves is pinnately divided in two or more pairs of opposite-facing leaflets. The few stem leaves are unstalked and reduced in size (similar species on p. 35).

Traditional use As the common name suggests, the leaves are bitter. However, they were nibbled on and used in soups.

Etymology The genus name, *Cardamine*, was the name Greek botanist Pedanius Dioscorides (AD 40–90) used for cress, and the common name cress means "to eat" or "to nibble on." The species name, *hirsuta*, means "hairy."

Origin Introduced from Eurasia.

Season Flowers in spring and autumn, depending on when the seeds germinate.

Reproduction By seed.

Concerns In moist rich soils, it can form dense colonies, which compete with vegetable crops for nutrients and moisture.

▶ DAME'S ROCKET   DAME'S VIOLET / SWEET ROCKET / PURPLE ROCKET

Hesperis matronalis

MUSTARD FAMILY Brassicaceae

Description Dame's rocket is a taprooted biennial or short-lived herbaceous perennial 0.6–1.2 m/2–4 ft. in height. Its velvet-like flowers may be white, pink, purple, or variegated. The lanceolate leaves can be as long as 20 cm/8 in. However, they are clasping and reduced in size upward.

Traditional use The young leaves' bitter taste did not stop them from being used in salads

Etymology The genus name, *Hesperis*, means "evening," in reference to the flowers becoming far more fragrant in the evening. Long ago, the flowers were a favourite of matrons; hence the species name, *matronalis*. From this expression later came the corrupted dame's violet. In medieval times, the word violet meant "flower."

Origin A garden escapee from Eurasia.

Season Flowers from the end of March to summer.

Reproduction By seed.

Concerns An alternate host of some vegetable viruses.

▶ HONESTY SILVER DOLLAR PLANT / MONEY PLANT

Lunaria annua

MUSTARD FAMILY Brassicaceae

Description Honesty is a taprooted annual or biennial to 60 cm/2 ft. in height. Its showy flowers are to 2.5 cm/1 in. across, have four petals, and are bluish purple, sometimes white. The leaves are 5–10 cm/2–4 in. long, heart shaped, and toothed. The stems and leaf stalks are hairy. The seed pods (siliques) are to 5 cm/2 in. long, green to start, and papery silver when ripe.

Etymology The genus name, *Lunaria*, comes from *luna*, "the moon," in reference to the flat round seed pods. The branches, with dried seed pods, make an attractive winter bouquet.

Reproduction By seed.

Concerns None. Usually an accepted volunteer in the garden.

▶ FIELD PEPPERGRASS FIELD PEPPERWORT / COW CRESS

Lepidium campestre

MUSTARD FAMILY Brassicaceae

Syn. *Neolepia campestre, Thlaspi campestre*

Description Field peppergrass is a short densely hairy annual or biennial to 50 cm/20 in. in height. Its tiny white flowers have yellow stamens and four petals and are borne in long terminal clusters. The seed pods (siliques) are up to 0.6 cm/0.25 in. long and egg shaped, with a notch at the top. The basal leaves are stalked and sit in a rosette. The stem leaves are unstalked, reduced in size, and clasping.

Similar species The seed pods of field pennycress (*Thlaspi arvense*) are similar to those of field peppergrass, except they are two to three times larger.

Traditional use The seeds have a peppery taste. They are a good mustard paste if ground and mixed with vinegar or white wine. The young shoots were used as a substitute for watercress (*Nasturtium officinale*).

Etymology The species name, *campestre*, means "from the pasture."

Origin Introduced from Eurasia.

Season Flowers from May to July.

Reproduction By seed.

Concerns Very competitive with field crops.

▶ WILD RADISH   JOINTED CHARLOCK / WILD RAPE / WILD KALE

Raphanus raphanistrum / Raphanus sativus

MUSTARD FAMILY Brassicaceae

Description Wild radish is a thick taprooted annual or biennial to 90 cm/3 ft. in height. Its showy flowers are usually pale yellow, fading to white, with purple venation. The seed pods (siliques) are to 8 cm/3 in. long, with 4 to 12 seeds. The basal leaves are 10–20 cm/4–8 in. long, pinnately divided, and hairy, with the stem leaves being reduced in size upward.

Similar species Garden radish (*R. sativus*) is very similar to wild radish. The main differences are the flowers and seed pods. Garden radish has seed pods 2.5–5 cm/1–2 in. long, with only one to three seeds.

Traditional use The roots, cleaned but not peeled, can be eaten raw when small or steamed when larger.

Etymology The common name jointed charlock refers to the jointed compartments on the seed pods.

Origin Introduced from Europe. Cultivated radishes were grown by the ancient Egyptians as early as 2700 BC.

Season Flowers from June to October.

Reproduction By seed.

Concerns Hosts mosaic viruses. Seeds contain glucosinolates; avoid eating in large quantities.

▶ HEDGE MUSTARD   SINGER'S PLANT / CRAMBLING ROCKET

Sisymbrium officinale

MUSTARD FAMILY Brassicaceae

Description Hedge mustard is a taprooted annual to 90 cm/3 ft. in height. Its pale-yellow flowers have four petals and are borne in clusters that elongate as the seed is produced. The seed pods (siliques) are to 1.5 cm/0.5 in. long, erect, and held tightly to the stem. The basal leaves are to 20 cm/8 in. long, pinnately divided, hairy, and reduced in size upward.

Similar species Two closely related species are common tumble mustard (*S. altissimum*) and Loesel's tumble mustard (*S. loeselii*). They are called tumble mustards because they break off at the ground when the seeds are ripe and tumble in the wind. (This is how the seeds are dispersed.)

Traditional use The young leaves, picked before the flowers, are good in salads and cooked as potherbs. Infusions of the plant were used to treat throat illnesses. The French called it the singer's plant. It was used to cure the loss of voice, as happened to many singers.

Origin All three species are native to Eurasia.

Season Flowers from April to July.

Reproduction By seed.

Concerns Competes with field crops. It is also known to host mosaic viruses.

▶ PENNYCRESS FIELD PENNYCRESS / MITHRIDATE MUSTARD / STINKWEED

Thlaspi arvense

MUSTARD FAMILY Brassicaceae

Description Pennycress is a taprooted annual to 80 cm/32 in. height. Its tiny white flowers have four petals and are borne in compact terminal racemes that elongate as the seeds are produced. The seed pods (siliques) are 1.3–1.7 cm/0.5–0.7 in. long, roundly heart shaped, and flattened, with a notch at the top. The basal leaves are formed in a rosette. They are larger and more oval than the alternate lanceolate upper leaves.

Traditional use The young shoots and leaves can be eaten raw or cooked; they were typically eaten with other vegetables. In the middle ages, pennycress was used in the complicated mixture mithridate, a mustard thought to be an antidote to poisons.

Etymology The common name pennycress is from the dried seed pods' resemblance to pennies. Crush the leaves of the plant and you will know why it's also called stinkweed.

Origin Native to Asia; introduced from Europe in the early 1700s.

Season Flowers from April to August.

Reproduction By seed.

Concerns A single plant can produce 20,000 seeds.

▶ BUTTERFLY BUSH SUMMER LILAC / ORANGE EYE

Buddleja davidii

FAMILY Buddlejaceae

Description The butterfly bush is a deciduous bush or shrub 2–5 m/6.6–16 ft. in height. Its fragrant flowers are borne in terminal racemes 15–25 cm/6–10 in. long. They range from light to dark purple, with an orange eye. The leaves are 15–25 cm/6–10 in. long, opposite, and lanceolate, with grey woolly hairs beneath.

Etymology As the common name suggests, the fragrant flowers are attractive to butterflies. The genus name, *Buddleja*, commemorates the 17th-century English botanist Adam Buddle. The species name, *davidii*, is for Armand David, the famous collector of Chinese plants.

Origin Native to China, the butterfly bush has jumped the garden fence and can be seen growing alongside most low-level highways.

Season Flowers from July to September.

Reproduction By seed.

Concerns By the ocean, it can form dense colonies and replaces the native flora.

► CREEPING BELLFLOWER PURPLE BELL / GARDEN HAREBELL

Campanula rapunculoides

HAREBELL FAMILY Campanulaceae

Description Creeping bellflower is a perennial to 90 cm/3 ft. in height. Its bell-shaped flowers are 3.5 cm/1.5 in. long, blue to light purple, nodding, and borne in the upper leaf axils. The lower leaves are to 7 cm/3 in. long, alternate, and long stalked. The upper leaves are reduced in size, stalkless, and lanceolate to egg shaped.

Traditional use The roots can be prepared like asparagus, and the leaves can be used in salads. Both are said to be of low quality.

Etymology The genus name, *Campanula*, means "little bell." The species name, *rapunculoides*, means "resembling rapunculus" or "rampion-like," which is diminutive of turnip (*Brassica rapa*), referring to the thick roots.

Origin A garden escapee; native to Eurasia.

Season Flowers from July to September.

Reproduction By seed and creeping roots.

Concerns This plant is best admired in other people's gardens and lawns, as it is very hard to eradicate.

► COMMON HOP EUROPEAN HOP / HOP

Humulus lupulus

HEMP FAMILY Cannabaceae

Description Common hops are herbaceous perennial vines capable of growing over 9 m/ 30 ft. annually. The vines are dioecious—they have male and female flowers on separate plants. Both types of flower arise from the leaf axils. The male flowers are in loose panicles 5–12 cm/2–5 in. long, and the female flowers are greenish yellow and cone-like, with overlapping bracts. The leaves are to 10 cm/4 in. long, opposite, lobed, and heart shaped.

Traditional use The young shoots can be prepared like asparagus. The fruit of the vines has been use in breweries since the 14th century. Many a fine ale and beer have been made from them. Over the centuries, common hop has been used to treat heart disease, nervous disorders, toothaches, earaches, and stomach and digestion problems.

Etymology The genus name, *Humulus*, is thought to be derived from *humus*, the rich soil the vine likes to grow in. The common name hop is from the Ancient Anglo-Saxon word *hoppan* ("climbing").

Origin Introduced from Europe.

Season The hops ripen from August to September.

Reproduction By seed.

Concerns When common hops get established, the aggressive vines overshadow the native flora.

► ROSE CAMPION

Lychnis coronaria

PINK FAMILY Caryophyllaceae

Description Rose campion is a woolly grey herbaceous perennial to 90 cm/3 ft. in height. Its showy red flowers are to 2.5 cm/1 in. across, have heart-shaped petals, and are borne singly at the end of the branched stems. The leaves are to 10 cm/4 in. long, woolly, grey, opposite, lanceolate, and often overlapping up the stem.

Etymology The genus name, *Lychnis*, is Greek for "lamp," referring to the flame-coloured flowers or that the leaves were used as wicks in lamps. The species name, *coronaria*, means "garlanding" or "forming a crown." Corn cockle (*Agrostemma githago*) is very similar in appearance to rose campion, with the exception that crown cockles' green sepals extend past the red petals and it is an annual.

Origin Introduced from Europe as a garden ornamental.

Season Flowers throughout the summer.

Reproduction By seed.

Concerns Can become a pest in cultivated gardens.

► SWEET WILLIAM CATCHFLY

Silene armeria

PINK FAMILY Caryophyllaceae

Syn. *S. glauca*

Description Sweet William catchfly is a taprooted annual with slightly sticky stems that can grow to 75 cm/30 in. in height. Its flowers are to 2.5 cm/1 in. across, pink to lavender, five petalled, and borne in flat-topped clusters. The leaves are to 5 cm/2 in. long, hairless (glabrous), spoon shaped, and mostly clasping.

Etymology The common name catchfly is from the stem exuding a sticky sap that traps small insects. The species name, *armeria*, is Ancient Latin for a species of *Dianthus*, which means "flower of the gods."

Origin Introduced from Europe as a garden ornamental.

Season Flowers from May to September.

Reproduction By seed.

Concerns Sweet William catchfly can be seen taking over low-elevation meadows and forest edges. In moist semi-shaded areas, it is overshadowing the smaller native flora.

▶ WHITE COCKLE   WHITE CAMPION / EVENING CAMPION / EVENING LYCHNIS

Silene latifolia ssp. *alba*

PINK FAMILY Caryophyllaceae

Syn. *Lychnis alba, S. alba, Melandrium album, S. pratensis*

Description White cockle is a stoutly taprooted annual, biennial, or short-lived perennial to 90 cm/3 ft. in height. Its fragrant white flowers are to 2.5 cm/1 in. across and dioecious (male and female flowers are on separate plants). The flowers open in the early evening and close at dawn. Both male and female flowers have a much-inflated calyx supporting the flower. The lower leaves are to 10 cm/4 in. long, lanceolate, opposite, and stalked. The upper leaves are reduced in size and stalkless.

Etymology The common name campion is from the garlands made from the flowers and placed on the heads of sporting "champions." White cockle and red campion (*S. dioica*) are very similar. When they are grown together, pink hybrids are known to occur.

Origin Introduced from Eurasia in the 1800s as a garden ornamental.

Season Flowers from May to September.

Reproduction By seed.

Concerns Competes with field crops for nutrients and light, and is also a host of mosaic viruses.

▶ CORN SPURRY   SPURRY / SANDWEED / PICKPURSE / STICKWORT / DEVIL'S GUTS

Spergula arvensis

PINK FAMILY Caryophyllaceae

Description Corn spurry is a small, taprooted annual 10–60 cm/4–24 in. long/tall. Its tiny white flowers have five petals and are borne in loose terminal clusters that droop as the seeds ripen. When the drooping seed capsules mature, the tips open, allowing the wind to scatter the seeds. A large plant can produce over 10,000 seeds. The needle-like leaves are to 5 cm/2 in. long, fleshy, and attached to the stem nodes in whorls of 6 to 10.

Etymology The genus name, *Spergula*, is derived from the Latin word *spargo*, "scatterer," in reference to the scattering of the seeds. The species name, *arvensis*, means "of the fields" or "of plowed fields," where this little plant is most at home.

Origin Corn spurry was introduced to North America from Europe as a forage crop.

Season Plants germinate in March and flower from May to the first frost.

Reproduction By seed.

Concerns Can become very invasive in lower-growing grain and vegetable fields and is a host to some mosaic viruses.

COMMON CHICKWEED MISCHIEVOUS JACK

Stellaria media

PINK FAMILY Caryophyllaceae

Description Common chickweed is a shade-tolerant, mat-forming annual to 80 cm/32 in. across. Its star-like flowers are to 0.6 cm/0.25 in. across, have five deeply notched petals, and are borne in both the leaf axils and in terminal clusters. The leaves are to 2.5 cm/1 in. long, opposite, and sharply egg shaped. The stems have a single line of hairs running up one side.

Traditional use The leaves can be added to salads or used as potherbs. The seeds can be dried, ground, and mixed with flour. Chickweed has been used for hundreds of years to treat inflammation, skin rashes, insect bites, and general itchiness.

Etymology The genus name, *Stellaria*, refers to the star-like flowers. The common name refers to the leaves and seeds being liked by most birds, especially chickens.

Origin Introduced from Eurasia.

Season Chickweed is in flower year-round, though it is most abundant in the cooler and wetter months of September to April.

Reproduction By seed and rooting at the stem nodes. A single plant can produce up to 15,000 seeds.

Concerns Chickweed's shade tolerance and ability to produce so many seeds per growing season have made it one of agriculture's most common weeds.

RUSSIAN ORACHE TWOSCALE SALTBUSH

Atriplex micrantha

GOOSEFOOT FAMILY Chenopodiaceae

Syn. *A. heterosperma*

Description Russian orache is a fleshy sprawling annual to 1.5 m/5 ft. in height. Its inconspicuous flowers are greenish and borne both in the leaf axils and in terminal spikes. The arrow-shaped leaves are to 5 cm/2 in. long, with the lower leaves opposite and the upper alternating. As with most oraches, the surfaces of the young leaves have a mealy white powder that disappears as they mature. The tiny seeds are borne in bumpy triangular bracts.

Etymology The species name, *micrantha*, means "small flowered." Garden orache, or French spinach (*A. hortensis*), has the largest leaves of the oraches and has long been used as a spinach substitute in Europe.

Origin Introduced from Eurasia.

Season Flowers from July to September.

Reproduction By seed.

Concerns Some species of *Atriplex* are alternate hosts for mosaic viruses.

► LAMB'S QUARTER
PIGWEED / WHITE GOOSEFOOT / WILD SPINACH

Chenopodium album
GOOSEFOOT FAMILY Chenopodiaceae
Syn. *C. lanceolatum, C. dacoticum*

Description Lamb's quarter is a taprooted annual 60–90 cm/2–3 ft. in height. Its tiny flowers are greenish grey and borne in dense clusters along the branch tips and leaf axils. The leaves are to 10 cm/4 in. long, fleshy, and shaped like lobed triangles or diamonds.

Traditional use The young leaves can be used in salads or cooked as spinach. It is not advisable to eat the leaves in large quantities or over long periods of time, as they contain oxalate salts.

Etymology The genus name, *Chenopodium*, is Greek for "goose foot," though the leaf does not look much like a goose's foot. The species name, *album*, refers to the white mealy or powdery scales on the leaves and stems. The common name lamb's quarter is from the plant's flowering on August 1, the first day of the Lammas Day festival.

Origin Introduced from Europe. In 1965, the seeds of lamb's quarters were discovered in a Danish bog and dated back to AD 200. There has been no evolutionary change in almost 2,000 years.

Season Flowers from May to October.

Reproduction By seed.

Concerns Very aggressive competitor with food crops.

► COMMON ORACHE
SPEARSCALE / SPREADING ORACHE / WILD ARRACH / SPEAR SALTBUSH

Atriplex patula
GOOSEFOOT FAMILY Chenopodiaceae

Description Common orache is a fleshy taprooted annual to 90 cm/3 ft. high. Its tiny flowers are greenish and borne both in the leaf axils and in dense terminal spikes. The arrow-shaped lower leaves are opposite, while the upper leaves are alternating. The surfaces of the young leaves often have a mealy white power that disappears as the leaves mature. The seeds are borne in conspicuous bumpy to smooth triangular bracts.

Traditional use The young leaves can be sliced and added to salads or cooked like spinach. The seeds can be dried, ground, and mixed with flour. Tinctures made from the seeds were used to treat headaches, pain, and early rheumatism.

Etymology The species name, *patula*, means "spreading," referring to the plant's sometimes reclining character. The common name orache is from *aurago*, "golden"; the seeds were mixed with wine and used to treat yellow jaundice.

Origin Common orache most likely originated in Eurasia.

Season Flowers from July to September.

Reproduction By seed.

Concerns Very few. Common orache is mainly found near the ocean, just above the high-tide line, where Canada geese forage on it.

WILD PROSO MILLET
MILLET / BROOM CORN MILLET / PANIC MILLET / PROSO MILLET

Panicum miliaceum

GRASS FAMILY Poaceae

Description Wild proso millet is a fibrous-rooted annual grass that grows to 30 cm/ 12 in. in soils and to 1.2–1.8 m/4–6 ft. in irrigated sites. Its flowers are in branched panicles 10–30 cm/4–12 in. long, with the lower florets being sterile and the upper fertile. The leaves are to 30 cm/12 in. long, 2.5 cm/1 in. wide at the base, and smooth to sparsely hairy. The seeds are smooth and shiny dark brown to black.

Traditional use It is extensively grown in Europe for cereals, flours, and poultry feed. In North America, it is mainly grown for birdseed. This may explain why it is often seen growing around duck ponds and bird feeders. Millet is thought to be very first of the cultivated grains.

Origin Introduced from Eurasia as a grain and forage crop.

Season Flowers from July to September, with the seeds maturing from August to October.

Reproduction By seed.

Concerns If growing in corn or bean fields, it will greatly reduce harvest production. As long as millet is used in commercial birdseed mixes, it will continuously be reintroduced in urban areas.

FIELD BINDWEED
SMALL-FLOWERED MORNING GLORY / JACK-RUN-IN-THE-COUNTRY / CORNBIND

Convolvulus arvensis

MORNING GLORY FAMILY Convolvulaceae

Description Field bindweed is a rhizomatous herbaceous perennial vine that can sprawl or climb to 3 m/10 ft. in length. Its trumpet-shaped flowers are to 3 cm/1.5 in. across, white to pink, and borne in clusters of one to four, arising from the leaf axils. The seeds are dull brown, three sided, and borne singly in conical capsules. The leaves are to 7 cm/3 in. long, alternating, long stalked and somewhat arrow shaped.

Traditional use In former times, a laxative was made from steeping the leaves, but all parts of the plant should be considered poisonous. The deleaved vines were once used as baler's twine.

Etymology The genus name, *Convolvulus*, is from the Latin word *convolvere*, "to entwine." The species name, *arvensis*, means "of cultivated fields," where this plant is most menacing.

Origin Introduced from Eurasia.

Season Flowers from May to October.

Reproduction By seed and rhizome.

Concerns Field bindweed is considered to be in the top 10 of the world's worst weeds. It is a carrier of the tobacco mosaic virus, so it should not be grown near any members of the potato family.

► HEDGE BINDWEED
MORNING GLORY / GREATER BINDWEED / BEARBIND / OLD MAN'S NIGHT CAP

Convolvulus sepium

MORNING GLORY FAMILY Convolvulaceae

Syn. *Calystegia sepium*

Description Hedge bindweed is a rhizomatous herbaceous perennial vine that can sprawl or climb to 3 m/10 ft. in height. Its large trumpet-shaped flowers are to 8 cm/3 in. long and pale pink with white stripes; they arise on long stalks from the leaf axils. The leaves are to 15 cm/6 in. long, alternating, sharp, pointed, and arrow shaped. Beneath the flowers are two large heart-shaped green bracts that appear to be holding the flower upright. The two bracts are good for distinguishing hedge bindweed flowers from field bindweeds, which have smaller bracts.

Traditional use All parts of the plant should be considered poisonous. Hedge bindweed has been used for hundreds of years as a laxative and as a remedy for jaundice. Modern herbal stores still sell morning glory as a laxative.

Etymology The species name, *sepium*, is from the Latin word *sepes*, "hedge," referring to where it grows. The common name bearbind refers to how strongly it binds plants together.

Origin Introduced from Eurasia.

Season Flowers from May to October.

Reproduction By seed and rhizome.

Concerns Overshadows and competes for moisture and nutrients with the native flora crops and vines.

► TEASEL
TEAZLE / VENUS'S BASIN / CARD THISTLE / BRUSHES AND COMBS

Dipsacus sylvestris

TEASEL FAMILY Dipsacaceae

Description Teasel is a prickly biennial to 1.8 m/5 ft. in height. Its purplish flowers are borne on cylindrical flower heads that are surrounded by long prickly bracts. The lower leaves are to 30 cm/1 ft. long, opposite, and lance shaped, with sharp prickles running down the midrib. A close inspection will reveal water collected where the base of the large leaves fuse together.

Traditional use An ointment made from the roots was said to be useful in removing warts and cankers, as was the water collected from the leaf bases.

Etymology The common name teasel is centuries old and comes from using the dried flower heads to raise (tease) the nap on cloth. The genus name, *Dipsacus*, is derived from the Greek word *dipsa*, meaning "thirsty," in reference to the water collected in the leaf bases.

Origin Introduced from Europe.

Season Flowers from July to September.

Reproduction By seed. In its first year, teasel sits as a leafy rosette. The next year, it sends up its armed stems and flowers.

Concerns Mainly seen as a roadside plant; however, it has been reported invading field crops.

▶ LEAFY SPURGE WOLF'S MILK

Euphorbia esula
SPURGE FAMILY Euphorbiaceae
Syn. *Euphorbia virgata*

Description Leafy spurge is a rhizomatous herbaceous perennial to 90 cm/3 ft. in height. Its flowers are yellowish green and borne in rounded terminal clusters. The tiny brown seeds are borne in exploding capsules that are capable of sending the seeds up to 4 m/13 ft. away. The leaves are to 6 cm/2.5 in. long, lanceolate, and mostly alternating.

Similar species Other introduced spurges to the Pacific Northwest are cypress spurge (*E. cyparissias*), petty spurge (*E. peplus*), thyme-leaved spurge (*E. serpyllifolia*), and ridge-seed spurge (*E. glyptosperma*).

Traditional use Concoctions of leafy spurge were used to relieve diarrhea, dysentery, and cholera.

Etymology The genus name, *Euphorbia*, commemorates Euphorbus, physician to the king of Mauritania, who used the milky latex medicinally.

Origin Introduced from Eurasia to North America in the 18th century.

Season Flowers from May to July.

Reproduction By seed and deeply rooted rhizomes.

Concerns The milky latex from *Euphorbia*s can cause skin irritations and blistering in humans—gloves are recommended when handling.

▶ CROWN VETCH

Coronilla varia
PEA FAMILY Fabaceae
Syn. *Securigera varia*

Description Crown vetch is a rhizomatous herbaceous perennial capable of sprawling or climbing to over 90 cm/3 ft. Its umbels (flower heads) consist of 10 to 20 pea-like flowers that are supported by a long stalk. The individual flowers are to 1.2 cm/ 0.5 in. long and range from white to pink to mauve. The seed pods are to 5 cm/ 2 in. long, curved, and chambered for each of the 3 to 10 seeds. The leaves are alternating and pinnately compounded into 11 to 19 leaflets.

Traditional use The seeds are thought to be toxic to humans. However, the plants are good forage for livestock.

Etymology The genus name, *Coronilla*, is Latin for "little crown," in reference to the attractive umbels. The species name, *varia*, refers to the different-coloured flowers.

Origin Crown vetch is an escaped cover or forage plant from Eurasia.

Season Flowers from May to September.

Reproduction By seed and rhizome.

Concerns A serious threat to the native vegetation. The rhizomes are so prolific that it is used for erosion control on steep banks and slopes. Once established, crown vetch is very hard to eradicate. It's even fire resistant—the rhizomes are protected under the ground.

BROAD-LEAVED PEAVINE

EVERLASTING PEA / PERENNIAL SWEET PEA

Lathyrus latifolius

PEA FAMILY Fabaceae

Description Broad-leaved peavine is a herbaceous perennial from rhizomes capable of climbing to 1.8 m/6 ft. Its pea-like pink flowers are scentless and borne in terminal clusters on stalks arising from the leaf axils. The seed pods are to 10 cm/4 in. long and smooth and house 10 to 25 seeds. The bluish-green leaves are to 15 cm/6 in. long, 5 cm/2 in. wide, and pinnately compounded with two leaflets. At the top of their tips, the leaves are branched, curling tendrils by which the plant climbs.

Traditional use All parts of the plant are considered poisonous, though the seeds were used in medicine.

Etymology The genus name, *Lathyrus*, is from the ancient Greek word *thouros*, "excitable." The species name, *latifolius*, refers to the broad leaves.

Origin Introduced from Europe as a garden ornamental.

Season Flowers from May to October.

Reproduction By seed and rhizome.

Concerns Not too much of a problem except in small gardens, where it can take over.

BIRD'S-FOOT TREFOIL

Lotus corniculatus

PEA FAMILY Fabaceae

Description Bird's-foot trefoil is a sprawling herbaceous perennial to 60 cm/24 in. long. Its bright-yellow flowers are to 1 cm/0.5 in. long and are often red tinged. They are borne in rounded umbels with two to eight flowers on stalks to 8 cm/3 in. high. The brown seed pods are to 2.5 cm/1 in. long and radiate like spokes from the stem ends. The leaves are stalkless and pinnately compounded into five leaflets.

Traditional use In the United Kingdom, a solution made from the plant was used for an eye wash.

Etymology The species name, *corniculatus*, means "horned," in reference to the spiked seed pods. The common name bird's-foot trefoil refers to the similarity of the seed pods to a bird's foot.

Origin Bird's-foot trefoil is an escaped forage plant from Eurasia.

Season Flowers from July to September.

Reproduction By seed and rooting at the nodes.

Concerns Not much of a problem yet; it is mainly seen along roadsides and in waste areas.

► ALFALFA
LUCERNE / BUFFALO HERB /
PURPLE MEDIC / MU-SU / JATT / YONCA

Medicago sativa

PEA FAMILY Fabaceae

Description Alfalfa is a deeply taprooted herbaceous perennial to 90 cm/3 ft. in height. Its flowers are bluish purple and borne in terminal clusters arising from the leaf axils. The seed pods are brown and spirally coiled at maturity. The leaves are alternating, hairy, and pinnately compounded into three leaflets.

Traditional use Alfalfa sprouts have in recent times become popular in salads and sandwiches. The Chinese have been using alfalfa since the sixth century to treat kidney stones and to reduce fluid retention and swelling. Early American settlers used it to treat scurvy, cancer, boils, bedsores, and urinary and bowel problems.

Etymology The genus name, *Medicago*, refers to Media, Ancient Persia, where the plant is thought to have first grown. The common name alfalfa is derived from the Arabic word *alfalfas*, which means "father of all foods."

Origin Introduced from Eurasia as a forage crop.

Season Flowers from May to September.

Reproduction By seed.

Concerns Mainly a roadside weed.

► WHITE SWEET CLOVER
WHITE MELILOT / HONEY
LOTUS / KING'S CLOVER /
HONEY CLOVER

Melilotus alba

PEA FAMILY Fabaceae

Description White sweet clover is a taprooted annual or biennial to 1.8 m/6 ft. in height. Its fragrant white flowers are borne in elongated racemes 5–15 cm/2–6 in. long that arise from the leaf axils. The leaves are alternating, veined, and typically clover-like, with three leaflets.

Similar species Yellow sweet clover (*M. officinalis*) (bottom photo) is very similar, except for its yellow flowers. Both plants are sweet smelling, especially when drying. The fragrance is from the chemical coumarin, which is also present in vanilla, fresh-cut hay, and woodruff.

Traditional use Plaster made from the plants was used to treat tumours and swelled joints. It was also used as an emollient and digestive. The flowers were used in a salve for skin sores.

Etymology The genus name, *Melilotus*, means "honey lotus," in reference to the amount of honey produced by the flowers.

Origin Introduced from Eurasia in the 1600s as forage crops and bee plants.

Season Flowers from May to August.

Reproduction By seed. Both sweet clovers can produce up to 100,000 seeds per plant.

Concerns If grown unnoticed, their abundant seeds can contaminate grain and flour crops.

▶ SPANISH BROOM   WEAVER'S BROOM

Spartium junceum
PEA FAMILY Fabaceae

Description Spanish broom is a deciduous shrub 2–4 m/6.6–13 ft. tall. The pea-like yellow flowers, to 2 cm/1 in. across, display themselves from June to July. By August, the flowers have morphed into black pods (legumes) to 10 cm/4 in. long. The lanceolate leaves fall away by summer, allowing the new shoots to act like leaves, undergoing photosynthesis and conserving water.

Traditional use Used medicinally, but the entire plant is considered poisonous.

Etymology The genus name, *Spartium*, is from *sparton*, a kind of grass used for weaving and cordage. The species name, *junceum*, means "rush-like," referring to the shoots. The shoots and stems have been used to make cloth, and the flowers to make a yellow dye.

Origin Introduced from the Mediterranean as an ornamental.

Season Flowers in August.

Reproduction By seed, which the plant is very prolific at.

Concerns Spanish broom is regarded as a noxious weed in California and in many Central American and South American countries.

▶ RED CLOVER   PURPLE CLOVER / MEADOW HONEYSUCKLE

Trifolium pratense
PEA FAMILY Fabaceae

Description Red clover is a well-recognized herbaceous perennial to 60 cm/24 in. in height. Its pink to red flower heads are to 2.5 cm/1 in. across, fragrant, and composed of 50 to 200 pea-like florets. The florets open from the bottom of the head and progressively upward. The alternating leaves are pinnately divided into three leaflets (or, rarely, four), with some of the leaflets having inverted V-shaped stripes known as chevrons.

Similar species White clover (*T. repens*) has smaller flowers and smaller, rounder leaflets.

Traditional use Clover leaves can be eaten raw in moderation. They are better suited as potherbs. The dried flowers make a pleasant tea that may treat bronchial problems and whooping cough.

Etymology The common name clover is derived from the Latin word *cava*, meaning "club," as in the "clover club" in playing cards and the three-pronged club used in combat by Hercules. The species name translates to "three-leaved plant from the meadows."

Origin Introduced from Eurasia as a forage crop.

Season Flowers from May to November.

Reproduction Red clover by seed; white clover by seed and rooting at the nodes.

Concerns White clover is very invasive in lawns. Both clovers host mosaic viruses.

LITTLE HOP CLOVER

Trifolium dubium

PEA FAMILY Fabaceae

Syn. *T. minus, T. filiforme*

SUCKLING CLOVER /
SHAMROCK / YELLOW CLOVER /
LESSER YELLOW TREFOIL

Description Little hop clover is a mat-forming annual 15–50 cm/6–20 in. long. Its rounded flower heads have up to 20 lemon-yellow florets. As the flower heads mature, they turn brown and produce small pods bearing one seed. The leaves are to 1 cm/0.5 in. long, finely toothed on the upper half, and trifoliate (they have three leaflets).

Similar species Black medick (*Medicago lupulina*) is similar looking, with the exception that its leaves are pointed and its black seed pods are coiled.

Traditional use The young, tender tips can be eaten by themselves or added to a salad.

Etymology Little hop clover is often considered the original shamrock used by St. Patrick; hence the common name shamrock. The species name, *dubium*, means "doubtful," referring to the uncertainty of its being an independent species. The common name little hop refers to the flower heads' resemblance to the cones of the hop plant.

Origin Introduced from Europe as a forage crop and soil conditioner.

Season The seeds germinate from January to February and flower as early as April. The flowers seem to disappear in the summer heat and reappear with the autumn rains.

Reproduction By seed.

Concerns Very hard to eradicate from lawns.

CRIMSON CLOVER ITALIAN CLOVER / LONG-HEADED CLOVER

Trifolium incarnatum

PEA FAMILY Fabaceae

Description Crimson clover is a taprooted annual 20–60 cm/8–24 in. in height. Its attractive crimson flowers are borne in dense terminal heads to 8 cm/3 in. long. The leaves are typical of clover: strongly veined and palmately compounded into three leaflets.

Etymology The species name, *incarnatum*, means "flesh coloured," referring to the crimson flowers.

Origin Crimson clover was brought over from Europe for cattle fodder and as a soil improver (for nitrogen fixing).

Season Flowers from April to June.

Reproduction By seed.

Concerns A very hardy annual that can displace the surrounding native flora. Mainly seen around farmland.

▶ GORSE FURZE / FIREWEED / PRICKLY BROOM

Ulex europaeus

PEA FAMILY Fabaceae

Syn. *Genista spinosa*

Description Gorse is a well-armed deciduous shrub 0.9–3 m/3–10 ft. in height. Its scented flowers are to 2.5 cm/1 in. long, pea-like, and bright yellow, with occasional purple tints. With help from the heat of the sun, the seeds are audibly ejected from the 2.5 cm/1 in. long pods. The alternating leaves have three leaflets that terminate in stiff grooved spines.

Traditional use An infusion of the flowers was used to treat scarlet fever in children. Ulexine, an alkaloid from the plant, is purgative and is used medicinally. Gorse is also known as a living fence; farmers planted impenetrable hedges to keep sheep and cattle confined.

Etymology The common name gorse is from the Anglo-Saxon word *gorst*, meaning "waste," in reference to the wastelands in which it can grow.

Origin A native to Europe; introduced from Ireland into Oregon in the 1890s as a garden ornamental.

Season Flowers mainly from February to July; however, some bushes can be seen in blossom year-round.

Reproduction By seed; however, it is known to spread vegetatively and to sprout back from a burnt or cut stump.

Concerns Competes with native flora. The high concentration of oils in the branches also make it a fire hazard.

▶ TUFTED VETCH COW VETCH / BIRD VETCH / STRANGLE TARE

Vicia cracca

PEA FAMILY Fabaceae

Description Tufted vetch is a herbaceous perennial vine that can climb or sprawl to over 1.8 m/6 ft. in length. Its pea-like flowers are to 1 cm/0.5 in. long, bluish purple, and borne in one-sided terminal racemes of 20 to 80. The seed pods are to 2.5 cm/ 1 in. long and smooth, with four to eight seeds. The leaves are pinnately compounded into 8 to 12 pairs of leaflets and terminated with grasping tendrils.

Traditional use Bees make an excellent honey from the flowers, but the seeds should be considered poisonous to both humans and livestock.

Etymology The genus name, *Vicia*, is from the Latin word *vincio*, meaning "to bind together," referring to the stems and tendrils twining to other plants and grasses. The species name, *cracca*, is Ancient Greek for "vetch."

Origin Introduced from Eurasia.

Season Flowers from May to November.

Reproduction By seed and spreading underground rootstocks.

Concerns The seeds can cause poisoning in livestock.

▶ TINY VETCH HAIRY VETCH / HAIRY TARE

Vicia hirsuta

PEA FAMILY Fabaceae

Description Tiny vetch is a taprooted annual vine that can climb or trail to 70 cm/30 in. in length. Its tiny flowers are white to very pale blue and borne three to eight in short-stalked racemes. The seed pods are to 1 cm/0.5 in. long and hairy, with two or three seeds. The alternating leaves are pinnately compounded into six to nine pairs of leaflets and terminated with branched tendrils.

Traditional use The seeds should be considered poisonous to humans.

Etymology The species name, *hirsuta*, means "hairy," referring to the hairy seed pods. The common name hairy tare refers again to the seed pods, and tare means "weed."

Origin Introduced from Eurasia.

Season Flowering starts at the beginning of May and continues through the summer.

Reproduction By seed.

Concerns If it is growing in the garden, children should be warned about possible poisoning from the seeds.

▶ COMMON VETCH

Vicia sativa

PEA FAMILY Fabaceae

Syn. *V. angustifolia, V. sativa* ssp. *nigra*

Description Common vetch is a herbaceous perennial vine that can climb or weakly support itself to 90 cm/3 ft. in height. Its sweet pea–like flowers are to 2.5 cm/1 in. long, light to dark purple, and usually borne in pairs originating from the leaf axils. The seed pods can grow to almost 7 cm/3 in. long and contain 4 to 12 seeds. The alternating leaves are pinnately compounded into four to eight pairs of leaflets and terminated with a branching tendril. Each leaflet is slightly notched and tipped with a slender bristle.

Traditional use The leaves, pods, and seeds can be eaten raw or used for potherbs.

Etymology Common vetch has been cultivated for centuries; hence the species name, *sativa*, meaning "cultivated" or "sown." It is a close relative of the fava bean, or broad bean, *V. faba*.

Origin Introduced from Europe as a forage crop and cover crop and for use in hay making and green manure.

Season Flowers from April to August.

Reproduction By seed.

Concerns Very little. It is edible and supplies the ground with nitrogen. Its only major flaw is that it could be confused with non-edible vetches.

▶ COMMON STORK'S BILL HERON'S BILL / RED-STEM FILAREE

Erodium cicutarium

GERANIUM FAMILY Geraniaceae

Description Common stork's bill is a reddish branched annual or winter biennial 5–25 cm/2–10 in. in height. Its pink to lavender flowers are to 1 cm/0.5 in. across, have five petals, and are borne in terminal umbrella-like clusters. The leaves are stiffly hairy and pinnately compounded so fine that the leaflets appear fern-like. True geranium leaves are palmately compounded.

Traditional use The young leaves can be eaten in salads or used as a potherb.

Etymology The shape of the mature seed pods gives the plant its common name stork's bill. The genus name, *Erodium*, is from the Greek word *erodios*, meaning "heron." This plant's name should be common heron's bill. The species name, *cicutarium*, means "resembling *cicuta*," or water hemlock, because the leaves of both plants are similar.

Origin Originally from the Mediterranean and introduced from Europe, most likely in a contaminated alfalfa bale.

Reproduction By seed. When the fruit ripen, they split apart into five pointed segments. As each segment dries, it twists like a corkscrew but straightens again when wet. This pushing and straightening actually pushes the seed into the ground.

Concerns When fields are heavily infested, common stork's bill will compete for moisture and nutrients.

▶ CUT-LEAVED GERANIUM CUT-LEAVED CRANE'S BILL

Geranium dissectum

GERANIUM FAMILY Geraniaceae

Description Cut-leaved geranium is a taprooted annual 15–60 cm/6–24 in. in height. Its flowers are to 0.5 cm/0.3 in. across, pink to purple, and usually borne in pairs on long stalks. The fruit capsules are to 2 cm/0.75 in. long, five parted, and hairy. The leaves are to 5 cm/2 in. across, opposite, and palmately dissected into five segments.

Traditional use The roots were cooked and used as famine food. An infusion made from the leaves and roots was used to treat diarrhea in children.

Etymology The genus name, *Geranium*, means "a crane," an allusion to the pointed beaks of the fruit capsules. A soft-brown dye can be obtained from steeping the dry flowers.

Origin Introduced from Eurasia.

Season Flowers from May to September.

Reproduction By seed.

Concerns Can become a pest in the garden.

▶ COMMON FUMITORY EARTH SMOKE / DRUG FUMITORY

Fumaria officinalis

FUMITORY FAMILY Fumariaceae

Description Common fumitory is a taprooted weak-growing annual to 50 cm/18 in. in height. Its unique flowers are to 1 cm/0.5 in. long, borne in axillary racemes, and pink purple with a darker-purple tip. The leaves are alternating and pinnately compound into many small fern-like leaflets.

Traditional use Common fumitory was used as a blood cleanser and to treat dropsy (edema), scurvy, gout, jaundice, and rheumatism. It was even smoked to treat mental disorders.

Etymology The genus name, *Fumaria*, is from the Latin word *fumus*, meaning "smoke." Legend has it that *Fumaria* did not germinate by seed but was created by smoke arising from the earth. In ancient times, it was believed that the smoke from the burning plant had the power to drive off evil spirits.

Origin Introduced from Eurasia as a garden ornamental.

Season Flowers from April to July.

Reproduction By seed.

Concerns Has not become a major problem yet.

▶ DOVEFOOT GERANIUM DOVEFOOT CRANE'S BILL / LAWN GERANIUM

Geranium molle

GERANIUM FAMILY Geraniaceae

Description Dovefoot geranium is an attractive taprooted annual 10–40 cm/4–16 in. in height. Its pink flowers are usually borne in pairs on long stiffly hairy stalks. The fruit capsules are to 0.7 cm/0.25 in. long and five parted. The basal leaves are kidney shaped and palmately divided into five to seven lobes, which are supported by long hairy stalks.

Traditional use True geraniums have a high tannin content in their roots and leaves. For this reason, they have been used medicinally in Europe for centuries to treat diarrhea, gum and mouth diseases, cholera, and cancer.

Etymology Someone must have been infatuated with birds when they named this plant. The genus name, *Geranium*, means "a crane," and the common name dovefoot refers to the shape of the leaves.

Origin Introduced from Eurasia.

Season Flowers from May to September.

Reproduction By seed.

Concerns Very hard to eradicate from lawns. If it is regularly mowed, it will flower at 2.5 cm/1 in. height.

▶ HERB-ROBERT

Geranium robertianum

GERANIUM FAMILY Geraniaceae

Description Herb-robert is a taprooted woodland annual 10–60 cm/4–24 in. in height. Its flowers are to 1 cm/0.5 in. across, pink to purplish, and usually borne in clusters of two. The fruit capsules are to 2.5 cm/1 in. long, five parted, and slightly hairy. The leaves are palmately divided into three to five sections, and these are then divided again.

Traditional use Modern herbal stores carry geranium oil and claim it calms the nervous system and lessens tension, pain, and inflammation. It is also considered an astringent.

Etymology Of the many stories about how this plant received its common name, my favourite is that it is associated with Robin Hood and Robin Goodfellow. (Robin is a derivation of Robert.)

Origin Introduced from Eurasia.

Season Flowers mainly from May to October but can flower year-round in protected spots.

Reproduction By seed.

Concerns Herb-robert does so well in our forests that it is overshadowing a lot of the low-growing native flora.

▶ PURPLE TANSY   FIDDLENECK / LACY SCORPIONWEED / LACY PHACELIA / BEE FOOD

Phacelia tanacetifolia

WATERLEAF FAMILY Hydrophyllaceae

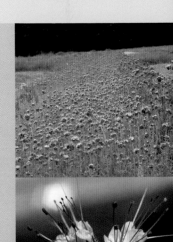

Description Purple tansy is an attractive annual 30–60 cm/12–24 in. in height. Its flowers are mauve to blue, with elongated stamens projecting past the petals. As the flower clusters mature, they curl much like a scorpion; hence the name scorpionweed. The leaves are to 20 cm/8 in. long and pinnately divided so finely they resemble ferns.

Traditional use In Europe, it is used as a green-manure crop and for honey production. It is listed as one of the top 20 honey-producing plants for honeybees.

Etymology The genus name, *Phacelia*, is from the Greek word *phakelos*, "bundle," referring to the clustered flowers. The common name purple tansy and the species name, *tanacetifolia*, both refer to the leaves' resemblance to common tansy's.

Origin Purple tansy is native to Arizona, California, Nevada, and Mexico.

Season Flowers from April to July.

Reproduction By seed.

Concerns Can become a problem in cultivated crops.

ST. JOHN'S WORT

Hypericum perforatum

ST. JOHN'S WORT FAMILY Hypericaceae

Description St. John's wort is a branched herbaceous perennial to over 90 cm/3 ft. in height. Its bright-yellow flowers are to 2.5 cm/1 in. across, five petalled, and borne in flat-topped clusters. Each of the petals is margined with purple dots and finely jagged. The seed capsules are to 0.8 cm/0.3 in. long, three chambered, and many seeded. The leaves are to 2.5 cm/1 in. long, opposite, lance oval shaped, and spotted with transparent dots.

Traditional use Use of St. John's wort in medicine dates back to early Greek and Roman times. Back then, it was used as a diuretic and to treat wounds and fevers. Over time, it has also been used to treat stomach ulcers, nervous disorders, depression, and anxiety.

Etymology The common name commemorates St. John the Baptist. It was thought that the bloody spots on the leaves appeared on August 29, the anniversary of his beheading. The genus name, *Hypericum*, is from the Greek words *hyper* ("above") and *eikon* ("picture"). Branches were placed above and hung in windows to keep evil spirits away.

Origin Native to Eurasia.

Season Flowers from June to October.

Reproduction By seeds and spreading rhizomes.

Concerns The aggressive way this plant can reproduce has made it one of the most noxious weeds in the Pacific Northwest.

YELLOW FLAG

WATER IRIS / YELLOW IRIS / SEGG / SHEGGS / DAGGER / JACOB'S SWORD

Iris pseudacorus

IRIS FAMILY Iridaceae

Syn. *I. aquatica, I. lutea*

Description Yellow flag is a semi-aquatic herbaceous perennial to 1.2 m/4 ft. in height. Its showy flowers are bright yellow with dark pencilled veins on the lower lips. Each flowering stem usually bears two flowers. The cylindrical capsules are to 8 cm/3 in. long and filled with flat, pellet-like seeds. The leaves are wider, to 4 cm/ 1.5 in., and taller, to 1.2 m/4 ft., than most irises.

Traditional use The fleshy rhizomes of yellow flag have long been used medicinally.

Etymology The common names segg and sheggs are Old Anglo-Saxon names for a small sword, referring to the leaves, which are also referenced by the common names dagger and Jacob's sword. It is thought that King Louis VII of France used this iris as his battle emblem. The flower was then known as fleur de Louis but was later changed to fleur-de-luce and, finally, to fleur-de-lis.

Origin Native to Eurasia.

Season Flowers from May to July.

Reproduction By seed and rhizome.

Concerns It is quickly taking over our native wetland plants. Its surface rhizomes are so thick they will not allow other seeds to germinate.

▶ GROUND-IVY CREEPING CHARLIE / ALEHOOF / GILL-OVER-THE-GROUND

Glechoma hederacea

MINT FAMILY Lamiaceae

Syn. *Nepeta glechoma*

Description Ground-ivy is a semi-evergreen trailing perennial to 40 cm/16 in. long. Its bluish-purple flowers are to 2.5 cm/1 in. long and trumpet shaped, with two lips. The flowers are borne three to four in whorls that originate in the upper leaves. The leaves are 2.5–5 cm/1–2 in. long, kidney shaped, and opposite, with rounded teeth. The square stems root at the nodes when trailing on the ground. Ground-ivy will lose its leaves in areas with hard frost.

Traditional use The leaves can be eaten raw and mixed with other salad greens. Medicinally, ground-ivy can be dated back to the first century AD—it was known as a cure-all (panacea). Infusions of the leaves have been used to treat diseases of the lungs and kidneys, asthma, and jaundice and to reduce fever and chronic coughs.

Etymology As its common name alehoof suggests, ground-ivy was used to flavour and clarify beer. Gill-over-the-ground comes from the French word *guiller*, "to ferment beer."

Origin Ground-ivy is thought to be one of the first edible herbal plants brought over from Europe by the settlers in the 1600s.

Season Flowers from March to July.

Reproduction By seed and vegetatively rooting at the nodes.

Concerns Can become invasive in shaded woodland areas with rich moist soil.

▶ YELLOW ARCHANGEL GOLDEN DEAD NETTLE

Lamiastrum galeobdolon

MINT FAMILY Lamiaceae

Description Yellow archangel is an evergreen perennial groundcover capable of covering hundreds of square metres or feet. Its helmet-shaped flowers are to 1 cm/0.5 in. long, yellow, and borne in whorls. The flowers have a hooded upper petal and a lipped lower petal. The lower lip serves as a landing pad for insects, and the reddish-brown markings act as nectar guides. The silver-green leaves are to 5 cm/2 in. long and ovate, with serrate edges.

Traditional use The young shoots and leaves can be used in salads or as potherbs. Medicinally, it was used to treat gout and joint pain, to stop bleeding, and to heal sores and ulcers.

Etymology The common name yellow archangel is from the colour of the flowers and because it is in flower on May 8, the day commemorating the archangel Michael. The genus name, *Lamiastrum*, refers to its resemblance to plants in the genus *Lamium*.

Origin Introduced from Eurasia as a garden ornamental.

Season Flowers from April to June.

Reproduction By seed, rooting at the nodes and stolons.

Concerns Once established, it can overshadow large areas of low-growing native plants. This is usually seen in moist soils at the forest edge.

▶ PURPLE DEAD-NETTLE
PURPLE HENBIT / PURPLE ARCHANGEL

Lamium purpureum

MINT FAMILY Lamiaceae

Description Purple dead-nettle is a taprooted annual 10–30 cm/4–12 in. in height. Its lavender flowers are to 1.2 cm/0.5 in. long and tube shaped, with an upper and lower lip, and are borne in whorls in the leaf axils. The leaves are heart shaped to triangular, fine toothed, and stalked.

Similar species Henbit dead-nettle (*L. amplexicaule*) is very similar. However, it has more coarsely toothed leaves that are all green, with the upper ones clasping. Purple dead-nettle's upper leaves are reddish and stalked. *L. hybridum* is a vigorous hybrid across between the two.

Traditional use In Sweden, the leaves were boiled and eaten as a potherb. The bruised leaves were applied to cuts and wounds to stop bleeding. A tea made from the dried leaves is said to promote perspiration, being useful in cases of chill.

Etymology The common name dead-nettle refers to the plant not stinging when touched, unlike stinging nettle. The common name henbit is from hens and roosters eating the small leaves.

Origin Native to Eurasia and Africa.

Season Flowers from February to May.

Reproduction By seed.

Concerns An invasive weed in gardens.

▶ GYPSYWORT
MARSH HOREHOUND / WATER HOREHOUND / EUROPEAN BUGLEWEED

Lycopus europaeus

MINT FAMILY Lamiaceae

Syn. *Lycopus europaeus* ssp. *mollis*

Description Gypsywort is a rhizomatous herbaceous perennial to 100 cm/40 in. in height. Its tiny flowers are white with purple dots on the lower lip and are borne in dense clusters surrounding the leaf axils. The leaves are to 10 cm/4 in. long, opposite, pinnately lobed, and slightly hairy on top.

Similar species Cut-leaved water horehound (*L. americanus*) is very similar, except its leaves are smooth (glabrous) on top and not hairy like gypsywort's.

Traditional use A tea or tincture made from the fresh leaves is said to be able to calm palpitations of the heart caused by excessive thyroid activity. The leaves and stems produce a permanent black dye that was used to dye wool and silk.

Etymology As the common name gypsywort suggests, gypsies used the dye from the leaves and stems to darken their complexions. The genus name, *Lycopus*, is Latin for "wolf's foot."

Origin Introduced from Europe.

Season Flowers from June to September.

Reproduction By seed and spreading rhizomes.

Concerns Very competitive with the native flora around lakes, ponds, and stream banks.

▶ HEAL-ALL SELF-HEAL / CURE-ALL / WOUNDWORT / CARPENTER'S WEED / BLUE CURLS

Prunella vulgaris

MINT FAMILY Lamiaceae

Syn. *Brunella vulgaris*

Description Heal-all is a fibrous-rooted herbaceous perennial 10–60 cm/4–16 in. in height. Its purple flowers are to 2 cm/0.75 in. long, two lipped, and borne in terminal spikes. The leaves are to 7 cm/3 in. long, mostly lance shaped, and opposite. The stems are square.

Traditional use As its common name suggests, heal-all has been used for centuries to treat almost every known ailment—whether it worked or not is another story. Its main use was as a tonic for sore throats and as a wound herb to stop bleeding. Seventeenth-century herbalist Nicholas Culpeper prescribed that it be taken inwardly in syrups for inward wounds, outwardly in unguents and plasters for outward wounds.

Etymology The common name woundwort refers to its use in stopping bleeding. The genus name, *Prunella*, is from the German word *braune*, meaning "quinsy," a disease of the throat, which it was used to treat.

Origin Although it is now a universal plant (even seen in places as cold as Sitka, Alaska), it is thought to be originally from Eurasia.

Season Flowers from May to October.

Reproduction By seed.

Concerns Can become invasive in lawns.

▶ SCOTCH BROOM BROOM TOPS / BASAM / BISOM / BRUM

Cytisus scoparius

PEA FAMILY Fabaceae

Syn. *Spartium scoparius, Genista scoparius, Sarothamnus scoparius*

Description Scotch broom is an unarmed deciduous shrub to 3 m/10 ft. in height. Its bright-yellow pea-like flowers are to 2.5 cm/1 in. long and project at all angles from the stems. When the flowering period is over, the bushes are draped with thousands of brown-black pods up to 5 cm/2 in. long. These split open when dry, forcing the seeds several metres or feet away from the parent plant. The leaves are short, narrow, and pressed close to the stems.

Traditional use In the United Kingdom, the young unopened flower buds were pickled and later washed or boiled and used as capers. The blossoms were made into a salve to treat gout. It is said that King Henry VIII drank a tea made from the flowers—I wonder why. The seeds and pods should be considered poisonous.

Etymology As the common names broom, basam, bisom, and brum suggest, the branches were tied together to make brooms. The species name, *scoparius*, is derived from the Latin word *scopa*, meaning "besom" or "broom-like."

Origin Introduced from Europe as a garden ornamental.

Season Flowers from April to August, but occasional flowers can be seen in any month.

Reproduction By seed. The trunks can regenerate if cut off at ground level.

Concerns Extremely invasive along the coastline, where it competes with the native flora and forestry seedlings.

▶ STAR OF BETHLEHEM

STARFLOWER / SLEEPYDICK / NAP-AT-NOON / DOVE'S DUNG

Ornithogalum umbellatum

LILY FAMILY Liliaceae

Description Star of Bethlehem is a bulbous herbaceous perennial with flowering stems to 30 cm/12 in. in height. Its star-shaped flowers are bright white with outer green stripes and are borne in flat-topped clusters of 5 to 20. The grass-like leaves are 15–30 cm/6–12 in. long and basal, with a thin white stripe down the keel.

Traditional use In ancient Europe, the bulbs were eaten raw, boiled, or roasted like chestnuts. Today, some authorities say the bulbs are poisonous to humans and livestock. Modern herbal stores sell tinctures of the plant with a 27 percent alcohol content for relief of naturally occurring nervous tension. I wonder if the alcohol has any effect.

Etymology The genus name is derived from the Greek words *orni*, "bird," and *gala*, "milk." The bulbs are thought to be the "dove's dung" mentioned in the bible, which were sold during the Babylonian siege of Jerusalem. The flowers of star of Bethlehem close at night and reopen when there is warmth and sun—they will not open on cold cloudy days.

Origin Introduced from Europe as a garden ornamental.

Season Flowers from April to June; then the leaves wither and disappear.

Reproduction By seed and bulblets.

Concerns None, unless the bulbs are poisonous.

▶ PURPLE LOOSESTRIFE

Lythrum salicaria

LOOSESTRIFE FAMILY Lythraceae

Description Purple loosestrife is a rhizomatous herbaceous perennial to 1.3 m/6 ft. in height. Its flowers are to 1 cm/0.5 in. long, pink to reddish to purple, and borne in dense terminal spikes. The leaves are 5–10 cm/2–4 in. long and lanceolate and can vary from opposite to whorled or even alternating, though mainly seen opposite.

Traditional use It was mainly used to treat dysentery, fevers, constipation, diarrhea, and cholera. An ointment was used to heal ulcers and sores.

Etymology The genus name, *Lythrum*, is derived from the Greek word *lythron*, meaning "blood" or "gore," referring to the colour of the flowers. The species name, *salicaria*, is from *salix*, "willow," referring to the willow-like leaves. The name loosestrife was given to plants (mainly *Lysimachia* spp.) that could rid a house or any dwelling of gnats, mosquitoes, flies, or evil spirits. The crushed leaves and branches were placed in mattresses, on sitting mats, in kitchens, and even around livestock, in the hopeful event of losing strife from the annoying visitors.

Origin Native to Eurasia.

Season Flowers mid- to late summer.

Reproduction By seed and rhizome.

Concerns If left unchecked, purple loosestrife will take over entire wetlands.

▶ DWARF MALLOW

COMMON MALLOW / CHEESES / CHEESE WEED

Malva neglecta

MALLOW FAMILY Malvaceae

Description Dwarf mallow is a short-lived herbaceous perennial to 60 cm/24 in. tall. Its flowers are to 2.5 cm/1 in. across, white to pale purple, and borne on short stalks originating from the axils. The long-stalked leaves are to 5 cm/2 in. across, five to seven lobed, and rounded to kidney shaped.

Traditional use The young leaves and seeds can be eaten raw, as potherbs; also a tea can be made from the dried leaves, flowers, or roots. See musk mallow for more uses.

Etymology The seeds are borne in round, flat carpels that somewhat resemble a wheel of cheese; hence the common names cheese weed and cheeses. The species name, *neglecta*, means "overlooked," in reference to the plant being overlooked for its many uses and benefits.

Origin Introduced from Eurasia.

Season Flowers from April to October.

Reproduction By seed. The seeds have been known to be viable for up to 100 years.

Concerns Can be a serious weed in vegetable crops and lawns.

▶ MUSK MALLOW

Malva moschata

MALLOW FAMILY Malvaceae

Description Musk mallow is a short-lived taprooted herbaceous perennial to 60 cm/24 in. in height. Its flowers are to 5 cm/2 in. across, have five petals, and range in colour from white to pink to purple. The leaves are to 8 cm/3 in. across and palmately compounded into several dissected linear segments.

Traditional use The young leaves and flowers are best used raw in salads. The leaves become very gluey or slimy when cooked. The seeds, when eaten raw, have a nutty flavour. Mallows have been used for centuries in poultices to treat bruises, ulcers, boils, sores, cuts, skin disorders, swelling, and inflammation.

Etymology The well-known spongy candy marshmallow used to be made from the gummy roots of the closely allied March mallow (*Althaea officinalis*). The species name, *moschata*, means musk-like, in reference to the musky scented leaves.

Origin Introduced from Eurasia.

Season Flowers from June to September.

Reproduction By seed.

Concerns Not many; usually seen as an attractive roadside escapee.

► EVENING PRIMROSE

PRIMROSE / EVENING STAR /
FEVER PLANT / KING'S CURE-ALL

Oenothera biennis

EVENING PRIMROSE FAMILY Onagraceae

Description Evening primrose is a night-scented biennial to 1.2 m/4 ft. in height. Its bright-yellow flowers are to 5 cm/2 in. across, have four petals, and are borne in leafy terminal spikes. The stem leaves are to 10 cm/4 in. long, alternate, lance shaped, and reduced in size upward. The seeds are contained in upright, hairy capsules to 3 cm/1.5 in. long.

Traditional use The leaves, flowers, seeds, and first-year roots can be eaten raw or as potherbs. The root is most often sought after and is cooked like carrots. For centuries, evening primrose was known as King's cure-all. It has been used to treat coughs, depression, cyclic nostalgia, high blood pressure, schizophrenia, eczema, diabetes, and premenstrual syndrome. Evening primrose oil is used in cosmetic creams, soaps, lip balms, lotions, and aromatherapy and massage carrier oils.

Etymology The common name evening primrose refers to the flowers fully opening at night. The flowers' sweet scent attracts nighttime pollinating moths. It used to be cultivated for its edible roots, but now it is grown primarily for the oil contained in the seeds.

Origin Native to the east coast of North America.

Season Flowers from June to September.

Reproduction By seed.

Concerns Mainly seen as a roadside weed; however, it can also contaminate crop fields.

► HELLEBORE

BROAD-LEAVED HELLEBORINE /
BASTARD HELLEBORE

Epipactis helleborine

ORCHID FAMILY Orchidaceae

Description Hellebore is a rhizomatous herbaceous perennial 0.3–1 m/1–3.3 ft. in height. Its greenish-brown flowers are to 2.5 cm/1 in. across and borne in leafy terminal racemes of approximately 24. The clasping stem leaves are to 10 cm/4 in. long, parallel veined, and reduced in size upward.

Similar species Giant hellebore (*E. gigantea*) is a taller but very similar plant that is not weedy.

Etymology Both the Greek genus name, *Epipactis*, and the Latin species name, *helleborine*, refer to the old names for helleborus, or Christmas rose. *Epipactis* is the only genus of the orchid family that has made a weed of itself. In the right conditions (light, shade, and moisture) it can be seen growing in the thousands.

Origin Native to Eurasia. It was first documented on the east coast in the 1970s, most likely as a garden ornamental.

Season Flowers from July to August.

Reproduction Mainly by seed. Small clumps can spread by rhizome.

Concerns None yet.

▶ YELLOW SORREL

CREEPING WOODSORREL / CREEPING OXALIS / SOUR CLOVER / YELLOW WOODSORREL

Oxalis corniculata

WOODSORREL FAMILY Oxalidaceae

Syn. *Oxalis repens, Xanthoxalis corniculata*

Description Yellow sorrel is a taprooted herbaceous perennial to 10 cm/4 in. in height. Tiny yellow flowers are borne in terminal clusters of two to five on long slender stalks. Sticky brown seeds are borne in greyish capsules to 2.5 cm/1 in. long, which explode at maturity. The clover-like leaves are often reddish purple and have three heart-shaped leaflets that fold toward each other. In the evening or in cold weather, the leaf stalks droop and the leaves close.

Similar species There is a similar-looking sorrel called *O. stricta*. It is distinguished by green leaves rather than reddish purple and is usually over 10 cm/4 in. tall.

Traditional use The leaves can be eaten raw or as a potherb but should not be eaten in large quantities, as they contain oxalic acid. The whole plant was used to treat scurvy, urinary tract infections, and diarrhea.

Etymology The genus name, *Oxalis*, is from the Greek word *oxys*, meaning "acid," "sour," or "sharp," in reference to the taste of the leaves.

Origin Introduced from Eurasia in the 1700s.

Season Flowers from June to September.

Reproduction By seed and rooting at the nodes.

Concerns Can be troublesome in the cracks of patio pavers and lawns.

▶ WELSH POPPY

Meconopsis cambrica

POPPY FAMILY Papaveraceae

Description Welsh poppy is a deeply taprooted herbaceous perennial to 16 cm/ 40 in. in height. Its showy flowers are to 8 cm/3 in. across, vary in colour from lemon yellow to rich orange to red orange, and are borne singly atop slender stems. The seeds are borne in ribbed capsules to 2.5 cm/1 in. long. The soft green leaves are to 18 cm/7 in. long and pinnately dissected with slightly alternating leaflets.

Etymology The genus name, *Meconopsis*, is derived from the Greek words *mekon*, "poppy," and *opsis*, "similar in appearance." The species name, *cambrica*, is from its origin in Wales–Cambria.

Origin Native to western Europe and the only species of *Meconopsis* that is not from the Himalayas, China, or Tibet.

Season Flowers from May to autumn.

Reproduction By seed and division; if the seed heads are cut off before they mature, the plants will continually flower.

Concerns In the Pacific Northwest it has become a serious invader in ornamental gardens.

AMERICAN POKEWEED COMMON POKEBERRY

Phytolacca americana

POKEWEED FAMILY Phytolaccaceae

Description Pokeweed is a herbaceous perennial to 3 m/10 ft. in height. Its flowers are white, five petalled, and borne in columnar clusters. The resulting fruit start off green and end a beautiful dark purple. The leaves are to 15 cm/6 in. long, alternating, and lanceolate.

Traditional use Pokeweed has a long history among Indigenous groups. The young shoots and leaves can be boiled twice to remove any toxins and eaten like asparagus or spinach. The leaves become toxic as they age. Pokeweed root capsules are sold in modern-day herbal shops. They are considered a blood cleanser. Pokeweed was being studied as a hopeful anti-AIDS drug and as a cure for childhood leukemia.

Etymology The genus name, *Phytolacca*, is from the Greek word *phyton*, "plant," and *lac*, referring to the dye extracted from the lac insect. The common names pokeweed and poke-berry are derived from *pocan*, an Indigenous word for a plant that yields a dye. Indigenous groups made a red dye from the berries for basket colouring and painting their horses.

Origin Native to eastern North America.

Season Flowers from July to August, with the berries ripening from September to October.

Reproduction By seed and division.

Concerns The raw berries are poisonous to humans and livestock.

RIBWORT PLANTAIN NARROW-LEAVED PLANTAIN

Plantago lanceolata

PLANTAIN FAMILY Plantaginaceae

Description Ribwort plantain is a herbaceous perennial 15–50 cm/6–20 in. in height. Its unusual flowers have four greenish petals and are borne in dense terminal clusters on leafless stalks. The leaves are 10–30 cm/4–12 in. long, basal, and strongly ribbed.

Traditional use A beautiful golden dye can be made by boiling the entire plant and letting the water sit for 24 hours. Although bitter, the young leaves of both ribwort plantain and common plantain can be eaten raw or as potherbs. The seeds can be dried, ground, and added to flour when baking. The leaves can be used externally to stop blood flow from cuts and wounds. Internally, it has been used to treat diarrhea, hemorrhoids, asthma, and gastritis. In the Tropics, the crushed leaves are used to treat insect bites and stings. Capsules of plantain are available at most herbal stores.

Etymology The species name, *lanceolata*, refers to the lance-shaped leaves.

Origin Introduced from Eurasia by the early settlers.

Season Flowers from May to October.

Reproduction By seed.

Concerns A serious lawn and garden invader.

▶ COMMON PLANTAIN
BROADLEAF PLANTAIN / GREATER PLANTAIN / BIRDSEED PLANTAIN

Plantago major

PLANTAIN FAMILY Plantaginaceae

Syn. *Plantago asiatica*

Description Common plantain is a fibrous-rooted herbaceous perennial 10–40 cm/ 4–16 in. in height. Its inconspicuous flowers are greenish white and borne in elongated clusters on leafless stalks. The leaves are 5–20 cm/2–8 in. long, basal, egg shaped, and strongly ribbed.

Traditional use A beautiful golden dye can be made by boiling the entire plant and letting the water sit for 24 hours. Although bitter, the young leaves of both ribwort plantain and common plantain can be eaten raw or as potherbs. The seeds can be dried, ground, and added to flour when baking. The leaves can be used externally to stop blood flow from cuts and wounds. Internally, it has been used to treat diarrhea, hemorrhoids, asthma, and gastritis. In the Tropics, the crushed leaves are used to treat insect bites and stings. Capsules of plantain are available at most herbal stores.

Etymology The genus name, *Plantago*, is from the Latin word *planta*, "foot sole," referring to the shape of the leaves and the way they lie flat on the ground.

Origin Introduced from Eurasia and first recorded in North America in the mid-1700s.

Season Flowers from May to October.

Reproduction By seed.

Concerns A hard plant to eradicate from lawns and gardens.

▶ COMMON KNOTWEED
PROSTRATE KNOTWEED / KNOTGRASS / WIREWEED / BIRDWEED

Polygonum aviculare

BUCKWHEAT FAMILY Polygonaceae

Syn. *P. arenastrum, P. littorale*

Description Common knotweed is a mat-forming taprooted annual 0.3–1 m/1–3.3 ft. long. Its tiny flowers are greenish, with white to red margins, and grow in clusters of one to five in the leaf axils. The bluish-green leaves are alternate and elliptical, with short stalks.

Traditional use The leaves can be steeped for a tea, eaten raw in salads, or used as a potherb. They are rich in zinc. The seeds can be dried, ground, and used in flour. The leaves have astringent and diuretic properties.

Etymology The species name, *aviculare*, is from *avis*, "bird," in reference to the many small birds that feed on the seeds. This is also the source of the common name birdweed.

Origin Native to Eurasia; thought to have come over at the beginning of the 1800s.

Season Flowers from May to October.

Reproduction By seed.

Concerns Mainly seen in sidewalk cracks and on roadsides. However, it is becoming a problem in lawns, gardens, and grain fields.

WILD BUCKWHEAT

BLACK BINDWEED / CLIMBING BUCKWHEAT / CORNBIND

Polygonum convolvulus

BUCKWHEAT FAMILY Polygonaceae

Syn. *Bilderdykia convolvulus, Fallopia convolvulus, Tinaria convolvulus*

Description Wild buckwheat is a sprawling and twining annual to 1.2 m/4 ft. in length. Its tiny flowers are greenish and borne both in the leaf axils and in terminal racemes. The black seeds are borne singly in three-sided capsules. The leaves are to 5 cm/2 in. long, alternating, and shaped like large arrowheads.

Similar species When not in flower, wild buckwheat can be confused with field bindweed (*Convolvulus arvensis*).

Traditional use The seeds can be dried, ground, and mixed with flour.

Etymology The species name, *convolvulus*, means "leaves like bindweed."

Origin Introduced from Eurasia, it is thought to have come over to the west coast in the 1860s.

Season Flowers from May to October or until the first frost.

Reproduction By seed. Each plant is capable of producing over 10,000 seeds.

Concerns It can be a serious invader in crop fields, where it competes for light and moisture.

MARSHPEPPER SMARTWEED

WATERPEPPER / SMARTASS / ARSSMART

Polygonum hydropiper

BUCKWHEAT FAMILY Polygonaceae

Description Marshpepper smartweed is a fibrous-rooted annual 30–90 cm/12–30 in. in height. Its flowers are greenish pink and borne in long slender racemes that sometimes droop at the tip. The leaves are to 8 cm/3 in. long, alternating, lance shaped, and fringed with hairs.

Traditional use The young leaves and shoots have a peppery taste and can be eaten raw or as a potherb. Infusions and decoctions made from the leaves have been used as a stimulant, diuretic, antiseptic, and desiccant.

Etymology The species name, *hydropiper*, literally means "waterpepper," referring to it growing in water and tasting like pepper. It is usually seen growing in areas that are flooded from autumn to spring. The common name smartweed refers to the smarting sensation a person receives when handling the plants and then rubbing their eyes or from eating the leaves.

Origin Introduced from Eurasia.

Season Flowers from July to August.

Reproduction By seed.

Concerns Very competitive with the native flora.

▶ LADY'S THUMB SPOTTED KNOTWEED / COMMON SMARTWEED

Polygonum persicaria
BUCKWHEAT FAMILY Polygonaceae
Syn. *Persicaria maculata, P. maculosa, P. vulgaris*

Description Lady's thumb is a taprooted annual 30–90 cm./12–36 in. in height. Its small pink flowers are borne in congested terminal racemes. The seeds are brown black and three sided. The leaves are to 10 cm/4 in. long, alternating, and lance shaped and usually have a dark splotch (hence the common name lady's thumb) in the centre.

Similar species Green smartweed (*Polygonum lapathifolium*) is very similar; however, it has yellowish hairs on the underside of the leaf and usually does not have the dark splotch.

Traditional use The peppery-tasting leaves and seeds can be eaten raw or as a pot-herb. The leaves are astringent and diuretic.

Etymology The genus name, *Polygonum*, is from the Greek, *polys* ("many"), and *gony* ("knee"), referring to the jointed stems. The species name, *persicaria*, means "from Persia," which is where botanists believe it originated.

Origin Introduced from Eurasia.

Season Flowers from June to July.

Reproduction By seed.

Concerns Can be very competitive for light, moisture, and nutrients in gardens and vegetable and crop fields.

▶ GIANT KNOTWEED SPREADING KNOTWEEDS / KNOTWEED

Polygonum sachalinense
BUCKWHEAT FAMILY Polygonaceae
Syn. *Reynoutria sachalinense, Fallopia sachalinense*

Description Giant knotweed is a rhizomatous herbaceous perennial 1.8–3.6 m/6–12 ft. in height. Its greenish-white flowers are to 0.3 cm/0.1 in. across and borne in dense panicles arising from the leaf axils. The stems are reddish brown and hollow, with bamboo-like joints. The leaves are 10–30 cm/4–12 in. long, alternating, and roundly egg shaped.

Similar species Japanese knotweed (*P. cuspidatum*) is very similar in appearance and aggressiveness. It is generally seen as a smaller plant with leaves that are abruptly pointed.

Traditional use Both species of giant knotweed are excellent vegetables. The new shoots with unfurled leaves can be treated as asparagus, and the rhizomes can be boiled or roasted. Resveratrol is an active component extracted from Japanese knotweed and red grapes that is being looked at to treat AIDS and cancer.

Etymology The species name, *sachalinense*, refers to Sakhalin Island, north of Japan, where giant knotweed is native.

Season Flowers from late June to October.

Reproduction By seed, but mostly by rhizome.

Concerns It is overtaking our native flora, and its hollow stems can become a fire hazard when the leaves drop.

SHEEP SORREL SOUR GRASS / WILD SORREL / RED SORREL

Rumex acetosella

BUCKWHEAT FAMILY Polygonaceae

Description Sheep sorrel is a rhizomatous, herbaceous perennial to 40 cm/16 in. in height. Its flowers are dioecious, with male and female flowers on separate plants. They are yellowish to red and borne in open terminal clusters. Being in the buckwheat family, the flowers have no petals. The mature leaves develop basal lobes, giving them an arrow-shaped appearance.

Traditional use The sharp-tasting leaves can be added to salads, soups, and stews. Medicinally, it was used as blood cleanser and gargle and to treat fevers, sores, and ringworm.

Etymology Sheep sorrel is also known as sour grass because of its sharp taste, like oxalic acid. Both the genus name and species name refer to the sour-tasting leaves.

Origin Introduced from Eurasia.

Season Flowers from April to October.

Reproduction By seed and slender rhizomes.

Concerns Sheep sorrel is the most invasive of the sorrels and docks. If left unchecked, it can take over entire pastures.

CURLED DOCK NARROW DOCK / SOUR DOCK

Rumex crispus

BUCKWHEAT FAMILY Polygonaceae

Syn. *Rumex elongates*

Description Curled dock is a taprooted herbaceous perennial to 1 m/3.3 ft. in height. Its small, unattractive flowers are greenish and borne in long terminal clusters. The spent flowers and seeds persist on the stalks through autumn and early winter. The basal leaves are to 30 cm/12 in. long, with curly edges, and the upper leaves are reduced in size.

Traditional use The young leaves can be used in salads or as potherbs. The seeds can be dried, ground, and mixed with flour. The taproots of curled dock have been used medicinally for centuries. Its astringent properties are thought to make it a good blood cleanser.

Etymology The long narrow leaves with curled margins make this dock one of the easiest docks to identify. The species name, *crispus*, means curly.

Origin Introduced from Eurasia.

Season Flowers from May through the summer.

Reproduction By seed. If curled dock's taproot is rototilled into the ground, the broken pieces will reproduce.

Concerns Curled dock can be extremely invasive in moist lowland pastures.

▶ BITTER DOCK BUTTER DOCK / BROAD-LEAVED DOCK

Rumex obtusifolius

BUCKWHEAT FAMILY Polygonaceae

Description Bitter dock is a large taprooted herbaceous perennial to 1.2 m/4 ft. in height. Its tiny flowers are a plain greenish brown and borne in dense elongated clusters. The basal leaves are to 30 cm/12 in. long, alternating, heart shaped at the base, and reduced in size upward.

Similar species Clustered dock (*R. conglomeratus*) is very similar. It can be distinguished by its segmented flower clusters.

Traditional use The young leaves can be used as potherbs, and the seeds can be dried, ground, and added to flour. Medicinally, the leaves were applied to burns, scalds, and nettle stings.

Etymology Until modern times, the large leaves were used to wrap bricks of butter; hence the common name butter dock. The species name, *obtusifolius*, means "blunt leaved."

Origin Introduced from Eurasia.

Season Flowers from June through summer.

Reproduction By seed. Like curled dock, if the taproot is rototilled into the ground, the broken pieces will reproduce.

Concerns Can be extremely invasive in moist lowland pastures.

▶ PURSLANE LITTLE HOGWEED / PIGWEED / PUSSELY / GREEN PURSLANE

Portulaca oleracea

PURSLANE FAMILY Portulacaceae

Syn. *P. neglecta*

Description Purslane is a prostrate succulent annual to 50 cm/12 in. long. Its showy yellow flowers are to 1 cm/0.5 in. across and are borne both in the axils and in terminal clusters. The succulent leaves are to 2.5 cm/1 in. long, alternating, wedge shaped, green above, and pale purple below. The flowers open on sunny days only, a common trait in the purslane family.

Traditional use The leaves can be eaten raw or as a potherb. The seeds can be dried, ground, and mixed with flour. Medicinally, purslane has been known since the time of Hippocrates. It was used by both Theophrastus and Pedanius Dioscorides for its diuretic, anti-parasitic, and cathartic properties.

Etymology The species name, *oleracea*, is given to plants that are vegetables and potherbs.

Origin Introduced from Eurasia; first seen on the east coast of North America in the 1670s.

Season The seeds germinate when the summer heat is full. Flowers from August to September.

Reproduction By seed. Each plant can produce over 200,000 seeds in a growing season. If the plant is pulled from the soil, it can still produce seeds from the reserves in its leaves.

Concerns If not being grown as a food crop, purslane can become a pest in the garden.

▶ CREEPING JENNY

MONEYWORT / WANDERING JENNY / CREEPING JOAN / LOOSESTRIFE

Lysimachia nummularia

PRIMULA FAMILY Primulaceae

Description Creeping jenny is a prostrate herbaceous perennial capable of covering hundreds of square metres or feet by rooting at the nodes and its spreading rhizomes. The cup-shaped flowers have five deeply-lobed yellow petals, which are borne singly on short stalks arising from the leaf axils. The leaves are to 2.5 cm/1 in. long, opposite, and oblong to circular in outline.

Traditional use The leaves and flowers can be steeped for a herbal tea. The bruised leaves were at one time applied to cuts and wounds for a blood stanch.

Etymology The species name, *nummularia*, means "coin shaped," referring to the shape of the leaves, which is also the source of its common name moneywort. Long ago, creeping jenny was called *serpentaria* from the belief that wounded snakes would lie on the leaves to heal their wounds.

Origin Introduced from Europe as an ornamental groundcover.

Season Flowers from June to July.

Reproduction By seed, but mainly by rhizomes and rooting at the nodes.

Concerns A hard plant to eradicate from the garden once it is established.

▶ SPOTTED LOOSESTRIFE

YELLOW LOOSESTRIFE / DITCHWEED

Lysimachia punctata

PRIMULA FAMILY Primulaceae

Description Spotted loosestrife is a rhizomatous herbaceous perennial 0.6–1.2 m/ 2–4 ft. in height. Its star-shaped flowers are to 2.5 cm/1 in. across and borne in whorls of three to five in the upper leaf axils. The leaves are to 10 cm/4 in. long, lance shaped, and opposite or in whorls of three or four.

Etymology Its genus name, *Lysimachia*, commemorates the Thracian king Lysimachus (c. 360–281 BC). It is said he calmed a raging bull with a sprig of loosestrife. The species name, *punctata*, means "spotted," referring to the lightly spotted stems.

Origin Introduced from Europe as a garden ornamental.

Season Flowers from June to July.

Reproduction By seed, but mainly by its spreading rhizomes.

Concerns Mainly a garden pest; however, it can also be seen in ditches and damp areas, where it competes with the native flora.

▶ TRAVELLER'S JOY OLD MAN'S BEARD

Clematis vitalba

BUTTERCUP FAMILY Ranunculaceae

Description Traveller's joy is a deciduous perennial climber to 15 m/50 ft. in length. Its creamy-white flowers are to 2.5 cm/1 in. across and slightly fragrant, with prominent stamens in the centre. The leaves are pinnately compounded into five leaflets, which are heart shaped and usually coarsely toothed.

Traditional use The leaves are analgesic and diuretic; a homeopathic remedy has been developed from them to treat rheumatism. All parts of the plant are considered poisonous.

Etymology The genus name, *Clematis*, is derived from the Old Greek word *klema*, meaning "climbing vine" or "tendril." The species name, *vitalba*, translates literally as "white vine," referring to the masses of white flowers.

Origin Introduced from Eurasia and North Africa as a garden ornamental.

Season The flowers hang in long panicles from mid-June to September. The fluffy seed heads remain on for most of the winter.

Reproduction By seed.

Concerns The woody vines are so strong and vigorous they can suffocate the surrounding native flora.

▶ MEADOW BUTTERCUP TALL BUTTERCUP / CROWFOOT / BLISTER PLANT

Ranunculus acris

BUTTERCUP FAMILY Ranunculaceae

Description Meadow buttercup is a fibrous-rooted herbaceous perennial 0.6–1.2 m/ 2–4 ft. in height. Its bright-yellow flowers are to 2.5 cm/1 in. across and shiny, with a central boss of yellow stamens that mature into a spiky ball of seeds. The leaves are to 10 cm/4 in. across and deeply divided into three to seven dissected leaflets.

Traditional use The leaves have been used to treat rheumatism, headaches, diarrhea, and colds and were well-known for removing warts and corns.

Etymology The genus name, *Ranunculus*, is from the Latin word *rana*, "frog," referring to the damp places where buttercups grow. The species name, *acris*, means "sharp" or "pungent," in reference to the plant's bitter juice.

Origin Introduced from Eurasia.

Season Flowers from the end of April to September.

Reproduction By seed; it does not have runners like creeping buttercup.

Concerns All parts of the plant are poisonous when fresh. The leaves are very acrid and can cause blistering when handled or eaten; hence the common name blister plant.

► LESSER CELANDINE   FIG BUTTERCUP / FIGWORT / PILEWORT

Ranunculus ficaria

BUTTERCUP FAMILY Ranunculaceae

Syn. *Ficaria verna, F. ranunculoides*

Description Lesser celandine is a low-growing herbaceous perennial capable of covering large areas. Its butter-yellow flowers are to 2.5 cm/1 in. across, have 8 to 12 glossy petals, and are borne singly on slender stalks arising above the leaves. The leaves are to 5 cm/2 in. across, glossy green, and heart shaped to kidney shaped. The bright-yellow flowers were William Wordsworth's favourite flower. In recognition of this, they were carved on his tomb.

Traditional use The plant should be considered poisonous. Lesser celandine has been used for hundreds of years for treating ulcers and hemorrhoids; hence the common name pilewort. The tubers and roots were used in Elizabethan times to fight the plague.

Etymology The species name, *ficaria*, means "small fig," referring to the fig-like tubers on the stems and roots.

Origin Introduced from Eurasia as a garden ornamental.

Season The leaves appear in January, and flowers appear from March to May.

Reproduction By seed, tubers, and rooting at the nodes.

Concerns Lesser celandine is a vigorous competing groundcover that forms extensive patches on the forest floor. Its early emergence in January prevents the smaller native flora from co-occurring.

► CREEPING BUTTERCUP

Ranunculus repens

BUTTERCUP FAMILY Ranunculaceae

Syn. *R. repens* var. *glabratus, R. repens* var. *pleniflorus, R. repens* var. *villosus*

Description Creeping buttercup is a fibrous-rooted herbaceous perennial to 30 cm/12 in. in height. Its cup-shaped yellow flowers are to 1 cm/0.5 in. across, have 5 to 10 petals, and are borne singly on stalks to 15 cm/6 in. long. The leaves are to 10 cm/4 in. across, alternating, and divided into three dissected leaflets. The leaf stalks can be up to 40 cm/16 in. long and freely root at the nodes.

Etymology The species name, *repens*, refers to the plant's creeping habit.

Origin Introduced from Eurasia.

Season Flowers from May to October.

Reproduction By seed, but more often by rooting at the nodes on the elongated stems.

Concerns Creeping buttercup has invaded most of North America. It prefers moist rich soils, such as in fields, in gardens, at forest edges, and in lawns. Once established, it is very hard to eradicate.

CAUTION Like most members of the buttercup family, creeping buttercup is considered poisonous. Just removing the plants from the garden can cause bare hands to blister.

▶ NORWEGIAN CINQUEFOIL ROUGH CINQUEFOIL

Potentilla norvegica
ROSE FAMILY Rosaceae
Syn. *P. monspeliensis*

Description Norwegian cinquefoil is a taprooted annual, biennial, or short-lived perennial to 90 cm/36 in. in height. Its showy yellow flowers are to 2 cm/0.75 in. across, have five petals, and are borne in leafy terminal clusters. The leaves are to 10 cm/4 in. across, alternating, hairy on both sides, and palmately compounded into three leaflets.

Traditional use It has been used to treat sore throats, ulcers, and cancer and as a pain reliever.

Etymology The genus name, *Potentilla*, is from the Latin word *potens*, meaning "powerful," from its reputed potent medicinal properties. The species name, *norvegica*, means "from Norway." The common name cinquefoil refers to most of the species having five leaflets.

Origin Native to North America and Eurasia, but most likely introduced to the west coast.

Season Flowers from June to October.

Reproduction By seed.

Concerns Can become a problem in cultivated fields. Norwegian cinquefoil will only grow in areas with high rainfall.

▶ ROWAN WITCH WOOD

Sorbus aucuparia
ROSE FAMILY Rosaceae
Syn. *Pyrus aucuparia*

Description Rowan is a small to medium-sized tree that rarely exceeds 13 m/43 ft. in height. Its flowers are creamy white, have five petals, and are borne in flat-topped clusters. The berries are to 1 cm/0.5 in. across, orange red, and, upon close inspection, shaped like miniature apples. The leaves are alternating, finely sawtoothed, and pinnately compounded into 11 to 15 leaflets.

Traditional use The berries are edible but bitter. They can be used to make an excellent rowan jelly.

Etymology The species name, *aucuparia*, is from the Latin word *aucupor*, meaning "bird catching"—the berries were used as bait to catch birds. For centuries, rowans were planted near English houses to protect the families from witches; hence the common name witch wood.

Origin A European garden escapee.

Season Flowers from April to May, with the berries ripening from September to October.

Reproduction By seed. The berries are a favourite food in late autumn among robins, flickers, and waxwings.

Concerns It can overshadow the native forest flora.

▶ LADY'S BEDSTRAW YELLOW BEDSTRAW / CHEESE RENNET

Galium verum

MADDER FAMILY Rubiaceae

Description Lady's bedstraw is a sprawling herbaceous perennial to 90 cm/36 in. in length. Its tiny yellow flowers are to 0.3 cm/0.1 in. across and borne in dense terminal panicles on square wiry stems. The thread-like leaves are 1–5 cm/0.5–2 in. long and borne in whorls of four to eight.

Similar species Cleaver (*G. aparine*) is the most common of the bedstraws. It is a cosmopolitan weed that is frequently seen on the west coast.

Traditional use The leaves and seeds can be eaten raw or as a potherb. A version of coffee can be made from roasting the seeds. The dried stems, leaves, and flowers are antispasmodic and diuretic. It has been strewn on flowers and furniture for a flea deterrent, used as stuffing for mattresses, made into dye, and used for curdling milk.

Etymology The genus name, *Galium*, is from the Greek word *gala*, meaning "milk."

Origin Introduced from Eurasia.

Season Flowers from July to August.

Reproduction By seed.

Concerns It is quickly becoming an invasive weed in crop fields on the west coast.

▶ IVY-LEAVED TOADFLAX

Cymbalaria muralis

FIGWORT FAMILY Scrophulariaceae

Syn. *Linaria cymbalaria*

Description Ivy-leaved toadflax is a delicate trailing or climbing vine to 90 cm/36 in. in length. Its violet-blue flowers are to 1 cm/0.5 in. long, yellow throated with two lobes, and borne singly on long stalks. The egg-shaped seeds are borne in rounded capsules. The leaves are to 2.5 cm/1 in. across, long stalked, and palmately rounded, with five to seven lobes.

Traditional use The leaves are bitter; however, they can be mixed with other greens in salads. Poultices made from the leaves have been used as a blood stanch.

Etymology The genus name, *Cymbalaria*, is from the Greek word *kymbalon*, meaning "cymbal," referring to the shape of the leaves. The species name, *muralis*, means "walls" and describes where the plant commonly grows.

Origin A garden escapee from Eurasia.

Season Flowers from April to November.

Reproduction By seed and rooting at the nodes.

Concerns Can be hard to control in brick or on stone patios. The vines prefer growing in crevices, where they can explode their seed capsules.

▶ FOXGLOVE FAIRY'S GLOVE / PURPLE FOXGLOVE / COMMON FOXGLOVE

Digitalis purpurea

FIGWORT FAMILY Scrophulariaceae

Description Foxglove is a fibrous-rooted unbranched biennial or short-lived perennial 1.5 m/5 ft. in height. Its bell-shaped flowers are to 5 cm/2 in. long, are usually borne in one-sided racemes, and range in colour from purple to pink to white. The basal leaves are to 30 cm/12 in. long, broadly lance shaped, coarsely toothed, and reduced in size upward.

Traditional use The important cardiac drug digitalis is derived from foxglove. The plant's original use in the 1700s was for dropsy (edema). However, the entire plant is considered poisonous.

Etymology The genus name, *Digitalis*, is from the Latin word *digits*, meaning "finger," referring to the flower's resemblance to fingers of a glove. The German name for foxglove is *fingerhut*.

Origin A European garden escapee.

Season Flowers from June to July.

Reproduction By seed. Each plant is capable of producing over 1 million seeds.

Concerns Not likely to be a problem. The first-year seedling sits as a basal rosette, which can be transplanted to more appropriate areas in the garden if not wanted where it germinated.

▶ EYEBRIGHT COMMON EYEBRIGHT / EASTERN EYEBRIGHT

Euphrasia nemorosa

FIGWORT FAMILY Scrophulariaceae

Syn. *E. americana, E. officinalis*

Description Eyebright is a taprooted annual to 30 cm/12 in. in height. Its tiny flowers are white to pale purple, with darker-purple guidelines and a yellow spot on the lower lip. The leaves are opposite, unstalked, and lance shaped to almost circular, with deeply sawtoothed margins.

Traditional use It has been used to treat colds, night sweats, hay fever, rheumatism, and coughs and in homeopathy for eye infections. The extracted juice was long used to treat diseases of the sight.

Etymology The genus name, *Euphrasia*, is derived from the Greek word *euphrosyne*, "to gladden" or "to delight," in reference to it bringing gladness to the person with restored eyesight. Using the diluted juice as an eyebath was said to make your eyes bright.

Origin A European garden escapee.

Season Flowers from June to September.

Reproduction By seed.

Concerns Usually seen growing on compacted dry soils, such as on pathways and roadsides and in waste areas.

DALMATIAN TOADFLAX

BROAD-LEAVED TOADFLAX / WILD SNAPDRAGON

Linaria dalmatica

FIGWORT FAMILY Scrophulariaceae

Syn. *L. genistifolia* ssp. *dalmatica*, *L. macedonica*

Description Dalmatian toadflax is a rhizomatous herbaceous perennial to 1.2 m/4 ft. in height. Its snapdragon-like flowers are bright yellow, have a basal spur, and are borne in long terminal spikes. The leaves are to 8 cm/3 in. long, bluish green, alternating, broadly lance shaped, and clasping.

Traditional use Toadflax has a long history in medicine. It has been used to treat jaundice, skin disorder, dropsy (edema), liver complaints, hemorrhoids, and ulcers. It should be considered poisonous to both humans and livestock.

Etymology The species name, *dalmatica*, is from Dalmatia, a region of Croatia on the east shore of the Adriatic Sea. The common name toadflax is probably a combination of the flowers looking like a toad's face and the leaves of common toadflax resembling flax.

Origin A garden escapee from Europe.

Season Flowers from May to August.

Reproduction By seed and rhizome. A single plant can produce up to half a million seeds annually.

Concerns Dalmatian toadflax is a serious weed in pastures and crop fields. Its height and deep roots compete for light, moisture, and nutrients.

PURPLE TOADFLAX

Linaria purpurea

FIGWORT FAMILY Scrophulariaceae

Description Purple toadflax is a taprooted herbaceous perennial to 90 cm/36 in. in height. Its small purple flowers have a white throat and are borne in dense terminal clusters that elongate as the plant matures. The leaves are to 5 cm/2 in. long, unstalked, whorled, and almost linear.

Traditional use Toadflax has a long history in medicine. It has been used to treat jaundice, skin disorders, dropsy (edema), liver complaints, hemorrhoids, and ulcers. It should be considered poisonous to both humans and livestock.

Etymology The species name, *purpurea*, refers to the purple flowers.

Origin Introduced from Europe as a garden ornamental.

Season Has a long blooming period, from July to October.

Reproduction By seed.

Concerns Can be seen on roadsides and in waste areas but is more of a pest in ornamental gardens. It can be easily dug out if not wanted.

COMMON TOADFLAX

BUTTER-AND-EGGS / YELLOW TOAD-
FLAX / PERENNIAL SNAPDRAGON

Linaria vulgaris

FIGWORT FAMILY Scrophulariaceae

Description Common toadflax is a rhizomatous herbaceous perennial to 90 cm/
36 in. in height. Its flowers are butter yellow with an orange throat, have a basal spur,
and are borne in dense terminal spikes. They are similar to but smaller than those of
Dalmatian toadflax. The leaves are to 10 cm/4 in. long, alternating, and almost linear.

Traditional use Toadflax has a long history in medicine. It has been used to treat
jaundice, skin disorders, dropsy (edema), liver complaints, hemorrhoids, and ulcers.
It should be considered poisonous to both humans and livestock.

Etymology The genus name, *Linaria*, is from the Latin word *linum*, meaning "flax"—
the thin leaves resemble those of flax. The name of the fabric linen, which is a
product of flax, is also derived from *linum*. The yellow flowers with orange throats
have given toadflax some of its common names: butter-and-eggs, eggs-and-collops,
and eggs-and-bacon.

Origin Introduced from Eurasia as a garden ornamental.

Season Flowers from May to August.

Reproduction By seed and rhizome.

Concerns Has become a very invasive weed in the interior rangelands.

YELLOW PARENTUCELLIA

YELLOW GLANDWEED /
STICKY PARENTUCELLIA /
YELLOW BARTSIA

Parentucellia viscosa

FIGWORT FAMILY Scrophulariaceae

Syn. *Bartsia viscosa*

Description Yellow parentucellia is a fibrous-rooted annual 30–50 cm/12–20 in. in
height. Its yellow flowers have two lips, with the bottom lip having three lobes, and
are borne in terminal clusters. The leaves are 2.5–5 cm/1–2 in. long, alternating,
lanceolate, and hairy.

Etymology The genus name commemorates Tommaso Parentucelli, Pope Nicholas
V, the founder of the Botanic Garden at Rome. The species name, *viscosa*, means
"sticky" or "clammy," referring to the plant being covered by short glandular hairs.

Origin A European garden escapee.

Season Flowers throughout summer.

Reproduction By seed.

Concerns It is not of significant quantities yet to be concerned. Yellow parentucellia is mainly seen growing in moist conditions at pond edges, in fields, and in waste
areas at lower elevations.

▶ MULLEIN GREAT MULLEIN / VELVET DOCK / TORCHES / CANDLESTICK / BEGGAR'S BLANKET

Verbascum thapsus

FIGWORT FAMILY Scrophulariaceae

Description Mullein is a taprooted biennial 1.2–2.4 cm/4–8 ft. in height. Its yellow flowers are to 2.5 cm/1 in. across, stalkless, and borne in elongated terminal spikes. The velvet-like basal leaves are 15–45 cm/6–18 in. long, with woolly hairs. The second-year stem leaves are alternating and reduced in size upward. In the first year, mullein puts out a taproot and sits as a basal rosette of leaves. In the second year, it puts up a giant stem of leaves and flowers.

Traditional use A strained tea can be made from the hairy leaves and flowers. Mullein has long been used in medicine to treat respiratory diseases, diarrhea, gout, burns, ringworm, hemorrhoids, and warts. The leaves and stems were used to make candle wicks and shoe insoles and were dipped in fat or wax for torches.

Etymology The genus name, *Verbascum*, is thought to be a corruption of the Latin word *barbascum*, meaning "with bread." The species name, *thapsus*, refers to an ancient town in what is now Tunisia; it may also have been named for the Greek island of Thapsos.

Origin Introduced to North America from Eurasia as a medicinal plant.

Reproduction By seed.

Concerns Can become a pest in pastureland but is otherwise not much of a problem.

▶ SLENDER SPEEDWELL LAWN VERONICA / THREADSTALK SPEEDWELL

Veronica filiformis

FIGWORT FAMILY Scrophulariaceae

Description Slender speedwell is a creeping herbaceous perennial capable of covering extensive grassed areas. Its attractive pale-blue flowers are to 1.1 cm/0.5 in. across and borne singly on thread-like stalks arising from the leaf axils. The leaves are to 0.8 cm/0.3 in. across, opposite, round to kidney shaped, and softly hairy.

Similar species Another attractive lawn speedwell is Germander speedwell (*V. chamaedrys*), which is from Europe and has larger flowers and leaves.

Traditional use All species of Veronica are considered astringent.

Etymology The genus name is thought to be named after St. Veronica, who is said to have wiped the sweat from Christ's face. The species name, *filiformis*, refers to the thread-like flower stems.

Origin A garden escapee from Asia.

Season Flowers from March to June.

Reproduction By seed and rooting along stems.

Concerns Some people enjoy the flowers mixed in their lawn, while golf superintendents despise it.

▶ JIMSON WEED JAMESTOWN WEED / DEVIL'S TRUMPET / THORN APPLE / DEVIL'S APPLE

Datura stramonium

POTATO FAMILY Solanaceae

Description Jimson weed is a fibrous-rooted annual 0.6–1.5 m/2–5 ft. in height. Its showy flowers are to 12.5 cm/5 in. long, white to purplish, trumpet shaped with five points, and borne singly in the leaf axils. The leaves are 10–20 cm/4–8 in. long, alternating, irregularly toothed, and foul smelling. The thorny seed capsules are to 5 cm/2 in. long. They start off green and ripen to brown; they then split open and release up to 700 flat black seeds.

Traditional use The entire plant is poisonous. It contains hyoscyamine, atropine, and scopolamine. At high doses it can become a sedative, hypnotic, and hallucinogenic. At prescribed doses, it is used to treat asthma, muscle spasms, and Parkinson's disease.

Etymology Jimson is a corruption of Jamestown, Virginia, where British soldiers are said to have been purposely poisoned from the plant in 1676.

Origin Some authorities mention jimson weed as being indigenous to North America or Central America. Others believe it is indigenous to Asia and was introduced here.

Season Flowers from June to October.

Reproduction By seed.

Concerns The plants can be fatal to children or livestock if ingested. Even smelling the fragrant flowers can cause headaches and dizziness. Handling the plants can cause blistering.

▶ BITTERSWEET WOODY NIGHTSHADE

Solanum dulcamara

POTATO FAMILY Solanaceae

Description Bittersweet is a perennial vine to 3 m/10 ft. in length. Its unique flowers are bluish purple with folded-back petals (corolla) exposing the yellow anthers. The flowers are borne in open umbrella-like clusters on stalks arising from the leaf axils. The berries are to 1 cm/0.5 in. long; they start off green and then turn orange and finally brilliant red. The upper leaves are to 8 cm/3 in. long and alternating, with two lobes at the base.

Similar species The other, related species that can be distinguished by their white flowers are hairy nightshade (*S. sarrachoides*) and black nightshade (*S. nigrum*).

Traditional use All parts of the plant should be considered mildly poisonous. Bittersweet has been used to treat aches, whooping cough, arthritis, rheumatism, and asthma. It is available in modern herbal shops as a homeopathic remedy.

Etymology The genus name, *Solanum*, is from the Latin word *solor*, meaning "quieting" or "ease," probably referring to the effects of its medicinal properties. The species name, *dulcamara*, literally translates as "sweet bitter."

Origin Introduced from Eurasia.

Season Flowers from June to October.

Reproduction By seed.

Concerns It can reduce the value of bean crops.

▶ SPURGE LAUREL LAUREL-LEAVED DAPHNE

Daphne laureola

THYME AND DAPHNE FAMILY Thymelaeaceae

Description Spurge laurel is an evergreen bush to 1.5 m/5 ft. in height. Its scented flowers are to 1 cm/0.5 in. long, greenish yellow, and borne in dense clusters around the leaf axils. The egg-shaped berries (drupes) are to 1 cm/0.5 in. long and mature to shiny black. The dark glossy leaves are to 10 cm/4 in. long and alternating.

Traditional use All parts of the plant should be considered poisonous. Long ago, the leaves and bark were used to induce abortions.

Etymology The genus name, *Daphne*, was the original name for bay laurel (*Laurus nobilis*), from a nymph in Greek mythology. The species name, *laureola*, refers to the laurel-like leaves.

Origin Introduced from Eurasia.

Season Flowers from February to April.

Reproduction By seed.

Concerns Children should be warned not to eat the berries (or any berries they do not know).

MARINE PLANTS

▶ GREEN ALGAE

Enteromorpha sp.

GREEN SEAWEED FAMILY Ulvaceae

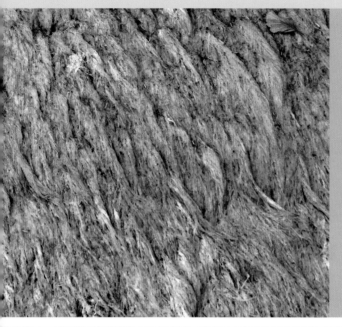

Description Green algae have tangles of tubular blades to 25 cm/10 in. long. The blades often fill with oxygen, which makes them float on water.

Etymology The genus name, *Enteromorpha*, is Greek for "intestine form."

Habitat Can be seen in upper pools, mudflats, and seepage areas on cliffs above the ocean, from Alaska to northern California.

Edibility Unknown.

▶ SEA HAIR

Enteromorpha sp.

GREEN SEAWEED FAMILY Ulvaceae

Description Sea hair has hollow yellowish-green blades to 20 cm/8 in. long. The blades are so thin they are often referred to as maiden hair.

Etymology The genus name, *Enteromorpha*, is Greek for "intestine form."

Habitat Can be found on rocky areas in the mid to upper intertidal zone, from Alaska to Mexico.

Edibility Small amounts have been used to flavour stews.

SEA LETTUCE

Ulva fenestrata

GREEN SEAWEED FAMILY Ulvaceae

Description Sea lettuce is bright green and to a length of 51 cm/20 in. The blades are so delicate that they are translucent when looked at in the sunlight.

Season The genus name, *Ulva*, is Latin for "marsh plant."

Habitat Tide pools and rocky shorelines in the lower to upper intertidal zones, from Alaska to California.

Edibility Edible.

TURKISH TOWEL

Chondracanthus corymbifera

FAMILY Gigartinaceae

Description Turkish towel blades are spiny, red to purplish, to 51 cm/20 in. long, and 20 cm/8 in. wide. The intensity of the colours is much greater when the plants are young.

Etymology The genus name, *Chondracanthus*, is Greek for "spiny."

Habitat The lower intertidal zone to depths of 18 m/ 60 ft., from BC to California.

Edibility Edible.

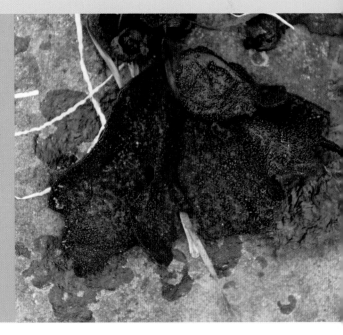

► YELLOW SEAWEED

Mazzaella parksii

FAMILY Gigartinaceae

Description Yellow seaweed has lobed reddish-yellow blades to 5 cm/2 in. in height. The stands are densely packed.

Etymology The genus name, *Mazzaella*, commemorates Angelo Mazza, an Italian phycologist.

Habitat Found in the rocky upper intertidal zone, from Alaska to California.

Edibility Unknown.

► SEA SAC

Halosaccion glandiforme

FAMILY Palmariaceae

Description Depending on age, sea sacs range from red purple to yellow brown. The sausage-like hollow sacs grow to 15 cm/6 in. in length and are found in clumps.

Etymology The genus name, *Halosaccion*, is Greek for "sea sac."

Habitat Rocky shores in the middle intertidal zone, from Alaska to California.

Edibility Unknown.

WINGED KELP

Alaria marginata

FAMILY Alariaceae

Description Winged kelp is so named for the spore-producing winged blades growing from its base. The main blade has a midrib and is light brown to dark brown, wavy edged, and to 3 m/10 ft. in length.

Etymology The genus name, *Alaria*, is Latin for "wine."

Habitat Rocky areas in the lower intertidal zone, from Alaska to California.

Edibility Edible.

FEATHER BOA

Egregia menziesii

FAMILY Alariaceae

Description Feather boa ranges from olive brown to dark brown. The main stem (stipe) is to 6 m/20 ft. long and is decorated with small blades and elongated floats.

Etymology The genus name, *Egregia*, is Latin for "remarkable."

Habitat Rocky shores in the lower intertidal zone, from BC to California.

Edibility Has been used as a soil booster on farms.

▶ BROAD-RIB KELP

Pleurophycus gardneri

FAMILY Alariaceae

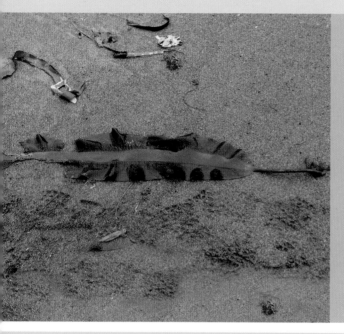

Description Broad-rib kelp is so named for its central broad rib that runs the length of the blade. The blade is dark brown to black and to 1.5 m/5 ft. long. It is supported by a 50 cm/20 in. stem (stipe) and holdfast.

Etymology The genus name, *Pleurophycus*, is Greek for "ribbed seaweed."

Habitat High-current areas in the lower intertidal zone, from Alaska to California.

Edibility Unknown.

▶ OLD GROWTH KELP

Pterygophora californica

FAMILY Alariaceae

Description Old growth kelp is unusual among the brown seaweeds, for the reason that it can live up to 25 years. Most brown seaweeds are annuals. It is dark brown and can grow to 3 m/10 ft. in height. The top half of the stem (stipe) has smooth blades to 90 cm/35 in.

Etymology The genus name, *Pterygophora*, is Greek for "bearing wings."

Habitat Grows in the lower intertidal zone, from BC to California.

Edibility Unknown.

▶ ROCKWEED

Fucus gardneri

FAMILY Fucaceae

Description Rockweed is one of the most common seaweeds along the Pacific Northwest coast. Its colour varies from dark green to yellowish brown, and it grows to 50 cm/20 in. long. The swollen terminal ends hold the eggs and sperm.

Etymology The genus name, *Fucus*, is Greek for "seaweed."

Habitat Grows on rocks in the semi-protected mid to lower intertidal zones, from Alaska to California.

Edibility Unknown.

▶ LITTLE ROCKWEED DWARF ROCKWEED

Pelvetiopsis limitata

FAMILY Fucaceae

Description Little rockweed is light green to olive green; it is lighter in colour than rockweed. It grows to only 18 cm/7 in. long and has swollen terminal ends.

Etymology The genus name, *Pelvetiopsis*, commemorates François Alexandre Pelvet, a French naturalist.

Habitat Prefers to grow on rocks in the high intertidal zone, from southern BC to California.

Edibility Unknown.

▶ SEERSUCKER RIBBED KELP

Costaria costata

FAMILY Costariaceae

Description Seersucker is light brown to dark brown in colour, with elliptical blades to 2 m/6.6 ft. long and five defined ribs. When growing in the semi-protected waters of the lower intertidal zone, the blades are wider than when growing in harsher waters.

Etymology The genus name, *Costaria*, and species name, *costata*, are both Latin for "rib."

Habitat Found in the lower intertidal zone, from Alaska to California.

Edibility Edible when young.

▶ SMALL PERENNIAL KELP GIANT KELP

Macrocystis integrifolia

FAMILY Laminariaceae

Description Small perennial kelp is yellowish to dark brown in colour and can grow to 30 m/100 ft. in length. The individual blades are to 35 cm/14 in. long and have a pointed float at the end.

Etymology The genus name, *Macrocystis*, is Greek for "giant bladder."

Habitat Grows in rocky areas in the lower intertidal zone, from Alaska to California.

Edibility Edible.

▶ SEA PALM

Postelsia palmaeformis

FAMILY Laminariaceae

Description Sea palm is an apt name for this aquatic palm tree. It is light green when young and brown when mature, and it grows to 60 cm/24 in. in height. The serrated blades hang over the top of the stipe, giving it a palm tree–like appearance.

Etymology The genus name, *Postelsia*, commemorates Alexander Filippovich Postels, an Estonian naturalist hired by Czar Nicholas I of Russia to explore the Pacific coast.

Habitat Grows on wave-swept rocky shores in the mid to lower intertidal zone, from BC to California.

Edibility Edible.

▶ SPLIT KELP

Laminaria setchellii

FAMILY Laminariaceae

Description Split kelp is dark brown to almost black in colour. The stipe can grow to 80 cm/31 in. high with terminal split blades to 80 cm/31 in. long.

Etymology The genus name, *Laminaria*, is Latin for "thin leaf."

Habitat Prefers wave-swept exposed rocky areas in the lower intertidal zone, from Alaska to California.

Edibility Edible.

▶ SUGAR WRACK

Laminaria saccharina

FAMILY Laminariaceae

Description Sugar wrack is so called because of its sugary taste. The blades are dark brown and grow to 3 m/10 ft. in length. They are held firmly in place by a small stipe and holdfast.

Etymology The species name, *saccharina*, is Latin for "sugar."

Habitat Found in rocky areas in the lower intertidal zone, from Alaska to California.

Edibility Edible.

▶ BULL KELP

Nereocystis luetkeana

FAMILY Laminariaceae

Description Bull kelp is one of the most recognized kelps in the Pacific Northwest and one of the largest, attaining lengths of over 30 m/100 ft. The long brown stipe is kept afloat by a large pneumatocyst (float), which is decorated with over 20 blades, each to 3 m/10 ft.

Etymology The genus name, *Nereocystis*, is Greek for "mermaid's bladder."

Habitat Grows on rocky areas in the lower intertidal zone, from Alaska to California.

Edibility Edible.

▶ SEA CAULIFLOWER

Leathesia difformis

FAMILY Leathesiaceae

Description The sea cauliflower, often called the sea potato, is a brain-shaped yellowish-brown alga to 15 cm/6 in. across. It can grow on other algae (epiphytic) or on rocks.

Etymology The genus name, *Leathesia*, commemorates Reverend G.R. Leathes, a British naturalist.

Habitat Found in the mid to lower intertidal zone, from Alaska to Mexico.

Edibility Unknown.

▶ JAPANESE WIREWEED

Sargassum muticum

FAMILY Sargassaceae

Description Japanese wireweed was introduced to the west coast accidentally, in the 1930s. It is olive brown and to 2 m/6.6 ft. long, with hundreds of small rounded floats.

Etymology The genus name, *Sargassum*, is Spanish for "seaweed."

Habitat It is mainly seen in protected bays in the lower intertidal zone, from Alaska to Mexico.

Edibility Unknown.

► LYNGBYE'S SEDGE

Carex lyngbyei

SEDGE FAMILY Cyperaceae

Description Lyngbye's sedge grows to 1 m/3.3 ft. The leaves have reddish-brown sheaths; the inflorescence is stiff nodding spikes. It spreads by rhizome.

Habitat Found in mud flats, tidal flats, and salt marshes, from Alaska to California.

Edibility It is a favourite forage for grizzly bears, migratory geese, and trumpeter swans.

► SCOULER'S SURF GRASS

Phyllospadix scouleri

EELGRASS FAMILY Zosteraceae

Description Scouler's surf grass leaves are to 1.5 m/5 ft. long and only 0.4 cm/0.15 in. wide. Male and female flowers are borne on separate plants (dioecious).

Habitat Grows on rocky shores in very exposed areas of the lower intertidal zone. Alaska to Mexico.

Edibility The rhizomes were harvested by west coast Indigenous peoples.

► MARINE EELGRASS

Zostera marina

EELGRASS FAMILY Zosteraceae

Description Marine eelgrass has leaves to 1.2 m/ 4 ft. long and 1 cm/0.5 in. wide. A dwarf introduced eelgrass (Z. *japonica*) can often be seen growing with common eelgrass. The dwarf eelgrass has shorter, thinner leaves.

Habitat Prefers protected bays and mud flats. Found from Alaska to Mexico.

Edibility The seeds and rhizomes were harvested by west coast Indigenous groups.

► SEA ASPARAGUS AMERICAN GLASSWORT

Salicornia virginica

GOOSEFOOT FAMILY Chenopodiaceae

This species is described on page 39, among other members of the Goosefoot family in the Flowering Plants section.

BLACK SEASIDE LICHEN SEA TAR

Verrucaria maura

FAMILY Verrucariaceae

Description Black seaside lichen can be found in patches ranging from under 15 cm/6 in. to over 5 m/ 16 ft. wide. Some patches look as if an oil spill has occurred.

Etymology The genus name, *Verrucaria*, is Latin for "water wart." It supposedly dries up warts if it is drunk with water.

Habitat Very common along exposed rocks in the high intertidal zone, from Alaska to California.

FAUNA

BIRDS

▶ GOLDEN EAGLE

Aquila chrysaetos

HAWK FAMILY Accipitridae

Description The golden eagle has a length of 70–90 cm/28–35 in. and a wingspan of 2.4 m/7.9 ft. On adults, the neck has golden feathers, while the rest of the body is dark brown. The legs are heavily feathered down to the talons.

Etymology The genus name, *Aquila*, is Latin for "eagle."

Habitat Grasslands and forests, from canyons to high mountains, from Alaska to California.

▶ BALD EAGLE

Haliaeetus leucocephalus

HAWK FAMILY Accipitridae

Description The bald eagle is probably North America's most recognized bird. It is the national symbol of the United States. Benjamin Franklin originally wanted the wild turkey to be the national symbol because he thought the bald eagle was a bird of bad moral character. The bald eagle has a length of up to 1 m/3.3 ft. and a wingspan to 2 m/6.6 ft. It can weigh up to 6.5 kg/14 lb. It takes five years to get its snow-white head, neck, and tail. Bald eagles are known to wait patiently in high trees observing ospreys diving for fish. When the osprey finally catches a fish, the eagle will swoop down and steal the catch.

Etymology The scientific name, *Haliaeetus leucocephalus*, means "sea eagle with white head." The common name bald comes from *piebald*, meaning "contrasting colours" or "black and white."

Habitat Common throughout North America, wherever there is water.

► NORTHERN HARRIER MARSH HAWK

Circus cyaneus

HAWK FAMILY Accipitridae

Description Northern harriers, like other harriers, have distinct colour and size differences between the sexes. As with most raptors, the male is smaller. It is to 400 g/14 oz., while the female is to 750 g/26 oz. The mature male's plumage is grey blue on top and white on the underside. The female is brownish overall. Northern harriers have a longer wingspan (to 1.2 m/4 ft.) for their body size than any other raptor in North America.

Habitat Found over most of North America. They can be seen floating with their heads facing down 3–6 m/10–20 ft. above marshes, fields, and farmland, looking for mice, voles, and other small mammals.

► RED-TAILED HAWK

Buteo jamaicensis

HAWK FAMILY Accipitridae

Description The red-tailed hawk is the most common hawk in North America. It weighs 0.7–1.6 kg/1.5–3.5 lb. and has a wingspan of 1.1–1.4 m/3.6–4.6 ft. and a length of 45–65 cm/18–26 in. Males are smaller than females. The mature plumage is a mottled dark red brown on its back and the tops of its wings, with a lighter barred stomach and underwings. The tail ranges from orange red to brick red.

Etymology The scientific name, *Buteo jamaicensis*, means "buzzard from Jamaica."

Habitat Red-tailed hawks are extremely resourceful; they can adapt to urban situations, forests, deserts, and farmland. Their range extends from Alaska to Central America.

▶ COOPER'S HAWK

Accipiter cooperii

HAWK FAMILY Accipitridae

Description Cooper's hawk is a crow-sized raptor 375–700 g/13–25 oz. in weight, with a wingspan of 62–94 cm/24–37 in. and a length of 38–48 cm/15–19 in. The male is smaller than the female. Mature cooper's hawks have a dark cap, red eyes, blue-grey upper plumage, and light underparts with reddish-brown bars.

Etymology Cooper's hawk was named by French naturalist Charles Lucien Bonaparte, the nephew of French emperor Napoleon Bonaparte, in 1828. The species name, *cooperii*, commemorates William Cooper (1798–1864), an American zoologist and naturalist.

Habitat Prefers coniferous or deciduous forests for breeding and hunting. Ranges from southern Canada to northern Mexico but winters as far away as Central America.

▶ NORTHERN GOSHAWK

Accipiter gentilis

HAWK FAMILY Accipitridae

Description The northern goshawk is widespread and fairly common; however, it is secretive and not often seen. It is the largest member of the genus *Accipiter*. Females can weigh as much as 1 kg/2.2 lb. and have a wingspan of 1–1.2 m/3.3–4 ft. and a length of 46–66 cm/18–26 in. The upper plumage is slate grey, with barred grey on white below.

Etymology The species name, *gentilis*, means "noble–gentle," not an observation I would make if I were being hunted by one. The common name goshawk literally means "goose hawk."

Habitat Forested areas from the taiga border through the mountain ranges of Washington, Oregon, and California.

▶ MERLIN

Falco columbarius

FALCON FAMILY Falconidae

Description Formally known as the pigeon hawk, the merlin is a small falcon not much bigger than a robin. It weighs 150–200 g/5–7 oz. and has a wingspan to 61 cm/24 in. and a length of 25–30 cm/10–12 in. Males have blue grey upper plumage with dark tail bands. Females are brown above with lighter tail bands. Both have light-brown streaking on the undersides.

Etymology The species name, *columbarius*, means "dove pigeon."

Habitat Coniferous and mixed forests; open parkland; marshes; urban areas, especially around bird feeders; coastlines; and even deserts. It ranges from Alaska to Mexico.

▶ PEREGRINE FALCON

Falco peregrinus

FALCON FAMILY Falconidae

Description The peregrine falcon is the fastest-diving bird in the world, with speeds up to 320 kph/200 mph. It has a length to 50 cm/20 in. and a wingspan to 1.1 m/3.6 ft. The head is dark with a yellow eye ring and a dark moustache. It has a bluish-grey back and white underparts with dark barring and spots.

Etymology The genus name, *Falco*, means "curved blade," referring to the hooked beak. The species name, *peregrinus*, means "travelling" or "wandering," referring to the huge areas it can cover.

Habitat Nests on cliffs; also known to nest on high-rise buildings. It is the most widespread raptor.

▶ GYRFALCON

Falco rusticolus

FALCON FAMILY Falconidae

Description The gyrfalcon is the largest of the falcons; it can weigh up to 1.8 kg/4 lb., with a wingspan of 1.2 m/4 ft. and a length of 51–64 cm/ 20–25 in. The upper plumage is grey, and the undersides are white with grey markings. Medieval falconers and nobility considered the gyrfalcon the most skilful and graceful falcon.

Habitat Arctic tundra and high mountain forests from Alaska to British Columbia.

▶ OSPREY

Pandion haliaetus

FALCON FAMILY Falconidae

Description The osprey is called "fish eagle" in many countries, because its diet is almost exclusively fish. It weighs 1.4–2 kg/3–4.4 lb., has a wingspan to 180 cm/71 in., and can be up to 61 cm/ 24 in. in length. The upper plumage is dark brown, with white undersides. The head is mostly white, with a brown line to the eye.

Etymology The genus name, *Pandion*, is from the mythical Greek king Pandion. The species name, *haliaetus*, means "sea eagle."

Habitat Almost anywhere there are water and fish. It has a worldwide distribution in all continents except Antarctica.

▶ TURKEY VULTURE

Cathartes aura

VULTURE FAMILY Cathartidae

Description The turkey vulture is one of North America's largest birds of prey. It can weigh as much as 2.3 kg/5.1 lb., with a wingspan of up to 183 cm/72 in. and a length of 62–81 cm/24–32 in. The overall plumage is brownish black, with the underwing flight feathers having a silver tinge. The disproportionately small head is red and featherless, with an ivory-coloured beak.

Etymology The genus name, *Cathartes*, means "cleanser" or "purifier." The species, *aura*, name is from the Spanish word *auroura*, meaning "turkey vulture."

Habitat Beaches, forested hillsides, and back roads, looking for roadkill. Turkey vultures are mainly summer dwellers in most of Oregon, Washington, and southern British Columbia. They winter in the south.

▶ SNOWY OWL

Bubo scandiacus

TRUE OWL FAMILY Strigidae

Description Snowy owls are different from most owls in that they hunt in the daylight. They are large owls, to 2.9 kg/6.4 lb., with a wingspan of up to 1.5 m/5 ft. and a length of 51–68 cm/20–27 in. Their plumage can vary from being extremely barred to pure white. Males are usually less barred than females, and juveniles are heavily barred. Their heads are round, with piercing yellow eyes.

Etymology The genus name, *Bubo*, means "eagle owl." The species name, *scandiacus*, refers to Scandinavia.

Habitat Snowy owls are circumpolar, nesting and hunting in the North American tundra and in Eurasia. When their winter food source (lemmings) is scarce, they migrate south to open fields, marshes, and shorelines.

▶ GREAT HORNED OWL

Bubo virginianus

TRUE OWL FAMILY Strigidae

Description Great horned owls are the most widely dispersed owls in North and South America. They can weigh up to 2.5 kg/5.5 lb. and have a wingspan up to 1.5 m/5 ft. and a length of 46–64 cm/18–25 in. The upper plumage is a mottled grey brown, with thin horizontal barring below. The top of the head is flat, with large ear tufts on the sides.

Etymology The species name, *virginianus*, is from the Virginia colonies of eastern North America, which were named for the Virgin Queen, Queen Elizabeth I of England (1533–1603).

Habitat With the amount of area great horned owls cover, they have adapted well to and can be found in extremely diverse habitats, including forests, deserts, shorelines, and marshes. They range from Alaska to the tip of South America, from the east coast to the west coast.

▶ BARRED OWL

Strix varia

TRUE OWL FAMILY Strigidae

Description Barred owls are relatively new to the west coast. The first one observed in southern BC was seen in 1966. They are an average-sized owl with a weight up to 1 kg/2.2 lb., a wingspan of 1.1 m/3.6 ft., and a length of up to 55 cm/22 in. The upper plumage is a mottled brown with white spots. The throat has horizontal barring, while the chest has vertical streaking. The head is large and rounded, with dark eyes and a yellowish beak.

Etymology The genus name, *Strix*, is from the Greek word *strinx*, meaning "owl." The collective noun for owls is a parliament. The thought is that they are wise.

Habitat Observed year-round in the Pacific Northwest, mostly in mixed forests.

▶ GREAT GREY OWL

Strix nebulosa

TRUE OWL FAMILY Strigidae

Description The great grey owl is the tallest of the North American owls. It has a wingspan to 1.4 m/4.6 ft. and a length to 84 cm/33 in. It has a very large grey-and-white facial disc, with bright-yellow eyes and mottled-grey upper plumage and streaked underparts. West coast birders get quite excited when there is a sighting.

Etymology The species name, *nebulosa*, means "grey mottled" or "clouded," referring to its plumage.

Habitat Mainly a northern owl, hunting and nesting in fens and forests of the taiga.

▶ BARN OWL

Tyto alba

BARN OWL FAMILY Tytonidae

Description The barn owl weighs up to 700 g/25 oz. and has a wingspan up to 110 cm/43 in. and a length to 41 cm/16 in. The upper plumage is golden brown with light-grey spots. The underparts are white with dark spots. It is the white, heart-shaped face that distinguishes the barn owl. This great little mouser used to be a common sight at twilight perched on farmland fence posts, but with the disappearance of barns, the use of rodenticides, and habitat loss, the barn owl's numbers are dwindling.

Etymology The genus name, *Tyto*, is from the Greek word *tuto*, meaning "owl."

Habitat In the Pacific Northwest, it is mainly seen on farmland and in grassy fields with a good concentration of mice.

▶ SHORT-EARED OWL

Asio flammeus

TRUE OWL FAMILY Strigidae

Description Short-eared owls are medium sized and can often be seen hunting alongside northern harriers for mice and voles. They can weigh up to 475 g/17 oz. and have a wingspan of up to 110 cm/43 in., with a length of 43 cm/17 in. The upper and lower plumage is vertically streaked red brown, with the wings and tail being barred. The yellow-orange eyes are accented by mascara-like black rings.

Etymology The genus name, *Asio*, is mentioned by Pliny the Elder as a type of eared or horned owl. The species name, *flammeus*, means "flame" or "fire coloured."

Habitat Hovers over fields and marshes hunting for its almost exclusive diet of mice and voles.

▶ LONG-EARED OWL

Asio otus

TRUE OWL FAMILY Strigidae

Description The long-eared owl is a medium-sized owl with a length to 40 cm/16 in. and a wingspan to 1 m/3.3 ft. It has conspicuously long ear tufts and brownish plumage overall, with vertical streaking. The facial disc is orange with a white X separating the eyes.

Habitat Long-eared owls roost during the day and hunt at night, mainly for rodents. They range from northern Canada to Baja California.

▶ NORTHERN SAW-WHET OWL

Aegolius acadicus

TRUE OWL FAMILY Strigidae

Description The northern saw-whet owl is one of the smallest owl species in North America. It has a length to 20 cm/8 in. and a wingspan of 48 cm/19 in. Its round head has large yellow eyes, a dark beak, and a disc-shaped face with fine white streaks. The underparts are a soft mix of tan, brown, and white.

Etymology The species name, *acadicus*, is named after Acadia, a former region of eastern Canada and the northeastern United States.

Habitat A tough little guy to find, it camouflages itself in mixed forests during the day and hunts at night.

▶ WOOD DUCK

Aix sponsa

DUCK FAMILY Anatidae

Description The male wood duck has to be North America's best-dressed duck. It is medium sized with a wingspan of 43–52 cm/17–20 in. and a length of 46–53 cm/18–21 in. The male has multicoloured plumage; the head has a down-swept crest and is glossy green with white stripes, a white chin, and red eyes. The female is less coloured. She is greyish-brown with a white eye patch and a small head crest.

Etymology The genus name, *Aix*, means "diving bird." The species name, *sponsa*, means "bride," from the Latin word *spondere*, meaning "to pledge oneself." As the common name suggests, wood ducks nest in trees.

Habitat On lakes, ponds, and streams that are located close to a forest. Wood ducks are known to have two broods, one in spring and one in late summer.

▶ AMERICAN WIGEON

Anas americana

DUCK FAMILY Anatidae

Description American wigeons are medium-sized ducks with a wingspan to 84 cm/33 in. and a length of 46–58 cm/18–23 in. The males have cinnamon-brown plumage with a black rump. They have a cream-coloured forehead with green patches on the face and a black-tipped greyish-blue bill. The female is mottled brown with a flecked grey head.

Etymology The genus name, *Anas*, is from the Latin and means "duck." The collective noun for a group of ducks on the water is a raft, in the air a flock, and on the ground a brace.

Habitat In the Pacific Northwest, American wigeons winter on ponds or lakes, along quiet shorelines, and in parks—anywhere there is aquatic vegetation and lowland elevation.

▶ MALLARD

Anas platyrhynchos

DUCK FAMILY Anatidae

Description Mallards are the most widespread ducks in the northern hemisphere. They have a wingspan to 93 cm/37 in. and a length to 71 cm/28 in. The males have an iridescent green head, a bright yellow bill, a narrow white collar, a brown chest with lighter sides, blue exposed wing patches, and black curls above a white tail. The females have an orange bill with a black patch and mottled brown plumage. Both have bright-orange feet. The female has the classic loud quack that always brings a smile, *quack-wack-wack-wack*. The mallard is ancestor to the domestic duck, of which there can be seen some whiter hybrids.

Etymology The species name, *platyrhynchos*, is from the Greek word *platurhunkhos*, "broad billed."

Habitat City ponds, lakes, shorelines, and flooded fields—almost anywhere there is shallow water and vegetation.

▶ COMMON GOLDENEYE

Bucephala clangula

DUCK FAMILY Anatidae

Description The common goldeneye is medium sized, with a wingspan to 76 cm/30 in. and a length to 41–51 cm/16–20 in. The male's head is an iridescent dark green, with a round white cheek spot and yellow eyes. The plumage is black, with white streaks on the back and white underparts. The female has a brown head and bright-yellow eyes, with greyish-brown plumage.

Etymology The genus name, *Bucephala*, is from the Greek word *boukephalos*, meaning "bull headed," from *bous*, "ox," and *kephale*, "the head." The species name, *clangula*, means "to resound," referring to the whistling wings. Another common name for goldeneye is "whistler."

Habitat Most common goldeneyes that winter in the Pacific Northwest stay along the coastline, with some being content on lakes or ponds. In spring, they fly north to breed, making their nests in tree cavities.

▶ BARROW'S GOLDENEYE

Bucephala islandica

DUCK FAMILY Anatidae

Description The barrow's goldeneye is marginally larger than the common goldeneye. It has a wingspan to 76 cm/30 in. and a length to 48 cm/19 in. The male barrow's goldeneye differs from the male common goldeneye by having white crescent-shaped patches in front of its eyes and white barrings on the sides. The female has a darker-brown head.

Etymology The species name, *islandica*, means "Iceland." In Iceland, barrow's goldeneye is known as *húsönd*, "house duck." The common name commemorates Sir John Barrow (1764–1848), a world traveller and an English statesman.

Habitat Breeds in the Pacific Northwest on ponds, lakes, and streams. Spends the winter along the coastline of BC and Washington.

▶ BUFFLEHEAD

Bucephala albeola

DUCK FAMILY Anatidae

Description The bufflehead is the smallest diving duck in North America. It has a wingspan to 61 cm/24 in. and a length to 40 cm/16 in. The male has a large white triangular patch behind its eyes, an iridescent dark green–purple head, a black back, and white underparts. The female has an oval white cheek patch and is dark overall with paler underparts.

Etymology The species name, *albeola*, means "white." The common name bufflehead is a hybrid of *buffalo* and *head*. The buffalo look is most noticeable when the male puffs out its head feathers.

Habitat Breeds in lakes and ponds in Alaska and across northern Canada. Spends the winter along the Pacific coast.

▶ HOODED MERGANSER

Lophodytes cucullatus

DUCK FAMILY Anatidae

Description The male hooded merganser has to be in the running for the best-dressed duck. It has a wingspan to 66 cm/26 in. and a length to 48 cm/19 in. The male has handsome white crests bordered in black, cinnamon-coloured sides, and a black back with white streaks. The female has a solid rufous-coloured crest and grey-brown plumage.

Etymology The genus name, *Lophodytes*, means "crested diver." The species name, *cucullatus*, means "hood" or "cowl."

Habitat Ponds and lakes surrounded by forests, where it nests in tree cavities.

▶ COMMON MERGANSER

Mergus merganser

DUCK FAMILY Anatidae

Description Common mergansers are larger than hooded mergansers. They have a wingspan to 84 cm/ 34 in. and a length to 69 cm/27 in. The male has an iridescent dark green–black head, with black plumage on top and white plumage below. The female has a reddish-brown crest, a white breast, and a grey back. Common mergansers are equipped with serrated bills, which help catch and hold fish.

Etymology The common name and species name, *merganser*, means "water bird goose."

Habitat Breeds in Alaska and across northern Canada. In southern BC, Washington, and Oregon, they can be seen year-round.

▶ NORTHERN PINTAIL

Anas acuta

DUCK FAMILY Anatidae

Description Northern pintails are medium-sized freshwater ducks. They have a wingspan to 89 cm/ 35 in. Males are to 74 cm/29 in. in length, while females are to 56 cm/22 in. Males have a brown head, a black bill with grey sides, a white neck, a grey back and sides, and a long pointed black tail. Females have a pale-brown head, a blackish bill, mottled grey-brown plumage, and a shorter tail than males.

Etymology The species name, *acuta*, is in reference to the sharply pointed tail.

Habitat In the Pacific Northwest, we get to see pintails in late summer and autumn on ponds, in marshes, and in flooded fields.

▶ LESSER SCAUP BLUEBILL

Aythya affinis

DUCK FAMILY Anatidae

Description The lesser scaup is the most abundant diving duck in North America. It has a wingspan to 76 cm/30 in. and a length to 46 cm/18 in. Males have a rounded dark head with a greenish tinge, a thin blue-grey bill, and a black breast and hindquarters, with a dark wavy pattern on the upper plumage. The female has a brown head and a grey bill with a white patch at the base, with brownish plumage. The lesser scaup closely resembles the greater scaup (A. *marila*).

Etymology The genus name, *Aythya*, is from the Greek word *aithuia*, a seabird mentioned by Aristotle. The species name, *affinis*, means "related" or "allied."

Habitat Winters along the Pacific Northwest coast. Breeds in Alaska and across northern Canada in open forests and tundra.

▶ RING-NECKED DUCK

Aythya collaris

DUCK FAMILY Anatidae

Description Ring-necked ducks could be more appropriately named ring-*billed* ducks, as the rings on their bills are far easier to see than the thin brown ring on their necks. They are a medium-sized duck with a wingspan to 63 cm/25 in. and a length to 46 cm/18 in. The male has an iridescent green-purple head, a grey bill with two white rings, a black neck with a thin brown ring at the base, grey sides, and a black back and chest. The female has a white ring at the top of the bill, with dark-brown plumage.

Etymology The species name, *collaris*, means "collared."

Habitat Winters in the Pacific Northwest in ponds, lakes, bogs, and flooded fields. Breeds across northern Canada.

▶ NORTHERN SHOVELLER

Anas clypeata

DUCK FAMILY Anatidae

Description The northern shoveller is so named because of its large shovel-shaped bill. Its wingspan is to 81 cm/32 in and its length is to 51 cm/20 in. The male has a dark-green head, yellow eyes, a large dark bill, a white breast, brown sides, and black hindquarters. The female has an orangish bill and mottled brown plumage, much like a female mallard.

Etymology The genus name, *Anas*, is Latin for "duck." The species name, *clypeata*, means "shield bearing," in reference to the bill.

Habitat Feeds on vegetation in ponds, shallow lakes, and flooded fields. Breeds at the edges of shallow water near vegetation.

▶ GADWALL

Anas strepera

DUCK FAMILY Anatidae

Description From a distance, gadwalls could pass for mallards or wigeons. A closer look reveals that the males have an amazingly delicate pattern on their sides and chest, a brown head with a black bill, and greyish-brown plumage above. Females have a white wing patch, a yellowish bill, and mottled brown plumage. They have a wingspan to 84 cm/ 33 in. and a length to 58 cm/23 in.

Etymology The species name, *strepera*, means "to be noisy."

Habitat Year-round residents in the Pacific Northwest on ponds and marshes, where there is shallow water with aquatic vegetation.

► HARLEQUIN DUCK

Histrionicus histrionicus

DUCK FAMILY Anatidae

Description The male harlequin must be another North American duck in line for best-dressed duck. Harlequins have a wingspan to 64 cm/25 in. and a length to 53 cm/21 in. The male is slate blue with brick-red sides and underparts and white markings on its head, back, and sides. The female has reddish-brown plumage and white patches on its face.

Etymology The genus and species name, *histrionicus*, means "theatrical," like a harlequin, referring to the bright plumage of the male.

Habitat Breeds in mountain streams in spring and summer and returns to rocky ocean shorelines in autumn and winter.

► GREEN-WINGED TEAL

Anas crecca

DUCK FAMILY Anatidae

Description This beautiful little dabbling duck is smaller than other teals. It has a length of 35 cm/ 14 in. and a wingspan to 58 cm/23 in. The male has a rufous head, a dark-green ear patch, a white vertical bar on its side, yellowish-buff undertail feathers, and finely detailed greyish sides and back. The female is mottled brown, much like a female mallard. Both male and female have small dark bills.

Etymology The species name, *crecca*, is a Latinized word meant to mimic the sound of the duck.

Habitat A common winter resident in the Pacific Northwest. Found from August to May in lakes, ponds, and marshes.

► CANADA GOOSE

Branta canadensis

DUCK FAMILY Anatidae

Description The Canada goose is probably the most recognized goose in North America. When in Hyde Park, in London, England, I was told it was the scourge from Canada. Canada geese have a wingspan to 1.7 m/5.6 ft. and a length to 1 m/3.3 ft. The overall colour of the plumage is grey brown, with a black head, neck, and bill and white chin patches. Males can weigh over 5 kg/11 lb. Pairs bond for life.

Etymology The genus name, *Branta*, means "burnt goose," in reference to the black plumage.

Habitat Breeds mainly in the northern parts of North America, with many being permanent residents of the Pacific Northwest.

► CACKLING GOOSE

Branta hutchinsii

DUCK FAMILY Anatidae

Description The cackling goose has a length to 75 cm/30 in. and a wingspan to 1.5 m/5 ft. The main differences between the cackling goose and the Canada goose are that the cackling goose is smaller in size and has a shorter, stubbier bill and a more acute forehead.

Habitat Often seen in the Pacific Northwest swimming and foraging with Canada geese.

▶ GREATER WHITE-FRONTED GOOSE

Anser albifrons

DUCK FAMILY Anatidae

Description The greater white-fronted goose is also known as the specklebelly goose, from the brown barring on its underparts. It has a wingspan to 1.5 m/ 5 ft. and a length to 86 cm/34 in. The overall plumage is light to dark grey, with a white rump. The bill is pink, with a white base extending up the forehead.

Etymology The genus name, *Anser*, means "goose." The species name, *albifrons*, is derived from *albus*, "white," and *frons*, "the forehead."

Habitat Breeds in Alaska and across northern Canada. Migrates to the Pacific Northwest in October. Most commonly seen on freshwater marshes and ponds.

▶ SNOW GOOSE

Chen caerulescens

DUCK FAMILY Anatidae

Description Snow geese are to 81 cm/32 in. long, with a wingspan to 1.3–1.7 m/4.3–5.6 ft. They are bright white, with black wing tips and an orange to dark-pink bill.

Etymology The species name, *caerulescens*, is Latin, meaning, "becoming blue." This refers to a colour variation, a blue morph, that occurs occasionally within the species.

Habitat In winter, large flocks can be seen on farmland from southern BC to Oregon. By spring, the flocks have gone back north to breed.

▶ MUTE SWAN

Cygnus olor

DUCK FAMILY Anatidae

Description The mute swan derives its common name from being quieter than other swan species. It has a wingspan to 2.4 m/7.9 ft. and a length to 1.6 m/5.2 ft. The overall plumage is snow white; it has an orange bill with a black knob at the base.

Etymology Both the genus name, *Cygnus*, and the species name, *olor*, mean "swan."

Habitat Introduced from Europe and Asia. Resident populations can be seen from southern Vancouver Island to the San Juan Islands.

▶ TRUMPETER SWAN

Cygnus buccinator

DUCK FAMILY Anatidae

Description Trumpeter swans are the largest waterfowl in North America. They have a wingspan to 2.4 m/7.9 ft. and a length to 1.65 m/5.4 ft. The overall plumage is snow white, with a straight black bill. Juveniles have grey plumage.

Etymology The species name, *buccinator*, is from the Latin word *buccina*, a military trumpet.

Habitat Breeds in Alaska and northern BC. Migrates to the Pacific Northwest between October and November.

▶ SURF SCOTER

Melanitta perspicillata

DUCK FAMILY Anatidae

Description Surf scoters derive their name from how well they dive for shellfish in the rough ocean surf. They have a wingspan to 75 cm/30 in. and a length to 55 cm/22 in. The males have a large orange-and-white bill and black plumage, with white patches on the forehead and nape. The females have white patches on the face and dark-brown plumage.

Etymology The genus name, *Melanitta*, is from the Greek words *melas*, "black," and *netta*, "duck."

Habitat Breeds on lakes and forest bogs in Alaska and northern California. From October to November, tens of thousands of surf scoters, white-winged scoters, and black scoters arrive on the shores of the Pacific Northwest to winter.

▶ RHINOCEROS AUKLET

Cerorhinca monocerata

AUK FAMILY Alcidae

Description The rhinoceros auklet derives its name from the horn adults grow on their bills during breeding time. Its length is to 38 cm/15 in., and its wingspan is to 55 cm/22 in. The plumage is dark grey above and lighter below. The bill is orange brown, with a lighter-coloured horn when breeding. It also has thin white plumes on its face.

Etymology The species name, *monocerata*, is from the Greek words *monos*, "single," and *keras*, "horn."

Habitat Can be seen by small islands, near shorelines, and on open seas along the west coast, from Alaska to California.

TUFTED PUFFIN

Fratercula cirrhata

AUK FAMILY Alcidae

Description The tufted puffin is a beautiful pigeon-sized bird with a length to 38 cm/15 in. and a wingspan to 65 cm/26 in. The overall plumage is black, with a white face, a parrot-like orange bill, red-orange feet and legs, and creamy-yellow curved tufts during breeding season. Like other puffins, the tufted puffin is an excellent underwater swimmer.

Etymology The species name, *cirrhata*, means "curly headed," referring to the creamy yellow tufts.

Habitat Winters at sea and breeds on coastal islands and cliffs, from Alaska to the San Juan Islands in Washington.

PIGEON GUILLEMOT

Cepphus columba

AUK FAMILY Alcidae

Description The pigeon guillemot has a length to 35 cm/14 in. and a wingspan to 58 cm/23 in. Its breeding plumage is black with an irregularly shaped white wing patch; the legs and feet are red. If lucky to get close enough, you will see that it also has a bright-red bill lining.

Etymology The genus name, *Cepphus*, is from the Greek word *kepphos*, meaning "seabird."

Habitat Breeds on cliffs and coastal islands and sometimes on elevated wharves; spends winter offshore, from Alaska to California.

▶ MARBLED MURRELET

Brachyramphus marmoratus

AUK FAMILY Alcidae

Description The marbled murrelet has a length to 25 cm/10 in. and a wingspan to 40 cm/16 in. The non-breeding plumage is black on the head and neck and white on the underbody. The breeding plumage is brown above, with a brown-and-white-spotted throat and marbled brown-grey underparts.

Etymology The genus name, *Brachyramphus*, is from the Greek words *brachy*, "short," and *ramphus*, "bill." The species name, *marmoratus*, means "marbled."

Habitat Marbled murrelets can be found from Alaska to California. They nest in first- and second-growth conifers where present. Otherwise, such as in northern populations where there are very few to no trees, they nest on rocky islands and outcrops. It was not until 1974 that a marbled murrelet nest was discovered in the Pacific Northwest, in a Douglas fir over 30 m/100 ft. tall.

▶ COMMON MURRE

Uria aalge

AUK FAMILY Alcidae

Description The common murre is a penguin-like bird with a length to 46 cm/18 in. and a wingspan to 73 cm/29 in. When breeding, it has a black head, bill, back, and wings, with white underparts.

Etymology The species name, *aalge*, is Danish for "auk."

Habitat When breeding, the common murre can be seen around small coastal islands and cliffs, from Alaska to California.

▶ GREAT EGRET COMMON EGRET

Ardea alba

HERON FAMILY Ardeidae

Description Great egrets have a wingspan to 1.7 m/5.6 ft. and a length to 90 cm/35 in. They have snow-white plumage, a long yellow bill, and black legs and feet.

Etymology The genus name, *Ardea*, is Latin for "heron."

Habitat Marshes, ponds, and rivers, where it feeds on frogs, fish, insects, and small snakes. Common in California and southern Oregon.

▶ GREAT BLUE HERON

Ardea herodias

HERON FAMILY Ardeidae

Description Great blue herons are the largest herons in North America. They have a wingspan to 1.8 m/6 ft. and a length to 1.2 m/4 ft. The overall plumage is grey blue, the head is white with a black streak, and the foreneck and chest are white with black streaks.

Etymology The species name, *herodias*, is from the Greek *erodios*, "heron."

Habitat With the exception of areas where water freezes, blue herons are year-round residents in the Pacific Northwest. They tend to favour areas that have shallow water (either fresh or marine) and tall trees to construct their heronry (breeding ground).

BLACK-CROWNED NIGHT HERON

Nycticorax nycticorax

HERON FAMILY Ardeidae

Description The black-crowned night heron has a wingspan to 1.2 m/4 ft. and a length to 67 cm/26 in. It has a black crown and back, red eyes, a white face and underparts, and grey wings and tail. In breeding season, adults have three long white plumes on their heads.

Etymology The genus name and species name, *nycticorax*, means "night raven" and refers to the night heron's nocturnal feeding habits and its raven-like voice.

Habitat Lives in freshwater and saltwater marshes, lakes, and swamps, and in wooded streams. Hunts in the early morning and at dusk for fish, frogs, and snakes.

BROWN PELICAN

Pelecanus occidentalis

PELICAN FAMILY Pelecanidae

Description The brown pelican is the smallest of the eight species of pelican. It has a wingspan of 1.8–2.4 m/6–8 ft. and a length of 1–1.4 m/3.3–4.6 ft. The overall plumage is grey brown, with a white head and a large dark bill with a throat pouch. Brown pelicans will dive from heights of up to 9 m/30 ft. above water upon sighting a fish.

Etymology The species name, *occidentalis*, means "western."

Habitat Mainly coastal, from California to southern Vancouver Island.

► SANDHILL CRANE

Grus canadensis

CRANE FAMILY Gruidae

Description Sandhill cranes fly with their necks straight out and their legs and feet straight back. They have a wingspan to 2.3 m/7.5 ft. and a length of 1.2 m/4 ft. The overall plumage is sand coloured and the legs are black; the head has a red crown, a whitish cheek patch, and a long black bill.

Etymology The genus name, *Grus*, means "crane."

Habitat There are a few resident sandhill cranes in the Pacific Northwest. However, most are migratory. They feed on grain, aquatic vegetation, and small shellfish.

► DOUBLE-CRESTED CORMORANT

Phalacrocorax auritus

CORMORANT FAMILY Phalacrocoracidae

Description The double-crested cormorant will often take shortcuts over land, whereas the pelagic cormorant and the Brandt's cormorant always fly over water. They have a wingspan to 1.2 m/4 ft. and a length to 91 cm/36 in. Adults are black, while juveniles are brownish. They have a straight bill with a hooked tip, orange skin under the bill, and two white crests on the crown.

Etymology The genus name, *Phalacrocorax*, is from the Greek words *phalakros*, "bald," and *korax*, "raven." The species name, *auritus*, means "eared" or "having long ears."

Habitat Fishes on lakes, ponds, rivers, and oceans. Mainly coastal in the Pacific Northwest.

▶ BRANDT'S CORMORANT

Phalacrocorax penicillatus

CORMORANT FAMILY Phalacrocoracidae

Description Brandt's cormorant has a wingspan to 1 m/3.3 ft. and a length to 89 cm/35 in. It has black plumage overall, with a brownish throat patch and white tufts of whiskers. A blue throat pouch is visible in mating season.

Etymology The species name, *penicillatus*, means "tufted" or "with brush-like tufts." The common name commemorates German naturalist Johann Friedrich von Brandt (1802–1879).

Habitat Strictly coastal, it is found only along the Pacific coast. As with other species of cormorants, it is often seen perched on a rock or a log with its wings spread out to dry them off.

▶ PELAGIC CORMORANT

Phalacrocorax pelagicus

CORMORANT FAMILY Phalacrocoracidae

Description The pelagic cormorant is the smallest of the Pacific Northwest cormorants, to 71 cm/28 in. in length with a wingspan to 1 m/3.3 ft. It is black, with white patches on the rear sides that are visible when the bird is in flight. If you can get close enough, you can see that the pelagic cormorant has thin white plumes on its neck and head and a small red throat pouch.

Etymology The common name pelagic suggests that this cormorant is an offshore bird; however, it is not. It feeds and nests near the shore.

Habitat Common along Pacific Northwest shorelines from Alaska to California.

▶ BLACK OYSTERCATCHER

Haematopus bachmani

OYSTERCATCHER FAMILY Haematopodidae

Description Black oystercatchers are comical and boisterous. They have a wingspan to 84 cm/33 in. and a length to 45 cm/18 in. The overall plumage is dark brown to black, the legs and feet are pink, the long flattened bill is bright orange, and the eyes are yellow with red rings.

Etymology The genus name, *Haematopus*, means "blood foot." The species name, *bachmani*, commemorates John Bachman (1790–1874), an American naturalist.

Habitat Strictly a shore bird; feeds on mussels, oysters, chitons, and limpets.

▶ VIRGINIA RAIL

Rallus limicola

RAIL FAMILY Rallidae

Description The Virginia rail has a length to 25 cm/10 in. and a wingspan to 33 cm/13 in. Its breeding colours are an attractive range of red browns, with black-and-white barring. It has grey cheeks and a slightly curved red bill.

Etymology The species name, *limicola*, is Latin for "mud dweller." The Virginia rail has very flexible vertebrae, which allow it to forage in thick vegetation; hence the expression "skinny as a rail."

Habitat Marsh and pond edges with an abundance of semi-aquatic vegetation.

▶ SORA

Porzana carolina

RAIL FAMILY Rallidae

Description The sora has a length to 25 cm/10 in. and a wingspan to 36 cm/14 in. Its upperparts are a streaked chestnut brown, with a grey breast. The bill is short, yellow, and surrounded by a black mask.

Etymology The species name, *carolina*, indicates that the sora was first seen in the Carolinas.

Habitat The sora is very well distributed across North America but is extremely elusive. It lives in heavily vegetated freshwater marshes. Patience is needed to find one.

▶ SPOTTED SANDPIPER

Actitis macularius

SANDPIPER FAMILY Scolopacidae

Description The spotted sandpiper has a length to 20 cm/8 in. and a wingspan to 40 cm/16 in. In the breeding season, it has a beautiful dark-spotted neck and stomach; outside of breeding season, it is grey above and white below.

Etymology The species name, *macularius*, means "spotted."

Habitat In the Pacific Northwest, the spotted sandpiper can be seen from May to October along stream banks, ponds, and muddy riverbanks. In winter, I have photographed this sandpiper as far south as Panama.

▶ LEAST SANDPIPER

Calidris minutilla

SANDPIPER FAMILY Scolopacidae

Description The least sandpiper is one of the smallest shorebirds in the Pacific Northwest. It has a length to 12 cm/5 in. and a wingspan to 35 cm/14 in. Breeding adults are a variety of browns above and white below, with greenish-yellow legs and a short dark bill.

Etymology The species name, *minutilla*, means "little."

Habitat Flat muddy areas, pond edges, riverbanks, and coastal mud bays.

▶ LONG-BILLED DOWITCHER

Limnodromus scolopaceus

SANDPIPER FAMILY Scolopacidae

Description Long-billed dowitchers are social birds, often feeding in flocks of 30 or more. They have a wingspan to 51 cm/20 in. and a length to 29 cm/ 11 in. They have dark eyes and a long dark bill. In winter, the upper plumage is grey brown and the underparts are white. In breeding season, the underparts are rusty red.

Etymology The species name, *scolopaceus*, means "resembling a woodcock."

Habitat Breeds in Alaska and northern Canada. Migrates to the freshwater ponds, marshes, and flooded fields of the Pacific Northwest in October.

▶ DUNLIN

Calidris alpina

SANDPIPER FAMILY Scolopacidae

Description Dunlins have a wingspan to 40 cm/ 16 in. and a length to 20 cm/8 in. Their winter, or non-breeding, plumage is grey brown above and white below; the breeding plumage is cinnamon brown with black above and white with a large inky patch below. The bill is black, longer than the head, and slightly curved.

Etymology The genus name, *Calidris*, is from the Greek word *kalidris*, a grey-coloured waterside bird mentioned by Aristotle. The common name dunlin is from the dun plumage it has in winter.

Habitat Breeds in the Arctic in the summer months, and winters along the Pacific coast, where there are mud flats and sandy beaches.

▶ GREATER YELLOWLEGS

Tringa melanoleuca

SANDPIPER FAMILY Scolopacidae

Description Greater yellowlegs have a length to 33 cm/13 in. and a wingspan to 74 cm/29 in. They have brown-grey streaking above and white below. The bill is slightly curved up and is longer than its head. The legs are bright yellow through all seasons. Lesser yellowlegs (*T. flavipes*) are slightly smaller, to 25 cm/10 in. in length, and have a shorter bill.

Etymology The genus name, *Tringa*, is Greek for a white-rumped water bird.

Habitat Both greater and lesser yellowlegs are seen in the Pacific Northwest on their spring and fall migrations. They are common in shallow freshwater habitats, including bogs, mud flats, ponds, and lake edges.

SANDERLING

Calidris alba

SANDPIPER FAMILY Scolopacidae

Description Sanderlings have a length to 19 cm/ 7.5 in. and a wingspan to 43 cm/17 in wide. In winter, the birds are mostly white, except for a dark shoulder patch on their wings. In summer, they are grey above and rusty red on the face and chest. Sanderlings are enjoyable to watch, chasing waves and being chased by waves as they try to eat small washed-up invertebrates.

Etymology The genus name, *Calidris*, is from the Old Greek word *kalidris*, a term used by Aristotle for grey waterside birds. The species name, *alba*, refers to the bird's white winter colour.

Habitat During migration, sanderlings can be found on coastal sandy beaches and in mud flats and sand flats.

WHIMBREL

Numenius phaeopus

SANDPIPER FAMILY Scolopacidae

Description The whimbrel is to 46 cm/18 in., with a wingspan to 90 cm/35 in. It is grey brown, with a long decurved bill, and looks like an oversized sandpiper. The crown has a central stripe.

Etymology The common name whimbrel is thought to have originated from the bird's call. The genus name, *Numenius*, is the Latinized Greek for "new moon," referring to the whimbrel's curved bill. The species name, *phaeopus*, is Greek for "grey footed," for its grey legs and feet.

Habitat Whimbrels are migrants to the coastal Pacific Northwest. They breed in Alaska and northern Canada and winter from California to South America. When migratory, they feed along sandy beaches and salt marshes.

▶ WESTERN GREBE

Aechmophorus occidentalis

GREBE FAMILY Podicipedidae

Description Western grebes are the largest grebes in North America. They have a wingspan to 62 cm/ 24 in. and a length to 74 cm/29 in. Their heads are black brown, with red eyes and a long yellow-green bill. The throat, neck, and underparts are white; the upperparts are dark grey.

Etymology The genus name, *Aechmophorus*, means "spear carrier," referring to the long, spear-like bill.

Habitat Breeds in lakes, ponds, and marshes. Spends the winter along the Pacific coast.

▶ PIED-BILLED GREBE

Podilymbus podiceps

GREBE FAMILY Podicipedidae

Description The pied-billed grebe is the most wide-ranging grebe in North America. It has a length to 35 cm/14 in. and a wingspan of 45–62 cm/ 18–24 in. The overall colours are brownish grey with a reddish-brown neck and breast in the breeding season and in summer. Both the female and the male have a black ring on their short greyish bill.

Etymology The common name of pied-billed is in reference to the grebe's greyish bill with a black ring.

Habitat Breeds on freshwater lakes and marshes. Winters along the Pacific coast in protected bays.

► AMERICAN COOT

Fulica americana

RAIL FAMILY Rallidae

Description The American coot is a bit of an oddity, with its chicken-like head that bobs in time with its lobed paddling feet. It has a wingspan to 61 cm/24 in. and a length to 41 cm/16 in. It has a black head, red eyes, and a white bill with black rings; the overall plumage is grey black. The multicoloured feet are lobed, which assists the American coot when walking in mud or on lily pads.

Etymology The genus name, *Fulica*, means "lobed," referring to the bird's lobed toes.

Habitat Migrates from its northern range to areas where water does not freeze. There are quite a few permanent residents in the Pacific Northwest. It feeds on aquatic and terrestrial greens along with small insects.

► DOWNY WOODPECKER

Picoides pubescens

WOODPECKER FAMILY Picidae

Description The downy woodpecker is the smallest of the Pacific Northwest woodpeckers. It has a wingspan to 30 cm/12 in. and a length to 18 cm/7 in. It has a black-and-white head with a short black bill, white underparts, black wings with white spots, and a white patch on the back. Males have a red patch at the back of their head.

Etymology The species name, *pubescens*, means "pubescent" or "downy."

Habitat Common in mixed forests, urban parks with trees, and backyards with suet feeders. A year-round resident in the Pacific Northwest.

▶ HAIRY WOODPECKER

Picoides villosus

WOODPECKER FAMILY Picidae

Description The hairy woodpecker is a larger version of the downy woodpecker. It has a wingspan to 41 cm/16 in. and a length to 26 cm/10 in. It has a black-and-white head with a short black bill, white underparts, black wings with white spots, and a white patch on the back. Males have a red patch at the back of their head. The hairy woodpecker has a longer bill and less spotting on its wings than the downy woodpecker.

Etymology The species name, *villosus*, means "hairy."

Habitat Mixed forests and urban parks with trees. A permanent resident in the Pacific Northwest.

▶ PILEATED WOODPECKER

Dryocopus pileatus

WOODPECKER FAMILY Picidae

Description The pileated woodpecker is the largest woodpecker in North America. It has a wingspan to 74 cm/29 in. and a length to 48 cm/19 in. The head is white, with a black stripe from the eye and a red crest. The overall plumage is black, with a white patch on the wings. The male has a red moustache, and the female has a black moustache.

Etymology The species name, *pileatus*, means "capped."

Habitat Older mixed forests and larger urban parks with trees. A permanent resident in the Pacific Northwest.

▶ ACORN WOODPECKER

Melanerpes formicivorus

WOODPECKER FAMILY Picidae

Description The acorn woodpecker is aptly named for the way it stores acorns in the bark of trees. It is slightly smaller than an American robin. It has a wingspan to 30 cm/12 in. and a length to 23 cm/9 in. The male has a yellowish forecrown; the female has a black forecrown. Both have a black neck, black wings, a black tail, white underparts, white wing patches, and a white rump.

Etymology The genus name, *Melanerpes*, means "tree creeper" or "woodpecker." The species name, *formicivorus*, means "ant eating."

Habitat Common in Oregon and California, where there are oak trees. The acorn woodpecker gathers acorns in the autumn and stores them in snug holes for later consumption. Because of their soft bark, pines and Douglas firs are mainly used as storage trees.

▶ NORTHERN FLICKER

Colaptes auratus

WOODPECKER FAMILY Picidae

Description Unlike other woodpeckers, the northern flicker will forage on the ground for food, such as ants and fallen apples. It has a wingspan to 51 cm/20 in. and a length to 33 cm/13 in. It has a grey-brown head with a buffy head patch, a heavily black-barred back, a black crescent on its breast, white underparts with black spots, and pink red wing and tail linings. Males have a red moustache. It is often called the red-shafted flicker for the red feathers on the undersides of its wings.

Etymology The genus name, *Colaptes*, is from the Greek word *kolaptes*, "chiseler." The species name, *auratus*, means "gilded" or "ornamented with gold," in reference to the yellow-shafted flicker, another variation of the species.

Habitat Mixed forests, treed parks, and urban gardens. Flickers will announce their territory by banging on metal chimneys, flashings, and signs, or anything else that will make a loud noise. A year-round resident in the Pacific Northwest.

▶ RED-BREASTED SAPSUCKER

Sphyrapicus ruber

WOODPECKER FAMILY Picidae

Description The red-breasted sapsucker is unusual for a woodpecker, in that it drills small holes in trees and later returns to drink the sap and eat the insects caught in it. It has a wingspan to 38 cm/15 in. and a length to 23 cm/9 in. It has a red head and breast, yellowish-white underparts, and a white wing patch; the overall plumage is black with white.

Etymology The genus name, *Sphyrapicus*, is from the Greek word *sphura*, "hammer."

Habitat Mixed forests and treed urban parks. A year-round resident in the Pacific Northwest.

▶ BELTED KINGFISHER

Megaceryle alcyon

KINGFISHER FAMILY Alcedinidae

Description The male belted kingfisher has a wingspan to 56 cm/22 in. and a length to 35 cm/14 in. It is unusual in that the male is not as colourful as the female. It has a bluish-grey crested head, a white collar and underparts, and bluish-grey upperparts. The female also has a rusty-red band on the breast.

Etymology The genus name, *Megaceryle*, is from the Greek words *megas*, "great," and *ceryle*, "kingfisher." The species name, *alcyon*, means "kingfisher."

Habitat Marine coastlines, lakes, and rivers; almost anywhere in the Pacific Northwest where it can dive for fish.

▶ NORTHWESTERN CROW

Corvus caurinus

CROW FAMILY Corvidae

Description The northwestern crow is smaller than the more common American crow (*C. brachyrhynchos*). It has a wingspan to 83 cm/33 in. and a length to 43 cm/17 in. Adult crows' plumage, beak, legs, and feet are black.

Etymology The genus name, *Corvus*, means "raven." The species name, *caurinus*, means "northwest wind."

Habitat Northwestern crows are mostly marine shoreline birds, though some will take advantage of urban landfills and other birds' eggs and chicks. Crows can be seen dropping shellfish, such as mussels, clams, and oysters, and swooping down to see if the shell has been broken. They are very protective of their nests.

▶ COMMON RAVEN

Corvus corax

CROW FAMILY Corvidae

Description The common raven is an intelligent bird that is surrounded by west coast Indigenous myths. It has a wingspan to 1.4 m/4.6 ft. and a length to 69 cm/27 in. The adult raven is completely black; in certain light it seems to have an iridescent purple sheen.

Etymology The scientific name, *Corvus corax*, literally means "crow of crows."

Habitat Very widespread; found from the Aleutian Islands to California. It is an opportunistic feeder, eating shore life, garbage, and hikers' lunches and robbing nests.

▶ STELLER'S JAY

Cyanocitta stelleri
CROW FAMILY Corvidae

Description Steller's jay is the provincial bird of British Columbia. It has a wingspan to 48 cm/19 in. and a length to 30 cm/12 in. The crested head, neck, and upper back are black; with the exception of the black-barred wing tips, all other plumage is blue.

Etymology The genus name, *Cyanocitta*, is from the Greek words *kuands*, "dark blue," and *kitta*, "jay."

Habitat During mating season, Steller's jays are mainly seen in elevated coniferous forests. In autumn, they move to lower elevations, including urban areas.

▶ GREY JAY

Perisoreus canadensis
CROW FAMILY Corvidae

Description Grey jays have a wingspan to 46 cm/ 18 in. and a length to 30 cm/12 in. They have a black crown, a white face, and a white collar; the upper plumage is dark grey, and the lower plumage is light grey. Grey jays are known for storing their food (and campers' food) on trees, with their glue-like saliva. Grey jays are also called Canada jays (hence the species name, *canadensis*), whiskey jacks, and camp robbers.

Habitat Coniferous forests in Alaska, across northern Canada, and down the Pacific coast to northern California. Food protection bags are necessary when camping in grey jay territory.

▶ VARIED THRUSH

Ixoreus naevius

THRUSH FAMILY Turdidae

Description The varied thrush is considered the most beautiful of all of the thrushes in the Pacific Northwest. It has a wingspan to 38 cm/15 in. and a length to 25 cm/10 in. It has orange eyebrows and an orange throat, black cheeks and a black crown, a bluish-grey back, and orange wings with black barring. A dark collar separates the spotted orange stomach and orange neck.

Etymology The species name, *naevius*, means "spotted."

Habitat Can be found in thick coniferous and mixed forests. Mainly a mountain bird, except when snow falls. Then they can be seen in lower, more open areas, such as urban parks and backyards, foraging on the ground for fruit, berries, earthworms, and insects, much like the resident robins.

▶ AMERICAN ROBIN

Turdus migratorius

THRUSH FAMILY Turdidae

Description The American robin is probably one of the most recognized birds in North America. It has a wingspan to 38 cm/15 in. and a length to 28 cm/11 in. The head is blackish, with a yellow bill and vertical black stripes on the throat. The upper plumage is dark grey; the lower plumage is brick red on males and orangish on females. Juvenile robins have spotted breasts.

Etymology The genus name, *Turdus*, means "thrush." The species name, *migratorius*, means "migrant" or "wanderer."

Habitat Breeds across most of North America. Migrates in winter to areas that have berries, fruit, and earthworms. In some years, robins can be found drunk from eating fermenting mountain ash berries.

▶ CEDAR WAXWING

Bombycilla cedrorum

WAXWING FAMILY Bombycillidae

Description When first sighting a cedar waxwing, it looks as though someone's beautiful tropical bird has escaped. It has a wingspan to 30 cm/12 in. and a length to 20 cm/8 in. The crested head is tan brown, with a black-and-white mask. The belly is yellowish with a darker breast; the upper plumage is greyish brown with splashes of waxy red on the wing tips and a bright-yellow-tipped tail.

Etymology The genus name, *Bombycilla*, means "silk tail," referring to the bright-yellow-tipped tail. The species name, *cedrorum*, means "of the cedar trees."

Habitat Breeds in southern Canada and across the United States. Migrates in winter to areas that have fruit and berries.

▶ BREWER'S BLACKBIRD

Euphagus cyanocephalus

BLACKBIRD FAMILY Icteridae

Description Brewer's blackbird has a wingspan to 38 cm/15 in. and a length to 27 cm/11 in. The male has a purple-black head, yellow eyes, and a strong black bill. The overall plumage is black with a greenish-blue sheen. The female is grey brown overall with brown eyes.

Etymology Brewer's blackbird is named after Thomas Mayo Brewer (1814–1880), a naturalist and the author of *A History of North American Birds* (1874). The genus name, *Euphagus*, is from the Greek words *eu*, "good," and *phagos*, "glutton." The species name, *cyanocephalus*, means "dark-blue head."

Habitat Grain fields, urban areas, and thickets, where it feeds on grain, fruit, insects, and snails.

► RED-WINGED BLACKBIRD

Agelaius phoeniceus

BLACKBIRD FAMILY Icteridae

Description Red-winged blackbirds are known for forming huge flocks of thousands of birds when migrating. They have a wingspan to 30 cm/12 in. and a length to 24 cm/9.5 in. The male is black overall, with red and yellow shoulder patches. The female is streaked brown overall.

Etymology The genus name, *Agelaius*, means "flocking." The species name, *phoeniceus*, refers to Phoenicia, where the cities of Tyre and Sidon produced the celebrated Tyrian purple dye, from the secretion of a sea snail.

Habitat Open woodlands with marshes and fields. Almost anywhere that supports large areas of cattails (*Typha latifolia*). Red-winged blackbirds are migratory in most of Canada and the northern United States.

► YELLOW-HEADED BLACKBIRD

Xanthocephalus xanthocephalus

BLACKBIRD FAMILY Icteridae

Description The yellow-headed blackbird has a length to 25 cm/10 in. and a wingspan to 38 cm/15 in. The male is black, with a bright-yellow head and breast. A white wing patch can be seen when in flight. The female is not as colourful; she has a brown body and a dull-yellow throat and breast.

Etymology The genus name and species name, *xanthocephalus*, is from the Greek word *xanthos*, "yellow," and the Latin word *cephala*, "head."

Habitat Yellow-headed blackbirds nest in marshes and lakes that are covered in cattails (*Typha latifolia*). They are only summer residents in the Pacific Northwest, migrating to the southwest United States and Mexico for fall and winter.

► BROWN-HEADED COWBIRD

Molothrus ater

BLACKBIRD FAMILY Icteridae

Description Brown-headed cowbirds are the smallest of the blackbirds in North America. They have a wingspan to 30 cm/12 in. and a length to 20 cm/8 in. The males' head and throat are caramel brown, and the overall plumage greenish black. The female has greenish-grey plumage with streaked underparts.

Etymology The genus name, *Molothrus*, means "glutton" or "greedy beggar." The species name, *ater*, means "black."

Habitat Woodlands, urban parks, fields, and farms. They do not have a nest; the female lays her eggs in the nests of other bird species.

► EUROPEAN STARLING

Sturnus vulgaris

STARLING FAMILY Sturnidae

Description One hundred European starlings were introduced to New York City's Central Park in 1890. By 1950, they had spread to the west coast. They have a wingspan to 41 cm/16 in. and a length to 23 cm/9 in. In breeding season, they have a yellow bill and glossy black plumage. In non-breeding season, they have black plumage with white spots and a dark bill.

Etymology The genus name, *Sturnus*, means "starling." The species name, *vulgaris*, means "common," which they are.

Habitat Fields, farms, parks, and urban areas. They are very adaptable.

▶ KILLDEER

Charadrius vociferus

PLOVER FAMILY Charadriidae

Description Killdeer have a length to 25 cm/10 in. and a wingspan to 63 cm/25 in. They are grey brown above and white below, with two black bands on the breast. The bill is short and black, and the rump is orange brown, which is more obvious in flight. Killdeers are well-known for their broken-wing trick, which they display when a predator approaches their nest. They run around pretending to have a broken wing, making predators think they have an easy kill, which keeps them away from the ground nest.

Etymology The common name killdeer is from the sound of their repeated shrill, *killdeer, killdeer*.

Habitat In breeding season, killdeer are found in open fields with gravel, short grass, or weeds, or on even flat gravel roofs. Outside of breeding season, they can be found in mud flats, on beaches, in fields, and in lawns, from Alaska to South America.

▶ VIOLET-GREEN SWALLOW

Tachycineta thalassina

SWALLOW FAMILY Hirundinidae

Description The violet-green swallow has a wingspan to 28 cm/11 in. and a length to 14 cm/5.5 in. The male has a green head, black-and-white underparts that extend around the throat and above the eyes, and an iridescent violet rump and tail. The female has brown on her head and is slightly duller in colour.

Etymology The genus name, *Tachycineta*, means "moving quickly"; the species name, *thalassina*, means "sea green."

Habitat Breeds in the Pacific Northwest in parks, woodlands, farms, and swallow boxes placed above water. Migrates south in October.

▶ NORTHERN ROUGH-WINGED SWALLOW

Stelgidopteryx serripennis

SWALLOW FAMILY Hirundinidae

Description The northern rough-winged swallow's drab colours make it unappealing to a lot of birders. It has a wingspan to 30 cm/12 in. and a length to 15 cm/6 in. The upper plumage is dull brown, and the stomach is light grey, turning to light brown on the breast.

Etymology Both the genus name, *Stelgidopteryx*, and the species name, *serripennis*, refer to the hooked primary feathers, from which it also gets its common name.

Habitat Breeds in the Pacific Northwest and winters as far away as Central America.

▶ BARN SWALLOW

Hirundo rustica

SWALLOW FAMILY Hirundinidae

Description The barn swallow is the largest and most abundant swallow in North America. It has a wingspan to 30 cm/12 in. and a length to 18 cm/7 in. It has an iridescent blue-black head and upperparts, a dark rusty throat, and a lighter rusty stomach. The long forked tail adds length to the body.

Etymology The genus name, *Hirundo*, means "swallow." The species name, *rustica*, means "rural" or "rustic."

Habitat Originally, barn swallows bred in caves, but now their preference is human-made structures. You can see their mud nests under bridges, houses, barns, and building soffits.

▶ TREE SWALLOW

Tachycineta bicolor

SWALLOW FAMILY Hirundinidae

Description After the barn swallow, the tree swallow is the most abundant swallow in North America. It has a wingspan to 32 cm/13 in. and a length to 15 cm/6 in. The head and upperparts are an iridescent dark blue black; the throat and underparts are bright white.

Etymology The species name, *bicolor*, refers to the tree swallow's two contrasting colours.

Habitat Nests in abandoned woodpecker holes, tree cavities, and human-made nest boxes, always close to water. Like other swallows, it eats flying insects while in flight. Winters in the southern United States and Central America.

▶ ANNA'S HUMMINGBIRD

Calypte anna

HUMMINGBIRD FAMILY Trochilidae

Description Anna's hummingbird has a wingspan to 13 cm/5 in. and a length to 10 cm/4 in. Both the male and the female have iridescent green upperparts. The male has a dark rose-red crown, neck, and throat and greyish underparts. The female has a spotted throat and greyish-white underparts.

Etymology The genus name, *Calypte*, is from the Greek word *kaluptre*, a women's veil, referring to the shining hoods of the male hummingbirds. The species name, *anna*, commemorates Anne Debelle (1802–1887), princess of Essling and wife of collector François Victor Masséna, prince of Essling.

Habitat Woodlands, parks, and gardens. Some Anna's hummingbirds are permanent residents of the Pacific Northwest.

▶ RUFOUS HUMMINGBIRD

Selasphorus rufus

HUMMINGBIRD FAMILY Trochilidae

Description The rufous hummingbird has a wingspan to 13 cm/5 in. and a length to 10 cm/4 in. The male has rufous upperparts and sides with a white breast patch and an iridescent orange-red crown and throat. The female has green upperparts and white underparts with rufous sides.

Etymology The genus name, *Selasphorus*, is from the Greek words *selas*, "bright flame" or "flash of lightning," and *phorus*, "carrying."

Habitat Woodland edges, meadows, gardens, and backyard feeders. Early rufous hummingbirds show up in spring and migrate south by the end of August.

▶ MOURNING DOVE

Zenaida macroura

DOVE FAMILY Columbidae

Description The mourning dove has a length to 30 cm/12 in. and a wingspan to 43 cm/17 in. The overall plumage is greyish brown, with lighter underparts, dark spots on the wings, and one spot on each side of the neck.

Etymology The mourning dove is so named because of its call. The genus name, *Zenaida*, commemorates Princess Zenaide, the wife of Charles Lucien Bonaparte.

Habitat Found in a wide variety of areas, including fields, open forests, and parks and near bird feeders, from central BC to Mexico.

BAND-TAILED PIGEON

Columba fasciata

PIGEON FAMILY Columbidae

Description The band-tailed pigeon is the largest pigeon in North America. It has a wingspan to 66 cm/26 in. and a length to 38 cm/15 in. The overall plumage is blue grey, with a white bar on the back of the neck and a pale-grey band on the tail. The beak is yellow with a black tip.

Etymology The genus name, *Columba*, means "pigeon" or "dove." The species name, *fasciata*, means "banded" or "striped."

Habitat Breeds in coniferous forests in the Pacific Northwest. Its favourite foods are arbutus berries, cascara, holly, and Garry oak acorns.

EURASIAN COLLARED-DOVE

Streptopelia decaocto

DOVE FAMILY Columbidae

Description The Eurasian collared-dove has a length to 32 cm/13 in. and a wingspan to 50 cm/20 in. It is greyish pink overall, with darker tail feathers and a black-and-white half collar; hence its common name.

Etymology The genus name, *Streptopelia*, is from the Greek words *streptos*, meaning "collar," and *peleia*, meaning "dove."

Habitat The Eurasian collared-dove was first introduced to North America and Central America in the 1970s. It has rapidly spread and is becoming more common in urban and suburban areas with trees and seed sources.

▶ ROCK PIGEON

Columba livia

PIGEON FAMILY Columbidae

Description The rock pigeon was brought over to North America from Europe in the 17th century. It has a wingspan to 71 cm/28 in. and a length to 33 cm/13 in. The plumage on rock pigeons is variable; the most common is a dark-grey head, neck, and throat, with lighter-grey upper and lower parts, two black bars on the wings, and a black-tipped tail.

Etymology The species name, *livia*, means "blue grey."

Habitat Mostly an urban dweller; feeds on grain, garbage, grass, seeds, and public handouts.

▶ OLIVE-SIDED FLYCATCHER

Contopus cooperi

TYRANT FLYCATCHER FAMILY Tyrannidae

Description The olive-sided flycatcher is brownish olive on the upperparts, with white on the throat and the centre of the breast and belly. It is a medium-sized songbird, to 19 cm/7.5 in. long.

Etymology The genus name, *Contopus*, is from the Greek words *kontos*, "short," and *pous*, "foot." I will have to look at a flycatcher's foot the next time I see one.

Habitat The olive-sided flycatcher prefers open forest edges with tall trees and snags for perching on and foraging. It breeds mainly in Canada and spends its winters in South America.

▶ BLACK-HEADED GROSBEAK

Pheucticus melanocephalus

CARDINAL FAMILY Cardinalidae

Description The black-headed grosbeak is a common summer resident in the Pacific Northwest; however, its shyness makes it seem elusive. It has a wingspan to 30 cm/12 in. and a length to 20 cm/ 8 in. The male has a heavy conical bill; a black head, tail, and wings, with white barring on the wings and tail; and an orange neck and underparts. The female has a brown head and upperparts, a white eyebrow, and orangish-brown underparts.

Etymology The genus name, *Pheucticus*, means "shy," or "inclined to avoid." The species name, *melanocephalus*, means "black headed."

Habitat Thick brush and forests along rivers and streams. It is a summer migrant in the Pacific Northwest.

▶ CHESTNUT-BACKED CHICKADEE

Poecile rufescens

TITMOUSE FAMILY Paridae

Description The chestnut-backed chickadee has a wingspan to 20 cm/8 in. and a length to 13 cm/ 5 in. It has white cheeks, white underparts, and dark wings lined with white. It is much like the black-capped chickadee except it has a brownish-red back and sides and a dark-brown head and throat patch. The chestnut-backed chickadee's small nests are usually half hair or fur from coyotes, rabbits, and deer.

Etymology The species name, *rufescens*, is Latin for "becoming reddish."

Habitat It is a permanent resident in the Pacific Northwest, from southern Alaska to southwest California.

► BLACK-CAPPED CHICKADEE

Poecile atricapillus

TITMOUSE FAMILY Paridae

Description The black-capped chickadee has a wingspan to 20 cm/8 in. and a length to 13 cm/ 5 in. It has a black cap and throat patch, white cheeks, buffy sides, and white underparts; the dark wings are lined in white.

Etymology The genus name, *Poecile*, means "spotted" or "variegated." The species name, *atricapillus*, means "black capped."

Habitat These birds are constantly busy, jumping from branch to branch and hanging upside down foraging for insects and seeds.

► BUSHTIT

Psaltriparus minimus

TITMOUSE FAMILY Paridae

Description After hummingbirds, bushtits are the lightest birds in North America. They have a wingspan to 15 cm/6 in. and a length to 10 cm/4 in. These tiny birds have a brownish head and a small black bill; they are flat grey on top and lighter grey below. Males have black eyes, and females have yellow eyes.

Etymology The genus name, *Psaltriparus*, means "pygmy tit."

Habitat Bushtits are known for their amazing sock-like nests, made from moss, lichens, spiderwebs, and leaves. They are common in woodlands, parks, and urban areas.

GOLDEN-CROWNED KINGLET

Regulus satrapa

KINGLET FAMILY Regulidae

Description The golden-crowned kinglet is the smallest songbird in North America. It has a wingspan to 18 cm/7 in. and a length to 10 cm/4 in. Males have an orange-yellow crown patch with black sides and a white eyebrow, while females have a yellow crown. The upper plumage is grey brown, and the lower plumage is light grey; the wings have white barring.

Etymology The genus name, *Regulus*, means "prince." The species name, *satrapa*, means "viceroy" or "governor."

Habitat Mainly a woodland bird; found in mixed forests and urban parks. Feeds on insects from the branches of conifers, deciduous trees, and shrubs.

RUBY-CROWNED KINGLET

Regulus calendula

KINGLET FAMILY Regulidae

Description For such a small bird, the ruby-crowned kinglet is renowned for its very loud songs. It has a wingspan to 18 cm/7 in. and a length to 10 cm/4 in. Males have a red patch on the crown; females do not. The upper plumage is a greyish green and is lighter below. It has a darker wing with white barring.

Habitat Feeds and breeds mainly in coniferous forests in the spring and summer and mixed forests in the winter.

► MARSH WREN

Cistothorus palustris

WREN FAMILY Troglodytidae

Description The marsh wren has a length to 12 cm/ 4.7 in. with a wingspan to 15 cm/6 in. It has a dark head with white eyebrows and an orange stripe on the forehead. The plumage is brown above and greyish below.

Etymology The species name, *palustris*, means "marsh loving."

Habitat Wherever cattails grow, including marshes and wetlands. A very secretive bird that is always on the move.

► WINTER WREN

Troglodytes troglodytes

WREN FAMILY Troglodytidae

Description The winter wren is the only North American wren whose range extends across Europe and northern Asia. It has a wingspan to 14 cm/ 5.5 in. and a length to 11 cm/4.3 in. It has dark-brown barring on the back and sides. Like other wrens, it has a continuously flicking tail.

Etymology The genus name and species name, *troglodytes*, means "cave dweller"; males build their nests in cavities along stream banks and in roots and branches.

Habitat Winter wrens can be seen year-round hopping and flying from underbrush and fallen branches in mixed forests, parks, and gardens in the Pacific Northwest.

▶ BEWICK'S WREN

Thryomanes bewickii

WREN FAMILY Troglodytidae

Description Bewick's wren has a wingspan to 18 cm/ 7 in. and a length to 14 cm/5.5 in. It is brown above and white below, with a white eyebrow and a slightly down-curved bill. Its tail is long and banded and flicks from side to side.

Etymology The species name, *bewickii*, and the common name Bewick's wren commemorate Thomas Bewick, a 19th-century British naturalist.

Habitat A year-round resident the Pacific Northwest; found in open forests from BC to California.

▶ BROWN CREEPER

Certhia americana

CREEPER FAMILY Certhiidae

Description The brown creeper forages for insects by climbing spirally up a tree trunk and then flying to the base of another tree and doing it again. It has a wingspan to 20 cm/8 in. and a length to 13.5 cm/ 5.3 in. The bill is thin and downward curved, and it has a white streak above the eyes. The upper plumage is mottled brown, and the underparts are white.

Etymology The genus name, *Certhia*, is from the Greek word *kerthios*, a small tree-dwelling bird mentioned by Aristotle.

Habitat Mixed forests, open parks, and urban areas with trees.

▶ RED-BREASTED NUTHATCH

Sitta canadensis

NUTHATCH FAMILY Sittidae

Description Red-breasted nuthatches are bark-clinging birds that skilfully climb up and down tree trunks foraging for insects. They have a wingspan to 20 cm/8 in. and a length to 11 cm/4.3 in. The male has a black crown and black eye stripes, white cheeks and white eyebrows, blue-grey upper plumage, and red-orange underparts. The female is not as brightly coloured as the male.

Etymology The genus name, *Sitta*, is from the Greek word *sitte*, a bird similar to a woodpecker mentioned by Aristotle.

Habitat Red-breasted nuthatches are found year-round in the Pacific Northwest, in mixed forests and urban parks and at bird feeders with sunflower seeds and suet.

▶ YELLOW-RUMPED WARBLER

Dendroica coronata

WOOD WARBLER FAMILY Parulidae

Description There are two forms of yellow-rumped warblers in the Pacific Northwest. The Audubon's form has a yellow throat, while the myrtle form has a white throat and a black eye patch. Both forms have a length to 13 cm/5 in. and wingspan to 22 cm/9 in.

Etymology The genus name, *Dendroica*, is from the Greek words *dendron*, "tree," and *oikos*, "home."

Habitat Both forms are migratory, breeding in the Pacific Northwest in the summer and leaving for the southern United States and South America in the autumn.

▶ WILSON'S WARBLER

Cardellina pusilla

WOOD WARBLER FAMILY Parulidae

Description Wilson's warbler has a wingspan to 17 cm/7 in. and a length to 11 cm/4.5 in. The male has a black cap and dull-green upper plumage, with yellow underparts. The face has the brightest yellow. Females have a light-green cap.

Etymology The common name Wilson's warbler commemorates Alexander Wilson (1766–1813), the author of *American Ornithology* (1808). The species name, *pusilla*, means "very small."

Habitat A spring and summer resident in the Pacific Northwest. Can be found in openings in mixed forests.

▶ WESTERN TANAGER

Piranga ludoviciana

TANAGER FAMILY Thraupidae

Description The western tanager has a wingspan to 30 cm/12 in. and a length to 20 cm/8 in. In breeding season, the male has a black tail, black wings with white and yellow bars, an orange head, and yellow underparts. The female upperparts are greyish olive with white bars on the wings; the underparts are a lighter grey.

Etymology The genus name, *Piranga*, refers to a municipality in Brazil, and the species name, *ludoviciana*, means "of Louisiana."

Habitat The western tanager is a common summer migrant in the Pacific Northwest. It can be found in mixed forests from Alaska to California.

▶ AMERICAN GOLDFINCH

Spinus tristis

FINCH FAMILY Fringillidae

Description The male American goldfinch is one of the brightest-coloured songbirds in the Pacific Northwest. It has a wingspan to 20 cm/8 in. and a length to 13 cm/5 in. The breeding male has a black forehead, wings, and tail and is bright yellow overall. The female is yellow greenish overall, with black wings and tail.

Etymology The species name, *tristis*, means "dull" or "sad."

Habitat Edges of mixed forests, weedy fields, parks, and backyard feeders with thistle seeds and sunflower seeds. Its main diet in mid- to late summer is thistle and weed seeds.

▶ PINE SISKIN

Spinus pinus

FINCH FAMILY Fringillidae

Description The pine siskin, as its common name suggests, is found in areas with conifer seeds. It has a wingspan to 20 cm/8 in. and a length to 13 cm/ 5 in. The upper plumage is streaked brown, and the underparts are whitish and streaked brown. It has yellow on its wings and tail.

Etymology The genus name, *Spinus*, is from the Greek word *spinos*, "siskin," and the species name, *pinus*, lets you know it likes pine nuts.

Habitat Common near coniferous forests. A regular at bird feeders.

▶ SNOW BUNTING

Plectrophenax nivalis

FINCH FAMILY Fringillidae

Description Snow buntings have a wingspan to 33 cm/ 13 in. and a length to 18 cm/7 in. When snow buntings are not in the breeding season, which is when they are seen in the Pacific Northwest, they have an orange bill, back of the head, and breast, with white underparts and black barring on the back and wings.

Etymology The species name, *nivalis*, means "snowy."

Habitat Breeds in the tundra across the Arctic. Winters as far south as the Pacific Northwest. Prefers open sandy areas along the coast.

▶ HOUSE SPARROW

Passer domesticus

OLD WORLD SPARROW FAMILY Passeridae

Description The house sparrow was introduced to New York in 1850 from Europe to help suppress insects. It has a wingspan to 23 cm/9 in. and a length to 15 cm/6 in. Males have a grey crown and underparts, black-and-brown upper plumage, a black throat, and a white wing bar. Females have a pale eyebrow, grey-brown underparts, and mottled brown upper plumage.

Etymology The genus name, *Passer*, means "sparrow."

Habitat Farms, urban settings, grain fields, and parks. Very common.

▶ SPOTTED TOWHEE

Pipilo maculatus

NEW WORLD SPARROW FAMILY Emberizidae

Description The bright rufous sides of the spotted towhee add colour to the stark winter forest floor. It has a wingspan to 25 cm/10 in. and a length to 20 cm/8 in. Its head and throat are black, and it has black upper plumage with white spots, rufous sides, and white underparts.

Etymology The genus name, *Pipilo*, means "to chirp" or "to twitter." The species name, *maculatus*, means "spotted."

Habitat Wooded areas with low vegetation, where it can be seen scratching backward in leaf litter for insects.

▶ DARK-EYED JUNCO

Junco hyemalis

NEW WORLD SPARROW FAMILY Emberizidae

Description The dark-eyed junco has a wingspan to 23 cm/9 in. and a length to 15 cm/6 in. Males have a black hood and wings, brown sides, and white underparts. Females are duller coloured and have a grey-brown hood. Sixteen subspecies of dark-eyed junco have been recognized.

Etymology The species name, *hyemalis*, means "wintry" or "of winter."

Habitat Edges of mixed forests, treed parks, and backyards. Very common at bird feeders.

▶ FOX SPARROW

Passerella iliaca

NEW WORLD SPARROW FAMILY Emberizidae

Description The Pacific Northwest fox sparrow is named after the eastern fox sparrow, which has fox-red plumage. It has a wingspan to 28 cm/11 in. and a length to 18 cm/7 in. The upper plumage is mottled brown, with grey across the face; the underparts are white with rusty-brown chevrons.

Etymology The species name, *iliaca*, means "of the flanks (sides)."

Habitat Mixed woodlands with low vegetation. Common in the Pacific Northwest.

▶ HARRIS'S SPARROW

Zonotrichia querula

NEW WORLD SPARROW FAMILY Emberizidae

Description Harris's sparrow is relatively rare in the Pacific Northwest. When seen, it is unmistakable, with its black face, white streaked breast, and grey-and-black plumage. Its length is to 18 cm/7 in. and its wingspan is to 27 cm/11 in.

Etymology The species name, *querula*, means "whistle," referring to the bird's whistled song.

Habitat Harris's sparrow breeds in the stunted coniferous forests of northern Canada. During winter, it can be seen in the Pacific Northwest in parks and at bird feeders.

▶ WHITE-THROATED SPARROW

Zonotrichia albicollis

NEW WORLD SPARROW FAMILY Emberizidae

Description The white-throated sparrow has a length to 19 cm/7.5 in. and a wingspan to 25 cm/10 in. It has a white throat patch, yellow patches by its eyes, and a black-and-white-striped head. The upper parts are streaked brown, and the underparts are dull grey.

Etymology The species name, *albicollis*, is Latin for "white throat."

Habitat The white-throated sparrow is a common winter visitor in the southern part of the Pacific Northwest. It is mainly seen on the ground along forest edges foraging for seeds and insects.

▶ SONG SPARROW

Melospiza melodia

NEW WORLD SPARROW FAMILY Emberizidae

Description The song sparrow, as its name suggests, has a pleasant song in spring and summer. It has a wingspan to 25 cm/10 in. and a length to 18 cm/7 in. The song sparrow has a greyish-brown striped head and upper plumage, with a central breast patch and lighter grey-and-brown-striped underparts.

Etymology The genus name, *Melospiza*, is from the Greek words *melos*, "song," and *spiza*, "finch." The species name, *melodia*, means "a pleasant song."

Habitat In woodlands with lower vegetation, urban forests, and parks and at backyard feeders.

▶ GOLDEN-CROWNED SPARROW

Zonotrichia atricapilla

NEW WORLD SPARROW FAMILY Emberizidae

Description The golden-crowned sparrow has a wingspan to 25 cm/10 in. and a length to 18 cm/7 in. The male's gold crown is bordered by black eyebrows; it has mottled grey-brown upper plumage with lighter-grey underparts.

Etymology The genus name, *Zonotrichia*, is from the Greek words *zone*, "band," and *trikhos*, "hair," referring to the striped head.

Habitat Far less well distributed than the white-crowned sparrow. Winters along the coast, from southern BC to California.

▶ WHITE-CROWNED SPARROW

Zonotrichia leucophrys

NEW WORLD SPARROW FAMILY Emberizidae

Description The white-crowned sparrow has a wingspan to 25 cm/10 in. and a length to 18 cm/7 in. It has black-and-white head stripes; the upper plumage is brown with white streaking and greyish underparts.

Etymology The species name, *leucophrys*, means "white crowned."

Habitat Widespread distribution, from Alaska across northern Canada. Winters in woodlands, farms, parks, and cities on the coast of the Pacific Northwest.

▶ HOUSE FINCH

Carpodacus mexicanus

FINCH FAMILY Fringillidae

Description The house finch has a wingspan to 23 cm/9 in. and a length to 15 cm/6 in. The male has red on its crown and breast, brown upper plumage, and white streaked underparts. The female has brown-grey streaks on the overall plumage.

Etymology The genus name, *Carpodacus*, is from the Greek words *karpos*, "fruit," and *dakos*, "biter"— an animal whose bite is dangerous.

Habitat A native of Mexico and the southern United States, the house finch appeared in the Pacific Northwest in the 1930s. It is very common in urban areas and at backyard feeders.

▶ BONAPARTE'S GULL

Chroicocephalus philadelphia

GULL FAMILY Laridae

Description Bonaparte's gull is one of the most graceful flying gulls. It has a wingspan to 84 cm/ 33 in. and a length to 33 cm/13 in. When breeding, the male has a black head, bill, and wing tips; white underparts; and a grey back and wings. When not breeding, it has a white head with a dark spot on its ear.

Etymology Bonaparte's gull is named after Charles Lucien Bonaparte, a zoologist and the nephew of Napoleon Bonaparte.

Habitat Mostly coastal. Some are known to nest in trees that are common in the Pacific Northwest.

▶ MEW GULL

Larus canus

GULL FAMILY Laridae

Description The mew gull is so called because of its call. It has a wingspan to 1.1 m/3.6 ft. and a length to 38 cm/15 in. When breeding, the mew gull has a pure-white head, neck, and underparts; a small yellow bill; a grey back and sides; yellowish-green legs and black wing tips with white spots.

Etymology The genus name, *Larus*, means "greedy seabird." The species name, *canus*, means "grey."

Habitat Coastal areas, rivers, lakes, and farmland.

▶ CALIFORNIA GULL

Larus californicus

GULL FAMILY Laridae

Description The California gull has a wingspan to 1.4 m/4.6 ft. and a length to 55 cm/22 in. When breeding, it has a white head, neck, and underparts, with a slate-grey back and black wing tips, and the bill has a red-and-black spot. It is one of the few gulls to have greenish legs. A sign and statue in Salt Lake City, Utah, commemorate this gull for saving the crops by devouring a locust swarm in 1848.

Habitat Winters on the coast, from southern BC to Mexico. More common in summer.

▶ RING-BILLED GULL

Larus delawarensis

GULL FAMILY Laridae

Description The ring-billed gull is one of the most common city gulls; it can be seen anywhere there is human garbage. It has a wingspan to 1.2 m/4 ft. and a length to 46 cm/18 in. When breeding, it has a white head, neck, and underparts; yellow eyes; a yellow bill with a black band near the tip; a grey back and sides; black wing tips with white spots; and yellowish-green legs.

Etymology The species name, *delawarensis*, is named for the Delaware River.

Habitat Breeds inland in freshwater habitats. Winters along the coast of the Pacific Northwest.

▶ GLAUCOUS-WINGED GULL

Larus glaucescens

GULL FAMILY Laridae

Description The glaucous-winged gull is one of the largest gulls in North America. It has a wingspan to 1.4 m/4.6 ft. and a length to 64 cm/25 in. It has a white head, neck, and underparts; a huge yellow bill; a pale-grey back and sides; dull-pink legs; and black on the wing tips when breeding.

Habitat Breeds and winters along the coast of the Pacific Northwest.

▶ RINGED-NECKED PHEASANT

Phasianus colchicus

PHEASANT FAMILY Phasianidae

Description The ringed-necked pheasant is an Asian species that was introduced to the Pacific Northwest in the 1890s as a game bird. It has a wingspan to 83 cm/33 in. and a length to 73 cm/ 29 in. The female's plumage is mottled brown overall. The male has a red face, white neck rings, iridescent gold plumage with dark barring, and a magnificent long tail.

Etymology The genus name, *Phasianus*, means "pheasant." The species name, *colchicus*, refers to an ancient country on the eastern shores of the Black Sea, (modern-day Georgia), where the Argonauts saw many pheasants.

Habitat Agricultural areas, orchards, forest edges, and marshes. Feeds on grain, weed seeds, berries, nuts, insects, and earthworms.

▶ AMERICAN DIPPER

Cinclus mexicanus

DIPPER FAMILY Cinclidae

Description The American dipper is the only aquatic songbird in North America. It has a wingspan to 25 cm/10 in. and a length to 20 cm/8 in. The plumage is slate grey overall, with a black bill and pink legs. The American dipper has an extra eyelid for diving under the water.

Etymology The genus name, *Cinclus*, is from the Greek word *kinklos*, a small waterside bird mentioned by Aristotle.

Habitat Near fast-moving rivers and creeks. Hunts for caddis fly larvae and fish eggs.

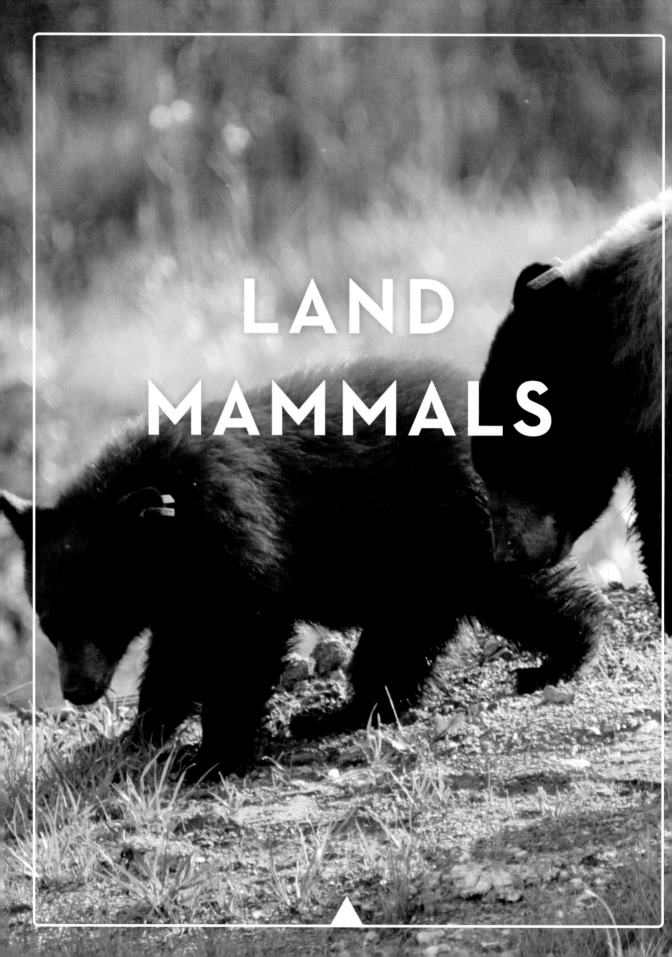

LAND MAMMALS

▶ ROOSEVELT ELK

Cervus canadensis roosevelti

DEER FAMILY Cervidae

Description Adult male Roosevelt elk are to 3 m/ 10 ft. in length and stand to 1.5 m/5 ft. to the shoulder. The body is brown tan, with a darker-brown neck and head and a yellowish-white rump. The Roosevelt elk is named for Theodore Roosevelt, the 26th president of the United States.

Etymology The scientific name, *Cervus canadensis roosevelti*, means "Roosevelt deer of Canada."

Habitat Old-growth forests that allow sunshine to reach the ground and open lands where they can graze on the grasses. Found from southern BC to Redwood National Park in northern California. There are approximately 5,000 elk in Olympic National Park, Washington. They were also introduced to Alaska in 1929.

▶ MULE DEER

Odocoileus hemionus

DEER FAMILY Cervidae

Description The mule deer is to 2.1 m/6.9 ft. in length and can stand to 1.1 m/3.6 ft. at the shoulder. It is tan brown with a whitish neck, face, and rump and a black-tipped tail.

Etymology The mule deer is so called because its large ears resemble a mule's.

Habitat In the Pacific Northwest, the mule deer can be seen in open forests, at forest edges, and in grasslands. It can be found from Yukon to California.

▶ BLACK-TAILED DEER

Odocoileus hemionus ssp. *columbianus*

DEER FAMILY Cervidae

Description The black-tailed deer is a subspecies of the mule deer. It is smaller than the mule deer, to 145 cm/57 in. in length and to 90 cm/35 in. at the shoulder. It is a darker brown than the mule deer, with a white rump patch and a black tail. The fawns are reddish brown with white spots. The buck sheds his antlers each winter and grows a new set in the spring.

Habitat Very common in open forests with undergrowth. Can be seen from the Alaskan Panhandle to California. The city of Victoria, on Vancouver Island, is overrun with black-tailed deer.

▶ GRIZZLY BEAR

Ursus arctos

BEAR FAMILY Ursidae

Description The grizzly bear is from 1.4 m/4.6 ft. to 2.8 m/9.2 ft. in length and can have a shoulder height from 0.7 m/2.3 ft. to 1.5 m/4.9 ft. It can range in colour from tan, to brown, to almost black. Most of the bears have white tips at the end of their hair, giving them a grizzled look.

Etymology The genus name, *Ursus*, is Latin for "bear"; the species name, *arctos*, is Greek for "bear."

Habitat The grizzly bear once ranged across a large portion of North America, including northern Mexico. In the Pacific Northwest, grizzly bears can be seen in coastal BC, especially when the salmon are spawning. They move from higher elevations to lower elevations when the berries are ripening and then move higher to follow the ripening fruit. Alaska has the largest concentration in North America.

▶ BLACK BEAR

Ursus americanus

BEAR FAMILY Ursidae

Description The black bear is to 1.8 m/5.9 ft. in length and can stand to 1.1 m/3.6 ft. at the shoulder. Though it is called the black bear, it can also be tan to brown. There is also the rare Kermode bear (*Ursus americanus kermodei*), which is white to creamy white. It is a subspecies of the black bear.

Habitat Forested areas, mountains, salmon streams and rivers, and garbage dumps, from Alaska to California.

▶ GREY WOLF TIMBER WOLF

Canis lupus

DOG FAMILY Canidae

Description The grey wolf has a length from 1.4 m/4.6 ft. to 2 m/6.6 ft. and a shoulder height to 1 m/3.3 ft. The fur colour ranges from nearly white to black, with grizzled grey being the most common. A dark coat usually indicates the wolf lives in dense forests; a lighter coat is common where there is lots of snow (when it is known as the Arctic wolf).

Etymology The species name, *lupus*, is Latin for wolf.

Habitat Along shorelines, in or beside dense forests, in the Pacific Northwest.

► COYOTE

Canis latrans

DOG FAMILY Canidae

Description The coyote is to 1.4 m/4.6 ft. in length, with a shoulder height to 60 cm/24 in. The colour of the fur varies geographically; in the Pacific Northwest, the fur is usually whitish grey with hints of red.

Etymology The species name, *latrans*, means "to bark."

Habitat Almost anywhere it can find food, including urban areas, parks, forests, and fields. The diet of the coyote is extremely varied, including mice, squirrels, birds, reptiles, and, when in season, berries. Found from Southern Alaska to California.

► COUGAR MOUNTAIN LION

Puma concolor

CAT FAMILY Felidae

Description The cougar is 1.5–2 m/4.9–6.6 ft. in length and has a shoulder height to 80 cm/31 in. The coat is a uniform tawny yellow to reddish brown. The throat, chest, and belly are whitish.

Etymology The genus name, *Puma*, comes from the Peruvian Quechua language, where it means "powerful."

Habitat Other than humans, the cougar has the largest natural distribution of any terrestrial mammal in the western hemisphere. In the Pacific Northwest, the cougar is most likely to be seen wherever there are deer.

NORTHERN RIVER OTTER

Lontra canadensis

WEASEL FAMILY Mustelidae

Description The northern river otter is to 1.3 m/ 4.3 ft. long and can weigh up to 14 kg/31 lb. The water-repellent fur is dark brown on the back and sides, with lighter underparts.

Etymology The genus name, *Lontra*, means "otter."

Habitat Common along the coast, from Alaska to California; can also be found inland in streams and lakes.

STRIPED SKUNK

Mephitis mephitis

SKUNK FAMILY Mephitidae

Description The striped skunk has a body length from 45 cm/18 in. to 80 cm/31 in. and a tail length from 20 cm/8 in. to 35 cm/14 in. It is black overall, with a white stripe that starts at the head, divides down the back, and rejoins at the rump.

Etymology The genus name and species name, *mephitis*, come from the Latin word *mephit*, which means "bad odour."

Habitat In the Pacific Northwest, the striped skunk can be seen in urban areas, parks, forested areas, fields, and lower mountains, from BC to California. It has become a pest in vegetable gardens and newly laid lawns.

AMERICAN MINK

Mustela vison

WEASEL FAMILY Mustelidae

Description The American mink is a semi-aquatic omnivore to 70 cm/28 in. in length. The luxurious fur is dark brown to black. Its anal scent glands secrete a foul odour, which is mainly used to define its territory.

Etymology The genus name, *Mustela*, is Latin for "weasel." The common name mink is from a Swedish word that means "stinky animal."

Habitat Mostly seen around waterways, ocean, rivers, streams, and ponds hunting for aquatic food. Can be found from Alaska to California.

COMMON RACCOON

Procyon lotor

RACCOON FAMILY Procyonidae

Description Raccoons are omnivorous mammals with a body length from 50 cm/20 in. to 80 cm/ 31 in. Their coat is greyish brown overall, with a black-and-white face mask and ringed tail.

Etymology The species name, *lotor*, is Latin for "washer," in reference to the way they seem to wash their food.

Habitat Mainly seen in urban settings close to water, trees, and forests. Native to the Pacific Northwest; found from southern BC to California.

AMERICAN BEAVER

Castor canadensis

BEAVER FAMILY Castoridae

Description The American beaver has a length from 74 cm/29 in. to 90 cm/35 in. and a weight of 11 kg/24 lb. to 32 kg/71 lb. It has dark-brown fur, webbed back feet, orange incisors, and a flat tail from 20 cm/8 in. to 35 cm/14 in. long. The American beaver is the largest rodent in North America; it comes in second in the world after the South American capybara. The beaver waterproofs its fur by coating it with castoreum, an oily secretion from its scent glands.

Etymology The genus name, *Castor*, comes from the secretion castoreum.

Habitat Ponds, streams, rivers, and lakes. Almost anywhere there is fresh water and deciduous trees.

EASTERN GREY SQUIRREL

Sciurus carolinensis

SQUIRREL FAMILY Sciuridae

Description The eastern grey squirrel is to 30 cm/12 in. in length with a tail to 25 cm/10 in. long. Though the common name suggests the squirrel is grey, it can also be dark brown to black. Grey squirrels were first introduced to the west coast in Stanley Park, in Vancouver, BC, around 1912.

Etymology The genus name, *Sciurus*, is from two Greek words: *skia*, meaning "shadow," and *oura*, meaning "tail," referring to the way the squirrel curls up its tail and sits in its own shadow.

Habitat Very common in low-elevation forests and parks and around bird feeders.

▶ CALIFORNIA GROUND SQUIRREL

Otospermophilus beecheyi

SQUIRREL FAMILY Sciuridae

Description The California ground squirrel is to 30 cm/ 12 in. in length, and its bushy tail is to 15 cm/ 6 in. long. The squirrel's upperparts are a mottled or spotted grey brown, and the underparts are a soft greyish yellow with black fur around the ears.

Etymology The species name, *beecheyi*, commemorates Frederick William Beechey, a 19th-century British explorer and naval officer.

Habitat Open, well-drained soils; roadsides; highland near beaches; and farms, especially where grain is grown. Quite common at roadside pullovers along the state highways through Oregon and California—the squirrels come out to get treats from the tourists.

▶ DOUGLAS SQUIRREL

Tamiasciurus douglasii

SQUIRREL FAMILY Sciuridae

Description The Douglas squirrel is to 20 cm/8 in. in length, and its tail is to 15 cm/6 in. long. It has two distinct coats, summer and winter. In summer, the underparts are deep orange and the upperparts are a grizzled grey brown. The winter coat is duller and greyer.

Etymology The species name, *douglasii*, commemorates David Douglas (1799–1834), the famous Scottish botanist who identified plants along the west coast of North America.

Habitat Found almost exclusively in coniferous forests from southern BC to California.

▶ YELLOW-PINE CHIPMUNK NORTHWESTERN CHIPMUNK

Tamias amoenus

SQUIRREL FAMILY Sciuridae

Description The yellow-pine chipmunk has a total length to 24 cm/9.5 in and can weigh up to 73 g/ 2.6 oz. These cute little rodents have five longitudinal black-and-white stripes on a cinnamon-coloured coat.

Etymology The species name, *amoenus*, means "beautiful" or "lovely."

Habitat In the Pacific Northwest, the yellow-pine chipmunk is usually seen at mid to high elevations that have coniferous forests.

▶ MARMOTS

SQUIRREL FAMILY Sciuridae

HOARY

VANCOUVER ISLAND

OLYMPIC

Hoary (whistler) marmot (*Marmota caligata*) Grows to 62–82 cm/24–32 in. long, up to 10 kg/22 lb. The shoulders and back are a silver grey (hoary), and the feet and lower legs are black. Makes a whistling sound, from which the Whistler Mountain gets its name. Common to slopes of the Cascade Range.

Olympic marmot (*Marmota olympus*) Smaller than the hoary marmot, and the male is considerably larger than the female in this species. Light brown fur with white patches. Occurs only on the Olympic peninsula in Washington State; a protected species in Olympic National Park.

Vancouver Island marmot (*Marmota vancouverensis*) Smaller than the hoary marmot, with rich dark brown fur and white markings. Endemic to Vancouver Island, particularly mountain slopes around Mt. Washington and Nanaimo; critically endangered, though numbers are increasing. Sightings of this species are rare.

▶ BLACK RAT

Rattus rattus

MOUSE FAMILY Muridae

Description The black rat has a body and head length to 20 cm/8 in. and a tail length to 20 cm/8 in. It is slightly lighter in weight than the Norway rat. The species is divided into subspecies according to colour: black, grey, or white. The black rat is also known as the roof rat, the ship rat, and the house rat.

Habitat Mainly found in coastal areas (hence the common name ship rat), it is an excellent climber and can be found in the top floors of apartments (which gave it the common name roof rat) and tall trees. It is not a frequent guest to sewers.

▶ NORWAY RAT

Rattus norvegicus

MOUSE FAMILY Muridae

Description The Norway rat is to 25 cm/10 in. long, with a tail to 20 cm/8 in. long. Its coarse fur ranges from brown, to dark brown, to grey; the underparts are lighter grey or brown.

Etymology The species name, *norvegicus*, and common name Norway rat refer to this rat having originated in Norway, which it did not. It is probably from Asia.

Habitat With the exception of Antarctica, it can be found almost everywhere humans are. Norway rats are not fussy about their diets or living conditions.

▶ LITTLE BROWN BAT

Myotis lucifugus

EVENING BAT FAMILY Vespertilionidae

Description Little brown bats have a length to 10 cm/4 in. and a wingspan to 25 cm/10 in. The glossy fur on the upperparts is dark brown to golden brown, with the underparts being paler.

Etymology The species name, *lucifugus*, is Latin for "fear of the light" or "shunning of the light."

Habitat The little brown bat occupies three types of roosts: night, day, and hibernation. The night and day roosts are usually in buildings or trees near water. The hibernation roost is usually in caves or old mines, where the temperature does not fall below freezing. Found from southern Alaska to California.

▶ RABBITS

SHOWSHOE
BRUSH
EUROPEAN

Snowshoe hare (*Lepus americanus*) At 36 cm/14 in. to 52 cm/20 in. long, the snowshoe hare is the smallest of the *Lepus* genus. It is well adapted to a snowy terrain, with white winter fur and long back legs and feet (see track photo). Found from Alaska to Oregon and eastward.

Brush rabbit (*Sylvilagus bachmani*) A relatively small rabbit, from 30 cm/11 in. to 37 cm/14.5 in. long, with a grey tail, white fur in winter with black-tipped ears. Found from the Columbia River to southern California, living among brambles along open areas; some sub-species are found only in old-growth forests.

European rabbit (*Oryctolagus cuniculus*) The European rabbit ranges from 15 cm/6 in. to 50 cm/20 in. long. The fur colour varies from white to grey, black, brown, and orange. Known for underground warrens; prefers open areas with low brush. Found abundantly in Victoria, Vancouver, and the Gulf and San Juan Islands.

AMPHIBIANS

AMERICAN BULLFROG

Rana catesbeiana

TRUE FROG FAMILY Ranidae

Description The American bullfrog is an introduced species that is to 15 cm/6 in. long. It is generally olive green to brown, with off-white underparts. It has noticeable eardrums behind the eyes. The American bullfrog is considered an invasive species that displaces native frogs.

Etymology The species name, *catesbeiana*, honours Mark Catesby, an English naturalist. The common name bullfrog comes from the sounds it makes, like a bull's.

Habitat Ponds and marshes from BC to California.

OREGON SPOTTED FROG

Rana pretiosa

TRUE FROG FAMILY Ranidae

Description The Oregon spotted frog is to 10 cm/ 4 in. long. Older frogs tend to be redder in colour; both juveniles and adults have blackish spots on their back and heads.

Etymology The genus name, *Rana*, means "frog," and the species name, *pretiosa*, means "precious"— precious frog.

Habitat Marshes, ponds, and lake edges from southern BC to Oregon. Not common anymore.

PACIFIC TREE FROG

Pseudacris regilla

TREE FROG FAMILY Hylidae

Description The Pacific tree frog is to 5 cm/2 in. long. It ranges in colour from bright green, to dark green, to brownish, with a black face mask. Some have black blotches on their body and head as well.

Etymology The genus name, *Pseudacris*, means "false locust"; the species name, *regilla*, means "regal." The sound this frog makes is like a locust's.

Habitat Shallow marshes and ponds. The Pacific tree frog is the most common frog in the Pacific Northwest. It can be found from BC to California.

NORTHERN LEOPARD FROG

Lithobates pipiens

TRUE FROG FAMILY Ranidae

Description The northern leopard frog is to 10 cm/ 4 in. long. It has several colour variations, from light green, to dark green, to brown, with brown to black spotting. The underparts are creamy white.

Etymology The species name, *pipiens*, means "peeping."

Habitat Ponds, marshes, and moist forests from BC to Oregon.

▶ NORTHWESTERN SALAMANDER

Ambystoma gracile

MOLE SALAMANDER FAMILY Ambystomatidae

Description The northwestern salamander is to 22 cm/ 8.7 in. long. It is brown all over. When in the larva stage it is a lighter tan colour with spots.

Etymology The genus name, *Ambystoma*, means "blunt mouth."

Habitat Adults live in moist forests and breed in ponds and marshes. Found from Alaska to California.

▶ WESTERN TOAD

Bufo boreas

TOAD FAMILY Bufonidae

Description The western toad is to 13 cm/5 in. long. It has a cream-coloured stripe from its head down its back. It has excellent camouflage colouring, including green, brown, and grey. The skin is usually dry and warty.

Etymology The genus name, *Bufo*, is Latin for "toad."

Habitat In the Pacific Northwest, the western toad is often seen in mountain meadows, from Alaska to California. It breeds in shallow ponds and at lake edges.

REPTILES

▶ RED-EARED POND SLIDER TURTLE

Trachemys scripta

POND TURTLE FAMILY Emydidae

Description The red-eared pond slider turtle is to 30 cm/12 in. long. The top of the shell (carapace) is dark green to brown. The bottom (plastron) is yellow. The tail, legs, and head are green with yellow stripes. The red-eared pond slider turtle was introduced to the Pacific Northwest from the southern United States and northern Mexico.

Etymology The red-eared pond slider turtle gets its common name from the red markings around its ears and its ability to slide off rocks and logs easily.

Habitat Soft-bottomed ponds, marshes, and lake edges, from BC to California.

▶ WESTERN PAINTED TURTLE

Chrysemys picta

POND TURTLE FAMILY Emydidae

Description The western painted turtle is named after the bright colours it has. It can grow to 25 cm/10 in. long. The top of the shell is dark green to black and smooth. The skin is green to black with red-and-yellow stripes on the tail, legs, and neck.

Etymology The species name, *picta*, is Latin for "colour."

Habitat Ponds, marshes, and lake edges with soft bottoms, from Alaska to California.

▶ GARTER SNAKE

Thamnophis sp.

COLUBRID SNAKE FAMILY Colubridae

Description The common garter snake ranges from 0.46 m/1.5 ft. to 1.4 m/4.6 ft. It generally has three stripes down its back, one in the centre and one on each side. The stripes can be yellow, green, blue, or white. It hibernates from early November to early April.

Habitat Just about anywhere on land. It is the most widespread snake in North America.

▶ NORTHERN ALLIGATOR LIZARD

Elgaria coerulea

LIZARD FAMILY Anguidae

Description The northern alligator lizard is to 27.5 cm/ 11 in. long. It ranges in colour from a mottled grey green to mottled brown, with a light-grey stomach. It has short legs and a long tail.

Etymology Its species name, *coerulea*, means "bluish."

Habitat The alligator lizard lives in a wide range of habitats, including mountains, dry forests, streamsides, and grasslands, from southern BC to California. It hibernates during winter.

▶ COMMON WALL LIZARD

Podarcis muralis

TRUE LIZARD FAMILY Lacertidae

Description The common wall lizard is an introduced species to 20 cm/8 in. long. It has variable colours and patterns but is generally greyish to brown, with yellow, green, white, or red spots. Its main diet is small insects; it is known to jump and catch moths and butterflies.

Etymology The species name, *muralis*, is Latin for "wall," which is where the lizard is found.

Habitat Becoming common in North America, especially in the Saanich area of Vancouver Island, where it was released from a zoo in 1970. It prefers rocky areas and dry stacked walls, where it can hide and bask in the sun.

INSECTS
AND
ASSOCIATES

▶ RED ADMIRAL

Vanessa atalanta

BRUSH-FOOTED BUTTERFLY FAMILY Nymphalidae

Description The red admiral has a wingspan to 5 cm/2 in. This beautiful butterfly has a brown body, black wing tips with white spots, and orange to red bands that cross all four wings.

Etymology The species name, *atalanta*, is in honour of Atalanta, the daughter of King Schoeneus of Scyros.

Habitat The red admiral can be seen in the Pacific Northwest from May to September. It then migrates south to California.

▶ PAINTED LADY

Vanessa cardui

BRUSH-FOOTED BUTTERFLY FAMILY Nymphalidae

Description The painted lady has a wingspan to 5 cm/ 2 in. The body is light brown, while the wings are spattered in orange, black, and white. The hind wings have a row of four or five dots, which can be black or blue or both.

Etymology The species name, *cardui*, refers to thistles, one of its favourite foods.

Habitat The painted lady is also known as the cosmopolitan, because it is one of the most widely distributed butterflies in the world. In the summer it is almost ubiquitous in gardens, parks, and fields and at beaches.

▶ WEST COAST LADY

Vanessa annabella

BRUSH-FOOTED BUTTERFLY FAMILY Nymphalidae

Description The west coast lady has a sharper and darker orange colour than the painted lady. It has a wingspan to 5 cm/2 in. The spattering of orange, black, and white on the wings is more refined than that of the painted lady. Each of the hind wings has four blue spots with black rings. The west coast lady is the most common lady butterfly in the Pacific Northwest.

Habitat Fields, parks, and dunes. In certain years, when the concentrations are high, they can be found just about anywhere.

▶ LORQUIN'S ADMIRAL

Limenitis lorquini

BRUSH-FOOTED BUTTERFLY FAMILY Nymphalidae

Description Lorquin's admiral has a wingspan to 7 cm/2.8 in. The body and wings are dark brown. Both the forewings and hind wings have elongated white spots that form an awkward-looking semicircle. The forewings have orange patches at the tips; hence another common name, orange-tip admiral.

Etymology The species name, *lorquini*, honours Pierre Joseph Michel Lorquin, a French naturalist who came to California during the gold rush.

Habitat Common in poplar forests, at streamsides, in orchards, and in fields.

▶ MOURNING CLOAK

Nymphalis antiopa

BRUSH-FOOTED BUTTERFLY FAMILY Nymphalidae

Description The mourning cloak's name comes from its colour and velvety appearance. Its wingspan is to 9 cm/3.5 in. The wings are a velvety dark brown with a creamy-yellow margin and a row of blue spots on the inside.

Etymology The common name mourning cloak refers to the traditional colour of a cloak worn during mourning.

Habitat The mourning cloak is one of the few butterflies that does not migrate. It overwinters in tree cavities, in woodpiles, or under loose bark and is one of the first butterflies to be seen in spring. It is common in open forests with willows and poplars.

▶ FIELD CRESCENT

Phyciodes pulchella

BRUSH-FOOTED BUTTERFLY FAMILY Nymphalidae

Description Field crescents have an average wingspan of 3.5 cm/1.4 in. The overall colour is dark brown, with orange and pale-yellow markings.

Etymology The species name, *pulchella*, means "pretty."

Habitat Open areas, fields, parks, meadows, and streamsides.

▶ MONARCH

Danaus plexippus

BRUSH-FOOTED BUTTERFLY FAMILY Nymphalidae

Description With a wingspan to 10 cm/4 in., the monarch is one of the largest butterflies in the Pacific Northwest. The wings are bright orange, with delicate black venation and white spots on the perimeter.

Etymology The genus name, *Danaus*, is the name of the great-grandson of Zeus. The species name, *plexippus*, is the name of one of the 50 sons of Aegyptus, the twin brother of Danaus.

Habitat Rare in the Pacific Northwest. Can be in seen open areas with milkweed. The west coast monarch migrates to California, while the eastern monarch migrates, by the millions, to Mexico.

▶ WESTERN MEADOW FRITILLARY

Boloria epithore

BRUSH-FOOTED BUTTERFLY FAMILY Nymphalidae

Description The western meadow fritillary has a wingspan to 4 cm/1.5 in., making it the smallest fritillary in the Pacific Northwest. The overall colour of the wings is orange, with dark brown to black spots, lines, and bars. The western meadow fritillary is also known as the Pacific fritillary. This is one of the first fritillaries to come out in the spring.

Etymology The genus name, *Boloria*, is from the Greek word *bolos*, "fishing net," referring to the pattern on the wings.

Habitat Prefers damp areas, streamsides, wet meadows, and open forest edges.

▶ PALE TIGER SWALLOWTAIL

Papilio eurymedon

SWALLOWTAIL FAMILY Papilionidae

Description The pale tiger swallowtail has a wingspan to 10 cm/4 in. The wings are white to creamy white; the tiger stripes and margins are larger than those of the western tiger swallowtails.

Etymology The genus name, *Papilio*, is Latin for "butterfly."

Habitat The pale tiger swallowtail is found most often in hilly areas in the Pacific Northwest. Food sources are cascara (*Rhamnus purshiana*) and California lilac (*Ceanothus* sp.).

▶ ANISE SWALLOWTAIL

Papilio zelicaon

SWALLOWTAIL FAMILY Papilionidae

Description The anise swallowtail has a wingspan to 8 cm/3 in. The wings are pale yellow, with black bands and margins. Near the end of each wing is a red-yellow spot with a black centre.

Etymology The species name, *zelicaon*, is from the Greek word *zelos*, "emulation."

Habitat The females oviposit (lay eggs) on plants in the carrot (Apiaceae) family. Common in the Pacific Northwest.

HOARY COMMA

Polygonia gracilis

BRUSH-FOOTED BUTTERFLY FAMILY Nymphalidae

Description The hoary comma is similar to the satyr comma except with fewer spots on the wings and two tapering commas on the underparts. It has a wingspan to 5 cm/2 in. The wings are a velvety orange brown, with dark-brown spots and margins.

Etymology The species name, *gracilis*, is Latin for "thin."

Habitat Common in the Pacific Northwest. Adult butterflies feed on tree sap and nectar.

MILBERT'S TORTOISESHELL

Aglais milberti

BRUSH-FOOTED BUTTERFLY FAMILY Nymphalidae

Description Milbert's tortoiseshell has a wingspan to 5 cm/2 in. The forewings are dark brown, with dark margins and two orange spots. The hind wings are dark brown with blue-spotted margins. Both sets of wings have yellow-orange banding.

Etymology The genus name, *Aglais*, is from the Greek word *aglaos*, "beautiful."

Habitat Found throughout the Pacific Northwest.

▶ SATYR COMMA SATYR ANGLEWING

Polygonia satyrus

BRUSH-FOOTED BUTTERFLY FAMILY Nymphalidae

Description The satyr anglewing has a wingspan to 5 cm/2 in. The wings are a velvety orange, with brown spotting and margins. The hind wings have a reduced margin.

Etymology The genus name, *Polygonia*, is from the Greek word *polygonos*, meaning "many angled," which refers to the wings.

Habitat Common in the Pacific Northwest. The larvae (caterpillars) feed on stinging nettles.

▶ WESTERN TIGER SWALLOWTAIL

Papilio rutulus

SWALLOWTAIL FAMILY Papilionidae

Description The western tiger swallowtail has a wingspan to 10 cm/4 in. The wings are bright yellow, with black tiger stripes and margins. Near the base of the tail are orange and blue spots. This is the most common swallowtail butterfly in the Pacific Northwest.

Habitat The western tiger swallowtail seems to like the cool coastal air. It can often be seen mudding, extracting moisture and nutrients. This is one of the best times to photograph them, as they do not often stay still.

CLOUDED SULPHUR

Colias philodice

SULPHUR, WHITE, AND ORANGE-TIP BUTTERFLY FAMILY Pieridae

Description The clouded sulphur has a wingspan to 5 cm/2 in. The wings are predominantly sulphur yellow, with black margins and two small dots.

Etymology The genus name, *Colias*, refers to an area in Attica, a historical region of Greece, noted for the temple of Aphrodite.

Habitat Found throughout the Pacific Northwest, mainly around alfalfa fields and clover fields.

PINE WHITE

Neophasia menapia

SULPHUR, WHITE, AND ORANGE-TIP BUTTERFLY FAMILY Pieridae

Description Pine whites have a wingspan to 5 cm/ 2 in. The wings are white, with black spots and black venation. Females have thicker veins than males and usually have red-orange margins on their wings.

Etymology The genus name, *Neophasia*, is Latin for "new phase." The common name pine white refers to the pine family being the primary food source of the larvae (caterpillars).

Habitat Common in the Pacific Northwest. Mainly found around Douglas fir forests.

▶ EYED SPHINX

Smerinthus cerisyi

CLEARWING MOTH FAMILY Sphingidae

Description The eyed sphinx has a wingspan to 9 cm/ 3.5 in. The forewings are dark grey brown, with light and dark lines. The hind wings are rose pink, with black-and-blue spots that resemble eyes.

Etymology The species name, *cerisyi*, honours Alexandre Louis Lefèbvre de Cérisy (1798–1867), a French entomologist.

Habitat Found mainly in valleys and at stream-sides. The larvae feed on willow and poplar.

▶ CEANOTHUS SILK MOTH

Hyalophora euryalus

WILD SILK MOTH FAMILY Saturniidae

Description The ceanothus silk moth has a wing-span to 13 cm/5 in. The wings are red brown, with two black spots on the apex of the forewings. The forewings have small comma-shaped yellow markings, while the hind wings have larger swoosh-shaped yellow markings, which gives it another common name, Nike moth.

Habitat Common in the Pacific Northwest. Being nocturnal, they are attracted to the night light. The larvae feed on ceanothus, Douglas fir, cherry trees, and willows.

▶ MARGINED WHITE

Pieris marginalis

SULPHUR, WHITE, AND ORANGE-TIP BUTTERFLY FAMILY Pieridae

Description The margined white has a wingspan to 5 cm/2 in. The wings of the spring form are white with greenish venation; the summer form is usually pure white.

Etymology The genus name, *Pieris*, is from the Pierides, the nine sisters of Greek mythology who challenged the Muses to a singing contest but were defeated and turned into birds.

Habitat Common throughout the Pacific Northwest. The larvae usually feed on native plants in the mustard family.

▶ CABBAGE WHITE

Pieris rapae

SULPHUR, WHITE, AND ORANGE-TIP BUTTERFLY FAMILY Pieridae

Description The cabbage white is an introduced butterfly with a wingspan to 5 cm/2 in. The wings are creamy white, with black tips on the forewing. There are two black spots on the centre of the forewings.

Etymology The species name, *rapae*, is from *Brassica rapa*, field mustard, a food source for the larvae.

Habitat Almost anywhere there are plants in the mustard family (also called the cabbage family). This butterfly was introduced to Canada accidentally, in 1860.

▶ YELLOW-SPOTTED TUSSOCK MOTH

Lophocampa maculata

TIGER MOTH FAMILY Arctiidae

Description The yellow-spotted tussock moth has a wingspan to 4.3 cm/1.7 in. The wings are deep yellow golden, with four light-brown bands. The larva has white hairs bristling from the entire body, with smaller black hairs at each end and dotting the back. Orange hairs fill the centre of the body.

Etymology The species name, *maculata*, is Latin for "spotted."

Habitat Common throughout the Pacific Northwest. The larvae feed on poplars, willows, maples, and birches.

▶ WOODLAND SKIPPER

Ochlodes sylvanoides

SKIPPER FAMILY Hesperiidae

Description The woodland skipper has a wingspan to 3 cm/1.2 in. The wings are orange, with dark brown margins and banding.

Etymology The genus name, *Ochlodes*, is Greek for "turbulent," referring to the skipper's flight pattern.

Habitat Very common in the Pacific Northwest, especially in the autumn, where it can be seen nectaring on Canada goldenrod and aster.

▶ EUROPEAN SKIPPER

Thymelicus lineola

SKIPPER FAMILY Hesperiidae

Description The European skipper has a wingspan to 3 cm/1.2 in. The wings are orange to orange brown, with dark margins and veins. In England, the European skipper is known as the Essex skipper.

Etymology The species name, *lineola*, is Latin for "small line," referring to the stigma of the male.

Habitat Not yet common in the Pacific Northwest, but it should be soon, as they reproduce quite rapidly. The larvae feed on timothy grass (*Phleum pratense*) and other grass species.

▶ OLIVE-GREEN CUTWORM

Dargida procinctus

OWLET MOTH FAMILY Noctuidae

Description The olive-green cutworm has a wingspan to 4 cm/1.6 in. The beautiful forewings are a combination of light- and dark-brown cross-hatchings. The larvae are to 3.5 cm/1.5 in. long. They are light green to olive green, with white, red, and black lateral bands.

Etymology The species name, *procinctus*, is Latin for "ready for battle." The common name olive-green cutworm comes from the colouring of the larvae.

Habitat Common on the west coast of North America. Mainly feeds on grasses; can become a pest in greenhouses.

ARCHED HOOK-TIP MOTH

Drepana arcuata

HOOK-TIP MOTH FAMILY Drepanidae

Description The arched hook-tip moth has a wingspan to 4 cm/1.6 in. The wings are hook tipped and yellow brown, with dark-brown lines.

Etymology The species name, *arcuata*, is Latin for "bent like a bow" or "arched."

Habitat Common in coastal forests. The larvae feed on paper birch and alder.

VIRGINIA TIGER MOTH

Spilosoma virginica

TIGER MOTH FAMILY Arctiidae

Description The Virginia tiger moth has a wingspan to 5 cm/2 in. The wings and body are pure white, with a few tiny black spots. The larvae are known as yellow woollybears.

Etymology The species name, *virginica*, is Latin for *virgin*. This moth was first seen and described in the state of Virginia, which was named after Queen Elizabeth I, England's Virgin Queen.

Habitat Common in the Pacific Northwest. The larvae feed on willow and rubus.

▶ CANARY-SHOULDERED THORN

Ennomos alniaria

GEOMETER FAMILY Geometridae

Description This aptly named moth is so called because of its canary-yellow thorax (shoulders). It has a wingspan to 4 cm/1.6 in. The forewings are light yellow and scalloped, with two crossbars. The adult moths are attracted to artificial light.

Etymology The genus name, *Ennomos*, is from a Trojan hero of the same name featured in *The Iliad*.

Habitat Becoming fairly common in the Pacific Northwest. The larvae feed mainly on red alder, paper birch, and native willows.

▶ ROUGH PROMINENT   WHITE-DOTTED PROMINENT

Nadata gibbosa

PROMINENT FAMILY Notodontidae

Description The rough prominent has a wingspan to 5 cm/2 in. The wings are light brown to dull orange, and the forewings have two silver-white dots. The rough prominent is attracted to artificial light.

Etymology The species name, *gibbosa*, means "swollen on one side."

Habitat Common in deciduous and mixed-wood forests.

LARGE YELLOW UNDERWING

Noctua pronuba

NOCTUID MOTH FAMILY Noctuidae

Description The large yellow underwing has a wingspan to 6 cm/2.4 in. The forewings range from light brown to dark brown. The hind wings are bright orange yellow, with a lower black band. The large yellow underwing is nocturnal and is attracted to light.

Etymology The genus name, *Noctua*, means "nocturnal."

Habitat Can be found around deciduous forests from BC to California.

WHITE-STRIPED BLACK MOTH

Trichodezia albovittata

GEOMETER FAMILY Geometridae

Description The white-striped black moth has a wingspan to 2.5 cm/1 in. The wings range from brown to black and have a white bar through the forewing.

Etymology The species name, *albovittata*, means "white striped" or "white banded."

Habitat The white-striped black moth is found from Alaska to northern California.

PACIFIC TENT CATERPILLAR MOTH

Malacosoma californicum

LAPPET MOTH FAMILY Lasiocampidae

Description The adult Pacific tent caterpillar moth has a wingspan to 4 cm/1.6 in. across. It is an attractive furry brown, with two lighter-coloured bands on the forewings. The antennae resemble finely dissected ferns. The caterpillars are to 5 cm/2 in. long and are patterned in yellow, black, and white.

Habitat Found in the coastal Pacific Northwest. It mainly feeds on red alders, cherry trees, and Pacific willows.

HUDSONIAN WHITEFACE

Leucorrhinia hudsonica

SKIMMER FAMILY Libellulidae

Description The Hudsonian whiteface has a body length to 3 cm/1.2 in. The male's abdomen is black and red, while the female's can be yellow or red. The wings are black netted, and the face is creamy white.

Etymology The common name Hudsonian refers to Hudson Bay, where it was first found.

Habitat Seen mainly around elevated lakes and ponds.

Flight season May to August.

NORTHERN BLUET

Enallagma annexum

NARROW-WINGED DAMSELFLY FAMILY Coenagrionidae

Description The northern bluet has a body length to 4 cm/1.6 in. The male's abdomen is mainly blue on the upper sides. The female is greenish to brown. The wings are transparent.

Habitat Common along marshy shores.

Flight season May to September.

BLUE DASHER

Pachydiplax longipennis

SKIMMER FAMILY Libellulidae

Description The blue dasher has a body length to 3.8 cm/1.5 in. The abdomen is dusted in blue. The wings are black netted.

Etymology The species name, *longipennis*, is Latin for "long wings."

Habitat Found where there is still water, bogs, marshes, or lakes.

Flight season June to September.

PACIFIC FORKTAIL

Ischnura cervula

NARROW-WINGED DAMSELFLY FAMILY Coenagrionidae

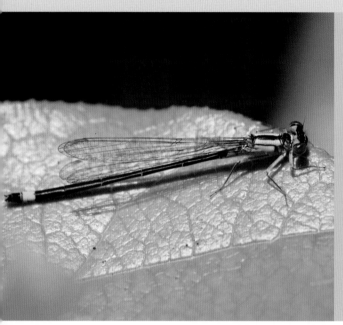

Description The Pacific forktail has a body length to 3 cm/1.2 in. The thin abdomen is black, with blue near the tip. The wings are black netted.

Habitat Very common around ponds, lakes, and slow-moving streams.

Flight season April to May.

BLUE-EYED DARNER

Aeshna multicolor

DARNER FAMILY Aeshnidae

Description The blue-eyed darner has a body length to 7 cm/2.75 in. The abdomen has large and small blue dots. The eyes are bright blue, and the wings are transparent.

Habitat Common around lakes, ponds, and marshes. Can also be found away from water sources.

Flight season May to October.

EIGHT-SPOTTED SKIMMER

Libellula forensis

COMMON SKIMMER FAMILY Libellulidae

Description The eight-spotted skimmer has a body length to 5 cm/2 in. The abdomen has yellow stripes on the sides; mature males also have a dusting of blue grey. The four wings are clear, with two black spots on each, making eight spots in total.

Habitat Common around muddy-bottomed lakes and ponds.

Flight season Late April to October.

FOUR-SPOTTED SKIMMER

Libellula quadrimaculata

COMMON SKIMMER FAMILY Libellulidae

Description The four-spotted skimmer has a body length to 4.3 cm/1.7 in. The abdomen is honey brown, with a black tip. The wings are clear, with a dark spot at the midpoint of each. The four-spotted skimmer is the state insect of Alaska.

Etymology The species name, *quadrimaculata*, means "four spotted."

Habitat Common around pools, rivers, and lakes.

Flight season May to October.

▶ CARDINAL MEADOWHAWK

Sympetrum illotum

COMMON SKIMMER FAMILY Libellulidae

Description The cardinal meadowhawk has a body length to 3.8 cm/1.5 in. The body and wing veins are cardinal red. The males are a more brilliant red than the females.

Habitat Lower elevations in the Pacific Northwest.

Flight season May to September.

▶ VARIEGATED MEADOWHAWK

Sympetrum corruptum

COMMON SKIMMER FAMILY Libellulidae

Description The variegated meadowhawk has a body length to 4 cm/1.6 in. As the common name suggests, the body, or abdomen, is of various colours, including bright red, golden brown, and pink. The wings are clear, with pinkish-orange veins.

Habitat Common near ponds and lakes.

Flight season May to October.

► EUROPEAN EARWIG

Forficula auricularia

EARWIG FAMILY Forficulidae

Description The European earwig has a length to 1.4 cm/0.6 in. The flattened body is dark reddish brown, the antennae are beaded, and the tip of the abdomen has two pincers. The male's pincers are curved, while the female's are straight.

Etymology The species name, *auricularia*, refers to the ear.

Habitat Common in food crops, where they can do substantial damage. Introduced from Europe at the beginning of the 20th century.

► PACIFIC DAMPWOOD TERMITE

Zootermopsis angusticollis

DAMPWOOD TERMITE FAMILY Termopsidae

Description The Pacific dampwood termite has a length to 2.5 cm/1 in. Nymphs have a white body and a red head. Soldiers are reddish orange brown, with pincers on their heads. The Pacific damp-wood termite is one of the largest termites in North America.

Etymology The species name, *angusticollis*, refers to the termite having a thin neck.

Habitat Usually seen in forests with rotting stumps and logs. Flying termites are females looking for a mate.

▶ SPITTLEBUG

Philaenus spumarius

SPITTLEBUG FAMILY Cercopidae

Description The spittlebug has a length to 0.6 cm/ 0.24 in. The colours of the nymph and adult are extremely variable, from yellowish, to brownish, to black with white spots. The foam produced is thought to protect the nymph from predators and dehydration.

Etymology The genus name, *Philaenus*, is Greek for "love." The species name, *spumarius*, means "sparkling," referring to the foam.

Habitat Common in garden beds and open forests.

▶ WHIRLIGIG WATER BEETLE

Gyrinus sp.

WHIRLIGIG BEETLE FAMILY Gyrinidae

Description The whirligig water beetle has a length to 0.6 cm/0.24 in. It is black all over, with reddish legs. Its eyes are split into two, one for looking up and one for looking down.

Habitat Common in still fresh water.

TEN-LINED JUNE BEETLE

Polyphylla decemlineata

LAMELLICORN BEETLE FAMILY Scarabaeidae

Description The ten-lined June beetle has a length to 3 cm/1.2 in. Its wing covers are green brown, with four long white lines and one short white line on each. The males have two large antennae.

Etymology The species name, *decemlineata*, means "10 lined." When threatened or picked up, they can make a hissing sound.

Habitat Common. The adults can be found around orchids; the larvae feed on the roots.

EUROPEAN CRANEFLY

Tipula paludosa

CRANEFLY FAMILY Tipulidae

Description The European cranefly was introduced to southern BC accidentally. Its body length is to 3 cm/1.2 in. The abdomen is light brown. The larvae, also known as leatherjackets, are to 2 cm/0.8 in. long.

Etymology The species name, *paludosa*, is Latin for "marsh loving."

Habitat Moist soils under lawns, in fields, and in wetland habitats.

▶ KAYAK POND SKATER

Limnoporus notabilis

WATER STRIDER FAMILY Gerridae

Description The kayak pond skater has a body length to 2.5 cm/1 in. It is generally a dull brown, with three pairs of legs. Its ability to walk on water is due to a combination of its long hydrophobic legs, the water's surface tension, and its weight distribution.

Etymology The species name, *notabilis*, is Latin for "remarkable" or "notable."

Habitat Calm waters in ponds, marshes, and lakes.

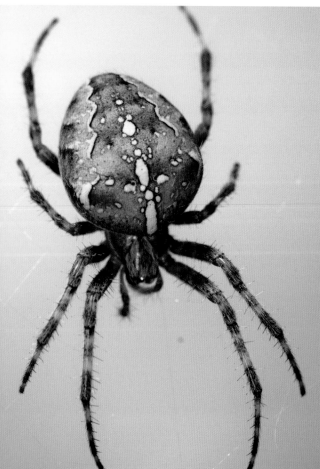

▶ ORB-WEAVER SPIDER

Araneus diadematus

ORB-WEAVER FAMILY Araneidae

Description The male orb-weaver spider's body is to 0.7 cm/0.3 in. across, and the female's is to 1.5 cm/0.6 in. across. The cross orb-weaver spider (see photograph) is red to brown, with a series of white dots that form a cross. Variations of colours and patterns can be found in different regions. This species is originally from Europe.

Etymology The genus name, *Aranaeus*, is from the Latin word *arane*, meaning "spider."

Habitat Most often seen at the end of summer and in autumn, spinning their orb-like webs.

▶ HARVESTMAN

Phalangium opilio

FAMILY Phalangiidae

Description The harvestman's body is to 0.6 cm/ 0.24 in. across. It can range in colour from light brown, to dark brown, to reddish, to grey. Harvestmen are not actually spiders; however, they are close relatives. Unlike spiders, they have one body section and two eyes. Harvestmen are also known as daddy longlegs.

Etymology The species name, *opilio*, means "shepherd" or "herdsman."

Habitat Harvestmen were introduced from Europe, and they are now widespread in the Pacific Northwest. They live in fields, grass, and forests.

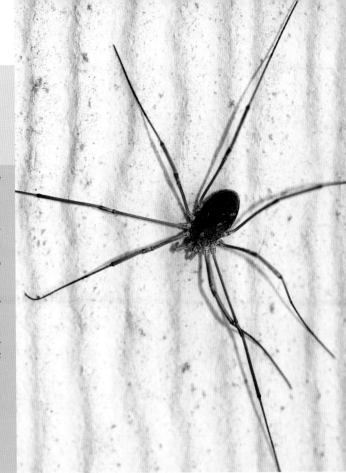

▶ WOLF SPIDER

Pardosa spp.

WOLF SPIDER FAMILY Lycosidae

Description There are over 500 species of wolf spider worldwide. The species found in the Pacific Northwest are 0.5–0.8 cm/0.2–0.3 in. in length. They are mainly dark grey brown. Wolf spiders do not spin a web; they hunt down their prey as a wolf would.

Habitat Common in the Pacific Northwest.

▶ WESTERN BLACK WIDOW

Latrodectus hesperus

COBWEB SPIDER FAMILY Theridiidae

Description The female western black widow's body is to 1.3 cm/0.5 in. in length and is black with a red hourglass mark on the lower abdomen. The male, which is considered harmless, is generally half the size of the female and a brown-tan colour. The female has a venomous bite that can be dangerous.

Etymology The species name, *hesperus*, is Latin for "from the west" or "western."

Habitat Found in warm, dry habitats in sheltered locations. I found two females in the woodpile in my basement. I wore gloves after their discovery.

▶ FLOWER CRAB SPIDER

Misumena vatia

CRAB SPIDER FAMILY Thomisidae

Description The flower crab spider has a body length to 0.9 cm/0.4 in. It can be white or yellow, depending on the colour of the flowers it typically hunts on. It is also known as the goldenrod crab spider, because it often perches on yellow flowers to hunt. It does not spin a web; it patiently waits to ambush its prey.

Etymology The species name, *vatia*, means "bow-legged."

Habitat Common on daisies, sunflowers, and goldenrods. Most commonly seen at the end of summer and in autumn.

GREAT GREEN BUSH-CRICKET

Tettigonia viridissima

BUSH-CRICKET FAMILY Tettigoniidae

Description The great green bush-cricket is 3.2–4.2 cm/1.3–1.7 in. long. Its antennae can be up to three times its body length. The females have an egg-laying organ (ovipositor) that can be as long as their body.

Habitat Great green bush-crickets are carnivores that spend most of their time in trees eating larvae, flies, and caterpillars.

DRUMMING KATYDID SMALL BUSH-CRICKET

Meconema thalassinum

BUSH-CRICKET FAMILY Tettigoniidae

Description The drumming katydid is light green and to 2.5 cm/1 in. long. The fragile-looking antennae can be up to 4 cm/1.6 in. long. The drumming katydid is a European species that has found its way west after being introduced to the east coast.

Etymology The species name, *thalassinum*, refers to the katydid's green colour. The common name drumming katydid is from the noise the males make by drumming on leaves.

Habitat Mainly found in deciduous trees.

▶ MIGRATORY GRASSHOPPER

Melanoplus sanguinipes

SHORT-HORNED GRASSHOPPER FAMILY Acrididae

Description The migratory grasshopper has a length to 4 cm/1.6 in. Its body ranges from green to brown. It has extremely powerful hind legs and is able to fly up to 16 m/53 ft.

Habitat One of the most common grasshoppers in the Pacific Northwest. It can be found in pastures and weedy fields.

▶ BANDED ALDER BORER

Rosalia funebris

LONG-HORNED BEETLE FAMILY Cerambycidae

Description The banded alder borer has a length to 4 cm/1.6 in. The wing covers are banded by three white stripes. The antennae are also banded black and white. The banded alder borer feeds on dead or dying alder trees and should not be considered a pest.

Habitat In the Pacific Northwest, they can be found anywhere there is an abundance of alder trees.

▶ RED-SHOULDERED PINE BORER

Stictoleptura canadensis cribripennis

LONG-HORNED BEETLE FAMILY Cerambycidae

Description The red-shouldered pine borer is to 2 cm/ 0.75 in. long. The male's wing covers are red and black; the female's are generally red.

Habitat Seen mainly on flowers along the coast.

▶ WESTERN CONIFER SEED BUG

Leptoglossus occidentalis

FAMILY Coreidae

Description The western conifer seed bug has a body length to 2 cm/0.75 in. The wings have a geometric design of whites, oranges, and browns.

Etymology The species name, *occidentalis*, means "of the west."

Habitat Found mainly in the tops of conifers feeding on young cones. It is becoming so common that it is flying into homes to overwinter.

▶ BRONZE CARABID EUROPEAN GROUND BEETLE

Carabus nemoralis

GROUND BEETLE FAMILY Carabidae

Description The ground beetle is an introduced species with a body length to 2.2 cm/0.87 in. The outer wing covers are iridescent blackish purple. Each wing has three rows of tiny dimples.

Etymology The species name, *nemoralis*, means "growing in groves" or "growing in woods."

Habitat Has become a welcome garden and forest predator.

▶ BLACK LAMPYRID

Ellychnia hatchi

FIREFLY BEETLE FAMILY Lampyridae

Description The black lampyrid has a length to 1.6 cm/ 0.6 in. The body is black, and the head has two red side margins.

Habitat Commonly found in damp Pacific coast forests in the spring.

► APHIDS

Aphis spp.

APHID FAMILY Aphididae

Description There are over 4,000 known species of aphids; they range in colour from translucent green, to brown, to black, to yellow, to white, to bronze. They range in size from 0.1 cm/0.04 in. to 1 cm/0.5 in. They are usually pear shaped and soft bodied and may or may not have wings.

Etymology The common name in plural form, aphids, is an anglicized form of the word for the Latin genus name *Aphis*, whose origin is unclear.

Habitat Aphids feed, and live, on many different plants, sometimes very destructively. Different species often favour specific plants.

► BLACK AND YELLOW MUD DAUBER

Sceliphron caementarium

SPHECID WASP FAMILY Sphecidae

Description The black and yellow mud dauber has a length to 2.8 cm/1.1 in. It has a black body with yellow markings.

Etymology The species name, *caementarium*, is Latin for "mason" or "builder of walls," referring to its mud nests.

Habitat Common. The adults nectar on flowers and can often be seen hanging around humming-bird feeders. Their nests are made from mud obtained from puddle and pond edges.

▶ THIMBLEBERRY STEM GALL WASP

Diastrophus kincaidii

SAWFLY FAMILY Cimbicidae

Description The adult thimbleberry stem gall wasp has a length to 0.5 cm/0.2 in. The adult wasps are dark brown to black. The gall (growth) itself is 5–10 cm/ 2–4 in. In the spring, the adult female lays her eggs, and after a week, the eggs have hatched. In autumn, they pupate, and by spring, they emerge as adults and start the cycle over. It is much easier to identify this wasp by looking at the galls a plant produces around the larvae than by actually looking at the wasp, since it is so small and its adult life is short.

Habitat Very common in areas that have thimble-berries.

▶ BLACKJACKET

Vespula pensylvanica

WASP FAMILY Vespidae

Description The blackjacket has a length to 2 cm/ 0.8 in. It has a white face and large black eyes. The thorax and abdomen have black and white alternating bands and spots. The stinger can sting repeatedly.

Etymology The species name, *pensylvanica*, refers to it first being seen in Pennsylvania.

Habitat Common in the Pacific Northwest.

▶ PAPER WASP

Polistes dominula

WASP FAMILY Vespidae

Description The paper wasp has a length to 1.8 cm/ 0.7 in. The abdomen is black with yellow bands. The head and thorax are black with yellow spots. The paper wasp builds its nest with only a single layer of papery cells, which allows observers to see into it.

Habitat Common. Their nests are constructed on covered walls and under overhangs.

▶ YELLOWJACKET

Vespula spp.

WASP FAMILY Vespidae

Description Yellowjackets are to 1.5 cm/0.5 in. They are yellow and black, with alternating bands on the abdomen. Yellowjackets have a barbed lance-like stinger that can sting repeatedly.

Habitat Very common in forests and urban areas in the Pacific Northwest. Their nests can be found in trees and rodent burrows.

EUROPEAN HONEYBEE

Apis mellifera

BUMBLEBEE AND HONEYBEE FAMILY Apidae

Description The European honeybee is to 2 cm/ 0.8 in. long. The abdomen, thorax, and head are woolly and yellow and black. The black antennae are bent.

Etymology The genus name, *Apis*, is Latin for "bee." The species name, *mellifera*, means "honey bearing."

Habitat Mainly found in human-made hives. European honeybees were introduced to North America in the 1600s. They are native to Europe, Asia, and Africa.

YELLOW-FACED BUMBLEBEE

Bombus vosnesenskii

BUMBLEBEE AND HONEYBEE FAMILY Apidae

Description The queen yellow-faced bumblebee is to 1.9 cm/0.75 in. long. Males and workers are to 1.4 cm/ 0.6 in. long. The hairs on the head and lower abdomen are yellow, with the rest of the body being black.

Etymology The genus name, *Bombus*, means "buzzing."

Habitat The yellow-faced bumblebee is a west coast species. It ranges from BC to Baja California, Mexico.

▶ MIXED BUMBLEBEE

Bombus mixtus

BUMBLEBEE AND HONEYBEE FAMILY Apidae

Description The mixed bumblebee is to 1.3 cm/ 0.5 in. long. The head and body are covered in yellow and black hairs. The tip of the abdomen is red brown.

Etymology The species name, *mixtus*, refers to the mixed colours.

Habitat The mixed bumblebee is a west coast species that feeds on nectar.

▶ ORCHARD MASON BEE

Osmia lignaria

BEE FAMILY Megachilidae

Description The female orchard mason bee is to 1.4 cm/0.6 in. long. The male is smaller, to 1.2 cm/ 0.5 in. long, and has a light-coloured tuft of hair on the front of its head. Orchard mason bees appear to be black; however, they are actually metallic blue green.

Etymology The common name mason bee is derived from the way females use mud to build separate cells for each egg.

Habitat Orchard mason bees are native to the Pacific Northwest, which makes them ideal to use as pollinators in orchards and blueberry fields.

▶ CYANIDE MILLIPEDE

Harpaphe haydeniana

POLYDESMID MILLIPEDE FAMILY Polydesmida

Description The cyanide millipede has a length to 4 cm/1.6 in. The upper body is black, with rows of yellow spots on the sides. It has approximately 20 body segments and 30 to 31 pairs of legs.

Etymology The common name millipede means "having a thousand feet."

Habitat Moist Pacific coast forests with lots of decaying vegetation.

▶ GARDEN CENTIPEDE

Lithobius sp.

CENTIPEDE FAMILY Lithobiidae

Description The garden centipede has a length to 4 cm/1.6 in. The adult's body is orange red, with 15 pairs of legs (not 50 pairs, as its name suggests).

Etymology The genus name, *Lithobius*, is from two Greek words: *lithos*, "stone," and *bio*, "life."

Habitat Common in dark, damp areas, such as under stones and logs.

▶ PILL BUG

Armadillidium vulgare

WOODLOUSE FAMILY Armadillidiidae

Description The pill bug has a length to 1.8 cm/ 0.7 in. It is slate grey, with seven pairs of legs and two visible antennae. As a defense mechanism, the pill bug can roll up into a ball. It is not an insect but a terrestial crustacean. It is an introduced species.

Etymology The species name, *vulgare*, means "common."

Habitat Common. Can be found in moist conditions under stones, logs, and hedges.

▶ SOWBUG SOW BEETLE

Porcellio scaber

FAMILY Porcellionidae

Description The sowbug is shaped like a miniature armadillo, with a length to 1.2 cm/0.5 in. It is generally slate grey and has seven pairs of legs and four antennae. It is not an insect but a terrestial crustacean. It was introduced from Europe.

Etymology The species name, *scaber*, is Latin for "rough."

Habitat Lives in moist areas: under flowerpots, in woodpiles or composts, and under damp concrete. It looks very similar to the pill bug (*Armadillidium vulgare*) but cannot roll up like a pill bug does.

PACIFIC SIDEBAND SNAIL FAITHFUL SNAIL

Monadenia fidelis

FAMILY Bradybaenidae

Description The Pacific sideband snail has a body length to 3.5 cm/1.4 in. The shell varies in shades of reddish brown and has a yellowish band. The body is dark brown to black, with pinkish bumps.

Etymology The genus name, *Monadenia*, means "one gland," referring to the mucous gland. The species name, *fidelis*, means "dependable."

Habitat Common in coastal forests. The Pacific sideband snail is endemic to the Pacific coast, from Alaska to California.

PACIFIC BANANA SLUG

Ariolimax columbianus

ROUND BACK SLUG FAMILY Arionidae

Description The Pacific banana slug has a length to 25 cm/10 in. Its colours can range from bright yellow (which gives it the common name of banana slug), to greenish, to brown, to black and brown (which gives it another common name, leopard banana slug), to white. Colours vary with age, diet, moisture, and light. The Pacific banana slug is the second-largest slug in the world.

Habitat Common in moist Pacific Northwest forests and gardens.

► CHOCOLATE ARION

Arion rufus

ROUND BACK SLUG FAMILY Arionidae

Description The chocolate arion has a length to 12 cm/ 4.7 in. Its colours vary from reddish brown, to orange, to black. The chocolate arion has wrinkles down its back and a respiratory pore at the front of its mantle (head), unlike the banana slug.

Etymology The species name, *rufus*, is Latin for "red."

Habitat Common in garden beds.

MARINE LIFE

▶ VARNISH CLAM DARK MAHOGANY CLAM

Nuttallia obscurata

SUNSET CLAM FAMILY Psammobiidae

Description The varnish clam has a length to 7 cm/ 2.8 in. The shells are oval shaped and shiny brown, with white at the hinge. The interior is light purple and white. The varnish clam was accidentally introduced to the west coast from Japan.

Etymology The species name, *obscurata*, means "dark" or "uncertain."

Habitat Buried in sand, gravel, or mud to 20 cm/ 8 in. deep.

▶ BUTTER CLAM

Saxidomus gigantea

FAMILY Veneridae

Description The butter clam is to 15 cm/6 in. long. The shell is white to greyish and etched with concentric lines. Indigenous groups have been harvesting the butter clam for thousands of years. The shells were used for trading.

Habitat Buried in sand, gravel, or mud to 35 cm/ 14 in. deep.

▶ PACIFIC RAZOR CLAM

Siliqua patula

FAMILY Pharidae

Description The shell of the Pacific razor clam is 8–15 cm/3–6 in. long. The polished-looking shells are tan to chestnut coloured, with variations of yellow and darker browns. The Pacific razor clam is an exceptionally fast-burrowing bivalve. This clam makes good eating. However, before harvesting any shellfish for food, check that the area is not closed to harvesting because of red tide or other issues. Red tide is caused by large algal blooms, which can bring serious harm to fish, shellfish, mammals, birds, and people.

Habitat Sandy exposed beaches from Alaska to California.

▶ NUTTALL'S COCKLE

Clinocardium nuttallii

TRUE COCKLE FAMILY Cardiidae

Description Nuttall's cockle is to 14 cm/5.5 in long. The thick shell is tan and mottled or banded with various shades of brown. There are more than 30 distinct radial ribs covering the shell. Nuttall's cockle has long been harvested by Indigenous groups.

Habitat Found in shallow depths in fine sandy mud, often in areas with eelgrass.

▶ PACIFIC OYSTER

Crassostrea gigas

TRUE OYSTER FAMILY Ostreidae

Description The Pacific oyster is to 30 cm/12 in. long. The shells are off-white and vary in shape according to the substrate they are growing on.

Etymology The genus name, *Crassostrea*, means "thick oyster." The species name, *gigas*, means "giant." The Pacific oyster is native to the Pacific coast of Asia.

Habitat Usually seen on hard rocky surfaces in calm shallow waters.

▶ CALIFORNIA MUSSEL

Mytilus californiensis

FAMILY Mytilidae

Description The California mussel is to 20 cm/ 8 in. long. The thick shell is blue and black and has coarse radial ribbing. The inside of the shell is pearly pale blue and white. The California mussel is native to the west coast and has been harvested by Indigenous groups for thousands of years.

Habitat Surf-exposed rocks, pilings, and wharves.

BLUE MUSSEL

Mytilus edulis

FAMILY Mytilidae

Description The blue mussel is to 11 cm/4.3 in long. The shell colour varies from blue black to brown. This mussel was introduced from the Atlantic for aquaculture. One of its main predators is the sea star.

Habitat Surf-exposed rocks, pilings, and wharves.

SPINY PINK SCALLOP

Chlamys hastata

SCALLOP FAMILY Pectinidae

Description The spiny pink scallop is to 9 cm/3.5 in. across. The shells vary from pink, to yellowish, to purple and have sharp spines radiating from two unevenly shaped tabs.

Etymology The species name, *hastata*, is Latin for "spear shaped," referring to the sharp spines.

Habitat Rocky shorelines from Alaska to California, to a depth of 150 m/490 ft.

▶ GIANT ROCK SCALLOP PURPLE-HINGE ROCK SCALLOP

Crassadoma gigantea

SCALLOP FAMILY Pectinidae

Description The giant rock scallop is a bivalve that can range from 15 cm/6 in. to 25 cm/10 in. across. The colour of the shell is pink to brown on the outside, with the inside being a shiny white. When young, the scallops are free swimming; as they age, they permanently attach themselves to a substrate. As with most scallop species, the giant rock scallop is highly prized as a food source.

Etymology The family name, Pectinidae, is from the Latin word *pecten*, meaning "comb," in reference to the comb-like structure of the shell.

Habitat Found on the ocean floor to depths of 80 m/260 ft., on or under large rocks and even on deep harbour pilings. Can be seen from BC to California.

▶ LEWIS'S MOONSHELL

Neverita lewisii

FAMILY Naticidae

Description Lewis's moonshell is to 14 cm/5.5 in. long. The rounded shell is yellowish tan to brown; it is composed of about six rounded whorls. It is one of the largest moonsnails on the west coast.

Etymology The species name, *lewisii*, and common name, Lewis's moonshell, honour Meriwether Lewis, American explorer, probably best known for the Lewis and Clark Expedition.

Habitat Sandy flat areas with calm waters and clams.

▶ RED TURBAN SNAIL

Astraea gibberosa

TURBAN SNAIL FAMILY Turbinidae

Description The red turban snail has a diameter to 10 cm/4 in. The beautifully whorled shell is red to brownish red. The snail is a herbivore, feeding on small giant kelp.

Etymology The species name, *gibberosa*, means "humped on one side" or "hunchbacked." Indigenous groups traded the shells.

Habitat On rocky shores from southern Alaska to northern Mexico.

▶ BLACK TURBAN SNAIL

Tegula funebralis

TURBAN SNAIL FAMILY Turbinidae

Description The black turban snail has a diameter to 4.5 cm/1.8 in. It is much smaller than the red turban snail. The shell is dark purple, with four whorls. The top of the shell is often worn down to the white interior layer.

Etymology The species name, *funebralis*, is from *funeral*, referring to the shell's dark colour.

Habitat On rocky shores from northern British Columbia to northern Mexico.

▶ BLUE TOP SNAIL

Calliostoma ligatum

FAMILY Calliostomatidae

Description The blue top snail has a diameter to 3 cm/1.2 in. The shell is beautifully striped brown and tan. Older, worn shells reveal the blue undercoating.

Habitat On rocky shores from Alaska to California.

▶ MUD-FLAT SNAIL

Batillaria cumingi

MUD-FLAT SNAIL FAMILY Batillariidae

Description The mud-flat snail is to 3.8 cm/1.5 in. long. The spiral-shaped shell has eight to nine whorls and is grey brown. The mud-flat snail was accidentally introduced to the west coast from Japan.

Habitat Does very well in calm bays with fine sandy mud; seen from BC to California.

▶ PURPLE OLIVE

Olivella biplicata

DWARF OLIVE FAMILY Olivellidae

Description The purple olive is a sea snail with a shell to just over 2.5 cm/1 in. long. The shiny shell varies in colour from greyish purple, to dark purple, to tan, to brown, to almost white. The shells of the purple olive have been collected and traded for thousands of years.

Habitat Common on sandy beaches from coastal BC to California. A distinctive sandy trail is visible where the purple olive has been. The empty shells are often taken over by hermit crabs.

▶ NORTHERN ABALONE

Haliotis kamtschatkana

ABALONE FAMILY Haliotidae

Description The northern abalone is to 18 cm/7 in. long. The exterior of the shell is red brown, with four to six respiration holes. The inside of the shell is the beautiful mother-of-pearl. Over-harvesting of the northern abalone has dramatically reduced its population to the point where it is now protected.

Etymology The species name, *kamtschatkana*, is named for the Kamchatka Peninsula in Russia.

Habitat Lower intertidal rocky beaches from Alaska to California.

RIBBED LIMPET

Lottia digitalis

FAMILY Lottiidae

Description The ribbed limpet is to 2.5 cm/1 in. long. The shell is green brown with grey-white blotches. The apex of the shell is slightly off-centre and has wavy ribs radiating down the shell.

Etymology The species name, *digitalis*, means "finger," referring to the ribs on the shell.

Habitat Rocky shores with strong waves, mainly in shady areas.

ROUGH KEYHOLE LIMPET

Diodora aspera

FAMILY Fissurellidae

Description The rough keyhole limpet is to 7 cm/ 2.8 in. long. The shell is grey white brown, with darker rays and an off-centre hole at the apex.

Etymology The genus name, *Diodora*, means "with a passage through," and the species name, *aspera*, means "rough."

Habitat Rocky shorelines from Alaska to California.

▶ PACIFIC PLATE LIMPET

Tectura scutum
FAMILY Lottiidae

Description The Pacific plate limpet is to 5 cm/2 in. long. The shallow shell is green brown grey, with a cream-coloured pattern.

Etymology The species name, *scutum*, means "shield."

Habitat Rocky shorelines from Alaska to California.

▶ ACORN BARNACLE

Balanus glandula
FAMILY Balanidae

Description The acorn barnacle is to 1 cm/0.5 in. tall and 1.8 cm/0.7 in. wide. The shell is white grey and cone shaped. The acorn barnacle is the most common barnacle in the Pacific Northwest.

Etymology The genus name, *Balanus*, means "acorn."

Habitat Along rocky shorelines from Alaska to Mexico.

▶ GIANT BARNACLE

Balanus nubilus

FAMILY Balanidae

Description The giant barnacle is to 12.5 cm/5 in. tall and 10 cm/4 in. wide. The shell is white grey, and the flesh is pinkish. It is one of the largest barnacles in the world. Indigenous groups roasted and ate this barnacle.

Etymology The species name, *nubilus*, means "cloudy."

Habitat Along rocky shorelines from Alaska to California.

▶ GOOSE BARNACLE

Pollicipes polymerus

GOOSE BARNACLE FAMILY Pollicipedidae

Description The goose barnacle is to 10 cm/4 in. long. The rubbery stalks are dark brown and covered in tiny spines. The plates (top portion) are white grey. The goose barnacle is edible.

Habitat Rocky shorelines from Alaska to California. Often seen growing with California mussels.

GREEN SEA URCHIN

Strongylocentrotus droebachiensis

SEA URCHIN FAMILY Strongylocentrotidae

Description The green sea urchin is to 8.3 cm/ 3.3 in. across. The shell is green brown, and the spines are pale grass green to light brown.

Edibility The green sea urchin is edible.

Habitat Found from Alaska to Washington; usually associated with kelp beds.

PURPLE SEA URCHIN

Strongylocentrotus purpuratus

SEA URCHIN FAMILY Strongylocentrotidae

Description The purple sea urchin is to 10 cm/ 4 in. across. The shell and spines are purple pinkish to greenish.

Etymology The genus name, *Strongylocentrotus*, means "ball of spines."

Habitat Rocky shorelines from Alaska to California.

▶ GREEN SHORE CRAB HAIRY CRAB

Hemigrapsus oregonensis

FAMILY Varunidae

Description The green shore crab is to 5 cm/2 in. across. The carapace (shell) varies from grey to green and is often mottled. The legs have very fine hair; hence the common name hairy crab. This crab is mainly a herbivore.

Habitat Loves flat muddy bays with eelgrass. Seen from Alaska to California.

▶ RED ROCK CRAB RED CRAB

Cancer productus

CRAB FAMILY Cancridae

Description The red rock crab has a carapace (shell) to 20 cm/8 in. across. Mature crabs have a brick-red carapace with rounded serrations at the edges.

Habitat Rocky shorelines and eelgrass beds from Alaska to California. The red rock crab, as its name suggests, prefers rocky ocean bottoms, whereas the Dungeness crab prefers sandy bottoms.

DUNGENESS CRAB

Cancer magister

CRAB FAMILY Cancridae

Description The Dungeness crab is to 25 cm/10 in. across. The carapace (shell) varies in colour from grey brown to red brown purple. The claws are yellow orange with white tips.

Habitat On sandy-bottomed areas from Alaska to California.

PURPLE SHORE CRAB

Hemigrapsus nudus

FAMILY Varunidae

Description The purple shore crab is to 5.5 cm/2.2 in. across. The carapace (shell) is dark purple to red brown. The claws have dark spots.

Etymology The species name, *nudus*, refers to the crab having no hair.

Habitat Found mainly under rocks in the intertidal zone from Alaska to California.

VEILED CHITON

Placiphorella velata
FAMILY Mopaliidae

Description The veiled chiton is to 5 cm/2 in. long.
The eight valves vary in colour from pink, to brownish reddish, to cream, to green. In younger chitons, the colours can be more vibrant.

Etymology The species name, *velata*, means "covered" or "veiled."

Habitat On exposed rocks and under rock ledges. Seen from Alaska to California.

HAIRY CHITON

Mopalia ciliata
FAMILY Mopaliidae

Description The hairy chiton is to 7.5 cm/3 in. long. The eight valves vary in colour from dark brown to light brown, and some have very bright blotches. The girdle surrounding the valves is covered in soft hairs. Chitons were a food source for Indigenous groups.

Etymology The species name, *ciliata*, means "fringed with hairs."

Habitat This chiton likes to hide under rocks and rock ledges. It can be seen from Alaska to California.

▶ BLACK KATY CHITON

Katharina tunicata

FAMILY Mopaliidae

Description The black katy chiton is to 12 cm/5 in. long. The eight valves are white or dirty green and are very noticeable due to being surrounded by a black leathery girdle.

Etymology The genus name, *Katharina*, honours Lady Katherine Douglas, who sent specimens of the chiton to England in 1815.

Habitat The black katy chiton is probably the most commonly seen chiton on the west coast. It can be found along rocky shorelines from Alaska to California.

▶ ECCENTRIC SAND DOLLAR

Dendraster excentricus

SAND DOLLAR FAMILY Dendrasteridae

Description The eccentric sand dollar is to 10 cm/ 4 in. across. The shells (tests) are covered in tiny spines, which give the sand dollar its colour, usually dark purple. White shells that have washed ashore are dead.

Etymology The genus name, *Dendraster*, means "tree star."

Habitat In sandy areas along the coast from Alaska to California.

PACIFIC SEA NETTLE

Chrysaora fuscescens

FAMILY Pelagiidae

Description The Pacific sea nettle's golden brown bell (body) is to 50 cm/20 in. across. This jelly-fish's maroon tentacles and white arms trail several metres or feet behind.

Etymology The genus name, *Chrysaora*, means "he who has a golden armament."

Habitat Open waters along the coast from Alaska to California.

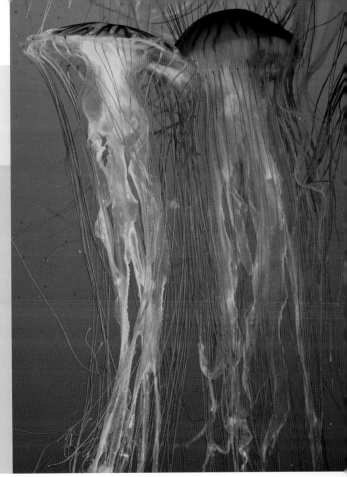

LION'S MANE JELLYFISH

Cyanea capillata

TRUE JELLY FAMILY Cyaneidae

Description The lion's mane jellyfish's bell is to 2 m/ 6.6 ft. across, with the tentacles trailing to 9 m/ 30 ft. behind. The bell is a translucent white red orange. It is the largest jelly in the world.

Etymology The species name, *capillata*, means "furnished with fine hair."

Habitat Found from Alaska to Mexico. Often seen floating near the surface of the water or stranded on the beach in summer.

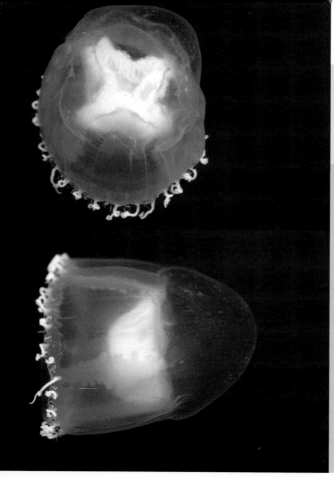

▶ RED-EYE MEDUSA

Polyorchis penicillatus

FAMILY Polyorchidae

Description The red-eye medusa is to 4 cm/1.5 in. high. The bell is a translucent blue grey, with up to 120 trailing tentacles. The common name is from the red spots around the perimeter that look like eyes.

Etymology The species name, *penicillatus*, means "brush"—having a tuft of hair like a paint brush.

Habitat Open coastal waters from Alaska to California.

▶ MOON JELLY

Aurelia labiata

FAMILY Ulmaridae

Description The moon jelly is to 38 cm/15 in. across. The bell is a translucent blue grey surrounded by small whitish tentacles. The four-leaf clover in the centre of the bell is gonads.

Etymology The species name, *labiata*, means "lipped."

Habitat Commonly seen near the surface of the water or stranded on beaches. Found from Alaska to California.

▶ MONTEREY SEA LEMON   DUSTY YELLOW NUDIBRANCH

Doris montereyensis
FAMILY Dorididae

Description The Monterey sea lemon, or sea slug, is to 15 cm/6 in. long. The body is generally yellow and covered in tubercles, some of which are tipped with black.

Habitat Rocky areas and pilings from Alaska to California.

▶ HOODED NUDIBRANCH

Melibe leonina
FAMILY Tethydidae

Description The hooded nudibranch is to 10 cm/ 4 in. long. The body is translucent white to green brown, much like a moon jelly's.

Etymology The species name, *leonina*, means "lion," referring to the tentacles, which look like a lion's mane.

Habitat Often seen near the surface of the water around wharves. Found from Alaska to California.

PACIFIC BLOOD STAR

Henricia leviuscula

FAMILY Echinasteridae

Description The Pacific blood star is to 12 cm/5 in. across. This star typically has five arms but may sometimes have four or six. It can be blood red, orange, or brown. Its diet is mainly sponges.

Habitat In rocky areas from Alaska to California.

VERMILION STAR

Mediaster aequalis

FAMILY Goniasteridae

Description The vermilion star is to 15 cm/6 in. across. This star has five equal-length arms and is brilliant red; hence the common name vermilion.

Etymology The species name, *aequalis*, refers to another common name, equal-arm star.

Habitat In rocky areas from Alaska to California.

GIANT PINK STAR

Pisaster brevispinus

SEA STAR FAMILY Asteriidae

Description The giant pink star is to 60 cm/2 ft. across. It has five bristly arms and is pink to whitish grey. The size of this star allows it to catch bigger prey, including clams, sand dollars, and giant barnacles.

Etymology The species name, *brevispinus*, refers to another common name of this star, short-spined star.

Habitat Areas with sandy mud where there are clams. Found from Alaska to California.

OCHRE SEA STAR

Pisaster ochraceus

SEA STAR FAMILY Asteriidae

Description The ochre sea star can be up to 35 cm/ 14 in. across but is more often seen around 25 cm/ 10 in. across. This common star has five arms and is yellow orange, purple, or brown. The network of white spines gives this star a rough, sandpaper-like feeling.

Habitat Common along rocky shorelines from Alaska to California.

SUNFLOWER STAR

Pycnopodia helianthoides

SEA STAR FAMILY Asteriidae

Description The sunflower star is to 1 m/3.3 ft. across. It can have up to 26 arms and is orange, pink, red, or purple.

Etymology The genus name, *Pycnopodia*, means "many legged." The species name, *helianthoides*, means "sunflower-like."

Habitat Along rocky and sandy areas (anywhere it wants). Seen from Alaska to California.

BAT STAR

Asterina miniata

SEA STAR FAMILY Asteriidae

Description The bat star is to 15 cm/6 in. across. It commonly has five arms; however, it sometimes has four or up to eight. It comes in a variety of colours: red, yellow, orange, purple, and more.

Etymology The genus name, *Asterina*, is from *aster* "star."

Habitat Exposed coastlines from Alaska to California.

GIANT GREEN ANEMONE

Anthopleura xanthogrammica

FAMILY Actiniidae

Description The giant green anemone is to 30 cm/
12 in. across and 30 cm/12 in. high. The body (disc)
and tentacles are a wonderful light blue green. The
colour comes from algae living in the tissues.

Habitat Very common along shorelines with shallow puddles and tide pools when tide is out. Found
all along the west coast.

PLUMOSE ANEMONE

Metridium senile

FAMILY Metridiidae

Description The plumose anemone is to 10 cm/
4 in. tall. It has fewer than 100 tentacles and is white,
orange, cream, or brown.

Etymology The species name, *senile*, means "aged"
or "white haired."

Habitat Very commonly seen on wharves, piers,
and pilings from Alaska to California.

▶ GIANT PLUMOSE ANEMONE

Metridium farcimen

FAMILY Metridiidae

Description The giant plumose anemone is to 1 m/ 3.3 ft. tall. It has more than 200 tentacles and ranges from pure white to pumpkin orange.

Habitat Commonly seen on wharves, piers, and pilings from Alaska to California.

▶ PAINTED URTICINA

Urticina crassicornis

FAMILY Actiniidae

Description The painted urticina is up to 25 cm/ 10 in. tall but is typically seen at 10 cm/4 in. tall. It varies in colour from green, to red, to yellow brown.

Etymology The species name, *crassicornis*, means "thick stem."

Habitat Likes being in protected areas, such as crevices or under ledges. Found from Alaska to California.

▶ BRANCHED-SPINE BRYOZOAN

Flustrellidra corniculata
FAMILY Flustrellidridae

Description The branched-spine bryozoan, or "moss animal," is to 10 cm/4 in. long. It is tan coloured and covered in tiny spines, giving it a rubbery appearance. It could easily be mistaken for a seaweed.

Etymology The species name, *corniculata*, means "with small horns."

Habitat Attached to rocks in the lower intertidal zone, from Alaska to California. They can be found washed up on shore after strong storms.

▶ ISOPOD

Ligia ssp.
FAMILY Ligiidae

Description There are an estimated 10,000 species of isopod in the world. The ones seen in the Pacific Northwest are most likely from the genus *Ligia*, also known as rock lice. They are to 3.5 cm/1.4 in. long and are related to the pill bug (*Armadillidium vulgare*) that we see in our gardens.

Habitat Common. Can be seen scurrying along coastal rocks from Alaska to California.

CALCAREOUS TUBE WORM

Serpula vermicularis

FAMILY Serpulidae

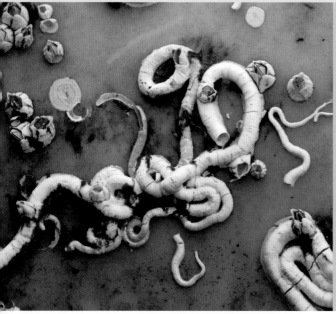

Description The calcareous tube worm is to 6.5 cm/ 2.6 in. long. The feathery tentacles are red, orange, or pink, and the tube is white and chalky.

Etymology The species name, *vermicularis*, means "worm-like."

Habitat Found on almost any hard surface under the ocean, from BC to California.

PACIFIC LUGWORM

Abarenicola pacifica

FAMILY Arenicolidae

Description The Pacific lugworm is to 15 cm/6 in. long. The body is tapered at both ends and is orange red. The coiled fecal castings are often all that are seen of this worm.

Habitat On flat sandy–muddy beaches from Alaska to California.

▶ NORTHERN FEATHER DUSTER WORM

Eudistylia vancouveri

FAMILY Sabellidae

Description The northern feather duster worm is to 25 cm/10 in. long. The tentacles on top of the worm are green and purple. The rubbery tubes can be as long as 60 cm/2 ft.

Etymology The species name, *vancouveri*, is from where the worm was first discovered, Vancouver Island.

Habitat Rocky shorelines, wharves, and pilings, from Alaska to California.

▶ GIANT PACIFIC OCTOPUS

Octopus dofleini

OCTOPUS FAMILY Octopodidae

Description The giant Pacific octopus is to 9 m/ 30 ft. across but is more typically seen at 2 m/6.6 ft. The body and eight legs are red to brown, depending on the colour of its habitat. It is the largest octopus in the world.

Habitat Along the coast from Alaska to California, sometimes in tide pools. I found the octopus in the photo below washed ashore on the west coast of Vancouver Island.

▶ NAVAL SHIPWORM

Teredo navalis

SHIPWORM FAMILY Teredinidae

Description The naval shipworm is not a worm; it is a marine bivalve (clam) with a worm-like body. It has two white calcareous plates that are up to 2 cm/ 0.8 in. long. The plates create bored tunnels that can be up to 60 cm/24 in. long and 1 cm/0.5 in. across.

Etymology The genus name, *Teredo*, means "wood gnawing."

Habitat Temperate and tropical oceans around the world.

▶ ORCA

Orcinus orca

OCEANIC DOLPHIN FAMILY Delphinidae

Description Male orcas range from 7 m/23 ft. to 9 m/30 ft. long. Females range from 6 m/20 ft. to 8 m/26 ft. long. Typically, they are black with a white chest, white sides, and white patches behind the eyes. Orcas are more closely related to dolphins than whales. The orca was originally named *Delphinus orca*, meaning "demon dolphin."

Habitat Common in coastal waters from Alaska to Oregon.

► PACIFIC WHITE-SIDED DOLPHIN

Lagenorhynchus obliquidens

OCEANIC DOLPHIN FAMILY Delphinidae

Description The Pacific white-sided dolphin is to 2.5 m/8.2 ft. long. It is dark grey to blackish with a creamy-white throat, chin, and underparts.

Etymology The genus name, *Lagenorhynchus*, means "bottle nose."

Habitat Mainly found away from shore, from Alaska to California. During the summer months, hundreds can be seen going through Active Pass in the Gulf Islands.

► PACIFIC HARBOUR SEAL

Phoca vitulina

HAIR SEAL FAMILY Phocidae

Description The Pacific harbour seal is to 1.8 m/ 6 ft. long. Their fur and spots vary in colour from brown, to white, to tan, to grey, to nearly black.

Etymology The genus name, *Phoca*, means "seal."

Habitat One of the most commonly seen sea mammals in the Pacific Northwest. Can be found from Alaska to California.

▶ HARBOUR PORPOISE

Phocoena phocoena

PORPOISE FAMILY Phocoenidae

Description The harbour porpoise is to 1.9 m/ 6.2 ft. long. It has a dark-grey back with lighter sides and a whitish belly.

Etymology The genus name and species name, *phocoena*, mean "big seal."

Habitat As its name implies, it is mainly a coastal mammal. It can be found from Alaska to California.

▶ STELLER SEA LION NORTHERN SEA LION

Eumetopias jubatus

EARED SEAL FAMILY Otariidae

Description Male Steller sea lions are to 3.3 m/ 10.7 ft. long, and females are to 2.9 m/9.5 ft. long. Males have a broader forehead than females and a light-tan head and rust-coloured body. Females are rust coloured all over.

Etymology The species name, *jubatus*, means "one with the broad forehead."

Habitat Rocky coastal waters from Alaska to California.

▶ CALIFORNIA SEA LION

Zalophus californianus

EARED SEAL FAMILY Otariidae

Description The male California sea lion is to 2.5 m/8.2 ft. long, and the female is to 1.7 m/5.6 ft. long. The California sea lion is smaller than the Steller sea lion and darker in colour.

Etymology The genus name, *Zalophus*, means "intense crest," from the mature male's protruding sagittal crest.

Habitat The California sea lion is a native to the west coast of North America. It enjoys rocky and sandy beaches and will haul itself out on wharves.

▶ SEA OTTER

Enhydra lutris

WEASEL FAMILY Mustelidae

Description The sea otter is to 1.5 m/5 ft. long and can weigh up to 45 kg/100 lb. The thick fur is usually dark brown to black; the head, throat, and neck are far lighter in colour. The sea otter has webbed hind feet, unlike the river otter.

Etymology The genus name, *Enhydra*, is Greek for "in the water."

Habitat Coastal bays with kelp beds from Alaska to California.

▶ HUMPBACK WHALE

Megaptera novaeangliae

RORQUAL FAMILY Balaenopteridae

Description The humpback whale is a baleen whale to 16 m/52 ft. long. It is dark grey to black and generally white below. Its flippers are to 4.5 m/15 ft., the longest of any whale.

Etymology The genus name, *Megaptera*, means "giant wing (flipper)."

Habitat Can be found in all oceans.

▶ GREY WHALE

Eschrichtius robustus

GREY WHALE FAMILY Eschrichtiidae

Description The grey whale is a baleen whale to 16 m/ 52 ft. long. It has dark-grey skin with light-grey-and-white mottling. It is often seen with barnacles growing on the skin.

Etymology The genus name, *Eschrichtius*, honours zoologist Daniel Frederik Eschricht.

Habitat Can be seen migrating from Alaska to California.

▶ SALMON

Oncorhynchus spp.

SALMON FAMILY Salmonidae

>> Chinook salmon

Oncorhynchus tshawytscha

Description The chinook salmon, also known as the spring salmon, is 61–91 cm/24–36 in. long and 9–23 kg/20–50 lb. Longer and heavier specimens have also been recorded. It is blue green on the back, with silver sides and a spotted tail.

Etymology The species name, *tshawytscha*, is Greek for "hood nose," referring to the hooked jaws of the males in mating season.

Habitat Ocean and coastal rivers from Alaska to California.

>> Coho salmon

Oncorhynchus kisutch

Description The coho salmon is on average 71 cm/ 28 in. long and 3.2–5 kg/7–11 lb. Longer and heavier specimens have also been recorded. It has a dark-blue back and silver sides.

Etymology The species name, *kisutch*, is from the Russian common name, *kizhuch*.

Habitat Ocean and coastal rivers from Alaska to Baja California, Mexico.

>> Sockeye salmon
Oncorhynchus nerka

Description The sockeye salmon can grow as large as 84 cm/33 in. long and weigh up to 6.8 kg/15 lb. It has a blue back and whitish sides. Sockeyes that don't migrate to the ocean and live in fresh water are known as Kokanee.

Etymology The species name, *nerka*, is the Russian name for the spawning, or anadromous, form.

Habitat Oceans and coastal rivers from Alaska to the Columbia River.

>> Chum salmon
Oncorhynchus keta

Description The chum salmon, also known as the dog salmon, is on average 60 cm/24 in. long and weighs 4.4–10 kg/9.7–22 lb. It is silvery blue green, with darker shading.

Etymology The species name, *keta*, is the Eastern Siberian word for "salmon."

Habitat The Pacific Ocean and coastal rivers from Alaska to California.

>> Pink salmon

Oncorhynchus gorbuscha

Description The pink salmon, also known as the humpback salmon, is on average 61 cm/24 in. long and weighs 2.2 kg/4.9 lb. In the ocean, they are a bright silver, before returning to their spawning rivers and streams where they turn greyish.

Etymology The species name, *gorbuscha*, is from the Russian common name, *gorbusa*.

Habitat Ocean and coastal rivers from Alaska to northern California.

▶ TIDE POOL SCULPIN TIDE POOL JOHNNY

Oligocottus maculosus

FAMILY Cottidae

Description Tide pool sculpins grow up to 9cm/ 3.5 in. long. Their colours change as camouflage according to their surroundings, ranging from grey, green, and brown to dark red. It often has several dark saddle markings down its back.

Etymology The genus name, *Oligocottus*, means "few sculpins." The species name, *maculosus*, means "spotted."

Habitat Very common in tide pools from Alaska to California.

NORTHERN CLINGFISH FLATHEAD CLINGFISH

Gobiesox maeandricus

FAMILY Gobiesocidae

Description The northern clingfish grows to 15 cm/ 6 in. long. It has a broad flat head and the body quickly narrows toward the tail. The colours range from different shades of browns and reds to grey, and there is usually a whitish band over the head extending from one eye to the other.

Etymology The species name, *maeandricus*, translates to "meandering colour streaks." The common name clingfish is from the sucking disk on its belly.

Habitat Commonly seen clinging to the underside of rocks, from Alaska to California. Can breathe air when out of the water.

CRESCENT GUNNEL BRACKETED BLENNY

Pholis laeta

GUNNEL FAMILY Pholidae

Description The crescent gunnel is an eel-like fish to 25 cm/10 in. long. Its colours are usually orangey-green to brown with mottling down the sides.

Etymology The species name, *laeta*, means "bright, vivid."

Habitat In summer and autumn the crescent gunnel can be seen in seaweed, under rocks, and in tide pools. It can breathe out of water. In winter they move farther out in the ocean. Common from Alaska to California.

ACKNOWLEDGEMENTS

This book could not be the quality it is without the help of many people, of whom I would like to acknowledge and thank the following: the University of British Columbia, with special thanks to the staff at the Beaty Biodiversity Museum: Karen Needham, Olivia Lee, Christopher M. Stinson, and Paul Kroeger; Douglas Justice at the UBC Botanical Garden; Amy Haagsma, who edited the manuscript; and the great staff at Heritage House Publishing, including senior editor Lara Kordic, editorial coordinator Lenore Hietkamp, and designer Jacqui Thomas. And finally, thanks for all the support from the Pena Family.

PHOTO CREDITS

All photos are by Collin Varner except as follows (all images have been altered to fit the layout).

All rights reserved (used with permission) Clingfish, p. 446, Ron Wolf, Flickr; Vancouver Island marmot, p. 359, Alena Ebeling-Schuld Photography, alenaesphotography.com

Public domain Scallop, p. 414, bottom, NatureDiver, Shutterstock; Grizzly, p. 352, bottom, Henry Lickorish; Chum, p. 444, bottom, Washington RCO, Flickr; Margined white, p. 380, Alan Schmierer, Flickr

Creative Commons Attribution 2.0 license (creativecommons.org/licenses/by/2.0/) Beaver, p. 357, top, Rosana Prada, Flickr; Brush rabbit, p. 361, Martin Jambon, Flickr; California hazelnut, p. 125, Superior National Forest, USFS, Flickr; Chinook, p. 443, top, Roger Tabor, USFWS, Flickr; Chinook, p. 443, middle, Zureks, Wikimedia; Chinook, p. 443, bottom, Lynn Ketchum, Oregon SU, Flickr; Chum, p. 444, top, W. Fischer, Alaska Fish Habitat Partnerships, Flickr; Coho, p. 443, bottom, Bureau of Land Management Oregon & Washington, Flickr; Creeping buttercup, p. 260, Tomasz Góralski, Flickr; Crescent gunnel, p. 446, SA, Flickr; Curled dock, p. 256 (both), Harry Rose, Flickr; Dowitcher, p. 313, Stephen Lester, Flickr; Dunlin, p. 314, Mike Prince, Flickr; Great green bush cricket, p. 397, bottom, Mark Bloemberg, Flickr; Great green bush cricket, p. 397, top, Matt Hewitt, Flickr; Grey whale, p. 442, bottom, Sam Beebe, Flickr; Grey wolf, p. 353, Patrick Rohe, Flickr; Hairy chiton, p. 425, Jerry Kirkhart, Flickr; Humpback, p. 442, top, Gregory Smith, Flickr; Marshpepper smartweed, p. 254, top, K. Kendall, Flickr; Mourning dove, p. 330, Robert Taylor, Flickr; Northern Bluet, p. 387, Don Henise, Flickr; Octopus, p. 437, top, Oliver Dodd, Flickr; Olympic marmot, p. 359, Chad Collins, Flickr; Pink salmon, p. 445, Joe Serio, USFS, Flickr; Scouler's willow, p. 149, Matt Lavin, Flickr; Sculpin, Jerry Kirkhart, Flickr; Sockeye, p. 444, bottom, USFS, Pacific Northwest Region, Flickr; Sockeye, p. 444, top, Pete Schneider, USFS, Flickr; Snowshoe hare, p. 361, NPS, Jacob W. Frank, Flickr; Sugar wrack, p. 278, J Brew; Sweet coltsfoot, p. 33, closeup, Peardg, Flickr; Villous cinquefoil, p. 90, Brewbooks, Flickr; Virginia rail, p. 311, top, Steve Arena, USFWS, Flickr; White-flowered hawkweed, p. 31, Tom Hilton, Flickr; White marsh marigold, p. 85, Steve Cyr, Flickr

BIBLIOGRAPHY

Acorn, John, and Ian Sheldon. *Bugs of British Columbia*. Vancouver, BC: Lone Pine Publishing, 2001.

Adolph, Val. *Tales of the Trees*. Delta, BC: Key Books, 2000.

Atkinson, Scott, and Fred Sharpe. *Wild Plants of the San Juan Islands*. Seattle, Washington: The Mountaineers, 1998.

Bird, David M. *Birds of Western Canada*. Toronto: Dorling Kindersley, 2013.

Cannings, Robert A. *Introducing the Dragonflies of British Columbia and the Yukon*. Victoria, BC: Royal BC Museum, 2002.

Cannings, Richard, Tom Aversa, and Hal Opperman. *Birds of Southwestern British Columbia*. Victoria, BC: Heritage House, 2005.

Clark, Lewis J. *Wild Flowers of British Columbia*. Sydney, BC: Gray's Publishing Ltd., 1973.

Corkran, Charlotte C., and Chris Thoms. *Amphibians of Oregon, Washington and British Columbia*. Rev. ed. Vancouver, BC: Lone Pine Publishing, 2006.

Craighead, John J., Frank C. Craighead, Jr., and Ray J. Davis. *A Field Guide to Rocky Mountain Wildflowers*. Boston: Houghton Mifflin Co., 1963.

Eder, Tamara, and Don Pattie. *Mammals of British Columbia*. Edmonton, AB: Lone Pine Publishing, 2001.

Forsyth, Robert G. *Land Snails of British Columbia*. Victoria, BC: Royal BC Museum, 2004.

Haggard, Peter, and Judy Haggard. *Insects of the Pacific Northwest*. Portland: Timber Press, 2006.

Harbo, Rick M. *Pacific Reef and Shore*. Madeira Park, BC: Harbour Publishing, 2006.

Haskin, Leslie L. *Wildflowers of the Pacific Coast*. New York: Dover Publications, 1977.

Hitchcock, C. Leo, Arthur Cronquist, Marion Ownbey, and J.W. Thompson. *Vascular Plants of the Pacific Northwest*. 5 vols. Seattle: University of Washington Press, 1955–69.

Lamb, Andy, and Bernard P. Hanby. *Marine Life of the Pacific Northwest*. Madeira Park, BC: Harbour Publishing, 2005.

Lederer, Roger, and Carol Burr. *Latin for Bird Lovers*. Portland: Timber Press, 2014.

Lyons, C.P. *Trees, Shrubs and Flowers to Know in British Columbia*. 1952. Reprint, Toronto: J.M. Dent and Sons, 1976.

Pojar, Jim, and Andy MacKinnon. *Plants of the Pacific Northwest Coast*. Vancouver, BC: Lone Pine Publishing, 1994.

Sargent, Charles Sprague. *Manual of the Trees of North America*. 2 vols. New York: Dover Publications, 1965. First published 1905 by Houghton Mifflin Co.

Sept, J. Duane. *The Beachcomber's Guide to Seashore Life in the Pacific Northwest*. Madeira Park, BC: Harbour Publishing, 1999.

Sept, J. Duane. *Common Mushrooms of the Northwest*. Sechelt, BC: Calypso Publishing, 2008.

Sheldon, Ian. *Seashore of British Columbia*. Edmonton, AB: Lone Pine Publishing, 1998.

Smith, Kathleen M., Nancy J. Anderson, and Katherine Beamish, eds. *Nature West Coast: A Study of Plants, Insects, Birds, Mammals and Marine Life as Seen in Lighthouse Park*. Victoria, BC: Sono Nis Press, 1988.

Stearn, T. William. *Stearn's Dictionary of Plant Names for Gardeners*. Portland: Timber Press, 2002.

Stoltmann, Randy. *Hiking Guide to the Big Trees of Southwestern British Columbia*. Vancouver, BC: Western Canada Wildlife Committee, 1987.

Turner, Nancy J. *Plant Technology of First Peoples in British Columbia*. Vancouver, BC: UBC Press, 1998.

Turner, Nancy J. *Food Plants of Coastal First Peoples*. Vancouver, BC: UBC Press, 2000.

INDEX

Scientific family names are indicated by SMALL CAPS, e.g., PEA FAMILY

abalone, northern 418
absinthium 202
acorn barnacle 420
acorn woodpecker 319
admirable bolete 175
admirals 371, 372
Alaska saxifrage 93
alcohol inky 164
ALDER FAMILY 142–43
alehoof 245
alfalfa 236
alpine coltsfoot 33
alpine fireweed 74
alpine pussytoes 27
AMANITA FAMILY 162–63
American beaver 357
American brooklime 101
American bullfrog 363
American coot 317
American dipper 349
American glasswort 39, 281
American goldfinch 340
American mink 356
American pokeweed 251
American raccoon 356
American robin 323
American searocket 35
American wigeon 294
anemones 84, 433, 434
angel wings 166
anise swallowtail 375
Anna's hummingbird 329
annual sow thistle 215

apargidium 32
aphids 401
apple, Pacific crab 148
arbutus 144
arched hook-tip moth 383
Arctic lupine 52
arnica, mountain 27
arrowhead 18
arrow-leaved groundsel 33
arrow-wood 135
arssmart 254
artist's conk 177
aspen, trembling 148
asphodel, western false 72
ASTER FAMILY 25–34,
    199–218
avens, large-leaved 88

bachelor's button 204
bald eagle 284
baldhip rose 136
banana slug, Pacific 408
banded alder borer 398
band-tailed pigeon 331
baneberry 83
Barbara's herb 221
BARBERRY FAMILY 34, 106
barnacles 420–21
barn owl 291
barn swallow 328
barred owl 290
Barrow's goldeneye 295
basam 247
bastard hellebore 250
bat, little brown 361
bat star 432
beach carrot 19
beach knotweed 81

beach morning glory 41
beach pea 52
beaked hazelnut 125
bearberry 48
bearbind 233
bears 352–53
beaver, American 357
bedstraw 91
bedstraws 91, 262
bee food 243
bees 404–5
beetle, sow 407
beetles 392–93, 398–99, 400,
    407
beggar's blanket 266
belle isle cress 221
belted kingfisher 320
berries 105–17
Bewick's wren 337
bigleaf maple 142
bigroot 42
bindweed 41, 232–33
birch 143
birdseed plantain 253
bird's-foot trefoil 235
birds nest fungi 190
bird vetch 239
birdweed 253
bishop's weed 195
bisom 247
bittecress, little western 35
bittercress, hairy 223
bitter buttons 216
bitter cherry 146
bitter dock 257
bittersweet 267
bitterweed 212
black alpine sedge 43

black and yellow mud dauber 401
black bear 352
blackberries 112, 113
black bindweed 254
BLACKBIRD FAMILY 324–26
blackcap 114
black cap, hairy 192
black-crowned night heron 308
black-eyed parasol 169
black gooseberry 111
black hawthorn 146
black-headed grosbeak 333
blackjacket 402
black katy chiton 426
black lampyrid 400
black lily 63
black oystercatcher 311
black raspberry 114
black rat 360
black seaside lichen 282
black-tailed deer 352
black turban snail 411
black twinberry 126
black widow, western 396
bleeding heart, Pacific 55
blistered cup fungus 191
blister plant 259
blue-berried elder 127
blueberries 108, 110
bluebill 298
blue buttons 198
blue curls 247
blue currant 110
blue dasher 387
blue elderberry 127
blue-eyed darner 388
blue-eyed mary, small-flowered 97
blue mussel 414
blue top snail 417
bogbean 70
bog blueberry 110
bog laurel, western 130
Bonaparte's gull 346

boneset 220
bracken fern 123
bracketed blenny 446
bracted lousewort 99
branch-spined bryozoan 435
Brandt's cormorant 310
Brewer's blackbird 324
bristly mushroom 170
brittle cinder 187
brittle prickly-pear cactus 36
broadleaf plantain 253
broad-leaved cocklebur 218
broad-leaved dock 257
broad-leaved fireweed 74
broad-leaved helleborine 250
broad-leaved peavine 235
broad-leaved stonecrop 41
broad-leaved toadflax 264
broad-rib kelp 274
bronze carabid 400
brooklime, American 101
broom corn millet 232
brooms 237, 239, 247
broom tops 247
brown creeper 337
brown-headed cowbird 326
brown pelican 308
brum 247
brushes and combs 233
brush rabbit 361
bryozoan, branch-spined 435
buckbean 70
BUCKWHEAT FAMILY 80–81, 253–57
buffalo herb 236
bufflehead 296
bull kelp 278
bull thistle 205
bulrush, hard-stemmed 44
bunchberry 40
burdock, common 201
bushtit 334
butter-and-eggs 265
butter clam 411
BUTTERCUP FAMILY 83–87, 259–60

butter dock 257
butterflies 371–78
butterfly bush 226
butterwort, common 58
buttons 216

cabbage white 380
cackling goose 301
calcareous tube worm 436
California ground squirrel 358
California gull 347
California hazelnut 125
California mussel 413
California poppy 79
California sea lion 441
California wax myrtle 133
camas 61, 66
Canada goldenrod 34
Canada goose 301
Canada thistle 205
Canadian buffalo berry 106
Canadian fleabane 29
canary-shouldered thorn 384
candlestick 266
candy stick 158
canoe birch 143
carbon antlers 187
cardinal meadowhawk 390
card thistle 233
carpenter's weed 247
CARROT FAMILY 18–22
cascara 145
cat's tongue 186
cattail 101
cauliflower mushroom 182
ceanothus silk moth 379
cedar (trees) 150, 151
cedar, ground 68
cedar waxwing 324
centipede, garden 406
chafeweed 207
changing forget-me-not 219
chanterelle, false 171
CHANTERELLE FAMILY 175, 191
cheese rennet 262

cheeses 249
cherry, bitter 146
cherry tree gummosis 189
chervil, wild 196
chestnut-backed chickadee 333
chickadees 333–34
chickweeds 38, 206, 230
chicory 199
chinook salmon 443
chipmunk, yellow-pine 359
chitons 425–26
chocolate arion 409
chocolate lily 62
Christ's thorn 198
chum salmon 444
cinquefoils 89–90, 261
clams 411–12
cleaver 91
climbing buckwheat 254
climbing honeysuckle 37
clotbur 218
clouded sulphur 378
clovers 53, 236, 237–38
CLUBMOSS FAMILY 68–69
clustered wild rose 137
coastal strawberry 116
coast boykinia 91
coast rhododendron 132
cockle, Nuttall's 412
cockfebur 218
coho salmon 443
coltsfoot 32, 33
columbine, red 84
comfrey 220
common burdock 201
common butterwort 58
common camas 61
common chickweed 230
common cocklebur 218
common daisy 203
common dandelion 216
common egret 307
common eyebright 263
common forget-me-not 219
common foxglove 263

common fumitory 242
common goldeneye 295
common groundsel 214
common hawkweed 208
common hop 227
common horsetail 45
common juniper 129
common knotweed 253
common mallow 249
common merganser 297
common murre 306
common orache 231
common periwinkle 198
common plantain 253
common pokeberry 251
common puffball 188
common raccoon 256
common raven 321
common smartweed 255
common sow thistle 215
common stork's bill 241
common tansy 216
common toadflax 265
common vetch 240
common wall cress 221
common wall lizard 369
Cooley's hedge-nettle 58
Cooper's hawk 286
copperbush 130
CORAL AND CLUB FUNGI FAMILY 182–84
coral root, spotted 159
CORMORANT FAMILY 309–10
cornbind 232, 254
cornflower 204
corn lily 66
corn sow thistle 214
corn spurry 229
cotton grass, narrow-leaved 44
cottonwood 147
cougar 354
cowbird, brown-headed 326
cow cress 224
cow parsnip 20
cow vetch 239
coyote 354

crab apple, Pacific 148
crabs 423–24
crambling rocket 225
cranberrry, highbush 117
cranefly, European 393
creeping bellflower 227
creeping buttercup 260
creeping Charlie 245
creeping Jenny 258
creeping Joan 258
creeping myrtle 198
creeping oxalis 251
creeping raspberry 115
creeping sow thistle 214
crescent gunnel 446
cress 221, 224
crested coral fungus 182
crickets 397
crimson clover 238
crow, northwestern 321
crowberry 107
crowded white clitocybe 165
crowfoot 259
crown vetch 234
cucumber cap 173
cudweed, marsh 207
cure-all 247
curled dock 256
CURRANT AND GOOSEBERRY FAMILY 110–12
cut-leaf blackberry 113
cut-leaved crane's bill 241
cut-leaved geranium 241
cutworm, olive-green 382
cyanide millipede 406
CYPRESS FAMILY 129, 150–51

dagger 244
daisies 29, 200, 203
Dalmatian toadflax 264
dame's rocket 223
dame's violet 223
dandelion, common 216
daphne, laurel-leaved 268
dark-eyed junco 342
dark mahogany clam 411

Davidson's penstemon 100
death camas 66
death cap 162
deer cabbage 70
DEER FAMILY 351–52
deer fern 120
devil's apple 267
devil's club 125
devil's guts 229
devil's paintbrush 208
devil's trumpet 267
dipper, American 349
disc mayweed 211
ditchweed 258
docks 253–55, 256–57, 266
DOGBANE FAMILY 23, 198
dog vomit slime mold 193
DOGWOOD FAMILY 40, 128,
   144
dolphin, Pacific white-sided
   439
double-crested cormorant 309
Douglas fir 155
Douglas fir collybia 166
Douglas maple 141
Douglas squirrel 358
dovefoot crane's bill 242
dovefoot geranium 242
doves 330, 331
dove's dung 247
downy woodpecker 317
dragonflies and damselflies
   386–90
drug fumitory 242
drumming katydid 397
DUCK FAMILY 293–304
duck potato 18
Dungeness crab 424
dunlin 314
dusty yellow nudibranch 429
dwarf dogwood 40
dwarf mallow 249
dwarf mistletoe 160
dwarf rockweed 275
dyer's polypore 179

eagles 284
early winter cress 221
earth smoke 242
earwig, European 391
eastern eyebright 263
eastern grey squirrel 357
eccentric sand dollar 426
edible thistle 28
eight-spotted skimmer 389
elder 127
elegant rein orchid 76
elfin saddle, fluted black 190
elk, Roosevelt 351
enchanter's nightshade 73
english daisy 203
english ivy 199
erythroniums 67–68
Eurasian collared-dove 331
European bugleweed 246
European cranefly 393
European earwig 391
European ground beetle 400
European honeybee 404
European hop 227
European rabbit 361
European skipper 382
European starling 326
evening campion 229
evening lychnis 229
EVENING PRIMROSE FAMILY
   73–74, 250
evening star 250
evergreen huckleberry 109
evergreen violet 104
everlasting pea 235
eyebright 263
eyed sphinx 379

fairy's glove 263
fairyslipper 75
faithful snail 408
FALCON FAMILY 287–88
false azalea 131
falsebox 139
false bugbane 86
false chamomile 212

false chanterelle 171
false charcoal 187
false dandelion 209
false lily of the valley 64
false solomon's seal 65
fan-leaved cinquefoil 89
fawn lilies 67
feather boa 273
fennel 197
fernleaf 99
ferns 118–23
fever plant 250
fiddleneck 243
field bindweed 232
field chickweed 38
field crescent 373
field pennycress 226
field peppergrass 224
field pepperwort 224
fig buttercup 260
figwort 260
FIGWORT FAMILY 96–101,
   262–66
FINCH FAMILY 340–41, 346
fine-leaved desert parsley 20
fir cone cap 166
fireweed 73–74, 239
firs 151, 152, 155
five-leaved bramble 115
flag, yellow 244
flathead clingfish 446
fleshy jaumea 31
flower crab spider 396
fluted black elfin saddle 190
fly agaric 162
flycatcher, olive-sided 332
foam flower 95
fool's huckleberry 131
fool's onion 60
forget-me-not, common 219
four-spotted skimmer 389
foxglove 263
fox sparrow 343
fried chicken mushroom 169
fringecup 95
fringed grass of parnassus 93

fringed quickweed 207
fritillarias 62–63
frogs 363–64
fumitory, common 242
furze 239

gadwall 299
garden centipede 406
garden harebell 227
garlic mustard 220
Garry oak 145
garter snake 368
geese 301–2
gemmed amanita 163
gem-studded puffball 188
GENTIAN FAMILY 55–56
GERANIUM FAMILY 241,
    242–43
giant barnacle 421
giant green anemone 433
giant hogweed 197
giant kelp 276
giant knotweed 255
giant pacific octopus 437
giant pink star 431
giant plumose anemone 434
giant rock scallop 415
giant vetch 54
gilled mushrooms 164–74
gill-over-the-ground 245
ginger, wild 25
GINSENG FAMILY 24, 125, 199
glacier lily, yellow 68
glaucous-winged gull 348
goat's beard 87, 138, 217
golden chanterelle 175
golden-crowned kinglet 335
golden-crowned sparrow 345
golden dead nettle 245
golden eagle 284
golden-eyed grass 56
goldeneyes 295
golden jelly cone 186
goldenrod 34
goldfinch, American 340
goose barnacle 421

gooseberries 111
gorse 239
goutweed 195
grand fir 152
grasshopper, migratory 398
great blue heron 307
great egret 307
greater bindweed 233
greater plantain 253
greater white-fronted goose
    302
greater yellowlegs 314
great green bush-cricket 397
great grey owl 291
great horned owl 290
great mullein 266
grebes 316
green algae 270
green-flowered wintergreen 51
green purslane 257
green sea urchin 422
green shore crab 423
green spleenwort 119
green-winged teal 300
grey jay 322
grey whale 442
grey wolf 353
grimsel 214
grim-the-collier 208
grizzly bear 352
grosbeak, black-headed 333
ground cedar 68
groundcone, Vancouver 161
ground-ivy 245
ground pine 69
groundsel 33
groundsels 33, 213–14
gulls 346–48
gummy gooseberry 111
gumweed 30
gypsywort 246
gyrfalcon 288

hairy bittercress 223
hairy black cap 192
hairy cat's ear 209

hairy chiton 425
hairy crab 423
hairy honeysuckle 37
hairy manzanita 129
hairy tare 240
hairy vetch 240
hairy woodpecker 318
harbour porpoise 440
hardhack 138
hard-stemmed bullrush 44
harebell, garden 227
hare's lettuce 215
hare, snowshoe 361
hare's thistle 215
harlequin duck 300
Harris's sparrow 343
harvest lily 60
harvestman 394
HAWK FAMILY 284–86
hawksbeard, smooth 206
hawkweeds 208–9, 212, 446
hawthorn, black 146
hazelnut, California 125
heal-all 247
heart-leaved twayblade 76
HEATHER FAMILY 47–50,
    107–10, 129–32, 144, 159
hedge bindweed 233
hedge garlic 220
hedge mustard 225
hellebores 66, 250
hemlocks 155–56
Henderson's shooting star 83
herb-robert 243
herons 307–8
heron's bill 241
highbush cranberry 117
himalayan blackerry 113
hoary comma 376
hoary marmot 359
hogweed, giant 197
holly 198
honesty 224
HONEYSUCKLE FAMILY
    36–37, 117, 126–28
honey clover 236

honey lotus 236
hooded merganser 296
hooded nudibranch 429
hoof fungus 180
Hooker's fairybells 62
Hooker's onion 59
hop, common 227
HORSETAIL FAMILY 45–46
horseweed 29
house finch 346
house sparrow 341
huckleberries 109
Hudsonian whiteface 386
hummingbirds 329–30
humpback whale 442

Indian celery 20
Indian hellebore 66
INDIAN PIPE FAMILY 158, 161
Indian plum 139
INK CAP FAMILY 164–65
IRIS FAMILY 56–57, 244
isopod 435
Italian clover 238
ivy, english 199
ivy-leaved toadflax 262

jack-go-to-bed-at-noon 217
jack-in-thehedge 220
jack-run-in-the-country 232
Jacob's sword 244
Jamestown weed 267
Japanese wireweed 279
jatt 236
jaumea 31
jays 322
jellied bird's nest fungi 190
jellyfish 427–28
JELLY FUNGI FAMILY 185–86
Jimson weed 267
jointed charlock 225
junipers 129, 150

kayak pond skater 394
kelps 274, 276–78
killdeer 327

kingfisher, belted 320
king gentian 56
kinglets 335
king's clover 236
king's cure-all 250
kinnikinnick 48
kinnikinnick hybrid 49
kneeling angelica 18
knitbone 220
knotweeds 80–81, 253–55, 255

Labrador tea 131
lacy phacelia 243
lacy scorpionweed 243
ladies' tresses 78
lady fern 120
lady's bedstraw 262
lady's thumb 255
lamb's quarter 231
large-headed sedge 43
large-leaved avens 88
large-leaved lupine 53
large yellow underwing 385
laurel-leaved daphne 268
lawn geranium 242
lawn veronica 266
leafy spurge 234
least sandpiper 313
leatherleaf saxifrage 92
lesser celandine 260
lesser scaup 298
lesser yellow trefoil 238
lettuces 210
Lewis' monkey-flower 98
Lewis's moonshell 415
lichen, black seaside 282
lichen agaric 167
licorice fern 122
LILY FAMILY 59–67, 71–72, 248
limpets 419–20
lion's mane jellyfish 427
lion's mane mushroom 181
lion's tooth 216
little brown bat 361
little hogweed 257

little hop clover 238
little prince's pine 47
little rockweed 275
little western bittercress 35
lizards 368–69
long-billed dowitcher 313
long-eared owl 292
long-headed clover 238
loosestrifes 248, 258
Lorquin's admiral 372
low cudweed 207
lugworm, Pacific 436
lupines 52–53
Lyngbye's sedge 280

maidenhair fern 119
mallard 294
MALLOW FAMILY 249
manroot 42
MAPLE FAMILY 141–42
marasmiellus 174
marbled murrelet 306
margined white 380
marine eelgrass 281
marmots 359
marsh cinquefoil 90
marsh cudweed 207
marsh horehound 246
marsh marigold, white 85
marshpepper smartweed 254
marsh wren 336
mayweeds 201, 211–12
meadow buttercup 259
meadow honeysuckle 237
meadowrue, western 87
Menzies' pipsissewa 47
mergansers 296–97
merlin 287
Merten's saxifrage 94
mew gull 346
migratory grasshopper 398
Milbert's tortoiseshell 376
milk cap, red hot 172
millet 232
millipede, cyanide 406
mink, American 356

MINT FAMILY 57–58, 245–47
mischievous Jack 230
mistletoe, dwarf 160
mithridate mustard 226
mixed bumblebee 405
mock orange 133
monarch 374
money plant 224
moneywort 258
monkey-flowers 97–98
Monterey sea lemon 429
moon jelly 428
moon shell, Lewis's 415
MORNING GLORY FAMILY 41,
    232–33
moths 379, 381, 382–86
mottled hawkweed 209
mountain arnica 27
mountain ash, Sitka 147
mountain bluet 204
mountain buttercup 85
mountain daisy 29
mountain fern 121
mountain hemlock 156
mountain lion 354
mountain lover 139
mountain monkey-flower 98
mountain sorrel 80
mountain sweet cicely 21
mourning cloak 373
mourning dove 330
mouse-ear cress 221
mouse-eared chickweed 206
mud-flat snail 417
mugwort 202
mule deer 351
mullein 266
mushrooms and toadstools
    162–76
musk mallow 249
mussels 413–14
MUSTARD FAMILY 220–26
mu-su 236
mute swan 303

naked broomrape 160

nap-at-noon 247
narrow dock 256
narrow-leaved cotton grass 44
narrow-leaved plantain 252
naval shipworm 438
nettles 58, 102, 245, 246, 427
nightshades 73, 267
ninebark 135
nipplewort 211
nodding beggarticks 28, 203
nodding onion 59
Nootka rose 136
northern abalone 418
northern alligator lizard 368
northern bluet 387
northern clingfish 446
northern feather duster worm
    437
northern flicker 319
northern goshawk 286
northern harrier 285
northern leopard frog 364
northern pintail 297
northern river otter 355
northern rough-winged swal-
    low 328
northern saw-whet owl 293
northern sea lion 440
northern shoveller 299
northwestern chipmunk 359
northwestern crow 321
northwestern salamander 365
Norway rat 360
norwegian cinquefoil 261
nudibranchs 429
nuthatch, red-breasted 338
Nuttall's cockle 412

oak, Garry 145
oak fern 122
oceanspray 135
ochre sea star 431
octopus, giant Pacific 437
old growth kelp 274
old-man-in-the-spring 214
old man's beard 259

olive-green cutworm 382
olive-sided flycatcher 332
Olympic marmot 359
one-flowered cancer root 160
one-sided wintergreen 49
onions 59, 60
opium lettuce 210
oraches 39, 230, 231
orange coral mushroom 183
orange eye 226
orange hawkweed 208
orange jelly 185
orange peel fungus 193
orange wax crust 192
orb-weaver spider 394
orca 438
orchard mason bee 405
ORCHID FAMILY 75–78, 159,
    250
Oregon grape 106
Oregon oxalis 79
Oregon spotted frog 363
osprey 288
otters 355, 441
oval-leaved blueberry 108
owls 289–93
ox-eye daisy 200
ox-tongue hawkweed 212
oyster, Pacific 412
oyster plant 217

Pacific banana slug 408
Pacific bleeding heart 55
Pacific blood star 430
Pacific crab apple 148
Pacific dampwood termite 391
Pacific dogwood 144
Pacific forktail 388
Pacific harbour seal 439
Pacific lugworm 436
Pacific madrone 144
Pacific oyster 413
Pacific plate limpet 420
Pacific razor clam 412
Pacific rhododendron 132
Pacific sanicle 22

Pacific sea nettle 427
Pacific sideband snail 408
Pacific silver fir 151
Pacific tent caterpillar moth 386
Pacific tree frog 364
Pacific white-sided dolphin 439
Pacific willow 149
paintbrush, red 96
painted lady 371
painted urticina 434
pale tiger swallowtail 375
panic millet 232
panther cap 163
paper birch 143
paper wasp 403
parrot's beak 99
parsley fern 121, 216
partridgefoot 88
pathfinder 25
PEA FAMILY 52–54, 234–40, 247
pearly everlasting 26
pear-shaped puffball 188
pelagic cormorant 310
pennycress 226
penstemons 100
pepper-and-salt 222
peregrine falcon 287
perennial snapdragon 265
perennial sow thistle 214
perennial sweet pea 235
periwinkle, common 198
pheasant, ring-necked 349
pickpocket 222
pickpurse 229
pied-billed grebe 316
pigeon guillemot 305
pigeons 331, 332
piggyback plant 96
pigweed 195, 231, 257
pileated woodpecker 318
pilewort 260
pill bug 407
pineapple weed 211

pine borer, red-shouldered 399
pinedrops 159
PINE FAMILY 151–56
pinesap 158
pine siskin 340
pine white 378
pink coral mushroom 184
pink corydalis 54
PINK FAMILY 38, 206, 228–30
pink monkey-flower 98
pink mountain heather 50
pink salmon 445
pink wintergreen 51
PLANTAIN FAMILY 252–53
plumose anemone 433
pokeweed, American 251
policeman's helmet 218
POLYPORE FAMILY 176–80
pond skater, kayak 394
poppies 79, 251
porpoise, harbour 440
prickly broom 239
prickly lettuce 210
prickly-pear cactus, brittle 36
prickly sow thistle 215
primrose 250
PRIMROSE FAMILY 74, 83
prince 168
prince's pine 47–48
princesss pine 69
proso millet 232
prostrate knotweed 253
PUFFBALL FAMILY 188–89
puffin, tufted 305
purple archangel 246
purple bell 227
purple clover 237
purple dead-nettle 246
purple foxglove 263
purple goat's beard 217
purple henbit 246
purple-hinge rock scallop 415
purple honeysuckle 37
purple loosestrife 248
purple medic 236

purple olive 418
purple rocket 223
purple sea urchin 422
purple shore crab 424
purple tansy 243
purple toadflax 264
PURSLANE FAMILY 82, 257
pussely 257

Queen Anne's lace 196
queen's cup 61
questionable stropharia 168
quick-in-the-hand 218
quickweed 207

rabbit, brush 361
rabbit, European 361
rabbits and hares 361
raccoon, American 356
radish, wild 225
raspberries 114–15
rats 360
rattlesnake plantain 75
raven, common 321
razor clam, Pacific 412
red admiral 371
red alder 142
red-belted polypore 176
red-berried elder 127
red-breasted nuthatch 338
red-breasted sapsucker 320
red clover 237
red columbine 84
red-eared pond slider turtle 367
red elderberry 127
red-eye medusa 428
red-flowering currant 112
red hot milk cap 172
red huckleberry 109
red-osier dogwood 128
red paintbrush 96
red rock crab 423
red root 195
red-shouldered pine borer 399
red sorrel 256

redstem ceanothus 134
red-stem filaree 241
red-tailed hawk 285
red turban snail 416
red twinberry 126
red-winged blackbird 325
rhinoceros auklet 304
rhododendrons 131, 132
ribbed kelp 276
ribbed limpet 419
ribwort plantain 252
rice root 63
ring-billed gull 347
ringed-necked pheasant 349
ring-necked duck 298
rockets 223, 225
rock lice 435
rock pigeon 332
rockweed 275
Rocky Mountain juniper 150
Roosevelt elk 351
rose campion 228
ROSE FAMILY 88–90, 112,
    114–17, 135–39, 146–47,
    148, 261
rough cinquefoil 261
rough keyhole limpet 419
rough prominent 384
rounded earthstar 189
round-leaved bog orchid 77
round-leaved sundew 45
rowan 261
ruby-crowned kinglet 335
rufous hummingbird 330
running clubmoss 69
Russian orache 230

salal 107
salamander, northwestern 365
salmon 443–45
salmonberry 115
salsifies 217
sand dollar, eccentric 426
sanderling 315
sandhill crane 309
SANDPIPER FAMILY 312–15

sandweed 229
sandwort, seabeach 38
sapsucker, red-breasted 320
sarsaparilla, wild 24
Saskatoon berry 117
satin flower 57
satyr anglewing 377
satyr comma 377
SAXIFRAGE FAMILY 91–96
scallops 414–15
scaup, lesser 298
scentless mayweed 212
Scotch broom 247
Scouler's surf grass 280
Scouler's willow 149
scouring rush 46
scrambled egg slime mold 193
sculpin, tide pool 445
scurvy grass 221
sea asparagus 39, 281
seabeach sandwort 38
sea blush 102
sea cauliflower 279
sea hair 270
seal, Pacific harbour 439
sea lettuce 271
sea lions 440–41
sea otter 441
sea palm 277
searocket, American 35
sea sac 272
sea tar 282
sea urchins 422
sea-watch angelica 19
seaweeds 270–79
SEDGE FAMILY 42–44, 280
seed bug, western conifer 399
seersucker 276
segg 244
self-heal 247
service berry 117
shaggy galinsoga 207
shaggy ink cap 164
shaggy mane 164
shaggy soldier 207
shamrock 238

sheep sorrel 256
sheggs 244
shepherd's purse 222
shooting star, Henderson's 83
shore bindweed 41
shore pine 154
short-eared owl 292
siberian miner's lettuce 82
silver burweed 26
silver dollar plant 224
silverweed 89
simson 214
singer's plant 225
Sitka alder 143
Sitka mountain ash 147
Sitka spruce 153
Sitka valerian 103
skunk, striped 355
skunk cabbage 24
sleepydick 247
slender blue penstemon 100
slender rein orchid 78
slender speedwell 266
slough sedge 42
slugs 408–9
small bush cricket 397
small-flowered alumroot 92
small-flowered blue-eyed
    mary 97
small-flowered morning glory
    232
small perennial kelp 276
small stagshorn jelly fungus
    185
small touch-me-not 219
smartass 254
smoky gilled woodlover 167
smooth hawksbeard 206
snails 408, 416–18
snakes 368
snapdragon, perennial 265
snowberry 128
snow bunting 341
snow goose 302
snowshoe hare 361
snowy owl 289

soapberry 106
sockeye salmon 444
solomon's seal 65
song sparrow 344
soopolallie 106
sora 312
sour clover 251
sour dock 256
sour grass 256
sowbug 407
spanish broom 237
sparrows 341–45
spear saltbush 231
spearscale 231
speckled jewels 218
speedwell, slender 266
spiders 394, 395–96
spinach, wild 231
spiny milk thistle 215
spiny pink scallop 414
spiny wood fern 121
spiraea 137–38
spittlebug 392
split kelp 277
spotted coralroot 159
spotted hawkweed 209
spotted knotweed 255
spotted loosestrife 258
spotted sandpiper 312
spotted touch-me-not 218
spotted towhee 342
spreading dogbane 23
spreading knotweed 255
spreading orache 231
spreading stonecrop 40
springbank clover 53
spring gold 20
spruce, Sitka 153
spurge laurel 268
SQUIRREL FAMILY 357–59
staggerwort 213
stammerwort 213
starfish 430–32
starflower 247
star-flowered solomon's seal 65
starling, European 326

star of Bethlehem 247
steeplebush 138
Steller sea lion 440
Steller's jay 322
stickwort 229
sticky gooseberry 111
sticky groundsel 213
sticky parentucellia 265
sticky ragwortl 213
stinging nettle 102
stink currant 110
stinking chamomile 201
stinking groundsel 213
stinkweed 226
St. James wort 213
St. John's wort 244
STONECROP FAMILY 40–41
strangle tare 239
strawberries 116
stream violet 103
stringy butt rot 178
striped skunk 355
subalpine buttercup 85
subalpine daisy 29
subalpine fir 152
subalpine spirea 137
suckling clover 238
sugar wrack 278
sulphur shelf 179
sulphur tuft 171
summer lilac 226
sundew, round-leaved 45
sunflower star 432
surf scoter 304
SWALLOW FAMILY 327–29
swallowtails 375, 377
swamp beacon 183
swamp gentian 55
swamp horsetail 46
swamp rose 137
swans 303
sweet coltsfoot 33
sweet gale 134
sweet rocket 223

sweet William catchfly 228
swine's snout 216

tall buttercup 259
tanager, western 339
tansies 216, 243
tansy ragwortt 213
teal, green-winged 300
teasel 233
ten-lined june beetle 393
tent caterpillar moth, Pacific 386
termite, Pacific dampwood 391
thale cress 221
thimbleberry 114
thimbleberry stem gall wasp 402
thistles 28, 205, 214–15, 233
thorn apple 267
threadstalk speedwell 266
thrushes 323
tide pool sculpin 445
tiger lily 64
tiger's eye 180
timber wolf 353
tinder polypore 180
tiny vetch 240
tippler's bane 164
toad, western 365
toadflaxes 262, 264–65
Tolmie's saxifrage 94
toothed jelly fungus 186
torches 266
trailing blackerry 112
traveller's joy 259
tree swallow 329
trefoils 235, 238
trembling aspen 148
trillium, western 63
trumpeter swan 303
tubaria 173
tube worm, calcareous 436
tufted puffin 305
tufted vetch 239

tule 44
turkey tail 176
turkey vulture 289
Turkish towel 271
turnip, wild 222
turtles 367
twinberries 126
twinflower 36
twisted stalk 71
twoscale saltbush 230

urticina, painted 434

VALERIAN FAMILY 102–3
Vancouver groundcone 161
Vancouver Island marmot 359
vanilla leaf 34
varied thrush 323
variegated meadowhawk 390
varnish clam 411
veiled chiton 425
velvet dock 266
velvet rollrim 170
Venus's basin 233
verbena, yellow sand 71
vermouth 202
vetches 54, 234, 239–40
villous cinquefoil 90
vine maple 141
VIOLET FAMILY 103–4
violet-green swallow 327
Virginia rail 311
Virginia tiger moth 383
viscid groundsel 213
vultures 289

wall lettuce 210
wandering jenny 258
wapato 18
warblers 338–39
wasps 401–3
water horehound 246
water iris 244
water parsley 21
water parsnip 22

waterpepper 254
water plantain 23
water smartweed 80
weaver's broom 237
welsh poppy 251
west coast lady 372
western anemone 84
western black widow 396
western bog laurel 130
western buttercup 86
western conifer seed bug 399
western dock 81
western false asphodel 72
western grebe 316
western hemlock 155
western meadow fritillary 374
western meadowrue 87
western painted turtle 367
western pasque flower 84
western pink fawn lily 67
western red cedar 151
western spring beauty 82
western star flower 74
western sword fern 123
western tanager 339
western tea-berry 108
western tiger swallowtail 377
western toad 365
western trillium 63
western varnish shelf 177
western white fawn lily 67
western white pine 154
western yew 156
wet-a-bed 216
whales 442
whimbrel 315
whirligig water beetle 392
whistler 359
whitebark pine 153
white bog orchid 77
white campion 229
white cockle 229
white-crowned sparrow 345
white-dotted prominent 384
white fairy fingers 181
white-flowered hawkweed 31

white-flowered rhododendron 132
white goosefoot 231
white marsh marigold 85
white melilot 236
white mountain heather 47
white rein orchid 77
white-striped black moth 385
white sweet clover 236
white-throated sparrow 344
white trunk rot 178
white-veined wintergreen 50
wild arrach 231
wild buckwheat 254
wild carrot 196
wild chervil 196
wild fennel 197
wild ginger 25
wild kale 225
wild lettuce 210
wild proso millet 232
wild radish 225
wild rape 225
wild sarsaparilla 24
wild snapdragon 264
wild sorrel 256
wild spinach 231
wild turnip 222
WILLOW FAMILY 147, 148–49
Wilson's warbler 339
winged kelp 273
wintergreens 49, 50–51
winter rape 222
winter wren 336
wireweed 253
witch wood 261
wolf 353
wolf's milk 234
wolf spider 395
wood betony 99
wood duck 293
woodland rose 136
woodland skipper 381
woodland strawberry 116
WOODPECKER FAMILY 317–20
wood saxifrage 94

woody nightshade 267
woolly chanterelle 191
woolly inkcap 165
woolly pine spike 172
woolly sunflower 30
wormwood 202
woundwort 247
wrens 336–37

yarrow 200
yellow archangel 245
yellow bartsia 265
yellow bedstraw 262
yellow cedar 150
yellow clover 238
yellow coral mushroom 184
yellow cypress 150
yellow-faced bumblebee 404
yellow flag 244
yellow glacier lily 68
yellow glandweed 265
yellow-headed blackbird 325
yellow iris 244
yellowjacket 403
yellow loosestrife 258
yellow monkey-flower 97
yellow parentucellia 265
yellow-pine chipmunk 359
yellow pond lily 72
yellow-rumped warbler 338
yellow salsify 217
yellow sand verbena 71
yellow seaweed 272
yellow sorrel 251
yellow-spotted tussock moth 381
yellow toadflax 265
yellow woodsorrel 251
yerba buena 57
yew, western 156
yonca 236

Zeller's bolete 174

ABOUT THE AUTHOR

Collin Varner is an arborist/horticulturalist at the University of British Columbia. Varner began his career at UBC in 1977, working at the Botanical Garden, and over the past forty years he has assumed the responsibility for conserving trees in all corners of campus, including those planted by graduating classes and ceremonial trees dating back to 1919. Today, he is the steward of 25,000 trees at the university's Point Grey campus, where he also teaches native plant studies through the Faculty of Science. He is a member of the International Society of Arboriculture and the American Society of Consulting Arborists. Varner is the author of *Gardens of Vancouver* (with Christine Allen) and a series of popular field guides, including *Plants of Vancouver and the Lower Mainland*, *Plants of the Whistler Region*, *Plants of the West Coast Trail*, and *Plants of the Gulf & San Juan Islands and Southern Vancouver Island*. An avid nature photographer and traveller, Varner has hiked in over fifty countries and cycled around the world. He has climbed Mount Everest, Mount Kilimanjaro, Mount Lebanon, and the Atlas Mountains in Morocco and Algeria, and he has hiked the West Coast Trail on Vancouver Island twenty-four times. For the past seventeen years, he has been collecting information and photographing plant and animal species up and down the coastal Pacific Northwest for this, his most ambitious book project to date. He lives in Vancouver, British Columbia.